Mastering

Manufacturing

Macmillan Master Series

Accounting
Arabic
Astronomy
Australian History
Background to Business
Banking
Basic Management
Biology
British Politics
Business Communication
Business Law
Business Microcomputing
C Programming
Catering Science
Catering Theory
Chemistry
COBOL Programming
Commerce
Computer Programming
Computers
Economic and Social History
Economics
Electrical Engineering
Electronics
English as a Foreign Language
English Grammar
English Language
English Literature
French 1
French 2

German 1
German 2
Hairdressing
Human Biology
Italian 1
Italian 2
Japanese
Manufacturing
Marketing
Mathematics
Modern British History
Modern European History
Modern World History
Nutrition
Pascal Programming
Philosophy
Physics
Psychology
Restaurant Service
Science
Secretarial Procedures
Social Welfare
Sociology
Spanish 1
Spanish 2
Spreadsheets
Statistics
Study Skills
Typewriting Skills
Word Processing

Mastering

Manufacturing

Gordon Mair

First published 1993 by
THE MACMILLAN PRESS LTD
Houndmills, Basingstoke, Hampshire RG21 2XS
and London
Companies and representatives
throughout the world

ISBN 0–333–54230–4

A catalogue record for this book is available
from the British Library.

Filmset by Wearset, Boldon, Tyne and Wear

Printed in China

10 9 8 7 6 5 4 3 2 1
02 01 00 99 98 97 96 95 94 93

Contents

x   *Contents*

⬡ **List of Figures**

Preface

A healthy manufacturing industry is of crucial importance to the wellbeing of a nation and every person within it. Our society depends on manufacturing industry to create wealth. This wealth is used to provide services such as health and education. The products produced by manufacturing industry form the fabric of our civilisation, whether they be used in transport, entertainment, telecommunications, or even within manufacturing industry itself. In short – without a manufacturing capability a country will soon go into economic and social decline!

It is therefore essential that a country contains individuals with the ability to understand how manufacturing industry works, and how to put that knowledge to profitable use. Acquiring this knowledge is a stimulating experience, and putting it into practice is challenging, exciting, and potentially financially rewarding.

This book has been written as a result of a conviction that there is a need for an introductory text covering the major elements found across the spectrum of manufacturing. There are many excellent books, some of them quite voluminous, that cover either the technology or the management of manufacturing. This book is different in that it shows most facets of the subject in one concise volume, thus allowing their interrelationships to be understood. Despite the broad range of the book each topic is covered in sufficient detail to provide a basic working knowledge. Suggestions for further reading are given at the end of each chapter to allow fuller study where desired. The book should therefore be useful as an introductory text to those beginning courses in manufacturing or engineering, and to others who need a background knowledge of the subject, for example those in business disciplines such as finance, human resource management, marketing, etc.

In Part I of the book the subject is introduced by showing the economic importance of manufacturing and considering the historical context. These chapters put the subject into economic, social, and technological perspective.

Going into more detail Part II considers the general organisation necessary for manufacturing, the materials used, and the design considerations that need to be made to create a competitive product. These three chapters provide the foundation for the engineering and management elements that follow.

The manufacturing processes used to create products form the content of Part III. How the raw material for manufacturing is obtained and the subsequent processes used to transform that material into products sale-able in the world market are all described. The knowledge gained from this chapter will allow an understanding of how the processes work, and their capabilities and relative advantages and disadvantages. This should produce the ability to decide on the fitness of a process for a particular task.

A knowledge of the technology alone is not sufficient to produce successful products. The basic inputs to a manufacturing operation are the 'M's of money, machines, materials, and manpower. The complex inter-relationship of these elements must be managed well. Part IV describes the various aspects of management that must be considered in a factory. The planning and control of the operation, the best way to organise work, the determination and control of costs, quality considerations, and human factors, are all examined.

Finally the fact that most modern factories take advantage of the benefits obtained from using automation and computers is acknowledged. Thus Part V has two chapters on the basic technological and managerial aspects of automation. Automation is shown to be applicable to all the elements of manufacturing discussed in the previous chapters of the book: design, e.g. computer aided design; control of processes and equipment, e.g. robotics; and management, e.g. computer integrated manufacture.

The environment within which manufacturing industry operates today is highly competitive. Manufacturers must consider their markets, and hence their competition, as existing on a global scale. Firms today want to be 'World Class Manufacturers'. This has stimulated them to rigorously examine their own operations and constantly compare themselves with other companies to ensure that their products stay ahead and their organisation remains dynamic. Since the competition is doing the same a state of constant change arises, hence the need for the 'Management of Change', a task recognised as necessary for company survival. Thus concepts such as 'Continuous Improvement', 'Towards Excellence', and 'Zero Defects' have been coined. Techniques have been formalised to assist achievement of these concepts, e.g. 'Total Quality Management', 'Just In Time Manufacture', and 'Simultaneous Engineering'. However these grand concepts cannot be put into practice unless the basic 'grass root' knowledge and infrastructure exists. It is hoped that this book will make a realistic contribution to providing this basic knowledge.

GORDON MAIR

⬡ Acknowledgements

I am very grateful to a number of individuals and companies for assistance in preparing this book.

In general my colleagues in the department of Design, Manufacture and Engineering Management at the University of Strathclyde have all been helpful in various ways. I would like to thank those who read over draft copies of the chapters, offered improvements, and assisted me with compiling the lists of further reading. These were: Neil Christie, Chris Larsson, Peter McKenzie, Bill Ion, and Stephen Warrington, all of my own department; also Tom Walmsley of the Department of Accounting and Finance, Christopher Baldry of the Department of Human Resource Management, Craig McLean and Graham Galbraith of the Department of Mechanical Engineering (in particular Graham for his contribution to the section on noise in Chapter 19), and Tom Mullen and Ronnie McMillan from the Strathclyde Graduate Business School.

I would particularly like to thank Mrs Sheena Nelson and the girls in the drawing office for their assistance in the preparation of the artwork; this was much appreciated.

I would also like to thank the following for permission to use sketches and illustrations. ABB Robotics AB, for Figures 2.1(b) and 21.6; The Science Museum London, for Figure 2.2; Image Select (Ann Ronan) Picture Library, for Figure 2.3 (a); Fanuc, for Figure 2.3 (b); Birmingham Museum of Science and Industry, for Figure 2.4; Graseby Ajax Ltd, for Figure 9.7(b); National Semiconductor (UK) Ltd, for the contents of Figure 13.3; IBM UK Ltd, for Figures 13.10 and 20.14(c); CACI Product Division, for Figure 14.2(e); MTTA, for Figure 19.2(a), from *Safeguarding Industrial Robots*; Herga Ltd, for Figure 19.2(b); CIBS, for Figure 19.11; Beaver Engineering Group plc, for Figure 21.5; Prentice-Hall International (UK) Ltd, for Figures 21.7 and 21.10–21.12, from G.M. Mair, *Industrial Robotics* (1988); Robot Simulations, for Figure 21.8; and Jungheinrich (GB) Ltd, for Figure 21.9.

Finally a special thanks to my wife Linda for her patience while I worked on this book, often in the 'wee sma' hours' of the morning.

G. MAIR

Part I
Introduction

① Essential manufacturing

1.1 Introduction

A few countries are rich due to having an abundance of natural resources, such as oil, or having some unique attribute, such as being a tax haven. These countries are in the minority. Most need to use the work of their population to create wealth. For them a healthy manufacturing industry is essential for prosperity. This chapter describes what manufacturing is, considers what is meant by the term 'prosperity', and shows why manufacturing is an indispensable creator of wealth.

Deriving from two Latin words, 'manus' meaning 'hand', and 'facere' meaning 'to make', 'manufacturing' is the process whereby materials are changed from one state into another by work. The new state is **worth** more than the old. Today the manufacturing process often involves the use of sophisticated machinery and complex organisations.

Without modern manufacturing techniques domestic goods would not be as affordable as they are. Labour saving devices like washing machines and vacuum cleaners are only possible at today's prices because of mass production techniques; the same applies to home entertainment equipment such as video recorders and music systems. The motor car, comprised of possibly up to 15,000 individual components, is now regarded by many families in developed countries as an essential possession, but unless produced using carefully designed and selected manufacturing methods it would be an unattainable luxury.

As well as the fabric of our way of life being held together by the use of manufactured goods, so also are the economics of our society dependent on manufacturing. The wealth created by manufacturing industry gives employment to individuals and enables a country to pay for services at a national level, such as health and education.

In order to put the rest of the book in perspective some aspects of the above statements are now looked at in a little more detail.

1.2 Wealth and prosperity

Consider first the economic environment within which we work. The economies we are concerned with are 'market economies', in that they operate on the basis that things, whether they be items or services, are bought and sold to bring benefit to the individual. The price of material, food, products, and labour, is determined by a combination of the demand for them and their availability or supply. Another type of economy, one that has not proved successful, is the 'centrally planned economy', in which the state owns the means of production and the means of distribution. In this type of economy the state, rather than market forces, would determine the level of wages and the price of goods.

The standard of living available in a country is determined by that nation's wealth. In our type of economy, 'wealth' consists of all things which satisfy human wants. These things can be transferred or exchanged, and because they are limited in supply they have **value** in exchange. By this definition not everything that we need and enjoy is 'wealth' in the economic sense. For example, without fresh air to breathe we would all die, but as air is unlimited in supply to all, it is not economic wealth. Sunlight is also essential for life, but as it is not limited in supply it would not be regarded as part of economic wealth. Thus by definition if something cannot be **bought** or **sold** it does not count in the measure of a nation's **economic** wealth.

It is now realised that the essentials of life such as fresh air and sunlight may no longer be regarded as being in unlimited supply forever. This is due to the manner of creation of the economic wealth described above and the pursuit of increasing standards of living, at the expense of damage to our natural environment. Those involved in manufacturing industry therefore have their part to play in ensuring that industry does not contribute unnecessarily to environmental pollution.

The creation of economic wealth on its own is no longer an adequate gauge of a country's true prosperity. It is significant that the word 'wealth' comes from the Anglo-Saxon word 'wela' meaning 'wellbeing' which is the condition of being contented, healthy, or successful. It is therefore the resulting **quality** of life, rather than the material standard of living, that is meaningful. The manner in which the wealth is created, and the equity with which it is distributed throughout the population, contribute to that quality of life. These concepts are not new. In 1862 the scholar John Ruskin wrote the following: 'There is no wealth but life, life including all its powers of love, of joy, and of admiration. That country is richest which nourishes the greatest number of noble and happy human beings'. More recently, in 1990, the United Nations Development Programme issued the *Human Development Report*. In this a country's progress towards true wealth is measured by using a 'human development index'. This index is derived from the factors of longevity, literacy, and real purchasing power of the average person, rather than the traditional Gross Domestic Product (GDP) or Gross National Product (GNP) per head explained below.

Despite these statements on the quality of life the most common criteria for judging the wealth of a country remain the Gross National Product and Gross Domestic Product. GNP is the total value of all the final goods and services produced annually and the GDP is the GNP minus the net incomes from investment in foreign countries. These criteria are therefore used here as indicators of the strength and energy of an economy, but it should be realised that they are not necessarily indicators of 'wealth' in the fullest sense of the word, **even when considered on a *per capita* (per head) basis**. Additionally, factors such as price levels and the distribution of income influence the reliability of the GNP per head as an indicator of a country's average standard of living. Figure 1.1 shows the GNP and the GNP per head of six of the world's largest market economies. However with the advanced economy countries considered here, the GNP per head figures are relatively high compared to underdeveloped and developing economies, and this does correlate to high standards of living. The importance of manufacturing to the total economy of a country is shown in Figure 1.2 for four of these six nations.

The vitality and competitiveness of an economy are often measured by the rate of growth of GNP, a rate of 3% usually being accepted as satisfactory. Although this is good evidence of the **potential** of a country to be truly prosperous, the country should also be asking itself: are the goods and services produced to provide this growth inherently valuable and beneficial; have benefits and the wealth created been fairly distributed throughout society; and has the production of these goods and services been made without detriment to other parts of society? If these questions can be answered satisfactorily, then it can be said that the wealth created by the country is contributing to the prosperity of the individual.

1.3   Manufacturing industry

In an economy, industry is generally regarded as existing at three levels,

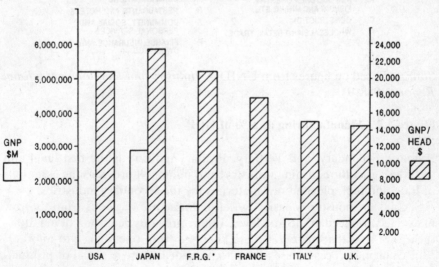

Source: Based on figures from *Europa World Yearbook* (1991)
(*West Germany before unification)

Figure 1.1   GNP and GNP per head for six of the world's largest economies

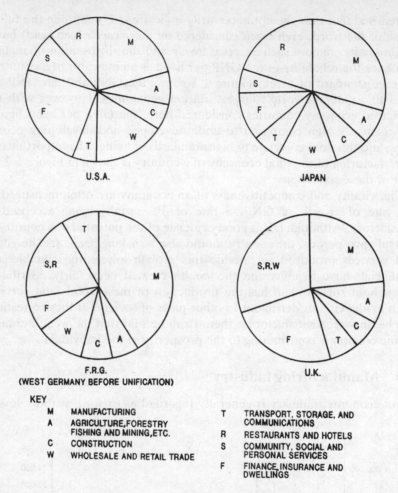

Source: Based on figures from UNIDO, *Industry and Development Global Report* (1988–9)

Figure 1.2   Manufacturing as a % of GDP

Primary, Secondary, and Tertiary. Primary industry is the first level and includes agriculture, fishing, forestry, and mining; it provides the essentials of food and fuel, plus the raw materials for the secondary industries.

Secondary industry is basically the manufacture of goods from the raw materials produced in the first level. In our previous definition of manufacturing we said that materials were changed from one state into another. This changing process causes **value** to be **added** to the material or product. For example if iron ore is taken, combined with certain other materials and melted, then steel ingots can be produced by pouring the melt into moulds. This steel is much more valuable than the raw ore because it is easier to put to use. If these ingots are now squeezed in a forging press to produce wheels for railway wagons, then once more value is added. An example of a product with very high value added would be a communications satellite, this requires many man-years of work in the form of research, development, and high skill manufacturing.

Tertiary industry involves services rather than extraction or manufacture. Examples of this type of industry are transport, entertainment, banking, police, health, and education.

Figure 1.3 shows the percentages of the total workforce, in five developed countries, occupied in various sectors of the economy. In each case the significance of manufacturing industry as a direct employer is evident. It is also important to realise that the primary and tertiary industries are very much dependent on the manufacturing sector. Estimates suggest that about half of those employed in the primary and tertiary industries depend indirectly on manufacturing industry for their jobs.

Efficient operation of the primary industries is dependent on the availability of manufactured goods. For example the efficiency of modern farming owes much to the use of tractors, combine harvesters, and other mechanised equipment. Fishing fleets require well made vessels with reliable navigation and communication equipment. Forestry workers use machines to cultivate the ground for tree planting, and to assist with felling and handling mature trees. Cost effective mining relies on the use of modern automated digging, cutting, and tunnelling machines. The primary industries rely on manufactured goods to keep themselves competitive in the world market, and to maintain safe and tolerable conditions for their employees. Food is now virtually a manufactured item when the amount of processing and packaging that is done on it is considered.

Tertiary industry also relies heavily on manufactured products. Transport services need reliable trains, buses, and lorries to operate satisfactorily. The entertainment industry uses many artifacts for sound and lighting, video recording, compact disc making, and of course there are communication satellites and the television and radio receivers in our living rooms. Banking requires the use of extensive computing facilities and customer terminals. The police use computers, communication equipment, and transport. The health service uses much of what has been mentioned already plus pharmaceuticals manufactured to stringent specifications. Education also uses many manufactured items; books are a good example. We can use this book you are reading to illustrate the way in which manufacturing stimulates economic activity.

1.4   Manufacturing as a stimulant

Initially, this book was written on a word processor. Thus the need to purchase the machine, which would first have had to be made. This, on its own, illustrates how manufacturing stimulates the need for further manufactures. Then communication between the author and the publisher had to take place, hence the need for communication systems which require

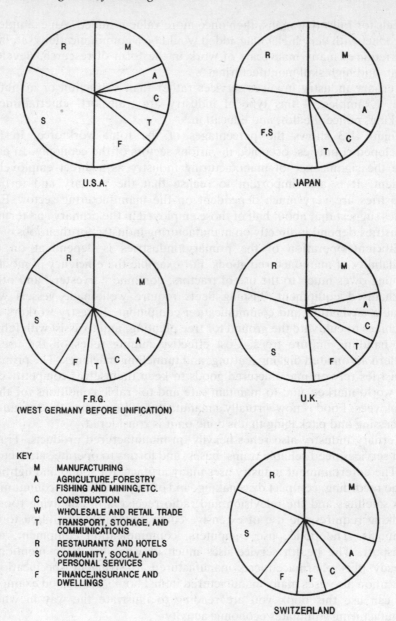

KEY

M	MANUFACTURING
A	AGRICULTURE, FORESTRY FISHING AND MINING, ETC.
C	CONSTRUCTION
W	WHOLESALE AND RETAIL TRADE
T	TRANSPORT, STORAGE, AND COMMUNICATIONS
R	RESTAURANTS AND HOTELS
S	COMMUNITY, SOCIAL AND PERSONAL SERVICES
F	FINANCE, INSURANCE AND DWELLINGS

Source: Based on figures from *Europa World Yearbook* (1991)

Figure 1.3   Manufacturing as a % of employed population

manufacture and operation. The process of producing the book involves the work of many people including the editor, the reviewers, and the people involved in production and printing of the book. The printing machines also had to be made, and the paper and ink produced. Transport facilities had to be used to distribute the book throughout the country. People were employed in the shop that sold it. Computers were required in the shop to monitor stock levels and raise orders. Throughout the whole process financial personnel would be involved in ensuring that money was available to finance the project and monitor the costs incurred. Sales and marketing personnel would also be involved in promoting the book.

It is obvious that the process of manufacturing even this small book contributes to the employment of many people, both directly and indirectly. In the case of this book none of the people involved, nor the machines used, were solely concerned with the product all of the time. In order to reduce the risk involved many books are manufactured by the publisher and the shop that sells it also stocks a wide variety of other books. It is also apparent from this that three types of manufactured goods are involved. The first is a producer, or investment, good, such as a printing press, usually sold to companies to produce other goods. The second type is an intermediate good which is a semi-finished product used by both manufacturers and consumers; paper would be the example here. The third is the consumer good, or consumer durable, sold to individuals, such as the book itself. This relationship is shown in Figure 1.4.

The previous paragraphs showed the stimulus to economic activity that arises from even a relatively simple product. Consider the vastly greater implications of manufacturing more complex products such as computers, motor cars, and aircraft, this last item possibly made of up to 4 million high quality components. The wages earned by all of those involved in the production process, and the profits made by the shareholders, are used to purchase more goods and services, so further stimulating the economy. Unfortunately this is all too apparent when working in reverse. For

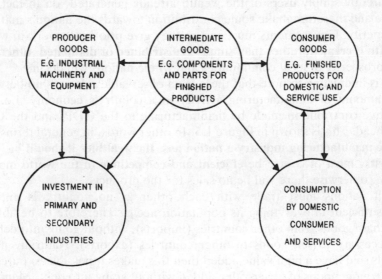

Figure 1.4   Types of goods

example if a large shipyard or steel making plant closes down a few thousand people may lose their jobs directly. But the numbers of unemployed do not stop there as there will be the companies that relied on their business for sub-contract work. These companies may have supplied materials and services. Trade in the surrounding community will also be affected as there will no longer be spare money available for the ex-employees to spend in the retail shops and the local entertainment and leisure industries – and so it goes on. These multiplier or 'knock on' effects are well known and verify the validity of the statement that a healthy manufacturing industry is essential for prosperity.

One of the most important characteristics of manufacturing industry is its inherent ability to **generate** economic activity and growth without recourse to other sectors of the economy. In fact manufacturing determines the prosperity of the other sectors. For example the advent of microprocessor based automation, in the form of computer controlled machines and industrial robots, has made it more economic to produce smaller batches of products and to change quickly from making one type of product to another. This flexibility has made it possible to do such things as offering a wide variety of car options to the customer, e.g. colour, trim, engine size, accessories, etc. This perpetuates itself as customers want more and more options, greater freedom of choice, and subsequently more frequent release of new models. This puts more pressure on the car industry to respond quickly to new styles and demands and so it needs to invest more heavily in capital equipment, . . . and so the cycle repeats itself.

Thus manufacturing is an extremely effective means of **creating** wealth. It is much more efficient than the service industries which, although apparently simply **users** of the wealth already generated, do in fact add value and therefore make some contribution towards the nation's material prosperity. Governments must ensure they give priority to work in which wealth is **created**, rather than simply **redistributed** or **dissipated**, otherwise the prosperity of local communities and whole nations will decline.

It is interesting to note that there is an observable relationship between the amount of manufacturing activity in a country's economy, i.e. the relative contribution made by manufacturing to the GDP, and the GNP per head. This is shown in Figure 1.5. In other words, in general terms, **the more manufacturing industry a nation has, the wealthier it should be**. This industry must of course be **efficient** and **competitive** in the world market place, otherwise there will be no sales for the products.

All nations must trade with each other as no country is entirely self-sufficient in everything its population needs. Therefore to be able to purchase goods **from** other countries (imports), without going into debt, it is necessary to sell goods **to** other countries (exports). Naturally if the goods sold have a high value added then this makes it possible to purchase many more goods of lower value added without going into debt. Manufactured products provide this high value added factor, hence the absolute

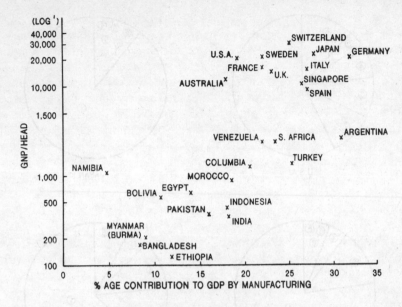

Source: Based on data from *Europa World Yearbook* (1991)

Figure 1.5   Relationship indicating that GNP per head generally increases as manufacturing activity increases

necessity for a country to have a strong manufacturing base to prevent increasing balance of payments problems.

Figure 1.6 shows the relative value of visible exports for five countries. It is apparent in each case that manufacturing industry is an absolutely essential contributor to exports. Switzerland is included because, according to the World Bank, it has in recent years consistently had the world's highest GNP per head. As may be expected, an essential part of the Swiss economy is its manufacturing industry. It is a country with no significant natural resources, yet it is famous for its precision engineering and machinery. Manufacture of pharmaceuticals, chemicals, and textiles is also important. It has a highly skilled labour force and is well organised to sell manufactured goods in the world market. These high value added commodities have helped provide its citizens with the high standard of living they presently enjoy.

This chapter has attempted to explain what wealth and prosperity are, and how a healthy manufacturing industry is essential for creation of that wealth and prosperity. Chapter 2 considers how manufacturing industry has developed over the years to reach its present level of importance.

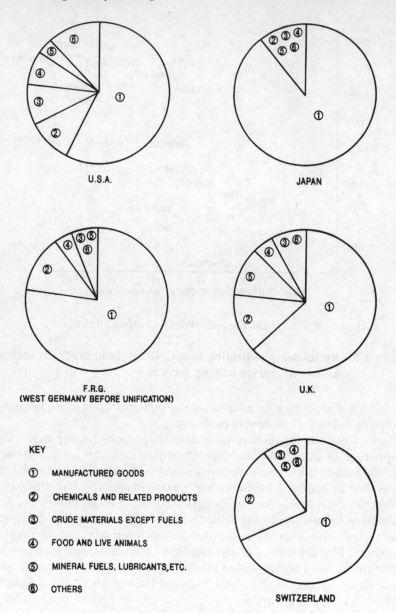

KEY

① MANUFACTURED GOODS

② CHEMICALS AND RELATED PRODUCTS

③ CRUDE MATERIALS EXCEPT FUELS

④ FOOD AND LIVE ANIMALS

⑤ MINERAL FUELS, LUBRICANTS,ETC.

⑥ OTHERS

Source: Based on figures from *Europa World Yearbook* (1991)

Figure 1.6   Relative value of visible exports

__ Review Questions __

1 What is a 'market economy'?
2 What is the basic indicator used to measure the wealth of a country? Why might this indicator not necessarily reflect the true prosperity of individuals within the country?
3 Describe the **three** levels of industry present in an economy, and discuss their composition.
4 What is the difference between 'producer', 'intermediate', and 'consumer' goods?
5 Explain what you understand by the term 'value added'.
6 In your own words, discuss why a healthy manufacturing industry is essential for a successful economy.

__ Further Reading __

1 'Economics of the Real World' by Peter Donaldson. 3rd Edition. Published by Penguin Books, 1992.
2 'Applied Economics: An Introductory Course', Edited by A. Griffiths and S. Wall. 4th Edition. Published by Longman Group Ltd. 1991.
3 'The Living Economy', Edited by Paul Ekins. Published by Routledge and Kegan Paul, 1986.
4 'Whatever Happened to Britain?', by John Eatwell. Published by BBC Publications, 1982.
5 'Manufacturing Into The Late 1990s' A Report by the PA Consulting Group. Published by HMSO, 1989.
6 'The Finniston Report' by Sir Monty Finniston. Published by HMSO, 1980.
7 'International Labour Office Yearbook of Labour Statistics' (use latest edition).
8 'Europa World Yearbook'. Published by Europa Publications Ltd. (use latest edition).
9 'Industry and Development Global Report 1988–89'. Published by the United Nations Industrial Development Organisation (1989).

② Manufacturing history

2.1 Man the toolmaker

In the classic science fiction film '2001 A Space Odyssey' there is a short scene that captures the essence of the following historical discussion. It occurs when an 'apeman' throws a bone into the air in triumph after he has discovered its usefulness as a weapon. As the bone spins into the air it is transformed by the camera into a rotating space station 'waltzing' to the strains of 'The Blue Danube'. Whether or not the apeman creature is a valid representation of early man the imagery is powerful. The word 'tool' comes from the Old Norse 'tol' meaning 'weapon'. From the first use of simple primitive tools for weapons and for cutting and crushing, man has developed the manufacturing technology and culture of today.

Although this scene is poetically inspiring, it also highlights the fact that man is unique in the animal kingdom in his ability to **design and make tools** (see Figure 2.1). He progressed from the selective phase of simply picking a natural object from the environment to use as a tool, just as a chimpanzee selects a twig to poke into anthills to catch ants. He also passed through the adaptive phase where a stone was chipped to create a sharp cutting edge. Man has now reached the inventive phase where an object not found in nature is conceived and manufactured, say a bow and arrow or a supersonic aircraft.

It is around two to three million years ago that we find the first archaeological evidence of toolmaking. An early manlike creature, *Australopithecus*, is thought to have made a simple cutting and chipping tool by striking the edge of one stone against another to produce a sharp edge. Since these creatures lacked dexterity the tool would have been held crudely, with the thick blunt end pressed against the palm, while being used to cut meat. These creatures lived in the open and probably cooperated in hunting.

Peking man, a form of *homo erectus*, lived between 400,000 and 200,000 years ago. These men were hunters and travellers but built camps and primitive huts for shelter. Many stone 'chopper' type tools of varying size and shape have been found from this period, though they do not differ much from those used during the previous two million years. There is evidence, however, that fire was used to harden the tips of sharpened wooden tools and weapons.

Between 70,000 and 30,000 years ago there lived Neanderthal man, an early member of *homo sapiens*. It is thought the average size of his brain could have been slightly larger than modern man and there is evidence that

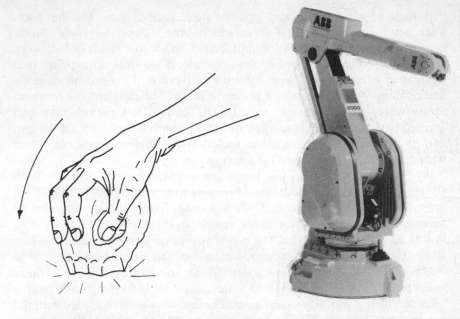

(a) Stone axe, c. 2 million BC

(b) Industrial robot, late
20th century
Source: ABB Robotics AB

The microprocessor controlled robot is much more complex than the stone axe, yet both are tools fashioned by man to improve his quality of life

Figure 2.1   Tools

he had a primitive religion. He was probably a well organised hunter working in groups to ambush animals or drive them over cliffs. The tools and weapons he used were still of fire hardened wood and shaped stone, although they were now more elegant in design.

2.2   The New Stone Age

Modern man, *homo sapiens sapiens*, appears just as Neanderthal man becomes extinct. The use of stone tools continued into the New Stone Age. This was the Neolithic period which lasted in south west Asia from about 9000 BC to 6000 BC, and in Europe from about 4000 BC to 2400 BC. Europe developed later as the last ice age finished here only 10,000 years ago. Even today in remote corners of the world there are a few tribes still living under Stone Age conditions. During the Neolithic period man made the change from a hunter gatherer to a farmer. Crop growing and cattle rearing were started. Tools had now become quite sophisticated although still made of wood, bone, and types of stone such as flint. The flint tools were often the master tools from which others could be made. Stone headed axes with bone handles, and knives and arrow heads of flint were common. Wooden hoes, and sickles originally made from setting flints into straight or curved bones, were used for cultivation. Clay pots were made and clothing was woven using a primitive loom. The sling and the bow and arrow were early inventions and, by the end of this period, man had learned to make as well as use fire and had produced the lever, the wedge, and the wheel. Since Neolithic society was relatively peaceful most weapons were probably used for hunting.

At this stage we can see the beginning of the primary industries. With the advent of agriculture man would be able to produce more food than his immediate community needed. This would create the opportunity of **trading** some of his food for other items, perhaps dried fish from a tribe that lived by the river or sea. The use of appropriate tools would allow him to increase the amount of food grown, and so this would stimulate him to make improvements in these tools. Some tribes may have lived near sources of flint. They would become adept at fashioning tools and a 'manufacturing' industry would arise. These tools would be traded with the fishers and farmers. The toolmakers were adding value to the flint by working it into shape, the fishermen adding value by drying the fish to prevent it from spoiling, and the farmers would be adding value to their produce by harvesting and transporting it to where it could be traded. These principles are unchanged today except of course money is now used to facilitate the sale and purchase of labour and goods.

2.3 The Bronze Age

Technological progress does not really begin to accelerate until about 5000 BC when we begin to move out of prehistory. The first urban civilisations existed along fertile riverbanks. These were the Sumerians in the valleys of the Tigris and Euphrates rivers in Mesopotamia, the Egyptians along the Nile, the Indus Valley civilisation in India, and the Chinese along the banks of the Yellow river. It is around this time that metal first began to be worked. Since metal has been the material that has allowed manufacturing industry to have such an influence on society, it is the production and use of metal that forms the core of the following sections.

Originally copper was used; it was probably obtained in its pure form and beaten into shape. Relatively soft in this state it has limited use for tools and was used mostly for ornaments. However it was soon found that when melted it could be alloyed with tin to produce a much stronger and harder material – bronze. The Bronze Age lasted from its beginnings with the Egyptians and Sumerians around 4500 BC to the start of the Iron Age around 1200 BC. Europe was about 1000 years behind Asia Minor in using bronze, with the Bronze Age in Britain lasting roughly from 2000 BC to 500 BC.

Pure copper became scarce in supply, therefore it was necessary to obtain or 'win' the metal by smelting copper rich ores. Excavations have been made of copper smelting furnaces built into the ground in beds of sand. Stones of varying size were used to support the internal walls of the structure and burning charcoal was used as a source of heat. The furnace pit was lined with mortar and had clay tubes set into the side for bellows' access. The bellows provided a forced draught to increase the furnace temperature. About 10 cm above the base of the furnace there was a tapping hole which led downwards into a tapping pit. As the ore was smelted the impurities would rise to the top of the melt and eventually be drawn off through the tapping hole. The pure copper would be left in the bottom of the furnace. Later it could be refined and alloyed by remelting in crucibles. Objects were made by casting in moulds and by beating the material into shape. Hammering of the metal also improved its hardness, enabling it to be used for items such as nails.

The Sumerians and Egyptians used war captives as slave labour. This allowed some of their own workers to have the time to develop their skills as craftsmen in the manufacture of bronze artifacts. Ploughs, hoes, and axes for farming, saw blades, chisels, and bradawls for carpentry, helmets, spearheads, and daggers for war, and ornaments, are just some of the items that were made out of bronze. Even after the use of iron became widespread bronze remained popular. Experience gained in alloying bronze with elements such as zinc and antimony ensured its continuing popularity.

As civilisation spread throughout the Middle East craftsmen such as metalworkers, potters, builders, carpenters, masons, tanners, weavers, and dyers were all to be found. The more skilled artisans, for reasons of economy and supply, lived in the larger towns and cities. They usually lived in their own identifiable areas and later, in the Middle Ages, they would organise into craft guilds that became powerful political groups.

2.4 The Iron Age

Iron, which is harder and tougher than bronze, was first used in its naturally occurring form. The original source, before smelting was feasible, was fallen meteorites, the ancient Egyptians calling it 'the metal from heaven'. The iron would be broken off, heated, then hammered into shape. The Hittites, who occupied the same area as the Sumerians had many years before, were the main workers in iron from about 2000 BC to 1200 BC. It is likely that they smelted their iron from bog ore. This ore occurs freely in marshy ground and can be obtained by simply sieving it out of the water. The ore is then smelted and the resulting iron 'bloom' hammered to remove the slag, i.e. impurities, before quenching in water. After repeating the heating, hammering, and quenching process several times an iron of useful strength is obtained. However widespread use of iron did not occur until the Hittite Empire was destroyed and the ironsmiths dispersed along with their skills. The design and use of tools in general was of course continuing in parallel with metallurgical developments. For example, primitive manually powered wooden lathes were in use around 700 BC for making items such as food bowls.

The use of iron was longer in developing than that of copper due to the difference in melting temperatures. Copper melts at 1083°C and iron at 1539°C, thus requiring much hotter and more efficient furnaces for smelting and casting. Eventually a primitive form of steel was produced by hammering charcoal into heated iron. The first iron ploughshare possibly came from Palestine around 1100 BC and by the the time of Christ the use of iron was widespread.

In Europe iron mining and smelting grew up in areas where the ore could be mined and there was a plentiful supply of wood from local forests. One of the main reasons for the Roman invasion of Britain in 55 AD was the attractiveness of the iron and tin mines. Iron was used for farm implements, armour, horseshoes, hand tools, and a wide variety of weapons. Iron wrought into beams had also been used in structural work by both the Greeks and the Romans. With increasing population the need for manufactured items was also increasing. This meant that there was now a need for the 'mass production' of some products. The Romans, for example, had 'factories' for mass producing glassware but these were very labour intensive and had low production rates compared with today's expectations.

We now take a time jump through the Dark and Middle Ages to around the beginning of the Renaissance period. The quality of iron had remained relatively poor and it was not until about the 15th century that furnaces using water powered bellows were sufficiently hot to smelt iron satisfactorily. This allowed better control of the material properties of the finished castings. In cannon and mortar manufacture, for example, the iron had previously been so brittle that the cannon often blew up in the users' faces. The higher quality iron that could now be produced prevented this. In the 16th century water power was also used for other metalworking processes and rolling mills were developed for producing the metal strips from which coins could be stamped.

As well as technology for manufacture, organisation of manpower is important and progress also occurred here. Leonardo da Vinci, who lived between 1452 and 1519, apparently found time to turn his attention to the manner in which work is carried out. He implemented a study of how a man shovelled earth and worked out the time it should take to move a specified amount of material using the observed method and size of shovel. This was an early example of the scientific analysis of work which is so important to the efficiency of modern manufacturing systems. Although Leonardo da Vinci and many others of this period were part of the great re-birth of interest in the arts and scientific discovery, it is not until the beginning of the 18th century that we find the manufacturing and engineering discoveries occurring that so changed the quality of life for the ordinary person.

The beginnings of the factory system were appearing in Europe during the 17th century in the woollen trade and cloth making. The **'factory system'** is typified by the 'specialisation', or 'division', of labour. This entails individual workers specialising in one aspect of the total work required to complete a product. The 'commission system' had also arisen during this period. A 'commission merchant' was someone who bought a product from a manufacturer and then sold that product to an end user. For instance he would buy wool from a sheep farmer and pay for it to be delivered to the wool cleaner. He would pay the cleaner, then pay for transport to the comber and pay him. This was repeated through the subsequent stages of carding, spinning, and weaving. The commission merchant then paid for transport of the finished cloth to the market, either at home or abroad. The merchant financed his operation from borrowing money from a 'capitalist'. Capitalists' wealth grew considerably from this type of investment. Initially these woolworkers were unlikely to be all together in the one 'factory' and were probably operating as individual 'outworkers' in their own homes. The division of labour could also be seen in woodworking: rather than general woodworkers, we find 'carpenters', wheelwrights, and cabinet makers beginning to appear.

It should be remembered that agriculture was still the main source of employment at this time. For example it has been estimated that in England in 1688 there were 4.6 million people employed in agriculture and only 246,000 in manufacturing. Between 1750 and 1850 the population of Britain trebled yet it remained self-sufficient in food, even though the number of workers in farming had dropped to around 1.5 million by 1841. This was due to the 'agricultural revolution' which was caused by new techniques such as planned crop selection and rotation, scientific animal breeding, and the development of new farming tools. Probably the most important invention of this time was the mechanical seed drill devised by Jethro Tull around 1701 which increased farming productivity. This was a good example of primary industry benefiting from a manufactured, or secondary industry, product. The advent of mechanisation on the farm would eventually lead to massive reductions in the numbers of labourers required; these were to provide a pool of workers for the blossoming industrial revolution.

2.5 The Industrial Revolution

A number of factors brought about the industrial revolution which is generally accepted as having been started in Britain during the course of the 18th century. One of these factors, the division of labour within a factory system of working, already existed. Two other elements that were to contribute were cheap and efficient power in the form of steam engines, and large supplies of good quality iron with which to make these engines and other products. An additional aspect was the development of transport systems. These initially appeared due to the economic stimuli of the elements mentioned previously, but they also, in themselves, assisted further industrial development. A growing canal network and rail system facilitated trade and transport domestically, and increasing sea transport provided the essential ability to sell manufactured goods overseas.

Iron had always been produced in relatively small quantities, but in 1711 in Coalbrookdale, England, Abraham Darby began to use coke to smelt large quantities of ore. He produced good quality cast iron that was suitable for forging as well as for casting. Soon iron was to replace copper, bronze, and brass for items such as pots and pans and other domestic goods.

Manufacturing industry at this time still relied on water power even although Thomas Savery had installed a steam engine to raise water from a mine in 1698, and an 'atmospheric' engine had been developed by Newcomen and Cowley in 1705. Many of the improvements in manufacturing technology during this period were concerned with the textile industry. In 1733 water powered looms were made possible by the invention of the 'flying shuttle' by James Kay, and in 1770 the 'Spinning Jenny' was patented by James Hargreaves. Replacing the spinning wheel, the Jenny was a frame containing a number of parallel spindles made to revolve by the use of a hand powered wheel and pulley belt. Where previously only one thread would have been spun by hand, eight could now be done and this was later improved to twenty or thirty.

The industrial revolution really got underway in 1776, when James Watt produced a much improved version of the steam engine. This was made a commercial possibility by the use of a boring machine made by John Wilkinson to produce the cylinders for the engine. Despite this, up until the beginning of the 19th century the relatively cheap Savery and Newcomen engines were often used in preference to the more expensive Watt engines. These were used on their own or as a supplement to water power.

Also at this time the basis of modern economics was laid down by Adam Smith in his book *The Wealth of Nations*. In this he further developed the concept of the division of labour to improve productivity and stimulate economic progress. The general adoption of this principle contributed to the success of the industrial revolution.

In 1784 Edmund Cartwright built a loom capable of being driven by steam power, and in 1788 James Watt devised the centrifugal governor for automatically controlling the speed of a steam engine. Thus we have the beginnings of manufacturing automation. Looms had originally been located close to hills to make use of water power and the same type of equipment as corn mills, hence the name 'mills'. With the advent of steam power they were relocated to areas where coal was plentiful.

Since the source of power for the early machines was a large, relatively expensive, steam engine, it was natural that all machinery driven by the engine should be located as close to it as possible. This also applied to associated activities. It was therefore now convenient for all workers to work within a short distance of each other and probably under the same roof. This was one factor that contributed to the rise of the factory. The other was social. People had been used to working to agricultural rhythms, but the new systems of work demanded tight organisation with workers expected to be available at specific times. Thus the time was ripe for the factory due to a combination of technological and social/organisational reasons. The factory was to peak in the early to mid-20th century with some employing around 70,000 people.

In 1794 in Britain Henry Maudsley created the first all metal lathe (see Figure 2.2). Meanwhile, in America in 1792, Eli Whitney had produced the cotton gin which greatly increased the productivity of the southern cotton workers, who at that time were predominantly slaves. In 1796 in Britain Joseph Bramah developed the hydraulic press which provided a means of greatly increasing the force a manual worker was able to exert. In 1804 in France we see Joseph Marie Jacquard introducing automatic control of a loom by the use of punched cards. The use of punched cards to contain information for computers and automatic machine control was to continue for the next 150 years.

We have already seen the emergence of two of the main ingredients of modern manufacturing, i.e. the 'factory' as a central manufacturing unit, and specialisation of labour. At this point, at the beginning of the 19th

Source: Courtesy the Science Museum, London

Figure 2.2   Maudsley's original screwcutting lathe, c. 1800

century, we see the appearance of three further major concepts, i.e. **mass production**, **standardisation**, and **interchangeability**.

One of the first instances of the manufacture of interchangeable components was in the USA in 1798 when Eli Whitney used filing jigs to produce parts for a contract of 10,000 army muskets. Although the parts were almost identical their manufacture did involve much manual labour in the filing to size of the components.

The manufacture of components using mechanised mass production techniques first occurred in 1803 in the Portsmouth Naval Dockyard in Britain. The components were pulley blocks for the Royal Navy. The machines for producing the blocks had been designed by the famous engineer Marc Isambard Brunel and manufactured by Henry Maudsley. There were forty five machines and they were powered by two steam engines. Eventually productivity was so improved that ten unskilled workers could produce as may blocks as had previously been produced by 110 craftsmen. By 1808 the production rate had risen to 130,000 per year.

In the USA two of the innovators in using machinery to make the close toleranced components necessary for interchangeability were Samuel Colt and his chief engineer Elisha Root. In the Colt armory in Connecticut they designed a turret lathe to facilitate the production of identical turned parts for the Colt revolver produced in 1835.

To achieve interchangeability of components not produced in the same factory, methods of **standardisation** had to be adopted for commonly used parts. One of the pioneers in this area was the British engineer Joseph Whitworth. Around 1830 he began developing precision measuring techniques and produced a measuring machine that utilised a large micrometer screw. These accurate measuring techniques and equipment were necessary for the inspection of components intended to be interchangeable. In 1841 he proposed a standard form and series of standard sizes for screw threads which were eventually adopted in Britain. It may be noted that although individual countries began to adopt their own national standards these were not necessarily compatible on a world wide basis. Even today much has still to be done to achieve international standardisation of manufactured items.

In the textile industry, which was the first industry to experience the effects of the industrial revolution on a large scale, workers began to be displaced from their jobs by encroaching mechanisation. This was resented so much that the Luddite movement was formed in England in 1811. The Luddites' purpose being to riot against the machinery, they caused considerable damage to equipment but refrained from violence against people. Repressive measures, including the shooting of a band of Luddites in 1812, did not put an end to the movement. They appeared in waves in various textile manufacturing areas. However, as the prosperity of individuals continued to increase so resistance to the machinery died out.

Greater possibilities for the improvement of working conditions in Britain were made possible by the repealing of the Combination Acts in

1824. This repeal allowed Trade Unions (combinations of workers) to be formed, thus providing the opportunity for organised resistance to exploitation. In the years 1833–40 Industrial Commissioners were appointed to investigate poor social conditions. These measures were necessary as there were many major problems to overcome.

Large numbers of people were now coming to work in factories in close proximity to each other. This meant that when working a, then normal, twelve hour day, they had to live near to the factory. Thus factory towns and cities increased in size and population density. Congested housing, often in the type of houses known as tenements, forced men, women, and children to live under very poor conditions. Rooms had poor lighting and ventilation, and were cramped and lacked privacy. There was also a 'ticket' system in operation for many workers. Under this system workers received tickets for their labour in lieu of money. To translate these tickets into the essentials of food and clothing, they had to be redeemed at the company store. Thus the company had a monopoly and was able to charge the highest prices for the poorest goods.

In the factories themselves, where many women and children were employed, working conditions were often poor. Low wages and long hours caused accidents, inefficient working, and poor health. The 'piecework' system also caused hardship. Under this system workers in their own homes, and eventually in what became known as 'sweatshops', worked on jobs sent out from the factories. They were payed per 'piece' produced and as they were forced to work at very low rates working conditions were often even worse than in the factories.

Considering the engineering aspects again, simple steam locomotives had been doing useful work in coalmines between 1813 and 1820, but it was not until 1825 that the first public railway was opened. This was between Stockton and Darlington in England. Improvements in manufacturing equipment and techniques were leading to stronger boilers and better fitting cylinders and pistons. Thus as the efficiency and power of the steam engines improved, so also did their ability to transport materials, products, and people over greater distances at higher speeds. By 1848 there were 5000 miles of railway track laid in Britain. The first successful steam ship had been built on the banks of the river Clyde in Scotland in 1812. This was the 'Comet' and it was the forerunner of ships such as the 'Sirius' and the 'Great Western' that began regular transatlantic service in 1838.

In his book *Days at the Factories* published in 1843 George Dodd remarked:

> The bulk of the inhabitants of a great city, such as London, have very indistinct notions of the means whereby the necessaries, the comforts, or the luxuries of life are furnished. The simple fact, that he who has money can command every variety of exchangeable produce seems to act as a veil which hides the producer from the consumer.

Obviously some things change little even over 150 years! Dodd differentiates between, 'mere handicrafts carried on by individuals of whom each makes the complete article', and the work that involves, 'the investment of capital and the division of labour incident to a factory'. He then goes on to describe the operation of various factories in the London of the early to mid-19th century. These were apparently well organised, with relatively sophisticated cost control systems, machines utilising steam power, and a variety of skilled, semi-skilled, and unskilled workers.

The confluence of improvements in iron and steel production, the development of precision machinery, mechanised processes, division of labour, mass production techniques, interchangeability of components, standardisation, the application of steam to transportation giving access to many new markets, and the beginnings of improvements in factory conditions, led into what has been termed the 'later factory period', beginning around 1850 (see Figure 2.3).

The acceleration in industrial development during the second half of the 19th century can be seen by considering the production of iron and the expansion of the rail network in Britain. The annual production of pig iron had risen from just over 17,000 tons in 1740 to 1.25 million tons in 1840, but by 1906 it had reached more than 10 million tons. In 1850 there were 6500 miles of railway in England; by 1900 this had risen to over 25,000. Working conditions were improving and by 1872 in Britain a basic nine hour working day had been agreed, although the working week was of six days. Manufacturing equipment continued to improve in quality and capability. For example in 1873 a fully automatic lathe was produced by Christopher Spencer. The movements of the machine elements were controlled by drum cams, or 'brain wheels' as they were called, forerunners of today's computer control systems (see Figure 2.4). By 1880 electric motors were being used to drive some machines. Coupled with the advent of the internal combustion engine at the end of the century, this meant that factories and other power reliant establishments would eventually be able to spread out and away from a central steam power source.

2.6 The 20th century

Many of the advances made in science, medicine, and engineering during this century have been possible due to parallel advances in manufacturing technology. The understanding of how best to organise and manage people at work has also increased. Toward the end of the 19th and the beginning of the 20th century great progress was made in the realm of 'scientific management'. This was concerned with finding the best ways of doing work, and became known as 'work study'; it was composed of 'work measurement' and 'method study'. As well as Leonardo da Vinci mentioned earlier, contributions had been made in this field by others. For example around 1750 in France Jean R. Perronet carried out a detailed study of the method of manufacture of pins. Also Charles Babbage, the British inventor of the mechanical digital computer, published a book in

Source: Courtesy Image Select (Ann Ronan) Picture Library

(a) The pen slitting room in the Hinks, Wells & Co. factory, Birmingham, c. 1850; note the specialisation of labour

Source: Courtesy Fanuc

(b) Fanuc factory in Japan, late 20th century; note the use of automation and the absence of labour)

Figure 2.3   The factory

Source: Courtesy Birmingham Museum of Science and Industry

Figure 2.4   Christopher Spencer's automatic lathe, 1873

1832 titled *On the Economy of Machinery and Manufactures*, in which he considered how best to organise people for improved productivity. However, widely recognised as the major contributors to work study are Frederick Winslow Taylor and Frank and Lillian Gilbreth. Their work has provided the basis for modern work organisation which is described more fully in Chapter 16 on 'Work Study'.

Whereas in the 18th and 19th centuries the textile industry had been a spur to, and a beneficiary of, much of the advances in manufacturing technology, at the beginning of the 20th century this role was taken over by the motor car industry.

One of the earliest examples of an assembly line was in the Olds Motor Works in Detroit, USA. In 'line production' the division of labour is fully utilised in that work is transported from worker to worker in a linear fashion, thus reducing work in progress and increasing productivity; in the Olds factory, which was rebuilt after a fire destroyed the original in 1901, the work was wheeled from worker to worker. But it is Henry Ford who is seen as the major pioneer of modern mass production techniques.

Ford seized on the assembly line concept and together with interchangeable mass produced components, a conveyorised production line, and specially designed assembly equipment, he made a tremendous contribution to manufacturing industry efficiency. Although the motor car engine was not made in a practical form until 1887, it has been estimated that Ford's Model T would have taken 27 days to build using the technology and techniques available at the time of the American Civil War (1861–5). By 1914 Ford was producing a Model T in just over an hour and a half. By 1918 he had cut the price from 850 dollars to 400 dollars; this of course increased sales which led to a demand for higher productivity and by the 1920s the production time for the Model T had been reduced to 27 minutes!

Laws were passed in the early 20th century to ensure tolerable working conditions in industry. For example in the UK there were laws relating to hours worked, the minimum age of workers, the amount of floor and air space per worker, and heating and lighting conditions. Also laws regarding the safety of machines were created; many machines used dangerous belt and shaft transmission systems and these had to be guarded. Employers were also to pay compensation for any injuries suffered by workers while carrying out their work.

The First World War of 1914–18 was a stimulus to technological progress. By the 1930s significant advances were being made in materials and manufacturing technology. For example the quality of steel was improving, tungsten carbide was being used, and new casting and extruding processes were developed. Plastics such as PVC and polyethylene were created. Automated machines for making screws and other items, and transfer machines capable of mechanically transporting parts from workstation to workstation, were also in use.

During the Second World War of 1939–45 industrial progress was rapid as the demand for manufactured goods for the armed forces mushroomed. For example, stick electrode welding was used for the first time on a large scale to fabricate ships. Production rates and quality and reliability of components had to be maximised. The integration of electronic control techniques with hydraulic mechanisms for gun and radar control was also to provide the foundation for the postwar automated machine tool industry.

By 1947 the General Electric Company (GEC) in the USA demonstrated how it was possible to control a machine tool using a magnetic tape. This was termed the 'record playback control' system. The machine element movements necessary to produce an initial workpiece were recorded on the magnetic tape. When the tape was played back the machine movements were duplicated using a servo control system so allowing further workpieces to be created automatically. Around this time a method of controlling a milling machine using punched cards was devised by J.T. Parsons, again in the USA. The coded pattern of holes on the cards was read automatically and the information fed to a controller to drive the milling cutter along the desired path. Through collaboration with the US Air Force and the Massachusetts Institute of Technology (MIT) the concept was further developed to produce a prototype three axis milling machine in 1952. In the same year the GEC method was improved by MIT and launched on the market by the Giddings and Lewis Machine Tool Company this was the first commercial numerically controlled machine tool system. About the same time Ferranti in Britain also developed a three axis machine controlled by magnetic tape.

In the technical journals at this time there was much talk about the 'automatic factory' as the possibilities of applying mechanisation coupled with electronic control began to be understood. By 1954 the first large scale automated production line was built. This was named 'Project Tinkertoy', and was used to produce and assemble electronic products. The first industrial robot, made in the USA by Unimation, was installed in 1961 for servicing a diecasting machine. These examples of automation were not the computer controlled systems of today. They either used mechanical devices or 'hard wired' electronics to effect control, and were therefore not easily reprogrammed to cope with changes of work. This only became possible with the advent of integrated electronic circuits.

1967 saw the first large scale integrated circuit manufactured which contained hundreds of electronic components. By 1970 the 'microprocessor' had been developed by Intel; this was a single electronic chip capable of interpreting and carrying out logical instructions. The cost of computing power was much reduced and 'minicomputers' could now be used for machine control, e.g. the first computer controlled industrial robot was produced by Cincinnati Milacron in 1974. Today microprocessor control is ubiquitous throughout manufacturing industry.

The 'unmanned factory' was again a popular concept in the 1980s, but it remains today an economic impracticality. Many unmanned manufacturing cells and larger units have been created through the use of computer control, but to take humans out of the system completely is still not feasible.

Around 10,000 BC the world population was about 10 million, by 5000 BC it was 100 million, by 1650 AD 500 million, and today it is 5000 million! Early man could survive off the land by hunting and gathering as the population increased so the need for planned agriculture arose to ensure an adequate food supply. Today, when the population of one city, São Paulo in Brazil, equals that of the early world, manufacturing industry has become an essential factor in creating the wealth necessary to support the world's 5 billion people.

Looking to the future, manufacturing could provide the whole world with the equipment for farming and fishing, the machines for food and materials processing, the land, sea and air transport facilities for distribution of food, materials and goods, and the production facilities for medicines and health care equipment. Naturally for access by all, a willingness to share at least some of the world's wealth will be necessary.

The history of man's use of tools shows how manufacturing industry has shaped our society. These first two chapters have attempted to show the significance of manufacturing. The following chapters now describe the composition and operation of the manufacturing industry of today.

Review Questions

1 What feature made *homo sapiens sapiens* different from his precursors, and how was this advantageous?
2 Why did Europe lag behind Asia in the development of metalworking?
3 Why did the full use of iron take longer than that of copper?
4 Why were improvements in the quality of items such as cannon barrels possible in the 15th century?
5 Explain the features that produced the 'factory system' of working in the 17th century.
6 Describe **four** factors whose combination produced the Industrial Revolution.
7 What was the principal reason for 'the factory' emerging as a central manufacturing unit?
8 Name and describe **three** major concepts in manufacturing that appeared during the initial years of the 19th century.
9 Briefly describe the production method, originally used by Olds, that Ford exploited to revolutionise car manufacture at the beginning of the 20th century.
10 What device led to the emergence of 'reprogrammable automation', and why is this type of automation important in today's economy?

Further Reading

1 'Industry and Empire', by E.J. Hobsbawm. Published by Penguin, 1969.
2 'Victorian Engineering', by L.T.C. Rolt. Published by Penguin, 1970.

3 'Manufacturing Industry Since 1870', by M. Ackrill. Published by Philip Allan Publishers, 1987.
4 'Where Did We Go Wrong? Industrial Performance, Education, and The Economy in Victorian Britain', Edited by G. Roderick and M. Stephens. Published by The Fahner Press, 1981.
5 'Technologies and Society', by Ron Westrum. Published by Wadsworth Publishing Co. (California), 1991.

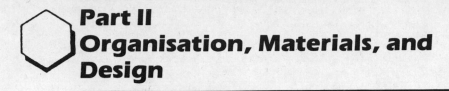

Part II
Organisation, Materials, and Design

Manufacturing organisation

3.1 Introduction

In Chapter 1 it was shown that the purpose of manufacturing industry was the **creation of wealth**. This should be used to improve the quality of life of the population. What, then, is the purpose of an individual manufacturing organisation within this industry? In line with the industry goal the individual company must also have wealth creation as its target. Just as wealth at a national level is measured by the GDP or GNP per head, so the success of the manufacturing company is measured by how well it performs at making **money**. In practice, this is measured by the profit it makes, by the ratio of this profit to the value of the resources it has to employ i.e. its 'return on investment', and by other factors such as the percentage share it has of the total possible market for its products. The fruit of a company that successfully makes money should be secure and well paid employment for the workforce, good working conditions, stimulation of the local economy around the manufacturing plant, incentives for further investment by shareholders and others to make the company 'grow', and of course a contribution towards the national economy.

The manufacturing company is therefore an organisation whose measure of health is its ability to make money. This chapter considers the individual elements of the organisation, and how they perform in concert to achieve the **corporate goal**. It is evident that manufacturing is concerned with the efficient use of resources to provide useful goods for the population. To do this the organisation, which comprises people, equipment, materials, and the necessary finance, must be managed well. The letter **M** for Manufacturing can be used as a mnemonic to remember these elements, i.e. Manufacturing involves the efficient Management of Manpower, Machines, Materials, and Money, in order to make more Money!

3.2 The manufacturing system

For the manufacturing organisation to fulfil its function, it must **make and sell products**. These products will sell at a high enough price to make a profit only if they are available at the right time and they are of the right cost, quality, and type to suit the market place.

- The essential stimulus is therefore the demand, or potential demand, for a product. This means that the organisation must be fully aware of the detailed requirements of the customer, otherwise competing companies will capture the market with their own products. If this happens there will be no inflow of cash from sales and the organisation will die. Figure 3.1 shows the manufacturing system in operation. The input to the system is the market need and the output is the satisfier of that need which, in the case of manufacturing, is a product.

- Subsequent to the identification of the need comes the **specification** of the product; this requires careful attention as all subsequent work will be useless if the specification is wrong. Using this 'spec' the designer is now able to form the **concept** of the product. This conceptual design is verified by marketing before a detailed **design** is produced. At the detailed design stage the designer will select appropriate materials and consider what manufacturing processes will be necessary.
- When the design has been thoroughly checked the next stage is the construction of a **prototype** of the product. How this is done will depend on the nature of the product, but it will usually involve craftsmen using general purpose machines and hand tools. This prototype will be

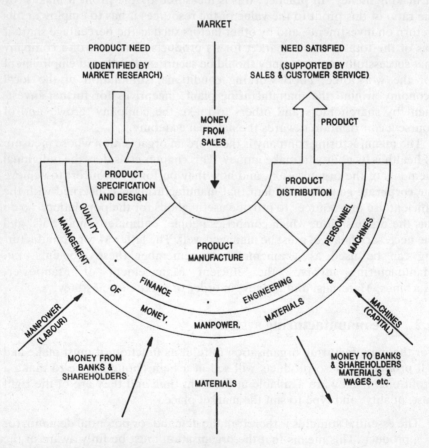

Figure 3.1 The manufacturing system

thoroughly tested to determine any problems that may necessitate design changes. Possible production difficulties should also be identified at this stage.

- The **final specification** of material and processes to be used should now be possible. Special tools needed for production will be designed and manufactured and the materials ordered. The actual production methods can also be planned, sequences of operations, the layout of the plant, and scheduling of the work can be initiated. How the product is to be inspected should also be determined, i.e. what dimensions and functions are critical, and at what stages inspection should be carried out.

- Assuming manpower, machines, and materials are all available the actual process of **production** can begin. If all foregoing steps have been properly implemented the product should now be able to be manufactured to the customer's requirements, and produced ready for on-time delivery. The individual elements of this production stage are covered later. Throughout the whole process **quality** of the product must be maintained; this is done by ensuring the quality awareness of all personnel, the provision of proper manufacturing methods, and strict adherence to inspection procedures. After the products are completed they will be given a final inspection and, if necessary, test before packing and despatch to the customer.

- Money will have to be made available for various items such as rent and rates, wages, and the purchase of equipment and materials; also costs incurred within the facility must be monitored and controlled; these are the responsibilities of the finance department.

- As can be seen from Figure 3.1, the sales and marketing functions form the **interface** between the company and the market. It is their responsibility to keep up to date with market demands and to ensure the product is sold.

- **Manufacturing Sub-systems**. From the previous description of the manufacturing system it is apparent that there must be various **sub-systems** working within it. The situation is analogous to a motor car. The car is a system composed of sub-systems, e.g. a transmission system, a braking system, a suspension system, and an electrical system. These systems can themselves be broken down into further systems, e.g. the electrical system can be broken down into the low tension and high tension systems. The same concepts apply in the manufacturing organisation. For example, there is the management system, the production control system, the financial control system, and the production system. The production system could be further broken down to describe individual production areas, groups of machines within these areas, individual machines, machine control systems, and eventually the individual hardware components used. This idea of 'systems within systems' is useful when considering control, and in particular computer control, which we will examine in Chapters 20 and 21.

3.3 Integrating the effort

Throughout this chapter, and indeed throughout the whole book, the manufacturing organisation and the functions, jobs, and processes involved, are described as objectively and unemotionally as possible. However it is worth noting that because **people** are involved in every area mentioned, subjectivity and emotion are factors that greatly influence much of what happens in a factory. In moderation, these factors add colour and excitement to the environment, but too much is a recipe for chaos. The personal ambitions of individuals, the different ways each person sees a situation, and attitudes, beliefs, and personalities, all lead to some inevitable disharmony in any work situation. This can be advantageous if not allowed to get out of hand, but excessive arguing, internal politics, and stubbornness must be avoided as the company would soon lose its way and become uncompetitive. Companies therefore look for ways in which they can structure their organisation to minimise human failings and optimise the functioning of the organisation as an entity in itself. Two examples are now considered.

(a) Simultaneous engineering

The systems mentioned earlier will not naturally operate in sympathy with each other. A great deal of effort has to be applied by the management and other individuals within the organisation to achieve full **integration**. Good **communication** between departments is essential to ensure the correct products are being produced to the correct specification at the correct time. This is not as simple as it sounds, and a conscious and determined effort must be made to create the proper environment for this communication. The concept of **simultaneous engineering** is an example of such an effort. The principle is shown in Figure 3.2 in comparison with the traditional sequence of events. Simultaneous engineering tries to ensure that all relevant problems associated with the design and manufacture of a new product are tackled in parallel, i.e. concurrently. This means that the design can be modified dynamically as manufacturing constraints and requirements are considered. Also the time between concept and actual manufacture is much reduced as problems are identified quicker, and machinery, materials, and manpower can be organised well in advance of the production start date.

(b) A common goal

The efforts and aims of each individual and group must be such that they act in concert. This can be achieved by the use of techniques such as **'Management by Objectives'** (MBO). MBO provides a structure within an organisation that ensures that the work done by each individual has as its aim a target that contributes directly towards the organisation's ultimate

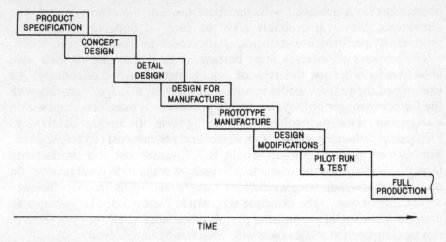

(a) Traditional event sequence

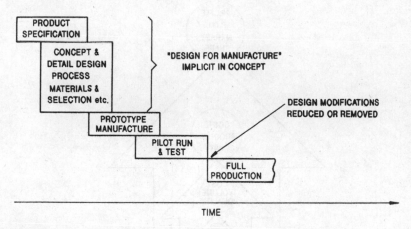

(b) Simplified simultaneous engineering event sequence

Figure 3.2 Design and manufacture of a new product: traditional and simultaneous engineering event sequence

goal. Therefore since we have said the ultimate goal of the manufacturing organisation is to make money, the sub-goals could be stated as an acceptable profit, return on investment, and market share. These sub-goals will be quantified to enable specific objectives to be set annually. A breakdown of these can then provide monthly objectives for the company and individual factories within the company. In each factory these objectives would be broken down further into objectives for the individual managers, supervisors, shop floor workers, and other staff. Obviously the objectives set at the level of individuals will not be specified as profit, return on investment (ROI), or market share. They will rather be objectives that if achieved will contribute towards the ultimate goal. For individuals, they will probably take the form of budgetary objectives, productivity performance statistics, quality levels and sales targets.

The workers themselves must participate in the setting of **their own objectives** in order for this type of management to work effectively. An example of the process would involve a production manager agreeing with the factory manager on, say, the number of products to be produced within a given time, the costs involved in producing them, the amount of labour to be used, and the maximum scrap, reject and rework costs to be incurred. The factory manager himself would have overall cost and productivity targets to achieve for the whole factory, whereas the individual production operator on the shop floor would have targets relating to his own efficiency and quality of work. The principle is shown in Figure 3.3. The system also provides a means of monitoring performance since each set of objectives can be compared at a later date with what has been achieved.

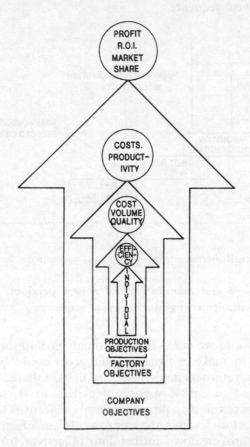

Figure 3.3 Hierarchy of objectives from an individual production worker to company level: the principle can be applied to all functions within the organisation

3.4   The formal organisation

(a) The structure

Manufacturing organisations are usually 'bureaucratic' in structure. The word 'bureaucratic' is not used disparagingly but rather in its true sense which implies a hierarchy of authority with a division of labour into bureaus, or departments. A pyramid type structure exists with each post at one level subordinate to a post at a higher level. Each person in the structure is responsible to only one person in the higher level. The division of labour, as explained more fully in Chapter 2, allows the advantages of **specialisation** to be obtained, i.e. each person has a specific, and often unique, task(s) to perform. Another characteristic of a bureaucratic organisation is the existence of an established system of rules to cope with various situations and to ensure impartial and just treatment of individuals.

Sometimes there is a distinction made in an organisation between 'line' and 'staff' personnel. For example in a large manufacturing company authority is clearly defined as running in lines down from the managing director, through the factory manager, production managers, foremen, to the shop floor operators. All of these people are directly responsible for production. However they all require the services of other people such as industrial engineers to select the appropriate methods of manufacture, and quality assurance personnel to ensure that the product is of an acceptable quality. These may be referred to as 'staff' functions, since they are an aid or support to the production function. In practice, the principles outlined earlier concerning good communication and integration must be followed by all concerned otherwise artificial barriers can arise and 'protectionist' attitudes occur between departments.

(b) The organisation chart

For a number of reasons it is advantageous to have an organisation chart constructed for the company. Assuming adequate descriptions or footnotes are appended, it allows everyone within the company to know who has responsibility for what function, and who should be approached to get something done. It can be shown to newly appointed personnel, or even interviewees, allowing them to appreciate their relative position within the structure. It is also useful to potential customers or quality approval bodies, to prove that a recognised structure of authority and responsibility exists.

Some disadvantages of organisation charts are that they can quickly become out of date if not regularly revised and if constructed retrospectively individuals may feel aggrieved at being placed lower on the chart than they had expected. Also formal charts cannot communicate **informal** relationships and roles that develop within the company due to personalities and individual knowledge and experience.

Organisation charts, or 'trees', are therefore useful but their limitations should always be remembered. A simplified chart for a manufacturing company is shown in Figure 3.4. It puts the job functions described in section (c) below in perspective. It should be noted that the actual titles used to describe the jobs, and even the jobs themselves, vary from company to company; however the actual tasks implied by the titles have to be done by someone no matter what terminology is used. In a large factory this pyramid type of structure becomes unwieldy. One way of overcoming this is to split the factory organisation into smaller units with as much **autonomy** for their actions as is practically possible. This can be done by product, e.g. keyboards, monitor units, and 'logic units' for a computer manufacturer, or by process, e.g. milling, turning, and grinding in a large machine shop. Another very effective means of improving efficiency, speeding up decision making, and reducing response time, is to remove many of the management layers. This has the effect of 'flattening' the pyramid. The use of computers and electronic communication networks has been an important factor in making this possible.

(c) The major functions

In a manufacturing organisation a number of major functions are per-

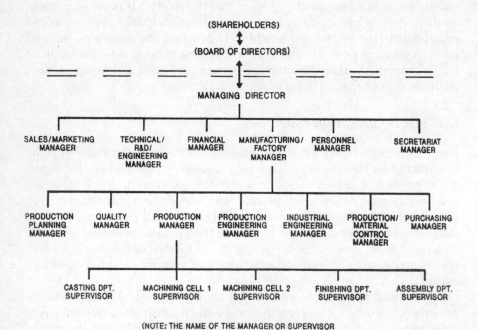

Figure 3.4 Simplified organisation chart: the name of the manager or supervisor would be added under each job title

formed by a variety of personnel. These personnel have specific jobs and titles, as is evident from Figure 3.4. It is the norm in a modern organisation to specify the job, then find an appropriate person to fill the post. The major functions and jobs within a manufacturing organisation are now listed.

- **The Board Of Directors**. This body is at the apex of the organisational structure of the company; it is appointed by the shareholders and represents the company ownership. In the company's Articles of Association and Memorandum of Association, all authority is delegated by the shareholders to the Board of Directors. The board's fundamental duty is to protect the interests of the shareholders; this implies protection of the company. It is the policy making body of the organisation, deciding broad objectives and the future direction(s) of the company. It is responsible for the appointment of company officers, e.g. the Chairman, Managing Director, and Company Secretary.
- **The Managing Director**. The Board of Directors delegates its authority to the Managing Director for the everyday running of the organisation. He or she is responsible directly to the Board for the successful achievement of the company's broad objectives. The 'MD' must be of high intelligence and integrity, and in a large company will probably have a wide business experience rather than being a specialist in any one area.
- **Manufacturing.** This function has the typical 'line' structure mentioned earlier. The largest number of people will probably be employed under this heading in either supervisory or direct and indirect operative roles. Activities such as production engineering, production planning, production control, work study, maintenance, quality, purchasing, and stores, etc. will be part of this function. The main objectives of Production are to produce the products required by the customer, at the correct time, at or below the budgeted cost, and at the agreed quality levels.

The **factory manager** (or manufacturing or works manager), is responsible to the managing director for the efficient operation of the manufacturing facility. He will have a large span of control, i.e. a large number of people will report directly to him. Under him will be the managers of production, production engineering, industrial engineering, production control, purchasing, maintenance, etc.

The **production manager** is responsible for ensuring that the product is completed as scheduled, within the budgeted costs, and at the specified quality levels. He has direct authority over the production labour force, which remains the largest grouping of people in many factories. Reporting to him will be various supervisors. Depending on the type of operation there could be further layers of foremen and section leaders, etc. before arriving at the pyramid base composed of the shop floor production workers or operatives.

The **production engineering manager** has the responsibility of ensuring that all production machinery and other equipment is appropriate to the task in hand and is working efficiently. He must also keep up to date with the latest technology and processes to ensure that the product is being made at a competitive cost.

The **industrial engineering manager** is responsible for the Work Study department. The task of this department is to create efficient work methods and determine accurately the times required to carry out the various jobs involved in making a product. This enables jobs to be costed properly, manpower requirements estimated, and productivity measured quantitively. The manager will also be responsible for making sure that the layout of the factory produces the minimum of movement of materials and manpower.

The **production or material control manager** coordinates the flow of material, components, and products within the production facility. It is his responsibility to provide all the necessary material for manufacture at the appropriate time and place. He must keep stores, work in progress, and stock to a minimum while making sure that no shortages occur on the production lines. This function is important since costs associated with parts and materials probably account for around 50% of the total manufacturing cost of a product, whereas direct labour constitutes only about 10%.

Each of the following functions will have its own manager or director depending on the company size and structure.

- **Finance.** This department has the responsibility of ensuring that funding is available for the smooth operation of the organisation. It also must compile budgets for the other departments; these will be set in cooperation with the managers concerned in a similar manner to other objectives. The department operates the cost and budgetary control systems by gathering and analysing costs and other financial data, before redistributing this information in the form of performance reports. Other activities are the keeping of all accounts including income and expenditure, the payment of wages, and participation in costing and pricing decisions.
- **Marketing**. In large organisations the marketing function will be composed of a number of sub-functions such as Advertising, Sales, Service, Distribution, and Market Research. Marketing has the responsibility of providing a steady flow of orders to the manufacturing facility to keep it producing at optimum production rates and to ensure that profits are maximised by striving to increase the company's share of the potential market.
- **Personnel**. With a broad range of responsibilities the personnel department attempts to relieve the other functions of the difficult and time consuming human problems, concerns, and decisions, that have to be made on both a short and a long term basis. Grouped under this heading might be found the responsibilities for welfare, industrial relations, training, safety, job evaluation, wage negotiations, and 'hiring, firing, and retiring' of personnel.

- **Technical**. Another broad departmental title that covers a variety of functions all related to the technical and engineering aspects of the organisation. For example, basic research of the scientific and technical factors that lead to new products, subsequent design and development of products resulting from this research, construction of prototypes, quality control and the setting of product specifications and standards are all part of the technical function. There will also be close liaison between the technical and marketing functions where customer service and complaints are concerned.
- **Secretariat**. Under the Company Secretary this function is concerned with the legal aspects of the company, the official recording of the work of the board of directors, and generally the handling of corporate level correspondence and books. The company secretary's office may also be responsible for the administration of pension schemes, insurance, patents, trade marks, and the handling of share issues and transfers of stock.

3.5 Types of manufacture

Manufacturing industry produces a broad range of products that range in size from microchips to oil tankers, and in production volumes from one to one million or more. While the size of the product has an obvious effect on manufacturing methods, it is the variance in volume that has the greatest influence on the type of organisation, equipment, and labour employed. There are a number of ways in which manufacturing can be classified; the terminology we will use here is Process, Mass, Batch, and Jobbing production. Figure 3.5 shows the relationship of these four types with respect to volume, variety, and cost per unit. Process and mass production are used for the highest volumes and least variety, they also produce the lowest unit cost; batch production has a medium unit cost for medium volumes and variety; jobbing production has the highest unit cost, greatest variety, and is used for single units. Before describing them further it should be noted that there is often a mixture of types used to create a finished product. For example although motor cars are mass produced, many of their components such as shafts, engine blocks, and conrods, etc. will be produced in economic batch quantities (EBQs). A large ship may well be the only one of its kind ever made, which implies jobbing production, but the steel plates that form its hull will have been produced by continuous casting and rolling which are really 'process production' techniques. There is also a 'blurring at the edges' where one type of production gives way to another. The classifications used here should therefore be simply regarded as useful labels to attach to various production systems when considering their organisation.

- **Process production.** This may also be referred to as 'continuous production'. It relates to that type of production in which the plant operates 24 hours per day for weeks or months without a halt. (This rarely happens

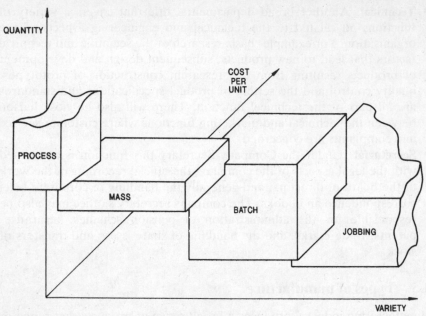

Figure 3.5   The four classes of production

in practice due to equipment breakdowns and planned maintenance.) The product being made will be required in 'bulk', and the plant output is likely to be measured in volume or weight rather than in numbers of discrete products produced. Oil refining, chemical manufacture, food processing, and steelmaking are all examples of processes that should ideally run continuously. The investment in the capital equipment will be high as it will probably be automated and specially designed and constructed for the product. Although plant and equipment costs will be high, the labour costs are likely to be low. The type of people employed here would be mostly technical and supervisory.

- **Mass production.** Again high volume production is involved, but this time it is discrete items that are produced rather than bulk quantities. Typical products made by this type of manufacture are motor cars, refrigerators, television sets, clocks, and radios. Individual components and sub-assemblies of these products may also be mass produced, e.g. batteries, refrigeration compressors, cathode ray tubes, transformers, and transistors. Just as in continuous production, mass production utilises expensive dedicated special purpose equipment. The variety of the product is kept to a minimum with standardisation and modularisation applied wherever possible. The workforce will have a large proportion of semi-skilled and unskilled workers for machine operation and assembly. In fact the work will be deskilled as much as possible to allow easy interchangeability of labour between jobs. Work is broken down into the simplest of operations to make operator training quick and simple. Because much of the work is tedious the use of industrial robots has become increasingly popular, especially in car manufacturing. Equipment, labour, and material supply are all highly organised to ensure a smooth flow of work through the plant and minimise the cost of each product unit.

- **Batch production.** Here, specific quantities of a product are required either in a single production run or in batches to be repeated at given times. Batch sizes may range from two or three to a thousand or more. Throughout its useful life each piece of manufacturing equipment will therefore be used for making many different products. This means that the equipment must be much more flexible than that used in mass production. Also as the labour force has to cope with a larger variety of work it will tend to be more highly skilled and higher paid. In a large factory many batches of different products of varying quantities, scheduled for different delivery dates and customers, will be being processed at any one time. As many of these products, though following different routes, will require to be worked on by the same machines and personnel, a complex control problem often arises. Since batch production manufacture contributes significantly to the national economy much effort has been given to ways of improving control, and hence efficiency. The use of computer controlled machines and computerised production control and management systems has greatly increased in an attempt to bring unit costs down towards those experienced in mass production. Examples of products produced in this type of manufacture are components and spares for aircraft, cars, buses, and construction equipment, machine tools, valves, pumps and compressors for the process industries, and furniture, etc.
- **Jobbing production**. Single unit quantities, usually made to a single customer's specification, are manufactured using this method. General purpose equipment and hand tools are used and the labour force is commonly composed of highly skilled craftsmen and technicians as well as the normal supervisory and administrative personnel. This type of manufacture produces the highest unit cost for a product and typical examples would be space satellites, ships, oil rigs, and special purpose manufacturing equipment.

3.6 Types of manufacturing equipment

It is possible to create a general classification for the types of equipment used in manufacturing; specific types of machine will be covered in later chapters in more detail. The process production industries use specially designed plant dedicated to the particular product being made. The massive investment required is apparent when oil refineries and chemical manufacturing plants are considered. The process industries require specialised treatment and, apart from the production of metals and plastics, this book does not examine them in detail.

- **Special purpose, dedicated** equipment is often found in mass production facilities. This type is built specifically to suit the product and is completely dedicated to the manufacture of that product. The equipment has therefore to be specially designed and built, making it very expensive; thus very long production runs are needed to justify the expense. Very high production rates will be achieved, and lower cost labour will be able to be used. The main disadvantage of this equipment is that when the product becomes obsolete, or has major design changes, then the equipment becomes redundant and has to be scrapped or broken down.

- **Computerised reprogrammable** equipment is now popular as it overcomes some of the limitations of the special purpose type. In today's environment product changes occur frequently as customer requirements change and new technology creates new product possibilities. This means that special purpose equipment cannot be used since production runs will not be sufficiently long to recoup expenditure. Examples of reprogrammable equipment in mass production can be seen in the industrial robots used for spot welding in car assembly lines. When a car model or style changes the robots can simply be reprogrammed and then resume working on the new design. Reprogrammable machines are also widely now used in batch production, as they are ideally suited to short production runs repeated at regular or irregular intervals. The programs for each batch can be stored away and reused when required.

- **Automation** is the term used to describe equipment that can operate on its own without continuous human control and monitoring. Most of the special purpose equipment used in process and mass production is highly automated. The reprogrammable equipment in the previous paragraph is automated. Sometimes the terms **hard** and **soft** automation are used. Hard automation refers to equipment, machines, and systems that are made to operate automatically but are not easily reconfigured to cope with changes in product or product design. Special purpose machines, machines controlled by cams, and 'hard wired' electronically controlled machines all usually fall into this category. Soft automation refers to equipment controlled by computers or other easily reprogrammed devices. Industrial robots, numerically controlled machine tools, and vision systems all come under this heading. The actual operation of these machines does not need highly skilled personnel.

- **General purpose** equipment is used for making prototypes and in jobbing production. Although electrically or hydraulically powered the machines will normally be manually operated and some may be numerically controlled. This is the most flexible type of equipment and can easily be used to produce any type of product. The hand held 'stick' welding system used in shipyards is an example of general purpose equipment; so also is the traditional centre lathe used for producing cylindrical type components. The skill levels of the equipment users are highest here as considerable training and experience needs to be gained before a good quality product can be produced.

There are also different ways of laying out a manufacturing plant, for example 'line' or 'cell' layout, or layout by product or process. These aspects of 'plant layout' will be covered later.

This chapter concludes the introductory section of the book. An appreciation of the economic importance of manufacturing, its history, and how it is structured has been given. The rest of the book explores more fully the manufacturing processes used to create products, and how people, material, machines and money need to be organised to optimise the creation activity.

Review Questions

1 Briefly describe how the success of a manufacturing company is measured.
2 State the major elements that must be properly managed in a manufacturing company.
3 List the main events that take place between the conception and the sale of a manufactured product.
4 Explain what is meant by the term 'manufacturing system'.
5 Explain what is meant by the term 'simultaneous engineering'.
6 Explain what is meant by the term 'management by objectives' (MBO).
7 Do you agree that a bureaucratic method of management is suitable for a manufacturing organisation? If so, why?
8 List the major job functions that need to exist within a manufacturing company.
9 Describe what is meant by the terms 'process', 'mass', 'batch', and 'jobbing' production.
10 Discuss what is implied by each of the terms 'hard' and 'soft' automation.

Further Reading

1 'Rethinking Organisation', Edited by M. Reed and M. Hughes. Published by Sage Publications Ltd. 1992.
2 'The Eternally Successful Organisation', by Philip B. Crosby. Published by McGraw Hill, 1988.
3 'The Machine That Changed The World: The Story Of Lean Production', by J.P. Womack, D.T. Jones, and D. Roos. Published by Rawson Associates 1990. ·
4 'Manufacturing: An Introduction For Accountants', by C.F. Lakin. Published by the Institute of Chartered Accountants in England & Wales, 1980.

5 'The Design of the Factory with a Future', by J.T. Black. Published by McGraw Hill Inc. 1991.
6 'Reinventing the Factory', by Roy L. Harmone and L.D. Peterson. Published by The Free Press Publishing, 1990.
7 'World Class Manufacturing Casebook', by R.C. Schonberger. Published by The Free Press Publishing, 1987.
8 'Organisational Structure and Information Technology', by Jon Harrington. Published by Prentice Hall, 1991.
9 'Implementing New Technologies: Choice, Decision, and Change in Manufacturing', Edited by E. Rhodes and D. Wield. Published by Basil Blackwell Ltd. in association with the Open University, 1985.
10 'Managing Manufacturing Operations in the UK', by Colin Weir. Published by BIM, 1986.

④ Manufacturing materials

4.1 Introduction

An engineer must have a good knowledge of the types and properties of materials from which a product can be manufactured. The material must not be so expensive as to make the product uncompetitive in the market place, yet it must possess all the characteristics necessary for the functioning of the product. Factors such as cost, strength, hardness, and how easily it can be worked must be considered carefully by the designer. Although there is already a wide range of materials available, research and development ensure that new ones are constantly being created. In plastics alone it is estimated that hundreds of new variants are developed each year. Advances in various areas of technology can often stimulate the need for new materials. For example, the possibility of building spacecraft created a requirement for materials, including metals, that could withstand extremes of temperature, pressure, and vibration.

We will mainly concern ourselves with metals and polymers which are the most common engineering materials. Other materials, such as composites and ceramics, are also considered. These materials are gaining in importance as more is learned about how to manipulate their structures to obtain desired properties.

One way of grouping materials is shown in Figure 4.1, i.e. into metals and non-metals. Metals are essentially chemical elements, such as iron, copper, gold and aluminium, or alloys of elements, such as steel and

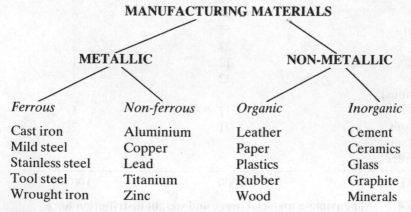

MANUFACTURING MATERIALS

METALLIC   **NON-METALLIC**

Ferrous	*Non-ferrous*	*Organic*	*Inorganic*
Cast iron	Aluminium	Leather	Cement
Mild steel	Copper	Paper	Ceramics
Stainless steel	Lead	Plastics	Glass
Tool steel	Titanium	Rubber	Graphite
Wrought iron	Zinc	Wood	Minerals

Figure 4.1 A simple classification of manufacturing materials

bronze. They are often lustrous when smoothed or polished, are usually good conductors of electricity and heat, and are likely to have a good strength to weight ratio. They can be further classified into the iron based metals, i.e. the ferrous metals, and the non-ferrous metals. The ferrous metals include the steels widely used in the construction of a broad range of products from pins and paper clips, through to motor cars, ships, and bridges. The non-ferrous materials are also used in a variety of familiar applications, e.g. electrical wiring made from copper, and strong light-weight aircraft components from aluminium.

The non-metallic materials can be split into organic and inorganic materials. Originally the organic materials were only those that had their origin in living organisms, e.g. wood and leather. Now organic materials are regarded as those based on carbon compounds generally, though it is interesting that the basic ingredients for even the synthetic polymers or 'plastics' are obtained from oil, natural gas, or coal, which in turn come from long-dead living matter. The inorganic materials come originally from the earth in the form of minerals. In the past they were used more in the construction industry than in manufacturing, but developments in ceramics and cements are producing many new manufactured products.

Where strength, at relatively low cost, is required metals are still by far the most common material used. Other materials, especially the plastics, are steadily gaining in ground in properties and popularity. For instance it is claimed that the volume of plastics sold is now greater than that of metals. Figure 4.2 shows the breakdown of materials by weight in a family

Material	Weight (kg)	Approx % of total car weight
Steel	675	68
Iron	82	8
Plastic	57	6
Rubber	53	5
Glass	27	3
Copper	12	1
Alloys (various)	12	1
Lead	11	1
Paint, oils, coolant, petrol, etc.	71	7
TOTAL	1000	100

Figure 4.2   Approximate material usage and weight distribution for a family car

sized motor car. Whilst acknowledging that steel is much heavier than, for example, plastic, Figure 4.2 does highlight the predominance of steel as a structural material due to its strength, manufacturability, and cost. The following notes therefore begin with a study of metals with particular emphasis on steel.

4.2   The structure of metals

(a) Atomic bonding

At this fundamental level we find that there are two ways in which atoms can be held together, i.e. primary and secondary bonding. Secondary bonding is a weak bonding which it is not necessary to consider here. The primary bonding is important as it is strong. Primary bonding has three types: (i) the Ionic bond in which electron transfer occurs, (ii) the Covalent bond in which electrons are shared, and (iii) the Metallic bond in which there is a structure of positive ions surrounded by universally shared wandering electrons. These electrons provide metals with their relatively high thermal and electrical conductivity. The structure can be deformed without the bonds breaking; this allows metallic bond materials to be changed in shape yet retain their original strength. The metallic bond is therefore of most relevance here; the covalent and ionic bonds will be mentioned later when ceramics are discussed.

(b) Atomic arrangement

This tells us how the atoms arrange themselves in a material. There are three types of structure: (i) Molecular as in water, (ii) Amorphous as in glass, and (iii) Crystal as in metals and most minerals. In crystal structures the atoms are arranged in a regular geometric array known as a space lattice. When metals solidify by cooling they adopt a crystalline structure and the atoms group themselves into one of these lattices. The three main types of lattice are body centred cubic or BCC, face centred cubic or FCC, and hexagonal close packed or HCP, see Figure 4.3. This structure helps determine how easily the material can be worked or deformed, e.g. FCC metals can usually be easily deformed without fracturing whereas HCP metals are difficult to work.

(c) Grain formation

As described above, when a metal solidifies atoms arrange themselves geometrically to form a crystalline structure. The initial lattices that appear become the nuclei or seeds from which the crystals of metal will grow. Many of these nuclei form in the initial stages of solidification but the direction in which each lies is random. As the crystals grow, the lattice

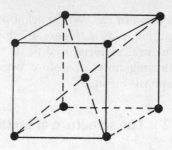

E.G.   CHROMIUM
        TUNGSTEN
        VANADIUM
        IRON (AT ROOM TEMPERATURE)

(a) BCC or body centre cubic

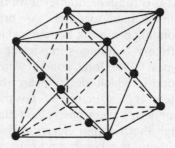

E.G.   ALUMINIUM
        COPPER
        GOLD
        SILVER
        PLATINUM
        NICKEL
        LEAD
        IRON (AT ELEVATED TEMPERATURES)

(b) FCC or face centre cubic: usually ductile

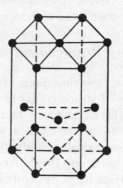

E.G.   BERYLLIUM
        CADMIUM
        MAGNESIUM
        TITANIUM

(c) HCP or hexagonal close packed: usually exhibits poor formability

Figure 4.3   Three main types of metal crystal structure

pattern of the source seed is maintained as successive lattices align themselves with their predecessors. Eventually when one growing crystal comes into contact with another of different orientation, growth of both will stop. The surfaces where they meet will be irregular in nature and will form part of a 'grain boundary'. This process is illustrated in Figure 4.4. It is interesting to note that some high quality jet turbine blades are made from metal consisting of a single large crystal. This unusual and expensive material gives good performance at high temperatures.

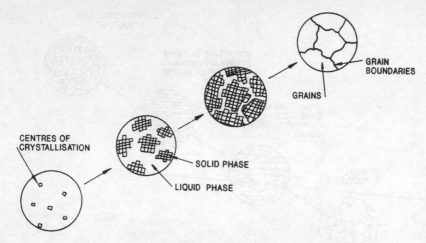

Figure 4.4   Crystal formation and grain growth

(d) Recrystallisation

This is an important feature in manufacturing with metals. When a metal composed of many crystals, i.e. a 'polycrystalline metal', is deformed the crystals are twisted and strained. If the metal is now heated to a high enough temperature new equiaxed and unstrained crystals will be formed from the original distorted grains. This process is known as recrystallisation and is illustrated in Figure 4.5. The temperature at which it occurs is different for each metal and varies with the amount of cold deformation which has previously taken place, i.e. the more deformation the lower the temperature at which recrystallisation will occur. The recrystallisation process tends to produce uniform grains of comparatively small size. As properties of metal tend to diminish as grain size increases, good control is important to keep the grain size small, or at the optimum level for the application. Generally if metals are allowed to cool slowly after being taken above their recrystallisation temperature, large crystals will form; if they are cooled rapidly, small crystals will result.

When metals are deformed **below** their recrystallisation temperature, **cold working** is said to take place. The structure consists of distorted grains and the metal is **strain hardened**; this can make it difficult to work the metal further. When deformation takes place **above** the recrystallisation temperature, **hot working** occurs. A recrystallised structure continually forms and no strain hardening is present. As metals may fracture if deformed too much it is common practice to recrystallise metal at intervals during cold working processes. This restores ductility and prepares the metal for further deformation; this process is known as **recrystallisation annealing**.

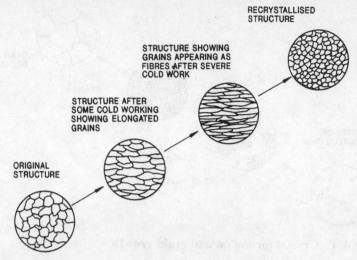

RECRYSTALLISED
STRUCTURE

STRUCTURE SHOWING
GRAINS APPEARING AS
FIBRES AFTER SEVERE
COLD WORK

STRUCTURE AFTER
SOME COLD WORKING
SHOWING ELONGATED
GRAINS

ORIGINAL
STRUCTURE

Figure 4.5   Effect on grain structure of cold working and recrystallisation

(e) The importance of grain structure

The grain size of a metal depends on the rate at which it was cooled and the extent and nature of the hot or cold working process. A metal with small, fine grains will have better strength and toughness compared to the same metal with large, coarse grains. This is due to the atoms being closer together in the smaller grained metal and causing more interference in the lattice structure when a force is applied. Larger grained metals are characterised by easier machining, more uniform hardenability during heat treatment, but with a greater tendency to crack when cooled by quenching. Additives can be added to a molten metal to promote a specific grain size, e.g. aluminium may be added to steel to promote fine grains.

Both hardness and grain size are affected by the temperature history of the metal. Quenching a hot metal quickly from a high temperature will usually harden it, whereas cooling it slowly will give it maximum softness. **Annealing** is the slow cooling of a metal from high temperature to increase the softness, toughness and ductility while also removing internal stresses.

When a metal is deformed the grains become elongated in the direction of metal flow. This gives the metal the appearance of having a fibre structure, similar to the grain structure in wood. Due to the creation of strain hardening and the fact that the intergranular boundaries will no longer be randomly oriented, the strength and other mechanical properties of the metal will not be the same in all directions, see Figure 4.6. This fact is exploited by engineers, with processes such as rolling and forging being used to impart such properties.

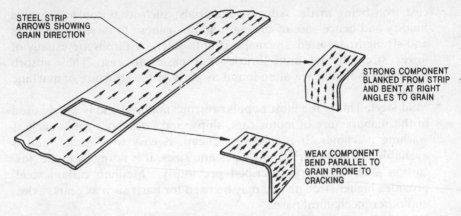

STEEL STRIP ARROWS SHOWING GRAIN DIRECTION

STRONG COMPONENT BLANKED FROM STRIP AND BENT AT RIGHT ANGLES TO GRAIN

WEAK COMPONENT BEND PARALLEL TO GRAIN PRONE TO CRACKING

Figure 4.6   Effect of grain direction on component strength

(f) Alloys

Alloys are formed when metals combine with other metals and, occasionally, with non-metals. The metals involved usually dissolve in each other in the liquid state to form a completely homogeneous liquid solution. In engineering, metals are normally used in the form of alloys. The most useful alloys contain a large quantity of one metal combined with a much smaller quantity of one or more added elements. These alloys are said to be based upon the metal which predominates in amount, e.g. iron or copper based.

Each alloying element has its own unique effect on a metal, the whole effect of two or more elements generally being greater than their individual sum. Carbon is an alloying element with iron which forms steel. The properties of steel are significantly affected by varying the quantity of carbon. Plain carbon steels are therefore referred to as being low (0.05%–0.3%C), medium (0.3%–0.6%C), or high (0.6%–1.4%C) 'carbon'. Below 0.05%C are the wrought irons and above 1.4%C are the cast irons. In the steels, tensile strength, yield strength, and hardness increase with carbon content, whereas impact strength and ductility are decreased.

(g) Some typical engineering metals

- **Wrought iron.** Though first made as long ago as the late 18th century, wrought iron is still a useful material where toughness and resistance to shock is required at relatively low cost. It usually has between 0.02% and 0.03% carbon, and may be used for such things as anchor chains and crane hooks.
- **Cast irons.** These are relatively cheap materials, made with various alloying elements, to give a range of types with differing properties. The carbon content varies from 2.0% to 3.6%, depending on the particular

cast iron being made. Alloying materials, such as silicon to improve fluidity and hence ease of casting, and manganese to increase hardness and strength, are used. In comparison to steel, cast irons are usually of lower strength and more brittle, but easier to cast. They absorb vibrations well and are often found as parts of the structure of machine tools.

- **Mild steel.** This is the most popular ferrous material and is widely used in the manufacture of motor cars, ships, and household goods such as washing machines. It is relatively cheap, is easy to machine, and is available in a wide variety of shapes and sizes. It is normally in the 'low carbon steel' category described previously. 'Medium carbon steel' provides higher strength and may be used for parts such as gears, axles, and other mechanical parts.

- **High carbon steels.** These steels can be hardened and tempered to give precise hardness, strength, and wear resistance characteristics. Cutting tools, screw drivers, press tools, cutlery, chisels, drills, and saws are some uses of this material.

- **Alloy steels.** Although all steels are alloy steels, i.e. they all contain carbon and other elements, such as molybdenum which increases strength and hardness, the 'alloy steels' have had a number of additional alloying elements added. Control of the manufacturing process is more precise than in the previous types to ensure a high quality metal that closely conforms to specification. Only a few of the possible alloying elements are noted here. The addition of nickel improves toughness and impact resistance. Chromium increases resistance to wear, abrasion, and corrosion; it also improves hardenability. Molybdenum increases hardenability and toughness. Vanadium improves impact and fatigue resistance. At high temperatures added tungsten will form hard tungsten carbides. When tungsten and vanadium are combined in steel the resulting material is known as High Speed Steel, HSS, which is used for cutting tool materials.

- **Tool steel.** This is an alloy steel able to be heat treated to give very good hardness for use in metal forming and cutting dies. Such steel may contain over 18% tungsten and will retain its hardness at high temperatures.

- **Stainless steel.** This is an alloy steel with more than 12% chromium and usually also containing nickel. It has very good resistance to corrosion and is used for cutlery, food processing equipment, sink units, valve and pump components, dies, etc.

These are only some of the wide range of ferrous materials commonly available. The non-ferrous materials also provide a wide variety of characteristics. Like the ferrous materials they are most useful in engineering in their alloyed forms.

- **Aluminium alloys.** These are used where light weight is required. In its pure form aluminium has good electrical conductivity and corrosion resistance. The alloyed form is much stronger but less corrosion resistant. Alloying elements such as copper, silicon, manganese and zinc are commonly used. For special applications, such as satellite construction where lightness and stiffness are required, lithium has been used. However lithium reacts explosively with water thus necessitating more expensive manufacturing procedures.

- **Copper.** Copper has extremely low electrical resistance and is corrosion resistant. However it is both soft and expensive in its pure form. It is therefore usually alloyed to provide bronze, brass, and other materials.
- **Bronze.** Bronze is an alloy of copper with tin, aluminium, manganese, or silicon. It is corrosion resistant and relatively strong.
- **Brass.** Brass is an alloy of copper with zinc. It has good corrosion resistance, is easily machined and cast, but can be less strong than bronze.
- **Titanium.** Titanium and its alloys, though expensive to produce, have generally high strengths up to 500°C and are highly resistant to corrosion. This makes them a cost effective solution to many problems in the aerospace and chemical industries.

(h) Heat treatment of metals

The final mechanical properties exhibited by a metal product are usually the result of three factors, i.e. the alloying materials, the way in which the metal was worked, and the heat treatment processes used. The first factor has already been explained, the second will become apparent as the various processes are studied later; heat treatment is briefly considered here. Heat treatment is usually employed to relieve internal stresses built up during cold working of the material, or to harden or soften the material to a specific value to suit a particular application.

- **Annealing**. The main purposes of annealing are to restore ductility and softness to a metal, and relieve internal stresses, after it has been hardened by cold working or rapid quenching from a high temperature. It is carried out by slowly heating the metal to an appropriate temperature, keeping it at this temperature for a specified time, then allowing it to cool slowly. The annealing process follows the stages of stress relief, recrystallisation, and grain growth, as was shown previously in Figure 4.5.
- **Hardening**. Steels with a carbon content greater than 0.3% can be hardenend by raising them to a high temperature, then rapidly cooling them in a liquid such as cold water. The temperature to which the steel needs to be raised depends on its carbon content and ranges between 720°C and 1100°C.

If the steel has a carbon content lower than, say, 0.3% then its surface can be hardened using a process known as **carburising**. Here the steel is heated to above 900°C in contact with a substance rich in carbon. The carbon in the substance will diffuse into the surface of the steel, forming a skin containing around 0.8% carbon. The carburising substance may be gas, liquid, or solid. When the steel is quenched it will be said to have been 'surface hardened'. It should now have a tough core and hard outer shell which will be wear resistant. In this process surface areas of the steel that do not require hardening can be protected against carbon penetration by a surface coating such as copper plating.

- **Tempering**. When a steel is fully hardened throughout, it is brittle and is likely to contain internal stresses. It is therefore necessary to reduce this hardness to that required for the application; this 'tempering' process will also restore toughness to the structure. Steel is tempered after hardening by reheating it to a specific temperature, usually below 550°C and then cooling it. The exact temperature to which it is reheated determines the final hardness of the metal. For example, a hardened chisel made entirely from high carbon steel would be too brittle to use, its edge would crack easily if dropped and, when hit by a hammer, the head would be liable to chip and cause an eye injury from flying particles. The chisel is therefore tempered, the edge is raised to a temperature high enough to remove the possibility of cracking yet ensuring that sharpness is maintained in use, and the head is raised to a higher temperature producing a softer but tougher composition that will not fracture.

Heat treatment of non-ferrous materials is often restricted to annealing to remove the effects of cold working. Some aluminium and copper base alloys can be hardened using a process called 'precipitation hardening'.

Where high strength is required at reasonable cost, metals are still the most likely engineering choice. Where special properties of light weight, heat resistance, and high strength to weight ratios are required materials such as polymers, ceramics, and composites are becoming more popular. However metals continue to be improved and new forms are always emerging from the world's laboratories. High stiffness steels capable of being useful in very thin lightweight sheets for car bodies, and ultra high carbon superplastic steels capable of 1000% deformation, have been developed. Advances like these should ensure that metals continue to be at least one of the most used engineering materials well into the next century.

4.3 Plastics

(a) Plastics and polymers

A 'plastic' is an engineering material that can easily be moulded into a desired shape, usually at an elevated temperature. After cooling the plastic retains its new shape. In the case of thermoplastics, reheating will allow the plastic to be remoulded. Thermosetting plastics retain their moulded shape even when reheated. Plastics can be transparent, translucent, or opaque. They can be produced in any colour or finish desired. They can be used for wrapping chocolate bars, housing computers, replacing human organs, or armour plating a tank. On average one new plastic is being created almost every day. In fact plastics are now so widely used and the variety is so great that major producers provide computer programs, free of charge to users, to assist with the appropriate plastic selection.

Plastics are generally synthetic polymers. Natural polymers have been used by man for many years. Latex is the sap of 'rubber trees' which, when mixed with certain chemicals and allowed to coagulate, can be processed with sulphur and placed in a mould. When the mould is heated a chemical reaction takes place called 'vulcanisation'; the product is a rubber product which has considerable mechanical strength and has the shape of the mould. Horn is another example. When heated horn becomes soft and able to be moulded. It was used for buttons and in thin translucent sheets was used as we now use glass. In fact the word 'lantern' comes from the term 'lanthorn', an early application of the natural polymer.

(b) The chemical structure of plastics

Plastics are polymers made by man from organic molecules using the process of synthesis. An organic molecule has carbon atoms as its base; an example of this is the ethylene molecule shown in Figure 4.7(a). In the production of plastics this ethylene molecule is known as a 'monomer' which means 'one part'. In the process of synthesis used to manufacture the plastic, conditions of high temperature and pressure may be created, causing one of the links in the central double bond to break. This allows the individual monomers to link up and form a chain, or 'polymer', as shown in Figure 4.7(b) and (c). Around 1000 to 20,000 of these monomers combine to form one polymer of 'polyethylene' which is a simple plastic composed only of carbon and hydrogen atoms. By introducing other atoms or groups of atoms plastics with different properties can be created. For example chlorine is used to produce polyvinylchloride or PVC, and fluorine can be used to create polytetrafluoroethylene or PTFE.

(c) The physical structure of plastics

The manner in which the polymer chains arrange themselves with respect to each other influences the properties of the final plastic. In the thermosetting plastics the molecular chains are designed so that further chemical linking can occur between the chains themselves. This produces a three dimensional **network** structure which forms as the plastic is being moulded under heat, see Figure 4.8(a). This produces a very strong plastic with good hardness and stiffness but usually brittle. Such plastics do not soften on reheating.

In the thermoplastics there is considerable scope for organisation of the

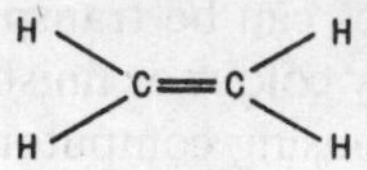

(a) Ethylene molecule

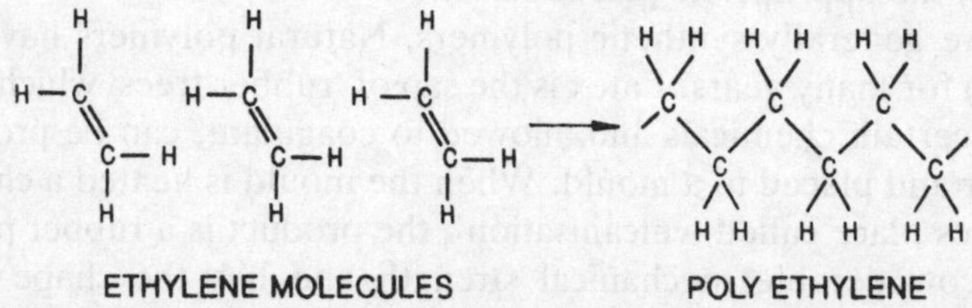

ETHYLENE MOLECULES   POLY ETHYLENE

(b) Ethylene molecules and polyethylene

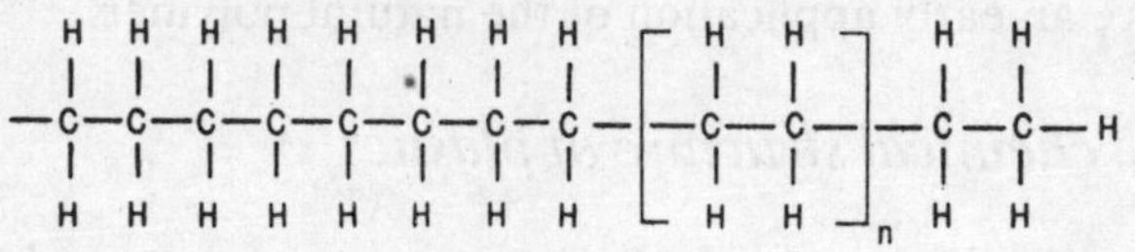

(c) Polyethylene chain: $n = 1000 - 2000$

Figure 4.7   Organic molecules

chains to provide different properties. Plastics such as PVC, polyethylene, and the acrylics and nylons have **linear** structures, see Figure 4.8(b). Since the chains are linear they can slide over each other, thus providing a certain flexibility to the plastic. Polyethylene is so flexible it can be used as wrapping film, whereas PVC is relatively rigid unless a 'plasticiser' is used. Plasticisers are liquid or semi-liquid additives which tend to separate out the polymer chains thus allowing them to slide over each other more easily. Thermoplastics can also have **branched** structures, see Figure 4.8(c), which are less dense and have an apparently higher strength than the linear ones. Both linear and branched structures often exist together in the one plastic. It is also possible to introduce a **crystalline** structure into plastics during processing. This improves hardness and stiffness, increases density, and decreases ductility.

(d) Some common plastics and their properties

Generally, plastics provide light weight, corrosion resistance, low electrical and thermal conductivity, and a low cost to weight ratio. It is also possible to produce plastic products directly in any colour or degree of transparency and with any type of surface finish desired, with no need for secondary operations such as machining or painting. As mentioned earlier, new

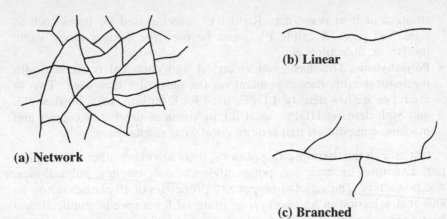

(b) Linear

(a) Network

(c) Branched

Figure 4.8   Polymer chains: network, linear, and branched structures

plastics are being introduced at the rate of a few hundred per year; we therefore concern ourselves with only a few basic types that highlight typical properties available.

Thermosetting plastics now include a wide range of materials. For example there are the **Epoxies**. These have very good mechanical and electrical properties, good elasticity, toughness, resistance to heat and chemicals, and strong adhesive qualities. They are often fibre reinforced and used in structural components such as tanks for holding chemicals. Another group are the **Phenolics**. These are relatively strong and hard but brittle. Widely used for products such as telephone cases, handles, and electrical insulators, they are available in many forms, e.g. sheet, rod, or tube. There are many other thermosetting plastics, e.g. **Alkyds**, **Aminos**, **Polyamides**, and **Silicones**, all exhibiting their own individual combinations of properties.

Thermoplastics are available in an extremely broad range and some of them are considered below.

- **Acrylics.** These plastics have good strength properties, especially impact strength, and have very good optical transparency. They can be used for vehicle windshields, goggles, lenses, and windows, etc.
- **Polyamides.** These include the nylons and aramids. Nylon is tough, has good abrasion resistance, and is self-lubricating. It is therefore used for gears, bearings, fasteners, etc. In monofilament form it is used for fishing lines and climbing ropes. Aramids have high tensile strength and stiffness and are used in bullet proof vests and pneumatic tyres.
- **Polycarbonates.** These have high strength and toughness and good impact resistance. Safety helmets, bottles, and machinery guards are some applications.
- **PVC.** A relatively inexpensive plastic, PVC has a wide range of properties and can be made either rigid or flexible. It does not have high

strength or heat resistance. Rigid PVC can be used for items such as signs and pipes. Flexible PVC can be used for flexible tubes, cable insulation, floor tiles, etc.

- **Polyethylene.** This has good electrical and chemical resistance with mechanical properties dependent on the particular type used. Two of the types are low density, LDPE, used for litter bins, toys, bottles, etc. and high density, HDPE, used for products as diverse as canoes and machine components that require good wear resistance.

Just as with the thermosetting plastics, there are many other thermoplastics. Examples of some are: polypropylenes, polystyrenes, polysulfones, and polyesters. The variety of types and properties of all plastics is now so vast that selection of an appropriate material for a specific application is best done using the material supplier's own updated computer program or product information catalogues.

4.4   Ceramics

Ceramics, first developed over 7000 years ago for making clay pots, are now used today to protect the surface of the Space Shuttle. With the demand for materials that can function at increasingly high temperatures and speeds, and yet retain their properties of strength, hardness, and electrical and chemical resistance, there has been a resurgence of interest in ceramics. Even at normal temperatures ceramics can provide a combination of hardness, lightness, stiffness, and resistance to corrosion that most other materials could not better. The main disadvantage, however, is that they are brittle.

Ceramics have been widely used for some time now as electrical insulators in electrical power systems and in items such as sparking plugs where high temperature strength is required. Other applications have been in cutting tools using tungsten carbide, and grinding wheels using silicon carbide as an abrasive. Now many new applications are seen as improved understanding of their constituents, and strict quality controls during manufacture, produce less brittle ceramics.

The structure of a ceramic material is a compound of metallic and non-metallic elements. The covalent and ionic bonds that hold the atoms together in a ceramic material are much stronger than metallic bonds, thus giving the ceramic greater hardness and thermal and electrical resistance than, for example, steel. The structure of a ceramic may be single crystal, or polycrystalline where the smaller the grain size the better the strength and toughness.

Examples of more recent ceramic products are ball bearings and turbine blades. Motor car manufacturers are particularly interested in using them. Ceramic exhaust liners, coatings for pistons, and catalytic converters, are already in wide use, but in the future it is hoped that much more of a car's engine will be made out of ceramics. Conventional piston engines that can run at high temperatures without the need of a radiator or ceramic gas turbine power units are some of the possibilities.

4.5   Composites

The composites are probably the materials with the highest strength to weight ratio of all the types previously considered. They are relatively expensive compared to metals but in many applications the extra cost is acceptable. One of the least expensive composites is glass fibre which is widely used for boat hulls, flat components for motor cars such as bonnets, sports rackets, and fishing rods. The simplest form has short fibres of glass randomly oriented in a matrix of plastic. By using longer fibres and arranging them all to run in the same direction within the matrix greater strength is obtained. By using sheets of these, and laminating them so that each layer has fibres runnning in different directions, structural aircraft components can be made. Further strength and stability can be obtained by using, within the plastic matrix, fibres that have been woven into a three dimensional pattern; this is used in products such as skis.

The plastic matrix is usually an epoxy or, less commonly, a polyester. This supports the fibres, protects the fibres from damage, acts as a crack arrestor, and transfers stresses to the fibres. The fibres themselves are usually high strength stiff materials, but brittle. A composite therefore exhibits the best properties of the plastic matrix and the integral fibres to give a tough, strong, lightweight structure. Typical fibres used are glass, graphite or carbon, and the organic aramid 'Kevlar'.

The latest composites use materials from all the types we have so far looked at, i.e. metals, polymers, and ceramics. They are used as the fibres or as the matrix. For example, silicon carbide fibres in a matrix of titanium, a metal matrix composite, is suitable for high speed aircraft structures. Advanced ceramic, metal, and polymer matrix composites are expensive, but they do appear to be attractive materials for the emerging high performance machines, motor cars, and aircraft of the near future.

4.6   Properties and testing of materials

Engineers are normally interested in the physical, chemical, and mechanical properties of materials. Typical physical properties are: density; this is important for weight, e.g. a good strength to weight ratio is imperative in aircraft structures; thermal and electrical conductivity; melting point; this is important in manufacturing as it determines the ease with which the material can be cast and also the amount of energy required for the process; magnetic properties; colour; and coefficient of thermal expansion. Chemical properties such as the ability to resist corrosion are also important. However it is the mechanical properties that often have the greatest influence on the manufacturing methods used to work the materials. Tensile, compressive, and shear strength, hardness, ductility, and impact and fatigue resistance are all relevant. They are described more fully below.

(a) Stress, strain, and the strength of materials

It is essential to understand the meaning of these the terms 'stress' and 'strain' before proceeding further. When a material is subjected to an axial load, as shown in Figure 4.9, two things happen to it. (i) It becomes **deformed**; this deformation is termed 'strain' and is defined quantitively as the change in length divided by the original length. (ii) **Internal forces** are set up within the material to resist the applied forces; this is called 'stress' and it is defined quantitively as the force exerted by the load divided by the cross sectional area of the material.

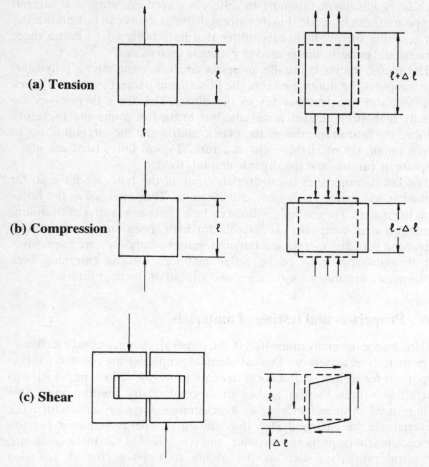

Figure 4.9   Tensile, compressive, and shear loading and resulting strain effects

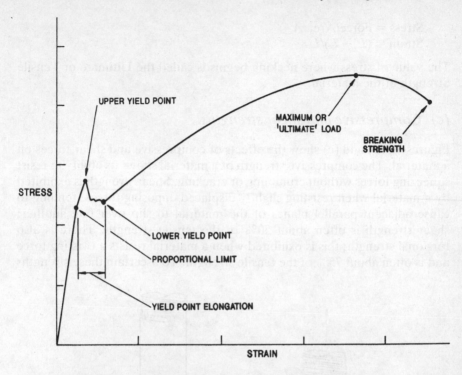

Figure 4.10   Stress/strain diagram for a low carbon steel

A simplified stress strain diagram for a low carbon steel is shown in Figure 4.10. Up to the proportional limit the material obeys Hooke's Law which states that stress is directly proportional to strain; this ratio is known as Young's Modulus or the modulus of elasticity. Either on, or just above, the proportional limit, the elastic limit occurs; beyond this point increases in strain do not require proportionate increases in stress. Elongation is now unrecoverable and is known as plastic deformation; usually when this happens the metal is said to have 'failed'. It is in this plastic region, before rupture occurs, that plastic deformation is used to shape a metal product in many manufacturing processes.

(b) Tensile strength

This is the strength exhibited by a material when it is being pulled apart from two opposing directions. Tensile strength is determined by pulling on the two ends of a specimen machined, as shown in Figure 4.11. When the specimen is pulled the smaller diameter section necks down from an area A to an area A', and the guage length increases from L to L'. For most engineering purposes the area A is used in all calculations since A' is difficult to measure. From the data collected while pulling the specimen a curve can be plotted from the two values of stress and strain where:

Stress = Force/Area A
Strain = $(L' - L)/L$

The value of stress where necking begins is called the Ultimate or Tensile Strength of the material.

(c) Compressive and shear strengths

Figures 4.9(b) and (c) show the effects of compressive and shear forces on a material. The compressive strength of a material shows its ability to resist squeezing forces without crumbling or cracking. Shear strength is exhibited by a material when resisting slightly displaced opposing forces, tending to cause adjacent parallel planes of the material to slip over one another; shear strength is often about 50% of the tensile strength. There is also torsional strength; this is exhibited when a material resists a twisting force and is often about 75% of the tensile strength. To ascertain these strengths

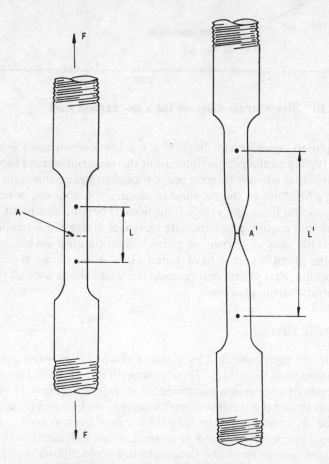

Figure 4.11   Tensile test

the material can be subjected to compressive, shear, and torsional stresses and strains, and in each case the appropriate load values noted at point of failure.

(d) Hardness

There are several techniques used for determining the hardness of a material, but most industrial methods measure the resistance of the material to penetration of a small sphere, cone, or pyramid. Initially the penetrator and material are forced into contact with a predetermined initial load. An increased load is then applied to the penetrator, and the hardness reading is obtained by noting the difference in penetration caused by the final load as compared to the initial load. One of the more common scales used is the 'Rockwell' test in which the load applied and shape of the penctrator are specified, see Figure 4.12.

(e) Ductility

The ductility of a material indicates how much it can be bent, drawn, stretched, formed, or permanently distorted, without rupture. Normally a material that has high ductility will not be brittle or very hard. Conversely, hard materials are often brittle and lack ductility. The tensile test can be used as a measure of ductility by calculating the percentage elongation of the specimen upon fracture.

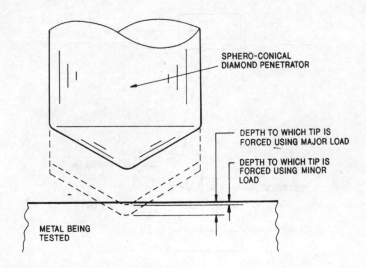

Figure 4.12   Rockwell hardness test

(f) Impact resistance

A material may be hard and have a high tensile strength, but it may still be unsuitable for an application that requires it to withstand impact or sudden load. A number of tests are used to determine this impact resistance. Two common tests are the Izod and the Charpy test, in which a notched specimen is struck by an anvil mounted on a pendulum. The energy required to break the specimen is an indication of the impact resistance of the material. For some common engineering materials this energy can vary quite dramatically with temperature, even at temperatures close to ambient. The Izod test is illustrated in Figure 4.13.

(g) Fatigue resistance

The yield strength is useful for designing components that are subjected to a static load, but for cyclic or repetitive loading the endurance or fatigue strength has to be known. This is found by loading the part and subjecting it to repetitive stress. Usually a number of specimens of a material are tested at various loadings and the number of cycles to failure are noted.

4.7   Conclusion

The variety of materials available to the engineer is vast. He must make optimum use of them if his product is to be competitive in the market place. A knowledge of materials is therefore essential not only for product design but also for consideration of how the product will be manufactured.

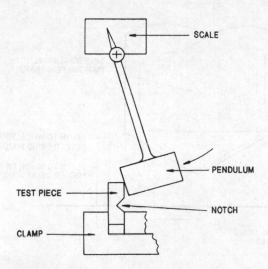

Figure 4.13   Izod impact test

Review Questions

1 Give an example of each of the following types of material together with a typical use: (a) ferrous, (b) non-ferrous, (c) organic, (d) inorganic.
2 What type of atomic bonding is exhibited by metals, and what implication has this with respect to their properties?
3 What is meant by 'grain formation' in metals?
4 Discuss the significance of grain structure, and the importance of recrystallisation.
5 What is an alloy?
6 In steels, how are properties generally affected by carbon content?
7 Describe **two** ferrous alloys, and their uses.
8 Why are ferrous metals hardened and tempered?
9 What are polymers, and why are they useful?
10 What is the main difference between a thermoplastic and a thermosetting plastic?
11 Describe **two** polymers and their uses.
12 What combination of properties makes ceramics attractive for today's product designers?
13 Why have 'composites' become desirable for products such as the structural elements of aircraft?
14 What do the terms 'stress' and 'strain' imply when materials are subjected to an axial load?
15 Briefly review the types of material properties of interest to product designers and manufacturers.

Further Reading

1 'Manufacturing With Materials' from 'Materials in action Series', edited by L. Edwards and M. Endean. Published by the Open University and Butterworths, 1990.
2 'Properties of Engineering Materials', by R.A. Higgins. Published by Edward Arnold, 1977.
3 'Selection and Use of Engineering Materials', by J.A. Charles and F.A.A. Crane, 2nd Edition. Published by Butterworths, 1989.
4 'Materials Science for Engineers', by L.H. Van Vlack. Published by Addison-Wesley, 1970.
5 'Light Alloys: Metallurgy of the Light Metals', by J. Polmear. Published by Edward Arnold, 1989.
6 'Mechanics of Engineering Materials', by P.P. Benham and R.J. Crawford. Published by Longman; 1987.
7 'Mechanics of Composite Materials' by R.M. Jones. Published by Scripta Book Co. 1975.

⬡5 Design for manufacture

5.1 Introduction

If a manufacturing company is to survive, it is essential that it produces well designed products. Should a company's products not be designed to satisfy the needs of the consumer, then competitors' products will be purchased and the company will fail. This applies equally to domestic and export markets. The contribution made by manufacturing to a nation's economy was emphasised in Chapter 1: inability of a company to sell its products leads inevitably to its demise. If this applies throughout a country's manufacturing industry it can be seen that good or bad product design has an extremely significant effect on the success or failure of the national economy.

Within the company, elements such as a good sales and marketing effort, tight cost controls, and high productivity, are useless if the design of the product is not what the customer wants.

It must also be remembered that most of the cost of manufacturing a product is determined at the initial design stage: estimates of 70% in the car industry and 80% in the aerospace industry have been made. Materials and processes to be used are dictated by the product design. Therefore subsequent improvements in, for example, manufacturing efficiency, serve only to **reduce** the costs that have already been **created** by the original design.

For all of these reasons, the design process requires careful attention if a world class product is to be produced.

Different products have different design priorities. For example fashion clothing has as its main priority aesthetic appeal; functional characteristics are less important, it is the 'style' that sells the product. At the other end of the spectrum we find products such as the microprocessor. Aesthetic appeal is irrelevant as the chip is not intended to be seen in use; however, functional aspects such as processing speed will be critical in determining whether or not it will be a success. In the first type of product the designer with artistic flair will have the most important input, although he will also require a knowledge of natural and synthetic clothing materials and how they are produced. In the second type it is the engineering design that is important and specialist circuit designers using computer aided design systems (CAD, see Chapter 21) will be required. Most products today demand consideration of a full range of attributes. For example, a motor car must be aesthetically pleasing as well as providing performance and safety.

Ecological or 'green' issues continue to increase in priority. Obvious everyday examples are the use of recyclable packaging, recycled paper, catalytic convertors, and unleaded petrol. Product designers must also remember that recycling and 'environment friendly' products are only a partial solution to pollution and waste. Acid rain destroying forests and buildings and industrial effluent poisoning rivers and the atmosphere can best be reduced by considering the methods of manufacture. Good product design will ensure that the manufacturing processes used will cause minimal environmental damage without recourse to the very expensive methods that treat the industrial waste after it has been produced. These solutions involve chemically or physically separating the toxic elements of the industrial waste and then converting or burying them somewhere. Long term solutions to environmental damage must rely on products being designed to produce the minimum of environmental damage as they are manufactured.

5.2   The product life cycle

Design can be novel or incremental. Some novel designs have had important implications for society, the internal combustion engine and television being two examples. However, most design is **incremental**, that is each design is an improvement on what has gone before. Internal combustion engines today are much more fuel efficient and their power to weight ratios higher than that of their ancestors. Similarly the design of a modern television with a large, flat, high definition colour screen, with 'picture in picture', teletext, and stereo digital sound facilities, is quite a different product from the small low definition monochrome screen of the massive, valve operated sets of half a century ago.

It is therefore apparent that the design process is not a once and for all event. If we consider each improvement as a new product then we can see that the initial and subsequent products will have a distinct lifetime. This is recognised as the Product Life Cycle and it is shown in Figure 5.1. In region *A* the new product design is introduced into the market. In this area the marketing department has the major task of promoting the new product and ensuring that sales growth begins. In region *B* the new product is accepted by the market; it enjoys increasing demand, and it experiences exponential growth. However, during this period competitors will have observed the success of the new product; this will stimulate them to produce their own competing design. In region *C* the product reaches maturity; it has already made its initial impact on the market, and it will probably be now competing with alternative designs by other manufacturers. In region *D* the sales of the product decline due to the availability of newer products possibly incorporating better technology.

It is therefore important for the company that designed and built the initial product to maintain technological progress through research and development (R&D). By doing this it can stay one step ahead of its

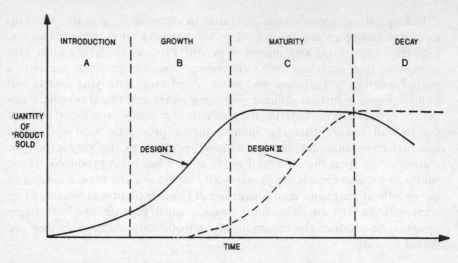

Figure 5.1   The product life cycle

competitors' designs and ensure that it maintains its market share. Products used to have life cycles of a few years, now they are much shorter; in the electronics industry some products have a life cycle of only a few months. The beneficial effect of incremental design improvements is shown by the dotted lines in Figure 5.1. Naturally the technology alone will not ensure success; other factors such as quality, price, and after sales service will also be important in creating the right package for the customer.

5.3   The design process

Product design and product manufacture must be considered concurrent: the development of the design should evolve in parallel with the knowledge of how the product will be made. Only by doing this can the company ensure that the most competitive and profitable product will be manufactured.

Traditionally, a chronological development of a design through a number of stages has been recognised. The first stage is the identification of a market 'need'. This provides the initial **idea** for a product to satisfy that need. Secondly a clear and unambiguous **specification** is created that fully describes all the attributes the product must have to satisfy the market need. Thirdly at the concept design stage a product **concept** is created, usually after having considered a number of alternatives, to satisfy the specification. Fourthly **detail design** of the product is carried out. Finally the **production design** stage occurs in which the design is modified to ensure the product can be manufactured economically. The problem with this traditional approach is that although it appears to follow a logical progression, and each stage is an essential activity, the process becomes 'compartmentalised'. Thus even if an apparently optimum design is obtained at each stage, an optimum for the 'total design' is lost.

The practical way to ensure the 'best' total design is to integrate all design activities and provide an environment conducive to good communications: good total design requires a team effort. For example, although a mechanical engineer involved in evaluating stress–strain relationships to maximise the strength of a product may produce a functioning design, he may not be fully aware of the manufacturing processes implied. A design must not only satisfy the product design specifications, it must also be able to be manufactured economically. The mechanical designer may also not be aware of the implications of his design for the aesthetic appeal of the product. It is therefore necessary to ensure that the mechanical engineer develops the design concurrently and in collaboration with the manufacturing engineer and, if appropriate, with an industrial designer. Here again the concept of **simultaneous engineering** is important. As mentioned in Chapter 3 an approach using a team is adopted, this team comprising representatives from the whole spectrum of manufacturing including engineering, purchasing, manufacturing, and even outside suppliers of components and raw materials. The approach attempts to integrate the product design with manufacturing process design to achieve a minimum total life cycle cost for the product, i.e. it is 'designed for manufacture'!

Figure 5.2 traces the design process, highlights the design goals, and

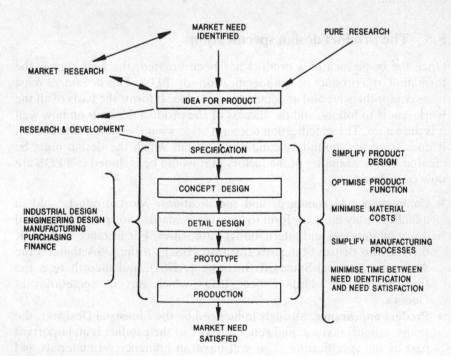

Figure 5.2   The design process

illustrates the information flow necessary to obtain a well designed product. The central spine shows the events that occur, the 'ribs' on either side show the information paths and the design goals that all exist concurrently.

5.4   Identifying the market need

In the beginning there is usually a perceived market need. This is observed and noted by the market research group in a large company, or by an individual such as an entrepreneur or inventor. From this need, or 'market gap', springs the idea for the product.

In a large company the idea may also emerge from a research and development group. If a company has the financial resources, and wishes to continue being a leader in its field, then it will carry out pure, or 'blue sky', research. Should it not be large enough to fund this on its own then it may work in collaboration with other companies and organisations, such as universities and government or private research laboratories. This type of research may not have an immediately obvious commercial worth, but it is conducted in the hope of future benefits and to ensure that an innovative advantage is maintained over the competition. 'Applied' research has more obvious and immediate commercial applicability; it has the short term goal of producing a process or product suitable for immediate commercial exploitation.

5.5   The product design specification

Once the basic idea of a product has been created, the next step is the formation of a product design specification, or 'PDS'. This document must be as comprehensive and as detailed as possible. It forms the basis of all the work that is to follow, and the success of the product depends on how well it is drawn up. The specification does not state what the design is to be, but it does state the 'boundary conditions' within which the design must be created. Some examples of the factors that would be included in a PDS are now considered.

- **Conformance to standards and specifications.** Most products sold in quantity today must conform to certain standards and specifications laid down by national and international authorities. For instance in the UK there is the British Standards Institute (BSI), in the USA there is the American National Standards Institute (ANSI), and then there is the International Standards Office (ISO) which has its secretariat in Geneva.
- **Product appearance.** Strongly influenced by the Industrial Designer, the shape, colour, texture, and general 'style' of the product is an important part of the specification. This will have an influence on materials and manufacturing processes to be used.

- **Product performance.** Depending on the product, this may take many forms. Speed of operation, number of work cycles expected in product life, intermittent or continuous working, loads to be withstood, etc. are typical considerations.
- **Life expectancy.** There will be a certain minimum product lifetime expected by the customer and a guarantee will normally have to be given with the product. This part of the specification will state how long the product should remain in working order provided reasonable care and maintenance is provided by the customer.
- **Maintenance.** How frequently and easily the product is to be maintained must be specified. If the product is to be maintenance free then costs may be increased due to the need for more expensive self-lubricating bearings, etc.
- **Working environment.** The conditions under which the product is likely to be used, stored, and transported must be specified. The product may experience extremes of temperature, pressure, and humidity. It may be subject to vibration, radiation, or chemicals. It may have to operate in explosive or corrosive atmospheres. All of these factors will strongly influence the product design.
- **Quantity.** The total quantity of the product expected and, more importantly, the production rates and batch sizes required, should be specified. This will have implications for the types of manufacturing equipment and work organisation necessary.
- **Size and weight.** These factors obviously have a strong effect on the design. If the product has to be particularly small the cost may be decreased if material volume is reduced; conversely the cost may be increased if more precise manufacturing processes are demanded. Weight restriction will also influence materials to be used; this in turn will influence the manufacturing processes chosen.
- **Ergonomics.** This is concerned with how easy the product is to use by the targeted market. For example, the median anthropomorphic dimensions for the adult male and female population will be used when designing the driver's seating, instruments, and controls in a car. This aspect is examined further in Chapter 21.
- **Safety.** The product must conform to all relevant safety standards within the countries where it will be sold. The specification should also state the possible abuse and misuse the product might be subjected to. Warning labels and instructions on safe operation of the product should be given, and these should be included in the PDS. It is important to remember that the designer can be held responsible for any accidents that may occur due to poor product design.

Some other factors to be included in the PDS are: likely methods of transportation; type of packaging necessary; quality and reliability expected; the time the finished product may lie around or be stored before use, i.e. the 'shelf life'; cost limitations; and the testing procedures that will be necessary. Consideration of the company's existing manufacturing capabilities should be made, since these will determine if the product can be made 'in house' or if it will have to be made by a sub-contractor. This will influence cost and lead time. Also at this stage a search of existing patents, relevant literature, and product data should be carried out. An analysis of competitors' products used to satisfy the same, or a similar, market need should be thoroughly investigated. Comparison of competitors' designs with the PDS will highlight any omissions, weaknesses, or strengths of the forthcoming design. The product design specification is an essential document, but it must not be immutable. Subsequent to its creation, at any part of the following design process, it should be changed should any opportunity for improvement appear.

5.6 Concept design

The next stage is the 'concept design' stage, in which a design solution to the demands set by the specification is achieved. It is therefore essential that the specification exists, since it is only by using this as a datum that the adequacy of the conceptual design can be evaluated. Initially there should be a number of alternative solutions obtained before a final selection of the 'best' one is made. The resulting solution should be a synthesis of all the characteristics and attributes expected of the product.

A concept design may come from an inspired individual; this does not happen very frequently and, for a large company, it is not a particularly reliable means of obtaining a steady supply of new products. Once again the importance of a 'synergetic' team approach to design cannot be overemphasised. 'Synergy', in this context, is a term which implies that the effectiveness of a group of people working together is greater than the total effect of these people working individually. Teams, comprised of the individuals mentioned earlier in the chapter, can use various techniques such as 'brainstorming' to produce a number of possible design solutions. These will be presented for further consideration and discussion in the form of annotated drawings, textual explanations, physical 3D models, and graphical computer simulations.

All of the possible designs should now be critically evaluated. It may be that an aspect of one design does not exactly conform to the PDS. This design should not be discarded until the PDS has been checked to see if it should be changed to suit any advantages found in the product design. Each potential design should be fully analysed for performance, etc. by carrying out all necessary calculations. This is often now done on computer to allow a speedy, efficient, comparison of alternatives.

5.7 Detail design

Following this there will be the 'detail' design in which the individual components and sub-assemblies will be designed. Depending on the product, detailed calculations will be carried out on, for example, mechanical, electrical, or thermodynamic aspects of the design. For some products such as aircraft, motor cars, ships, and some of their sub-assemblies and components, e.g. engines, scale models will be made and tested, and computer simulations carried out, to ensure that designs are optimised. These stages correspond to the 'development' part of the 'research and development' function.

Design engineers with specialist knowledge will be involved here. Electronic circuit designers, thermodynamic engineers, mechanical stress analysts, dynamic vibration specialists, are typical of the people who may be carrying out the detailed calculations and making decisions regarding the component design. Decisions affecting the details of the manufacturing process to be used will also be made here, e.g. to what dimensions will the product be made, what tolerances can be allowed on the size and geometry of the components, and what surface finishes are desired? In industry around three-quarters of the total design activity is occupied by detail design; unless the product design specification and concept design stages have been properly implemented, this time may easily be wasted.

5.8 Production

Once the design has been completed on paper or computer the first prototype of the product can be made. For large products only one prototype may be made but for smaller ones a number may be produced. These prototypes will undergo testing allowing design modifications to be made before production.

Finally a number of trial production runs will be made. This is necessary as the equipment and labour used for full production is quite different from that used for prototyping. Prototypes are often made using highly skilled craftsmen and technicians and general purpose machinery. Full production usually involves unskilled or semi-skilled labour operating special purpose equipment. Trial production allows any last minute changes to tooling and methods to be made. The tooling and production methods will have been designed in concert with the product design during the earlier stages. Although changes to the product design will still be possible at this late stage, they will be expensive.

The amount of design changes and modifications necessary as the design progresses are minimised by the integrated approach previously mentioned. Figure 5.2 shows that at all stages there must be a close collaboration between all functions. Depending on the complexity of the product various individuals will be involved in this collaboration.

5.9 Contributors to the design

The Industrial Designer often has the responsibility of finalising the general design and appearance especially in consumer products such as kettles, irons, radios, lamps, and telephones, and larger products such as cars. He or she should have a good engineering background coupled with artistic training and aesthetic flair. He will have an up to date knowledge of modern materials and their characteristics, and manufacturing processes and their capabilities. He will be aware of design trends, have a strong sense of 'style' regarding the finished appearance of the product, and will be concerned about 'ergonomics', i.e. how easy the product is to use. Specialist Engineers from appropriate disciplines will be responsible for the functional aspects of the design, e.g. electronic circuit design or strength of the product. The Production Engineer will be fully conversant with the details of modern manufacturing processes and materials. He will know such things as the precision of each process, the surface finish that can be produced, relative process costs, and their suitability for different production rates and volumes. Provided all these individuals have an input to the design process from PDS to production, the time from start to finish of the project will be reduced and the total cost will be minimised.

Concurrent with the above aspects there will also need to be an input from purchasing and planning personnel. Purchasing can provide present and anticipated costs for materials and components. Planning Engineers will be aware of the availability of company equipment and the capabilities of sub-contractors. They will also be able to plan in advance any reorganisation necessary, plant layout changes, and new tooling and machinery needed to manufacture the new design.

5.10   Some principles of product design

The basic tenet here is that a good design is **simple**, i.e. all functions of the product should be satisfied with the minimum of complexity. Following on from this guidelines have been developed that help to ensure that a product will be competitive in the market place; some of these are now considered.

- First, in general terms, the **product function** should be optimised. This involves getting the correct balance between all the operating factors. For example in a car an optimum solution has to be found for each market segment regarding speed, acceleration, fuel consumption, load pulling ability, and interior space. Different customers have different priorities, e.g. one customer may want a sports car, another a family car capable of towing a caravan, and yet another a small town car for commuting and shopping. The product must also be designed to be easy to use. Then material costs should be minimised; i.e. by selecting the appropriate material the designer can ensure that performance and manufacturability are optimised.
- Secondly, but no less important, the product must be 'designed for manufacture'. The design must allow the product to be **made** simply. This will minimise production costs by ensuring that low cost machinery and labour are used wherever possible. For example, if only twenty or

so metal components are to be made then machining may be acceptable, however if the number is to be 200,000 then the product should be designed to allow a process such as die casting to be used. This process has a higher initial cost than machining due to the special tooling necessary, but where large numbers are required the cost per part produced is much less. Also the labour required to operate the die casting machine is less skilled and hence less expensive than that for machining. Some other goals are as follows:

1 Keep the number of individual parts in the design to a minimum, e.g. if more than one part must be used then use integral clips for joining rather than separate nuts and bolts or screws.
2 Make components as similar as possible; this reduces the variety of manufacturing processes involved. Similarities may be in material, e.g. all plastic; shape, e.g. all cylindrical or prismatic; or specific process, e.g. shapes that can be extruded, etc.
3 Avoid redundancy, i.e. do not have two parts performing the same function (unless necessary for safety, e.g. a back up braking system in a bus or a back up computer system in a manned space vehicle).
4 Design for ease of assembly by allowing one component to be assembled to the next by vertical stacking movements. This also aids automation of the assembly process.
5 Avoid using floppy components in a design as they are difficult to handle, especially if automated manufacturing is to be used.
6 If possible design individual components so that they can be made to a wide tolerance yet still function when assembled together; this greatly reduces manufacturing time and cost.
7 Use standardisation and modularisation wherever possible. This last goal is of particular importance to today's world manufacturing environment; it is therefore dealt with more fully in the following section.

5.11 Standardisation and modularisation

As noted in Chapter 2, it was at the beginning of the 20th century that Henry Ford pioneered the mass production line methods that have brought the economies of scale essential to support today's consumer society. However the original techniques restricted the design of the product, e.g. 15 million of the Model T were produced over a period of 18 years, but they were all virtually identical – and all black! Today customers demand greater variety in their product and the designer has the task of trying to achieve the economies of scale typified by the Model T era, yet satisfying a wide range of requirements for discerning customers. One means of doing this is by utilising the complementary concepts of standardisation and modularisation.

- **Standardisation.** This is the concept of using the minimum number of parts for the maximum number of purposes while considering the overall cost and performance of the finished product. It has the overall effect of lowering the product design cost; removing the need for special tooling, e.g. drills, reamers, milling cutters, etc.; eliminating research, development, and planning costs; and removing drawing costs. As a rough guide, a product that has been created by using 'off the shelf' components from a catalogue might provide only about 90% of the performance of a product that uses specially designed components; however it will probably also have only about 50% of the cost. In products where performance is not critical this is likely to be a decisive competitive advantage. As an example, suppose an engineer calculates for strength purposes that a particular product requires six 4mm, ten 5mm, and six 6mm diameter bolts. The concept of standardisation would say that the design should be changed so that all bolts will be 6mm diameter. This will mean that they are all of adequate strength and that, where large numbers of products are concerned, economies of bulk buying will be achieved. Also one size of drill and tap will be used for drilling and threading the bolt holes; this will reduce storage space and stock control costs, the purchasing department will have a simplified task, and material handling will be more efficient. The principle of standardisation can be applied to all aspects of product design, e.g. materials, components, and processes.

- **Modularisation.** This is the broader concept of applying standardisation to produce modularised sub-assemblies. A car, computer, or even a ship can be completely designed and assembled as a series of these modules. As well as bringing all the benefits of standardisation the concept also has other implications. For example, new modules can be designed on an individual basis to directly replace existing ones, and if a number of these are introduced at the one time a new product is effectively created. Using the car as an example again – dashboards with associated instrumentation, sunroof 'kits' with glass and electric motors, door 'cassettes' containing the door shell, glass, winders, locks, and stereo speakers, and seats including their frames and upholstery, are each produced as complete ready to install modules by factories specialising in their manufacture. They are delivered to the main car factory where they are assembled, often by industrial robots, to other modules on the production line. To avoid the final assembly company tying up its money in purchased modules, which also occupy valuable floor space, precise timing of delivery is important so that they arrive just as they are needed. This is called 'just in time' manufacture or JIT, and it is discussed in Chapter 15. Another implication of this is that if the module manufacturers wish to obtain maximum benefit from their investment in their manufacturing equipment then they must try to achieve economies of scale. This means that they may sell their modules to more than one end user, thus making it possible to find exactly the same modules in the products of different manufacturers. Subsequently end users will spend much of their design effort in making their products attractive through styling and the overall package presented to the customer.

5.12   A design for manufacture example

Consider the design of a car engine alternator as shown in Figure 5.3(a) and (b); this is used to illustrate a few design for manufacture (DFM) principles. The reader will appreciate the significance of the following exercise more fully after reading the rest of this book; however, by putting the example in here the importance of the designer having a knowledge of manufacturing processes and associated costs is highlighted. Since the alternator is a purely functional item hidden under the car bonnet no aesthetic considerations will be necessary.

Figure 5.3 shows a much simplified section through the assembly. Figure 5.3(a) shows the original prototype design and Figure 5.3(b) shows the design improved for manufacture. The following points explain the changes.

1 In (a) the pulley and fan are separate items and are made of different metals. The pulley was machined from mild steel bar material and the fan was pressed from aluminium strip. By designing the pulley and fan as one item, as in (b), to be made from one polymer moulding a number of cost savings are made.
● The costs of the mild steel bar and machining for the pulley are saved.
● The aluminium strip and presswork tooling costs for stamping out the fan are saved.
● The costs of holding separate stocks of finished pulleys and fans are reduced, as are the costs of transporting and assembling the parts since only one component is now involved.
2 In (b) the use of lock nuts, a washer, and a threaded armature spindle to hold the pulley and fan assembly in place have been replaced by a simple circlip to retain the composite pulley/fan on a splined spindle. The pulley/fan will have a mating internal spline as part of the mould design. This system will be sufficient to prevent rotational slippage of the pulley/fan and also retain its axial position on the spindle. The new arrangement reduces the number of parts and makes assembly much quicker.
3 The need for the retaining plate and associated bolts has been removed by adding stepped diameters to the shaft. As well as removing the need for four parts, assembly of the whole product is much improved since a 'stacking' sequence can now be followed. Previously the left hand end plate assembly would have to be completed as a 'sub-assembly' before completing the final assembly of the product. Removal of the retaining plate allows the right hand section of the alternator to be used as the 'base' for assembly into which the other components can be stacked sequentially. This means that only one fixture need be used to hold the work, and also that automatic assembly of the product becomes economically attractive.

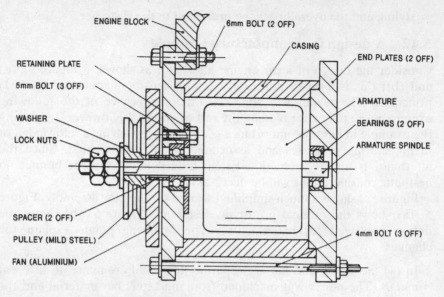

ENGINE BLOCK

6mm BOLT (2 OFF)

CASING

RETAINING PLATE

5mm BOLT (3 OFF)

WASHER

LOCK NUTS

END PLATES (2 OFF)

ARMATURE

BEARINGS (2 OFF)

ARMATURE SPINDLE

SPACER (2 OFF)

PULLEY (MILD STEEL)

FAN (ALUMINIUM)

4mm BOLT (3 OFF)

(DEVELOPED FROM SKETCHES IN "A KNOWLEDGE BASED SOLUTION
TO THE DESIGN FOR ASSEMBLY PROBLEM" BY E. KROLL et al.
IN MANUFACTURING REVIEW VOL 1. No. 2 JUNE 1988 PP104-8)

(a) Prototype design, simplified sketch

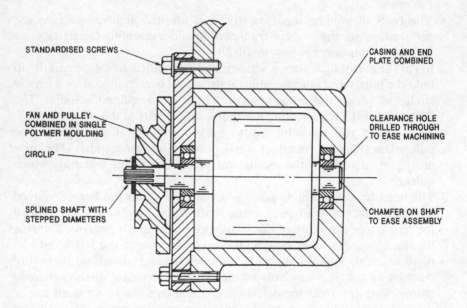

STANDARDISED SCREWS

CASING AND END
PLATE COMBINED

FAN AND PULLEY
COMBINED IN SINGLE
POLYMER MOULDING

CIRCLIP

CLEARANCE HOLE
DRILLED THROUGH
TO EASE MACHINING

SPLINED SHAFT WITH
STEPPED DIAMETERS

CHAMFER ON SHAFT
TO EASE ASSEMBLY

(b) Assembly redesigned for ease of manufacture

Figure 5.3 Alternator assembly for a car power unit

4 The use of stepped diameters removes the need for the two spacers, again reducing the number of parts, simplifying assembly, reducing assembly time, and lowering handling and storage costs.

5 A chamfer has been added to the right hand side of the armature spindle to ease assembly.

6 The right hand end plate can be combined with the casing into one casting. As well as reducing the number of parts, this type of design change also reduces the effect of tolerance build up, i.e. the mating faces of the end plate and casing no longer exist therefore machining of them to within specified sizes is no longer required.

7 The 4mm nut, bolt, and washer arrangement for holding the assembly together is no longer necessary once step 6 is accepted. Thus cheaper hexagonal headed screws can be used for assembly, again reducing material and labour costs. This principle is also applied to the 6mm bolts holding the alternator to the engine block. In practice a check would need to be made to ensure that the clamping forces remained adequate and that vibration would not loosen the screws.

8 By standardising the size of all the screws to 6mm diameter and making the lengths the same, savings are again possible by introducing the opportunity for reduced costs due to high quantity buying, and by simplifying storage, material handling, and assembly. An additional advantage to the customer is that maintenance is easier since only one size of tool is now necessary for removal and disassembly.

5.13 Conclusion

This chapter has indicated the importance of, and means of achieving, a good product design. The significance of design for manufacture has been highlighted. It is now worth mentioning in closing a few specific techniques that have been developed to achieve an optimal design.

- **Value Analysis** was originally developed by H. Erlicher and L.D. Miles in the USA after the Second World War. It is an organised and critical approach that questions the function of each part of a product with respect to its cost. 'Value analysis' is the term used when examining **existing** products, its aim being to achieve the same performance as the original design at a lower cost without affecting the quality or reliability of the finished product. 'Value Engineering' is the term used when applying the technique to **new** products.

- **DFA**, or **Design for Assembly**, is based on work by Boothroyd and Dewhurst and aims to minimise the cost of assembly by reducing the number of parts, and then ensuring that those remaining are easy to assemble. Another method, pioneered by Taguchi, uses statistical design of experiment theory to analyse the product design.

- Finally Professor Stuart Pugh has developed an approach that aims to take into consideration the complete commercial and technical environment within which the design process is taking place. This approach is termed **Total Design** and Pugh defines it as 'The systematic activity necessary, from the identification of the market/user need, to the selling of the successful product to satisfy that need – an activity that encompasses product, process, people and organisation'.

In conclusion, no matter what specific technique is used, the end result must be a product the cost of which over its whole life cycle will be such that it at least holds its own in the market place and returns an adequate profit to the company that sells it.

Review Questions

1 Explain why good product design is essential for the survival of a manufacturing company, and why it is important economically at the national level.
2 What is meant by the term 'Product Life Cycle', and what are its implications for the product design activity?
3 Compare the traditional approach to product design with that of simultaneous engineering; discuss both differences and similarities.
4 How might the market need for a product be identified?
5 Why is it so important to get the product design specification correct?
6 Using the guidelines in Chapter 5, write a product design specification (PDS) for **one** of the following: a domestic electric food mixer; a car jack; a video camera.
7 Discuss briefly what takes place at the 'concept' and 'detail' design stages of the design exercise.
8 Describe the job functions that should be involved in creating a successful product for manufacture.
9 In general terms, name **three** criteria that a product designer should attempt to satisfy.
10 List **six** different criteria that should be satisfied when designing for manufacture.
11 Explain fully the advantages of standardisation and modularisation.

Further Reading

1 'Design and the Economy' by Roy Rothwell et al. Published by The Design Council 1983.
2 'Total Design' by Stuart Pugh. Published by Addison-Wesley 1990.
3 'Design For Manufacture' by J. Corbett, M. Dooner, J. Meleka and C. Pym. Published by Addison-Wesley 1991.

4 'Design For Assembly – A Designer's Handboook' by G. Booth-royd and P. Dewhurst. Published by Univ. of Massachusetts 1983.
5 'Design for Assembly' by M. Andreason and T. Lund. Published by IFS Publications UK, 1988.
6 'Engineering Design Methods' by N. Cross. Published by John Wiley and Sons Ltd. 1989.
7 'Introduction to Quality Engineering – Designing Quality into Products and Processes', by G. Taguchi. Published by UNIPUB/ Quality Resources, New York 1986.
8 'Engineering Design' by G. Pahl and W. Beitz. Published by The Design Council, 1984.
9 'Essentials of Engineering Design' by Joseph Walton. Published by West Publishing Co., 1991.
10 ' A Guide to Design for Production' Published by The Institution of Production Engineers (now the Manufacturing section of the Institution of Electrical Engineers), 1984.
11 'Engineering Design Elements', by P. Polak. Published by McGraw Hill 1991.
12 'Manual of British Standards in Engineering Drawing and De-sign', Published by the British Standards Institution, 1984.

Part III
Manufacturing Processes

Introduction to manufacturing processes

6.1   Introduction

Manufacturing processes are the means used to change a material from one state to another state of higher value. For example iron ore is **smelted** to make pig iron which is **converted** to make steel. Next the steel might be **continuous cast** before **rolling** to make sheet steel. This can be **blanked** to make car body frames; these frames are then **assembled** to other components to produce a finished car.

Although manufacturing is a secondary industry it relies on primary industries such as mining and quarrying to supply the raw materials. The range of materials used by manufacturing industry was examined in Chapter 4; in this chapter we will simply look at the metals: iron, steel, copper, and aluminium. Plastics will be considered in their own chapter (Chapter 12).

Most metals require to be mined since they are found in naturally occurring mineral deposits known as 'ores'. In the natural state the metals are usually combined with other, undesired, elements. This 'gangue', is removed to leave the concentrated ore ready for the metal extraction process.

6.2   Ferrous metals production

The development of iron and steel making was briefly noted in Chapter 2, and metal structure considered in Chapter 4; here we briefly consider their production.

(a) Pig iron

Pig iron is the initial raw material for all ferrous metals. The composition of the pig iron will determine how it will be used. Along with iron the alloys usually contain between 3 and 4% carbon plus a total of about another 3 or 4% of the elements silicon, manganese, sulphur and phosphorous.

Figure 6.1 shows the blast furnace which is used for smelting the ore along with coke and limestone. The ore may be of different types depending on its source – Magnetite, which is 72% iron; Haematite, 70%; Limonite, 60–65%; Siderite, 48%; and Taconite, which although containing only 20–27% iron is normally pre-processed close to where it has been

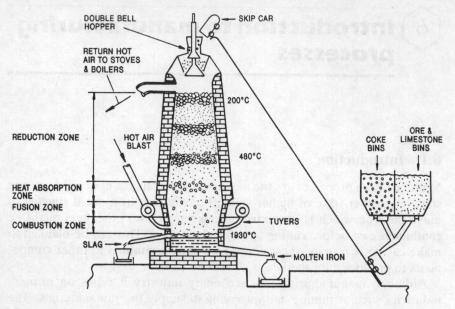

Figure 6.1   Blast furnace for making iron

mined to produce pellets which are 63% iron and suitable for the blast furnace. Together with heat the coke and the limestone produce the necessary chemical reactions in the ore.

The actual process is as follows. The blast furnace is composed of an outer shell of steel plates encasing a lining of refractory bricks, thus creating a hollow cylindrical chamber approximately 60m high and 8m in diameter. The process is a continuous one with the furnace operating 24 hours per day. The daily capacity of a typical furnace ranges from 1000 to 4000 tonnes. To produce 1000 tonnes of pig iron the total charge might consist of about 2000 tonnes of ore, 800 tonnes of coke, 500 tonnes of limestone, and 4000 tonnes of hot air. The heated air is blasted into the furnace through water cooled nozzles called tuyers; these can be seen at the base of the furnace in Figure 6.1. Passing through the incandescent coke the air causes large volumes of carbon monoxide to be produced; this together with the carbon in the coke causes a chemical reaction in the ore called 'reduction', a term for the removal of oxygen from a substance. Thus the iron oxides are reduced to iron. The limestone promotes the reduction process and additionally combines with the undesired oxides of calcium, magnesium, silicon, and aluminium to form a 'slag'. This slag is lighter than the molten iron and therefore floats to the surface where it can easily be drained off. The ore, limestone and coke are fed in constantly at the top of the furnace while the molten pig iron at the bottom is tapped off about every five hours.

(b) Cast iron

Using a combination of pig iron and scrap, cast iron is produced in a furnace called a 'cupola' using coke as fuel. In a manner similar to that used for pig iron the molten cast iron is tapped off at the bottom. Cast iron composition, discussed earlier in Chapter 4, is also similar to that of pig iron. The major difference between the two types is in the form of supply. Pig iron is supplied as cast bars called 'pigs', whereas cast iron is supplied in the form of castings of a design specified by the customer. Even this distinction is blurred in practice, as extremely large castings are sometimes made by using pig iron direct from the blast furnace.

(c) Steel

Steel is an alloy of iron with a little carbon plus other alloying elements to provide specific desired properties. The major problem with early steel was the slag waste from the ore which, especially when trying to make large volumes, would remain in the finished structure of the steel and so weaken it. However in the second half of the 19th century the Bessemer process was developed which allowed large volumes of steel to be produced as cheaply as cast iron had been. The principle of the process was to force air through the melt and so oxidise the excess carbon. A few years after its introduction another process – the open hearth furnace – was introduced. This also allowed the production of good quality steel by melting the ingredients of the charge in such proportions that the excess carbon and oxygen were driven off in the form of carbon monoxide. These two processes have now largely been superseded by the basic oxygen process and the electric arc furnace.

- **The basic oxygen process.** Between 65 and 80% molten pig iron from a blast furnace is used plus scrap, lime and fluorospar. The production rate is around 300 tonnes of steel every 45 minutes. The scrap is first loaded into a vessel lined with refractory material, then the pig iron is poured in. The vessel is held vertically, as shown in Figure 6.2, and a

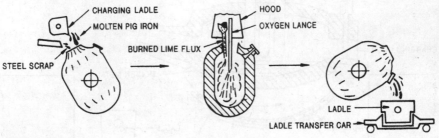

Stage 1: charging   Stage 2: refining   Stage 3: tapping

Figure 6.2   Stages in the basic oxygen steelmaking process

water cooled oxygen carrying lance is lowered to a height of between 1 and 2 metres above the molten charge. When the oxygen is blown through the lance and over the surface of the bath the metal immediately ignites and the temperature rises close to the boiling point of iron which is around 1650°C. Carbon, silicon, and manganese are oxidised and the lime and fluorospar added to collect various impurities such as phosphorous and sulphur in the form of slag. Unlike pig iron production steel making is not a continuous process. When a batch of steel is complete, the oxygen is shut off and the lance is retracted through the hood. The furnace is then tilted in one direction to pour off the slag, then after testing the melt it is tilted in the opposite direction to allow the steel to be poured into the ladle transfer car.

- **The electric arc furnace.** A sketch of the furnace is shown in Figure 6.3. Instead of pig iron it is charged with carefully selected steel scrap and alloying materials. The production rate is around 150 tonnes every 3 hours. Typically it will be used to produce melts for ingots and castings of stainless steel, tool steel, heat resistant steels, and other general purpose alloy steels. The recycled scrap is loaded through the charging door or the top of the furnace. Three graphite electrodes are held in the roof and arranged to sit just above the scrap heap. A three phase current arcs back and forward between the electrodes and the charge creating the necessary heat for the process.

(d) The integrated steel plant

The most efficient way to produce steel is to create an integrated plant.

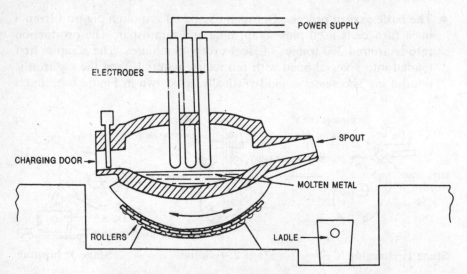

Figure 6.3   Electric arc furnace for steelmaking

These complexes require many square kilometres of land, kilometres of roads, expensive equipment, and labour. Typically the raw materials of ore, coal, limestone, and alloying materials arrive and are stored and blended. The coal is changed to coke in in a coking plant; the materials are then loaded into the blast furnace for the production of pig iron. This can then be transferred in its molten state to the basic oxygen furnace for conversion to steel. The molten steel can then be poured into the mould of a continuous casting plant for direct production of steel slabs, or into an ingot mould (see Chapter 7). The ingots are then transported to a rolling mill (see Chapter 8), for rolling into slabs. The slabs from either the rolling mill or the continuous casting process are then taken to other rolling mills for rolling into strip, plate, bars, or other forms. The advantages of an integrated plant are savings in energy, transport, and organisational costs. However at present there is overcapacity in the world's steel production capability, with many newly industrialised countries installing their own steel plants. The utilisation of other materials has also led to a reduction in the requirements for steel in many products. These factors have led to the demise of some steel plants in countries where steelmaking was previously a major industry.

6.3   Non-ferrous metal production

Non-ferrous metals are seldom used in their pure state since they lack physical strength, in fact less than 20% of metals used in industrial products are non-ferrous. However since they do have useful properties such as resistance to corrosion, high electrical conductivity, and malleability, they are often used as alloys with other materials. The natural colour of metals such as aluminium, copper, tin, and their alloys, also provides a selection of materials that are aesthetically pleasing and can enhance the appearance of a product. Casting of these materials is usually simple but welding is often difficult especially with those of lower density. Machining of some, such as aluminium and copper alloys, is easier than that of steel whereas titanium and nickel are more difficult.

(a) Copper production

The major sources of copper are the sulphide ores such as Copper Pyrites, Chalconite, and Bornite. When mined these minerals are found mixed with waste so that only about 4% of the mined material is copper. To obtain the copper from the raw material a number of production stages can be identified, as show in Figure 6.4.

In the first stage the ore is crushed to reduce it to a fine powder. It is then concentrated by a flotation process in which a tank is filled with a suspension of powdered ore in water. Small quantities of frothing agents are added and air is bubbled through the suspension. The desired particles are carried to the surface where they form a froth which can be removed by

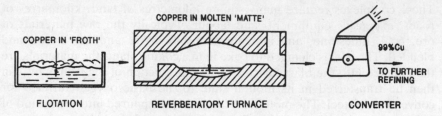

COPPER IN MOLTEN 'MATTE'

COPPER IN 'FROTH'

99%Cu

TO FURTHER
REFINING

FLOTATION   REVERBERATORY FURNACE   CONVERTER

Figure 6.4   One method of copper production

skimming, the undesired residue remaining in the tank. In the second stage the concentrate is heated with other materials called fluxes which allow a molten mixture of copper and iron sulphides to form under a slag which contains most of the remaining waste. The slag is run off continuously and the metal sulphides are periodically tapped and transferred in the molten state to the next stage. The furnaces used are termed 'reverberatory', because the heat from the melt is reflected back downwards by a low roof, and they are fuelled by gas, oil, or pulverised coal. In the third stage the melt is poured into a large cylindrical vessel lined with refractory material; this is termed the 'converter'. Air is blown through tuyers and into the melt. This causes the iron to oxidise and when silica is added to the melt they combine to form a slag; this can then be tapped off, thus effectively removing the iron. Continued blowing removes unwanted sulphur as sulphur dioxide gas is created. After a period of approximately 10 hours crude molten copper which is about 99% pure is left in the converter. This can either be cast into slabs termed 'blister copper', or while still molten it can be transferred to a fourth stage for further refining. Using electrolytic refining copper up to 99.99% pure can be obtained.

(b) Aluminium production

The main source of aluminium is Bauxite. This is a naturally occurring mixture of gibbsite and diaspore containing 45–60% aluminium. The impurities present are typically iron and titanium oxides and silica. The main producers of the ore are countries like Jamaica and Australia. However production of aluminium demands large amounts of electricity, around 13–18 kilowatt hours per kilogram. High volume production therefore started near sources of hydro-electricity such as in Scotland, Norway, and in the Niagara Falls area. Main users of aluminium today are countries like Japan and the USA who purchase the ore and then do their own refining. Two stages can be identified in aluminium production.

● In the first stage Alumina, i.e. aluminium oxide, is obtained by removing the water from the ore, crushing it, and placing it in a hot solution of caustic soda, i.e. sodium hydroxide, in a pressure vessel. Under high temperature and pressure the alumina is dissolved and the

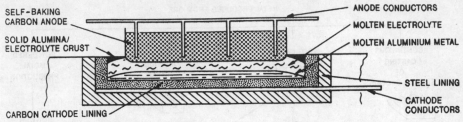

Figure 6.5   Electrolytic reduction cell for aluminium production

undissolved impurities precipitate out and settle as a red mud (which has to be carefully disposed of as it has been a troublesome pollutant). The separated liquid solution is cooled and aluminium is precipitated as hydroxide. Pure aluminium oxide is obtained by heating at about 1000–1500°C to drive off the combined water.

- In the second stage (see Figure 6.5), the electrolytic extraction of the aluminium is practicable only if the alumina is first dissolved in some other substance to form a liquid solution that is capable of conducting electricity. Cryolite, i.e. natural sodium aluminium fluoride, is used for this purpose. The solution, which is red hot and around 950°C, is held within a cell composed of steel plates and lined with carbon. Suspended in this are thick carbon anodes. Direct current is passed via the anodes through the electrolyte to the lining of the cell. This causes the alumina to split into aluminium and oxygen. The oxygen burns the anodes to form carbon monoxide and carbon dioxide. Molten aluminium is produced and, as its density is greater than that of the alumina and cryolite solution, it sinks to the bottom of the cell and forms a layer. This layer is then periodically tapped to provide aluminium which is 99.8% pure. It is sometimes refined further in a subsequent cell to provide aluminium 99.99% pure. It may also be noted that increasing amounts of 'scrap' aluminium are being used; this recycling is much more efficient as it uses only about 5% of the energy required for production from bauxite.

6.4   Forms of material supply

After the metal has been produced to sufficient purity, and alloyed with other metals to provide desired properties, it then undergoes further processing to produce a form suitable for further working. These forms are created by the 'primary processes', e.g. casting, rolling, forging, and extrusion. These processes, and others, are described in Chapters 7–11. Figure 6.6 illustrates some of the standard forms in which material is supplied to manufacturing companies.

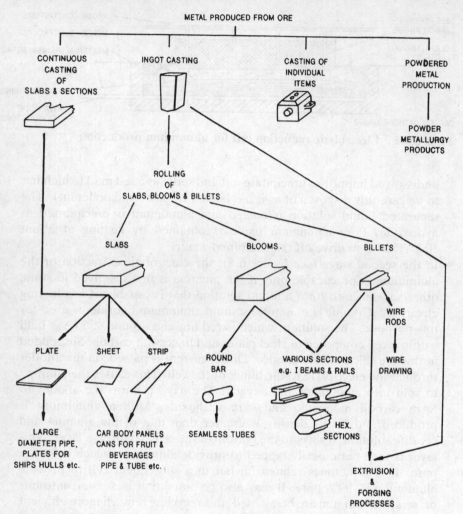

Figure 6.6   Primary processes and standard material forms

___ Review Questions _____

1 What are the main ingredients necessary to produce pig iron?
2 Briefly describe the process of pig iron production (no sketches are necessary).
3 Describe **one** modern method of steel production.
4 What is an 'integrated' steel plant, and what advantages are to be gained from the integration?
5 What is 'blister' copper, and how is it obtained?
6 Discuss why large scale aluminium production first started in areas where cheap electricity was available.
7 Sketch **five** different types of standard material form.

___ Further Reading _____

For Chapters 6–12 inclusive the following books provide comprehensive additional information. They also include good bibliographies and references for more detailed study.
1 'Manufacturing Processes for Engineering Materials', by Serope Kalpakjian. Published by Addison-Wesley, 1991.
2 'Materials and Processes in Manufacturing', by E.P. DeGarmo, J.T. Black and R.A. Kohser. 7th Edition. Published by Macmillan, 1990.
3 'Principles of Engineering Production', by A.J. Lissaman and S.J. Martin. Published by Edward Arnold, 1982.
4 'Introduction to Manufacturing Processes', by J.A. Schey. 2nd edition. Published by McGraw Hill. 1987.
5 'Machine Tools – Processes and Applications', by G.W. Genevro and S.S. Heineman. 2nd Edition. Published by Prentice Hall, 1991.
6 'Machine Tool Practices', by R.R. Kibbe, *et al.* Published by Prentice-Hall, 1991.

(7) Casting

7.1 Introduction

'Casting' is the process of pouring or injecting molten metal into a mould and then allowing it to solidify. Products weighing many tonnes or just a few grams can be produced in a variety of surface finishes and accuracies; internal cavities are also possible. It may be that casting is only the first process in a series of operations that will lead to the finished product, or the desired item may be cast with such precision that it can be fully utilised immediately in the 'as cast' condition.

The process is probably one of the earliest, dating from about 4000 BC, but in recent years much refinement has taken place and a variety of techniques have been devised to satisfy different needs. There are still some problems experienced generally with castings due to their metallurgical structure: relative to other processes they tend to have lower toughness and ductility, and porosity can occur.

As the metal cools in the mould from the molten state and solidifies, so it also begins to **contract**. This means that, if parts of the casting cool before others, depressions can appear on the surface and cavities can occur internally. The problem can be decreased by ensuring that there is always molten metal available to fill the spaces as they begin to grow. This is achieved by providing a 'head' of metal in reservoirs in the case of gravity fed moulds, and injecting the metal under pressure in the die casting processes.

7.2 Ingot casting

This is a preliminary process in which the metal is cast in the form of ingots. These are usually further worked by rolling, forging, or extrusion, to produce sheet, strip, rod, tube, or other forms such as 'I' beams for the construction industry. Any type of metal may be cast into ingots but steel is primarily considered here.

Steel ingots are often cast into large iron moulds. These hold several tonnes of metal and are tapered slightly so that the mould can be lifted clear of the cooled ingot. A phenomenon that appears here is 'piping'. This happens because of the relatively rapid cooling of the metal in contact with the mould surface; as the metal cools from the outside in so the shape shown in Figure 7.1(a) is formed. These 'pipes' are undesirable as impurities tend to gather in the vicinity of the pipe surface; this surface also

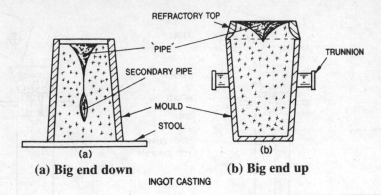

(a) Big end down   (b) Big end up

INGOT CASTING

Figure 7.1   Ingot casting and effect of mould orientation on piping

tends to oxidise. When the ingot is further worked, say by rolling, then this surface may become an internal feature of the rolled component and thus be a source of weakness in the finished product. Slow pouring of the metal can lessen the problem, or for smaller ingots reversing the mould and mounting it on trunnions to allow it to be rotated for ingot removal and using a 'hot top' as shown in Figure 7.1(b) also provides good results. In both methods the top region must be cut off and rejected due to the high impurity content.

7.3   Continuous casting

Continuous lengths of slabs, bar, and other sections, are produced in ferrous and non-ferrous alloys using this process. The product may be used as cast or further worked to give stronger directional properties. Continuous casting is a process that has become very popular for producing steel slabs for rolling work. It is more efficient for this than casting ingots, transporting them to energy hungry 'soaking pits' which reheat them to hot working temperature before being rolled by a massive rolling mill into slabs. It also removes the problem of rejecting the top part of the casting because of impurities, the problems of piping and mould spatter, and the cost of the ingot mould.

Continuous casting installations often comprise part of an integrated steel plant as described in Chapter 6. The molten metal is poured into a water cooled mould open at the top and bottom, as shown in Figure 7.2. There are a number of variations in the process but the two methods given in Figure 7.2 illustrate the basic principle. The retractable base is drawn downwards at a rate that allows the metal to solidify and yet keeps pace with the metal being poured. As the metal passes through the water cooled moulds it is transported along a path using rollers. Careful control must be maintained over the cooling rate and speed of casting as the material uses

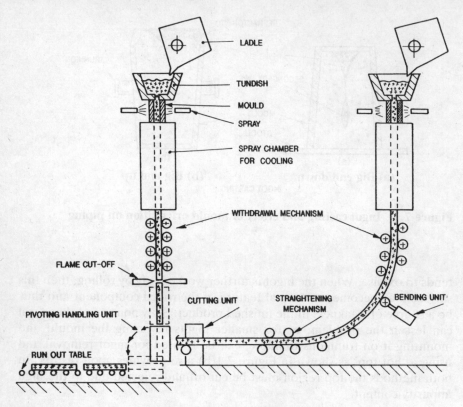

Figure 7.2   Two methods of continuous casting

its solidified skin to support itself. The mould is often made of copper and to ease the movement of the casting it is usually vibrated and lubricated with a graphite type material.

7.4   Sand casting

There are essentially two types of sand casting; these are 'green sand' and 'dry sand'. In the former the moist sand contains between 2% and 8% water. This is the most common method used to produce castings weighing from under half a kilogram to around 4 tonnes, and where high precision and surface finish are unimportant. It can be used for ferrous and non-ferrous metals, and the easy collapsibility of the mould reduces the stress and strain induced in the casting, so making it suitable for intricate work. The dry sand technique is used for large and very heavy castings. The sand is strengthened by giving the mould surfaces a refractory coating which is dried before pouring the molten metal. This section is primarily concerned with green sand casting.

Figure 7.3 illustrates the principal elements necessary for the green sand

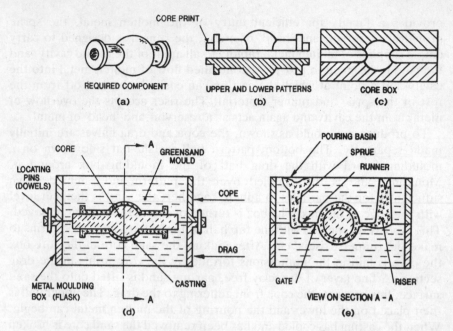

Figure 7.3   Sand casting elements

casting of the pipe shown in part (a). First a wooden pattern is made by a patternmaker. This pattern, shown in part (b), includes an allowance for contraction of the metal in the mould and if necessary a slight taper or 'draft' on the surface to allow easy removal of the pattern from the sand. As a hollow section is required a 'core' must be made. This necessitates the construction of the core box shown in part (c).

The sand for the main mould must have the following properties. It must be able to withstand high temperature, i.e. be refractory. It must be able to retain its given shape, i.e. be cohesive. And it must be able to permit gases to escape, i.e. be permeable. Most of the sand, up to 90%, is composed of silica which provides the refractoriness, between 4% and 8% is clay to provide cohesiveness, and the remainder may be composed of iron oxide, coal dust, and water, which contribute to the permeability once subjected to the heat of the molten metal. The core produced in the core box is composed of similar sand to the main mould, but it is further strengthened by additional bonding agents.

Parts (d) and (e) show an assembled mould. The moulding box containing the green sand mould has an upper portion, the 'cope' and a lower, the 'drag'. The two parts are held in precise relation to each other by means of the locating dowels.

As well as the mould cavity it can be seen that there is also a pouring basin, a sprue, runner and gate system, and a riser. The pouring basin provides a facility for efficient entry of the molten metal, the sprue provides a reservoir and 'head' of metal, the runner is designed to carry ample supplies of molten metal rapidly to all areas of the mould cavity, and the gate is designed to provide a controlled flow of molten metal into the cavity and a point at which the casting can easily be broken off from the rest of the sprue and runner material. The riser accepts the overflow of metal from the cavity and again acts as a reservoir and 'head' of metal.

To produce the mould as shown, the cope and drag halves are initially made separately. The bottom pattern half is laid flat side down on a moulding board with the drag half of the moulding box around it. Moulding sand is then riddled over the pattern and rammed down sufficiently for the particles to adhere together; the sand is then cut level with the edge of the box. The box is turned over and the pattern removed. This process is repeated with the top half of the pattern and wood forms to make the runners, risers, etc. After making the sand core in the core box the core is laid in the impressions formed by the core prints in the drag section. A fine layer of dry, clay free, parting sand is sifted onto the sand surface; this prevents the cope from adhering to the drag. The upper half is then placed on the lower and the pouring of the molten metal can begin. When the casting has cooled and has been removed the sand core is broken up and shaken out, thus leaving the completed hollow pipe. Although a simple product has been shown here the same technique is followed for most products made by this casting process.

The advantages of sand casting are that almost any metal can be used, there is virtually no limit on the size and weight of product, high complexity is possible, tooling costs are low, and the route is direct from pattern to mould. The disadvantages are that some machining is usually necessary, surface finish is poor, it is difficult to achieve close tolerances, and it is not practical to cast long thin sections.

7.5   Centrifugal casting

Long, hollow, cylindrical castings are commonly produced without the use of a central core, using this process. The permanent cylindrical metal mould is rotated at a high speed, usually between 300 and 3000 rpm, while molten metal is poured into it. The centrifugal force created by the spinning pushes the molten metal against the cylindrical surface of the mould; this produces a hollow cylinder of uniform wall thickness. A good dense structure is obtained with all of the lighter impurities concentrated on the inner face, thus allowing them to be easily removed by machining the bore.

The advantages of the process are that the centrifugal force facilitates complete filling of the mould, the gases and impurities concentrate on the inner surface for easy removal, a good solid outer surface is obtained, and the mould is relatively simple. The main disadvantages are that the process is limited to symmetrical products, and that if alloys of separable compounds are being cast these compounds may not be evenly distributed.

7.6 Shell moulding

This is essentially a sand casting process, in which the clay used for bonding in the green sand process is replaced by a synthetic material of the phenol- or urea-formaldehyde type. Figure 7.4 shows the five stages of the process. The patterns must be made of metal due to the relatively high temperature required for the setting of the bonding material. The process is carried out as follows: (1) The pattern and plate are heated to around 250°C and coated in silicone oil to aid stripping. The dump box containing the sand and the thermosetting resin mixture is attached. (2) The box, which is mounted on trunnions, is rotated and the sand mixture falls over the pattern. The resin melts and hardens, the resulting thickness of the shell depending on the pattern temperature and the length of time the sand is allowed to remain in contact with the pattern. (3) The box is again inverted and the uncured sand falls back into the box; the partially cured material is left adhering to the pattern. The shell thickness is usually about 3mm. The shell and pattern are then removed from the box and placed in an oven for about 2 minutes at 315°C; this finally cures the shell. (4) The hard shell is stripped from the pattern. (5) Two shells are fixed together to form the completed mould. They are usually placed in a pouring jacket and supported by sand or shot. The molten metal is then poured in.

This process provides a rapid production rate, a good grain structure,

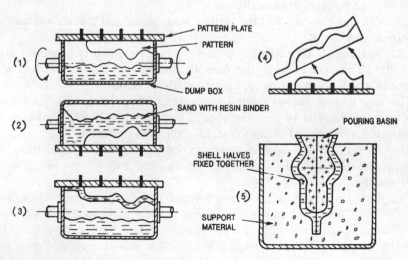

Figure 7.4   Stages in shell moulding

and a good surface finish and accuracy, thus minimising finishing operations. However it does require expensive patterns, equipment, and resin binder, and there is a limit to the size of part that can be made.

7.7   Full mould process

A consumable polystyrene pattern is used in this process. Complex product shapes, together with the pouring basin, sprue, and runner systems are formed in foamed polystyrene. The patterns are packed in sand and when the molten metal is poured they instantaneously vaporise. Though originally a one off type process suitable for prototype production, the process has been applied for large volume production using metal dies for mass producing the polystyrene patterns.

The process has the advantages that expensive wooden patterns do not require to be made and that as the pattern does not have to be withdrawn the need for taper or draft on the pattern is eliminated. Some machining is usually required to achieve the desired precision and surface finish, though this has been reduced due to improvements in the process.

7.8   Investment casting

Expendable patterns are again used here. However in contrast to the full mould process high precision products with good surface finishes are obtained in large volume production. The 'lost wax' investment casting process is described visually in Figure 7.5.

1 A metal die is made with a cavity conforming to the desired shape of the component. Wax is injected or poured into the die cavity. When the wax has cooled the die is opened and the wax pattern is removed. A large number of patterns are usually made.
2 The wax patterns are welded onto a wax sprue and runner system to form a 'tree'.
3 The wax tree is dipped into a fine slurry of refractory material and plaster. This will provide the smooth interior surface of the finished mould which is capable of replicating intricate detail.
4 The tree is now further coated by dipping or spraying with a coarser refractory material to give the mould additional strength. This step is repeated a number of times to increase the wall thickness.
5 The tree is placed upside down in an oven at a temperature of approximately 95°C. This melts out the wax and dries out the investment or coating.
6 The mould is now preheated in a furnace to a temperature of between 650 and 1050°C. This allows the poured molten metal to flow freely into all corners of the mould. It also promotes sympathetic contraction of the mould and casting thus providing better dimensional control. When the casting has cooled the mould is broken away leaving the finished

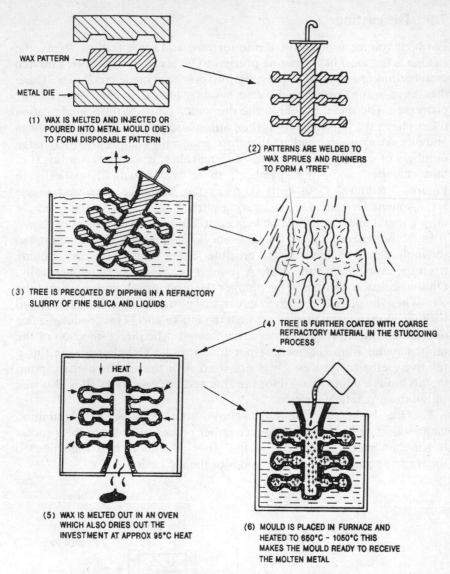

WAX PATTERN

METAL DIE

(1) WAX IS MELTED AND INJECTED OR POURED INTO METAL MOULD (DIE) TO FORM DISPOSABLE PATTERN

(2) PATTERNS ARE WELDED TO WAX SPRUES AND RUNNERS TO FORM A 'TREE'

(3) TREE IS PRECOATED BY DIPPING IN A REFRACTORY SLURRY OF FINE SILICA AND LIQUIDS

(4) TREE IS FURTHER COATED WITH COARSE REFRACTORY MATERIAL IN THE STUCCOING PROCESS

HEAT

(5) WAX IS MELTED OUT IN AN OVEN WHICH ALSO DRIES OUT THE INVESTMENT AT APPROX 95°C HEAT

(6) MOULD IS PLACED IN FURNACE AND HEATED TO 650°C - 1050°C THIS MAKES THE MOULD READY TO RECEIVE THE MOLTEN METAL

Figure 7.5 'Investment' or 'lost wax' casting process

components attached to the sprue and runner system.

The process provides high dimensional accuracy and an excellent surface finish, components of extreme intricacy can be produced in almost any metal, a good size range is available from a few grams to around 40 kilograms. The main disadvantage of the process is the high cost of the metal dies, and the time consuming manufacture of the moulds.

7.9 Die casting

For high volume production of non-ferrous, and some ferrous, items, die casting is the most likely casting process to be used. In this process molten metal is injected under high pressure into precision made metal dies. These dies have sprue, runner, and gate systems just as in the other casting processes. The metal is held in the die under pressure until solidification takes place; the finished item is then automatically ejected. The machines and dies are expensive and are therefore financially viable only where large numbers of castings are required. The machines come in two forms, i.e. 'hot chamber' and 'cold chamber'; these are shown schematically in Figures 7.6 and 7.7. In both sketches the hydraulic rams and toggle arrangement for clamping the moving portion of the die to the fixed die during metal injection would be located to the right of the chamber.

In the hot chamber process a 'gooseneck' duct is partially submerged in the molten metal held within the crucible. There is an intake port opening from the crucible into the duct. A plunger is shown operating vertically. On the downward stroke of the plunger the molten metal is forced into the die. When the plunger returns to its original position the chamber is refilled with the molten metal flowing through the intake port. This produces a fast operation, and short cycle times are obtained. The direct injection of the molten metal from the melting pot into the die chamber makes this a relatively efficient process. It is not used with the higher melting point metals but is commonly used for the zinc and tin base alloys. It is also well suited to automatic operation.

For the higher melting point alloys such as those of aluminium, magnesium, and copper, the cold chamber process is used. In this process the molten metal is ladled into the 'shot' chamber; it is then pushed forward by the plunger and injected into the die cavity.

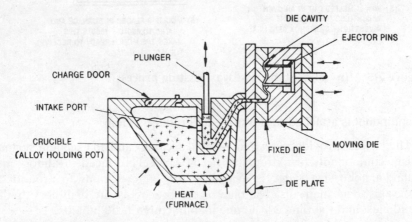

Figure 7.6   Schematic of 'hot chamber' die casting process

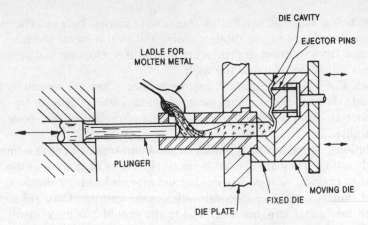

Figure 7.7 Schematic of 'cold chamber' die casting process

Due to the high pressures involved, e.g. in the hot chamber process the metal is injected at about 15MPa and in the cold chamber between 20 and 70MPa, large forces must be applied by the machines to keep the dies closed during operation. Thus die casting machines are rated according to the force they can apply, typically they range from about 25–3000 tonnes or approximately 200–27,000kN.

The advantages of die casting are: high production rates, high precision, high quality surface finishes, high integrity castings with low porosity and good grain structure, and complex castings with thin walls can be made. These advantages have to be paid for in the expensive machines and tooling that are required. It is therefore not a viable process to select if quantities and production rates are not high enough to produce an adequate return on investment.

7.10 Defects in castings

A number of defects can occur in casting; the more common are listed below with a comment on their likely causes.

1 **Shrinkage.** This is evidenced as internal porosity or cavities, or as depressions on the surface of the casting. Improvements and additions to the risers in the mould design should remove the problem.
2 **Scabs.** These are rough lumps of excess metal on the surface of sand castings. Probably caused by poorly rammed sand or sand with insufficient binding material.
3 **Fins.** This is the term given to the excess metal occurring along mould parting lines. It is caused by poor fitting of the mould halves and possibly other mould components such as cores and inserts.

4 **Blow holes.** Internal cavities in the casting caused by gas. The gas is originally present in the molten metal and as the metal solidifies it is rejected from solution so producing the cavities. Commercial degassing agents should be added to the melt.

5 **Blows.** Cavities on or near the casting surface. They are caused by poor mould venting and in the case of sand casting caused by gases emanating from the mould due to excess moisture and poor permeability.

6 **Inclusions.** These are slag, oxide, or sand particles evident in a finished sand casting. They are caused by poor skimming or fluxing of the melt prior to pouring, and poorly made sand moulds lacking cohesiveness.

7 **Cold shuts.** 'Seam' like discontinuities in the casting. They are formed when two metal streams meet inside the mould but have insufficient fluidity to allow them to break the oxide films which separate them. Improved mould design is necessary to ensure that the runner and gating system carries the molten metal rapidly enough to all areas of the mould cavity.

8 **Misruns.** Incomplete castings caused by the molten metal not penetrating throughout the mould. Usually caused by the metal being poured or injected at too low a temperature or pressure.

9 **Hot tears.** Cracks in the casting. Caused by stresses set up during contraction of the casting through poor mould design and in the case of sand casting through the use of cores lacking in collapsibility.

10 **Porosity.** This is said to exist if fluids can be transferred through the metal even though the pores are invisible. May be caused by contamination of the metal.

11 **Warping.** This is distortion of the finished casting due to poor mould design.

7.11 Cleaning of castings

When the casting is removed from the mould it is attached to the sprue, runner, and riser system. It must be separated from these and in addition any 'fins' or other surface protrusions must be removed. The sprue and runner system is removed at the gating points by hammering, flame cutting, grinding, or sawing. Pneumatic chisels may be used on larger castings. This initial process is termed 'fettling'. The sand left adhering to sand castings can be removed by vibration, or shot or sand blasting. For polishing and cleaning the casting surface and removing fins and rough edges, tumbling the castings in a cylindrical steel drum is sometimes used.

7.12 Summary of casting processes

Table 7.1 *Shows the processes involved*

Process	Typical tolerance (mm)	Surface texture μmRₐ	Weight of casting	Minimum section thickness	Costs Labour	Costs Equipment	Economic production levels
Sand casting	±1.5	5–25	Under 0.5kg–many tonnes	2.5mm	Low	Low	Unit, small and medium batch production
Centrifugal casting	±0.2	2–10	From approx 1kg–over 5 tonnes	2.0mm	Medium	Medium	Less than 1000
Shell moulding	±0.1	1–3	From 0.05kg–over 100kg	1.0mm	High	High	Over 100
Full mould process	±1.0	6–25	From under 0.5kg–over 1 tonne	3.0mm	Low	Low	Unit and small batch
Investment casting	±0.05	0.3–3	Usually under 0.5kg but over 100kg possible	0.4mm	High	Medium	100–5000
Die casting	±0.05	1–2	From under 0.05kg–about 50kg	0.5mm	Low	High	Minimum of 1000

Machining usually necessary;

Table 7.1 continued

Process	Advantages	Limitations	Typical products
Sand casting	Flexible process; any metal; no size or weight limit; high complexity possible; low tooling costs; short lead time	Machining usually necessary; poor surface finish; close tolerances difficult; long thin sections not practical	Wide variety, e.g. engine cylinder blocks, brake cylinders and drums, gearboxes, etc.
Centrifugal casting	High integrity castings; most impurities easily removed by machining; relatively simple; permanent mould	Limited to symmetrical components; alloys of separable components may not be evenly distributed	Pipes, lampposts, engine cylinders, large gun barrels, brake drums, and cylinder liners
Shell moulding	Rapid production rate; good grain structure; surface finish; accuracy	Patterns and equipment are expensive and size of part is limited	Good for products with thin wall sections, intricate re-entrant shapes such as holes, pockets and deep fins
Full mould process	No expensive patterns required; no draft necessary on pattern; short lead time; metal moulds can be used to produce patterns for mass production	Some machining is usually required	Prototyping and also large volume production of medium/ small components
Investment casting	High dimensional accuracy; surface finish; intricacy; almost any metal can be cast including high melting point alloys such as steel; good size range	Construction of dies for wax patterns and mould preparation is expensive and labour intensive (though automation is sometimes used)	Small–medium sized intricate components, e.g. impellers for pumps
Die casting	High production rates; precision, and surface finish; good grain structure and low porosity	Machines and tooling are expensive; not usually used for ferrous material, e.g. steel, as die life is reduced	Very large range of parts for domestic goods, motor cars, etc., e.g. handles for DIY equipment, toy cars, casings

7.13 When to use casting

There are a number of indicators that would suggest when it would be advantageous to select a casting process in preference to another manufacturing technique. These are outlined below.

1 When the product required has large heavy sections of complex shape, a process such as sand casting may be more efficient than fabrication and machining.
2 When using materials that are difficult to machine, e.g. refractory materials, casting to fine tolerances using investment casting may be an attractive solution.
3 When large production volumes of small to medium sized complex components are required in zinc or aluminium alloys, then pressure die casting is often appropriate.
4 When the desired component has a complex structure, possibly with re-entrant angles and internal cavities, then casting could be the only technique possible.
5 When vibration effects have to be absorbed, e.g. the damping of machine tools to decrease the effects of mechanical vibration and noise, then sand casting of components in grey cast iron is often carried out.
6 When it is necessary to produce items, such as machine pedestals and base plates, in which masses of metal have to be strategically placed, casting is usually preferable to fabrication.
7 When single items are required quickly, as in the case of prototypes, then the ability to produce a pattern rapidly, as in the full mould process, makes casting attractive.
8 When directional strength properties are not desired in the finished component.
9 When valuable or precious metals are to be used, casting provides a technique that minimises wastage.
10 When it is possible to design or redesign the product in such a manner that components that were originally separate can be integrated into one unit.

Review Questions

1 What is the phenomenon called 'piping' in ingot casting, and why is it undesirable?
2 Continuous casting is now more popular for making steel slabs than the rolling process. Discuss why this is so.
3 What is the difference between 'green sand' and 'dry sand' casting?
4 Describe **three** requirements for a good moulding sand.
5 State **one** further requirement of the moulding sand necessary during and after the casting has cooled.

6 What is the function of a 'core' in sand casting, and how is it made?

7 Explain the function of the following casting elements: sprue, runner, gate, and riser.

8 State why the structural integrity of products made by centrifugal casting is generally good.

9 Describe, with the aid of sketches where necessary, the stages of the shell moulding process.

10 Give **two** reasons why the full mould process is particularly suited to prototype manufacture.

11 Describe, without the aid of sketches, the lost wax process.

12 Discuss the differences between the hot and cold chamber die casting process, and state under what conditions each may be used.

13 List **six** defects commonly found in castings, and discuss how they could be avoided.

14 What is meant by the term 'fettling', and how is it carried out?

15 State the casting processes you would select to produce the following items and give reasons for your answer in each case:

(i) Small complex steel components, 50mm x 40mm x 10mm; a tolerance of ±0.05mm and a good surface finish is required; quantities will be 2000 per week.

(ii) Motor car wing mirror mountings. A tolerance of ±0.1mm and a special textured surface finish is required; the material will be a zinc alloy and 2000 per week are required.

(iii) Bowl shaped stainless steel pump casings for nuclear reactors. The outside diameter is 1m and the wall thickness is 150mm. The tolerance is ±2.5mm as the component will be finished by machining; 4 per month are required.

(iv) A seamless, steel, pressure vessel 2.5mm long, 0.5m diameter, with a wall thickness of 10mm; the tolerance required is ±1mm; 500 are required and a good sound casting with no internal flaws is necessary.

(v) A pedestal to hold a prototype cutting machine; accuracy and surface finish is unimportant, the material will be grey cast iron.

8 Deformation processes

8.1 Introduction

Deformation is one of the four main methods of producing a metal component, the others being casting, which was examined in Chapter 7, machining, and joining. There are at least three ways in which to classify deformation processes.

One is to use the terms 'bulk' deformation and 'sheet' forming. Bulk deformation implies that the ratio of the surface area to the volume is relatively small and that the process will significantly alter the cross sectional area and shape; an example of this is forging. Sheet forming involves changing the shape of material without significantly changing the cross sectional area; examples of this are blanking, bending, and drawing – these are considered in Chapter 10.

Another classification uses the terms 'primary' and 'secondary' deformation. Primary deformation signifies the changing of shape of a piece of material from its cast ingot form into another shape. Examples of this would be rolling, forging, and extrusion to produce standard shapes such as slabs, billets, or rods. Secondary forming processes take the output from the primary process and further work the material to produce a finished or semi-finished product. These processes may again be rolling, forging, or extrusion, but this time typical products would be foil, bolts, or window frames.

A third classification relates to the temperature at which the deformation work is carried out. Thus a deformation process may be termed 'cold', 'warm', or 'hot' working.

- **Cold working** is carried out when the material is worked well below its recrystallisation temperature (recrystallisation was discussed in Chapter 4). If the material is strain hardening then the deformation that occurs when cold working produces improvements in strength, hardness, and surface finish when compared to working at higher temperatures. No energy needs to be expended on heating and contamination of the component is minimised. Cold working also allows better dimensional control which in turn facilitates production of interchangeable components. However higher forces are required for deformation hence the necessity for heavier and more powerful equipment. Cold working also reduces the ductility of the material; this may cause it to fracture after a number of deformations have taken place unless annealing is carried out between deformations. Imparted residual stresses and directional properties can also be detrimental unless carefully.controlled.

● **Warm working** is carried out below the recrystallisation temperature but above normal cold working temperatures. Compared to cold working it has the advantages of reducing the forces required for deformation, and compared to hot working it provides better dimensional control. The exact temperature at which it can be carried out depends on the material.

● **Hot working** is carried out above the material recrystallisation temperature. At these elevated temperatures the material strength is reduced and its ductility increased thus making it easier and cheaper to deform. Large changes of shape can be made without the material cracking. The structure is improved as internal pores are welded shut and impurities distort and flow along the grain structure – this allows directional properties to be selectively imparted. Disadvantages are the need to heat the material, poor dimensional control, and the oxidation of the material surface. As well as producing a poor surface on the hot worked product the oxidised layer can also be disturbed and forced into the material as it is worked, making the achievement of a good surface finish difficult at subsequent machining operations.

8.2 Rolling

Rolling involves squeezing the material between rollers rather in the way that an old fashioned wringer was used to squeeze clothes dry. Large reductions in section are made by hot rolling the material. Only when finishing rods, strip, sheet, and foil is cold working used since changes in section are slight and high surface finishes are desired.

In the past the raw material for rolling was always a cast ingot; however, with the increasing use of continuous casting in integrated steel plants, more rolling of 'concast' slabs is carried out. Considering the most general case, that of rolling steel from the ingot, the process can be described as follows. While still hot, the ingots are placed in gas fired furnaces called soaking pits. There they remain until they have attained a uniform working temperature of about 1100°C throughout; this is well above the recrystallisation temperature but still below the melting point, which for steels is between 1370 and 1530°C. The ingots are then taken to the rolling mill where they are rolled into blooms, billets, or slabs. A bloom has a square cross section with a minimum size of approximately 150mm square. A billet is smaller than a bloom and may have any square section from about 40mm square to 150mm square. Slabs may be rolled from either an ingot or a bloom, they have a rectangular cross section with a minimum width of 250mm and a minimum thickness of approximately 40mm. The width is about three or more times the thickness, which can be over 300mm.

The principle of operation of a rolling mill and examples of some mill configurations are shown in Figures 8.1 and 8.2, respectively.

The mill used for rolling an ingot into a bloom is known as a 'cogging

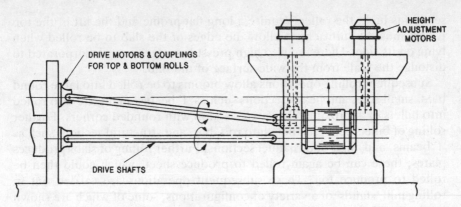

Figure 8.1 Principle of operation of a two high reversing mill for steel rolling

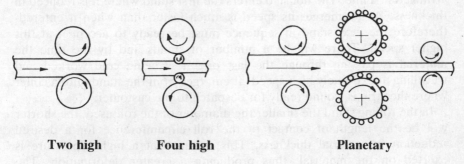

Two high   Four high   Planetary

Figure 8.2 Some rolling mill configurations

mill', and is generally of the two high reversing type. The heated ingot is placed on a conveyor comprised of powered rollers. These power driven rollers are provided at both sides of the mill and since they also are reversible the ingot can be passed to and fro between the pressure rollers. The whole process is monitored and controlled from an overhead pulpit which is equipped with instrumentation and closed circuit television screens. From here the power driven manipulators can be controlled which allow the ingot to be turned over, moved laterally, and even straightened, while on the conveyors. It is important to ensure that the metal is maintained at a uniform temperature, as this controls metal flow and plasticity. The rolls themselves are cooled by running water over them to ensure that they maintain their own strength and hardness properties. The rollers gradually wear in use and therefore require to be removed periodically for turning in a lathe to restore their original profile. The rollers for making smooth flat plates would be ground rather than turned.

The mill used for rolling ingots into slabs is known as a 'slabbing mill'. It is very similar in construction to a cogging mill, with a few differences. Since a slab is much wider than a bloom and the width to height ratio of the section is high, the rollers require a long flat profile and the lift of the top rollers must be sufficient to allow the edges of the slab to be rolled when lying on its side. There are also high pressure water sprays incorporated to dislodge the scale from the wide surface of the slab.

Subsequent rolling operations allow blooms to be rolled into large round bars, small slabs and heavy sections such as 'I' beams; many are also rolled into billets of approximately square section with rounded corners. Further rolling of billets converts them into rod, bar, and structural sections such as 'I' beams, and angle and channel sections. Further rolling of slabs produces plates; these can be again rolled to produce sheet, which could then be rolled to produce foil. These subsequent operations are carried out in rolling mill 'stands' of a variety of configurations, some of which are shown in Figure 8.2.

To produce strip from slabs, for example, a number of stands are arranged in a line. The hot slab enters the first stand where it is reduced in thickness. As it emerges its speed is much faster than when it entered, therefore the next stand in sequence must be ready to accept it at this higher speed. There will be a number of stands and by the time the material is passing through the last one it is being cold worked and travelling at extremely high speed. It emerges from the stand onto a coiler where the strip is wound ready for despatch to the customer.

In the rolling stand the smaller the diameter of the roll used, the shorter will be the length of contact of the roll circumference for a desired reduction in material thickness. This means that a higher pressure is exerted on the material, thus producing a greater deformation. The disadvantage is that the decreased size of the rolls reduces their stiffness. Therefore to prevent their deflection under load, back up rolls of thicker section are required. This leads to configurations such as the 'four high' and 'planetary' arrangements shown in Figure 8.2, which allow large reductions in section to be performed in a single pass.

Typical rolled products would be plates for building ships' hulls; structural beams of various sections for the construction industry; hexagonal section bar for making nuts and bolts; steel sheet for making panels for cars, washing machines, and cookers; copper alloy strip from which small components such as electrical terminals could be blanked; and aluminium foil.

8.3 Forging

As with rolling, forging can be carried out hot, warm, or cold, depending on the characteristics required in the finished product. In forging, plastic flow takes place in the material when it is subjected to compressive forces via presses or hammers. Figure 8.3(a) shows a drop hammer used for forging. Forging usually produces products of extremely good mechanical properties; they are much stronger, for example, than components produced by casting. The raw material for forging has often been already hot

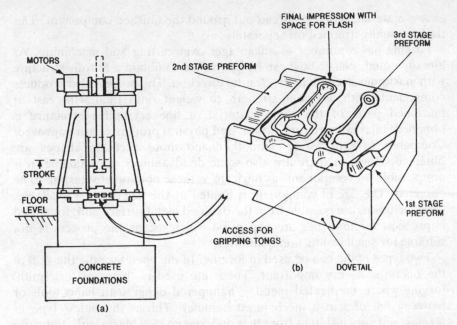

Figure 8.3   Friction drop hammer and lower half of closed impression die for conrod

worked, e.g. billets that have been hot rolled. Just as these billets have had their mechanical properties improved from that of the ingot from which they were made, so forging of them into a finished product further improves their properties.

Grain formation in metals and the importance of grain structure were mentioned in sections 4.2(c) and 4.2(e); forging provides a good method of controlling this grain structure. Consider the following. If a bar of rolled steel is sectioned longitudinally and the cut surface is smoothed and then deeply etched by a strong acid, then the surface will show closely spaced fine ridges indicating that the structure of the bar consists of fibres running in the direction of rolling. The properties of ductility, impact strength, and toughness will be found to be at a maximum when measured in this direction. As the axis of the material approaches 90° to that of the grain flow, the decrease in the ductility and impact strength is considerable (Figure 4.6). The direction of the grain flow can be controlled to a large extent by the sequence of operations in the forging process. For example, in the closed impression die for a conrod shown in Figure 8.3(b) the first operation is to bend, i.e. 'preform', the bar or billet to an approximate shape. The grain flow lines will then follow this shape in the finished forging. The subsequent stages shown in Figure 8.3(b) allow the billet to be taken to the finished shape progressively; this allows maximum control of the finished grain structure. Space is allowed in the final impression for excess material, flash, to spread out around the finished component. This flash is usually trimmed off separately.

Forging has a number of advantages over casting and machining. As already noted, plastic flow can be controlled to obtain a fibrous structure with maximum strength in the desired direction. The process also produces components with a higher strength to weight ratio than with cast or machined parts of the same material, a fine crystalline structure is obtained, internal pores are closed, and physical properties are improved. Compared to sandcasting, smoother and more accurate shapes are obtained. However there are also some disadvantages: for example, it is not possible for components as intricate as those obtained by casting to be obtained. The size of component is limited by the size of press available, scale inclusions are possible from the oxidised metal surface and, for closed impression forging, dies are expensive which means the process is not suitable for small production quantities.

Two types of die can be used in forging. In the open face die the skill of the operator is very important. These are used in 'hammer' or 'smith' forging where the heated metal is hammered either with hand tools or between flat dies in a mechanised hammer. This is the oldest type of forging, not very different from that undertaken by a blacksmith, but close accuracies are difficult to obtain and complicated shapes cannot be made. In closed impression die forging the die is made the shape of the desired finished product. Impact or pressure forces the material in its plastic state into the die cavity; this was the type shown in Figure 8.3(b).

Closed impression dies are used in drop and press forging. For example, in the gravity type hammer the impact pressure is developed by the force of the falling ram and die as it strikes upon the material placed in the lower fixed die, the force being entirely dependent on the weight of the hammer, the top die, and the distance dropped. In press forging a slow squeezing action is employed in contrast to the rapid impact blows of the hammer. The squeezing action thoroughly works the entire section of the material. The presses can either be mechanical or hydraulic, the latter being slower but able to exert higher forces.

8.4 Extrusion

In extrusion processes solid material is placed in a closed container and subjected to pressure which causes the material to flow out through a die. The shape of the die opening determines the shape of the section produced, analogous to squeezing toothpaste out of a tube or icing a cake. The principle has long been utilised in processes ranging from the production of brick, to pipe manufacture, to macaroni production. The principle of extrusion is shown in Figure 8.4. The following is a brief description of the operation of the process which can be carried out hot or cold, depending on the material.

A billet is placed inside an extrusion press container. The exertion of

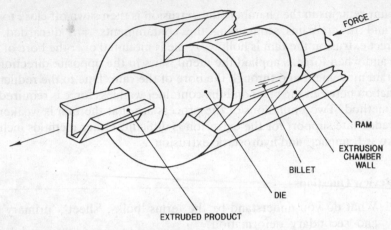

FORCE

RAM

EXTRUSION
CHAMBER
WALL

BILLET

DIE

EXTRUDED PRODUCT

Figure 8.4   The principle of extrusion

pressure on the billet via a ram causes the material to pass through the die opening. This rapidly creates a long product of the required section. The outer surface of the billet is chilled on contact with the container wall and is therefore less plastic than the core where flow initially takes place. Therefore during extrusion this outer skin containing scale and debris from the surface of the billet accumulates between the billet and the ram. This unwanted material eventually moves inwards to form a 'piping' defect in the last of the extruded material; this necessitates discarding the 'butt' end which may be as much as 10% of the total extruded material. Metals such as aluminium, lead, and tin, can be extruded cold, whereas others such as steel must be extruded 'hot'. The extrusion of plastics is very common, and is described in Chapter 12. Moulding trim, tubes, rods, structural shapes, and plastic or lead covered cables are typical products of extrusion.

The extrusion process is able to produce a variety of shapes of good strength, accuracy, and surface finish, at high production speeds. With the exception of casting no other process can provide as great a deformation or change of shape within a given time. The cost of dies is low relative to those required for casting and forging. Almost unlimited lengths of a continuous cross section can be produced from the one die and extrusion machine. For simple sections, production runs as short as 150m can be justified due to the low die cost. Shapes which would be difficult or impossible to roll, such as hollow bars and sections with re-entrant angles, can be extruded. However extrusion is about three times as slow as roll forming. The main disadvantage with extrusion is that for economic production the cross section of the product must remain constant over the full length.

There are various types of extrusion. For example in direct extrusion, shown in Figure 8.4, the flow of metal through the die aperture is in the same direction as the ram movement, the ram being the same diameter as the container. The metal is extruded through the die until only a small amount remains in the chamber; the extrusion is then sawn off close to the die and the remains, containing the contaminants, are discarded. In indirect extrusion the ram is hollow. A die is mounted over the bore of the ram and when force is applied the metal flows in the opposite direction of the ram movement and through the bore of the ram. Due to the reduction in friction between the billet and the container wall less force is required by this method. Two limitations of the process are that the ram is weakened and adequate support for the extrusion is difficult. Other methods include backward, impact, and hydrostatic extrusion.

___ **Review Questions** ___

1 What do you understand by the terms 'bulk', 'sheet', 'primary', and 'secondary' deformation?
2 Discuss what is meant by the terms 'hot', 'warm', and 'cold' working.
3 Outline the advantages and disadvantages of hot and cold working in terms of processing costs and finished product quality.
4 Describe the rolling process used to produce steel slabs.
5 Briefly discuss the use of rolled products.
6 Why does the forging process generally allow the optimum mechanical properties of a material to be realised in a finished product?
7 Briefly discuss the differences between hammer and press forging.
8 With the aid of a sketch, describe the extrusion process.
9 Discuss the advantages and disadvantages of metal extrusion.
10 List **five** typical metal products that would be made by extrusion.

⑨ Cutting

9.1 Introduction

There are a number of ways of cutting materials, and in this chapter we will consider some of the most popular. The first to be considered, and the most widely used in manufacturing industry, is machining. This generally involves using a cutting tool which removes material by chip formation. Another method, used particularly widely in shipbuilding, is thermal cutting. This involves separating metal by localised heat using for example gas, electric arc, or laser. Both of these methods are considered here in relation to metal cutting, although machining by chip formation is used for a wide variety of materials. Finally water jet cutting will be considered; this has become popular for cutting polymers and composite materials when using robots.

9.2 Sawing and filing

Both of these processes involve cutting the material by chip formation. In sawing, a narrow strip of metal called the blade has a series of cutting teeth arranged along its edge. Although hand saws of various types have been used in woodworking for hundreds of years, modern industrial power saws used for cutting metal in the manufacturing industry are normally of three types. First the hacksaw has a blade of limited length and is only slightly flexible; it is often used for cutting rods and bars to specified lengths. Secondly the bandsaw has a flexible blade formed into a continuous band. The blade is usually made mainly of flexible high tensile strength alloy steel with tungsten carbide or high speed steel teeth bonded to one edge. The blade passes round two wheels, one of which is driven while the other maintains the tension. The blade passes through a slot in a worktable on which the material to be cut rests. The bandsaw can be used for cutting shapes from sheet and plate materials. Finally the circular saw is a rigid disk with cutting teeth around the circumference. This is used for fast cut off operations and it usually leaves a clean smooth cut surface.

In filing, the cutting operation is similar to that of a saw except that the cutting teeth are much broader and arranged in series on a relatively broad rigid surface. Because only small amounts of material are removed filing is not used to separate or cut off material but is used to obtain precise shapes and dimensions on a workpiece. Files can vary greatly in size and shape. Large coarse files are used for removing large amounts of material quickly;

at the other end of the spectrum small fine toothed needle files are used for delicate work, and a wide variety of file sections are available, e.g. flat, round, square, triangular, etc. Filing machines use file segments joined to form a continuous band analogous to the bandsaw, circular files are used in disk filing machines, and straight solid files similar to those that are hand held, are used in reciprocating die filing machines.

9.3 Basic principles of machining

In machining, a 'cutting tool' is held in a 'machine tool' such as a lathe, drill, or milling machine. The machine causes relative movement of the tool with the work such that the material is cut. As the tool enters the work and moves through it a chip is produced, hence the term 'chip removal'; the operation of a single point tool is shown in Figure 9.1. Cutting tools may have more than one cutting edge; for example a drill usually has two, a milling cutter may have twenty-two, and the small hard particles which are the cutting edges on a grinding wheel can be numbered in their millions.

In lathe work a single point cutting tool is often used; it is also useful here for illustrating a tool's basic geometry, see Figure 9.2. It is apparent that the shape of a metal cutting tool is quite different from a knife or a woodworking chisel, i.e. the metal cutting edge appears much thicker. This is for two main reasons. First the tool is subject to very high loads when cutting strong and often hard metals, therefore the tool itself must be strong. It also has to be harder than the metal it is cutting, this makes it relatively brittle, hence the need for support behind and below the cutting edge.

A cutting tool requires to be hard, tough, and wear resistant. Until the early years of the 20th century alloy steel was able to satisfy these requirements. However as the need for higher cutting speeds increased so the need for cutting materials that held their hardness, toughness and wear resistance at high temperatures also increased. This led to the use of 'carbide' cutting tools in the 1930s. The tool composition was in fact particles of tungsten carbide bonded into a matrix of cobalt for cutting

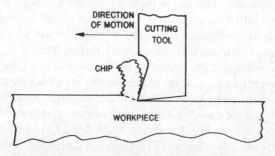

Figure 9.1 Two dimensional (orthogonal) cutting using single point tool

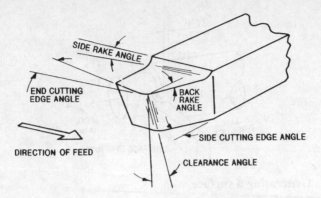

Figure 9.2 Single point cutting tool for lathe turning

non-ferrous metals and cast iron, or titanium carbide for use at higher cutting speeds when cutting harder materials such as steels. These tools are still used today in the form of disposable tool inserts, see Figure 9.3. Since then, other cutting tool materials have been introduced. Because of their cost they are used in the form of indexible inserts. Ceramic tools and cubic boron nitride, which is almost as hard as diamond, are examples. Suitable materials can also be used to coat the surface of a base material, e.g. titanium nitride can be used to coat high speed steel tools.

Cutting tools can be used to create the shape of a workpiece by either 'generating' or 'forming' the surface. In generating, the shape of the surface produced is determined by the nature of the movement of the cutting tool relative to the workpiece. Thus in turning, a cylindrical shape is generated when the tool moves parallel to the rotational axis of the workpiece, see Figure 9.4. Using turning again as an example, a surface can be formed as shown in Figure 9.5. In this case, the tool is fed straight into the work at right angles to the rotational axis and the final shape of the surface is determined by the shape of the cutting tool.

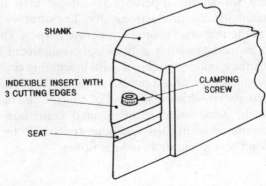

Figure 9.3 Indexible insert

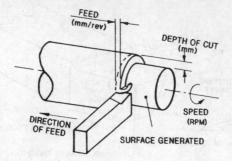

Figure 9.4 Generating a surface

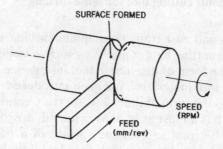

Figure 9.5 Forming a surface

Generally speaking, machining is the best manufacturing process for achieving high precision components with specific surface finish characteristics.

9.4 Machine tools

The variety of machine tools available is large; there are those that are manually operated, those that are computer controlled, and those that are specially designed for specific operations – these may be controlled mechanically, pneumatically, or electronically. The ones we will examine in this chapter are the universal manually operated types. These might be found in a toolroom where possibly only a single component is to be made at a time. Today lathes, milling machines, and machining centres are often 'numerically controlled', i.e. a computer is incorporated in the machine control system. No matter what the method of control, the basic principles of operation are the same as those mentioned here; however, further discussion on computer controlled machine tools will be included in Chapter 21 on Computer integrated manufacturing.

(a) The lathe

The lathe is used for turning, facing, and boring; it is the most widely used general purpose machine tool. Most machining operations on a lathe involve rotating the workpiece and generating a surface. When the surface is external and parallel to the rotational axis the cutting process is termed 'turning', when cutting an internal surface the term 'boring' is used, and when creating a surface at right angles to the rotational axis a 'facing' operation is being carried out, when cutting a component off from the material held in the lathe workholder, the process is called 'parting off'. Screw threads are often cut using a lathe and this operation is termed 'screwcutting'. These operations are shown in Figure 9.6.

Three critical parameters in machining are the speed of the cutting, the depth of cut taken, and the rate at which the cutting tool is fed into the work; this is illustrated for a turning operation in Figure 9.4. These are determined by considering the rate at which material is to be removed, the type of material being cut and the material of the cutting tool being used, the surface finish required, the power of the machine tool, and the amount of support given to the work. For a fast material removal rate the cutting speed, feed rate, and depth of cut all need to be maximised. Tough or hard materials being cut will reduce the material removal rate and hard and tough cutting tool materials will allow it to be increased. Generally speaking, high feed rates with single point tools produce coarse surface finishes, smooth surfaces being obtained by using high cutting speeds, low feed rates, shallow depths of cut, and cutting tools in good condition.

There are many different types of lathe, each suited to different production volumes and types of product. Three are outlined here to explain the essential principles of operation. The basic type is called a centre lathe since the workpiece may be held between a revolving powered centre in the lathe headstock and a free centre mounted in the tailstock. This type is also known as an engine lathe, the term arising from when they were first used in factories and driven via pulleys and shafts from a common steam engine. The basic construction of this lathe is shown in Figure 9.7.

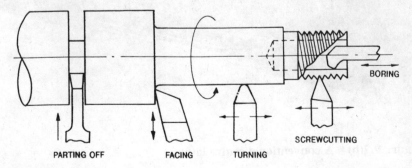

Figure 9.6 Some machining operations carried out on a lathe

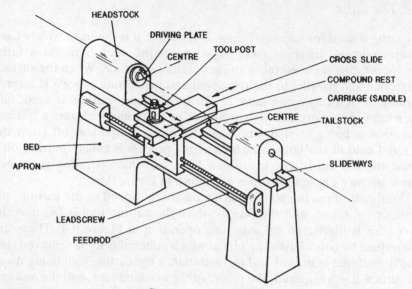

Figure 9.7(a)   Basic elements of a centre lathe

Figure 9.7(b)   A conventional centre lathe

Source: Graseby Ajax Ltd

The main body of the lathe is termed the bed. This supports and contains all the other lathe components; a large portion of it may be made from cast iron or other materials such as concrete or a granite–epoxy composite to absorb vibration. On the top of the bed are two sets of surface hardened precision machined slideways; these are parallel, straight, and flat. They hold the headstock and tailstock and guide the carriage. The precision of the whole lathe is determined by the precision of these slideways. The motors to drive the lathe may be mounted in the bed or 'headstock'. The headstock holds the gear trains to allow a variety of cutting speeds and feeds to be selected. The headstock also contains the hollow spindle which drives the workpiece holder. The gearing in the headstock transmits drive to the leadscrew and the feed rod. The leadscrew is engaged to the carriage when cutting screw threads. The feed rod rotates and causes movement of the carriage and cross slide during operation of the lathe. The apron contains the components for transmitting the movement from the lead-screw and feed rod to the carriage and cross slide. The carriage, or saddle, can move parallel to the major axis of the lathe and supports the cross slide. The cross slide rests on guides on the carriage and can move at right angles to the major axis; it holds the tool post which carries the cutting tools. When cutting the tool is clamped tightly into the toolpost or toolholder. The tool must be rigid with the minimum of overhang otherwise it will vibrate or 'chatter' and produce a poor surface finish on the component. Both the carriage and the cross slide can be fed by hand or machine drive by engaging or disengaging the transmission.

In operation, the workpiece is attached to the spindle via a number of alternative workpiece holders. For example, if the component being machined is long a centre will be inserted into the spindle and a driving plate attached; the other end of the work will be held in the centre contained in the tailstock. If the work is very long a roller support will be placed opposite the cutting tool to prevent deflection of the work due to cutting forces. More often a chuck will be used as the workholder, see Figure 9.8. These have either three or four jaws. The jaws of the three jaw chuck move in unison when clamping a component; they are therefore useful for holding circular bar or previously turned components. The jaws of four jaw chucks move independently and are therefore used for clamping and centring non-circular components. Collets are quicker to use than chucks and are again used for circular components, see Figure 9.9. They are hollow, therefore they can be used when machining components from long lengths of bar. The bar can be held in a support and passed through the hollow spindle and collet in the headstock. The collet clamps the material and the turning operation is carried out. On completion the component is parted off, the collet then unclamps, and the bar is fed through the required length for the next component.

Although the centre lathe serves well to explain the basic turning operations, it is not suitable for high volume production work. One that is suitable is the turret lathe. In this lathe a multi-sided indexible toolholder

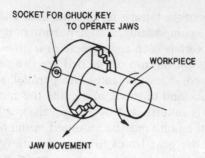

Figure 9.8   A three jaw chuck

Note Three and four jaw chucks are usually much larger than collets

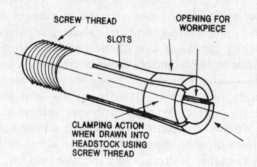

Figure 9.9   A round collet

Note For cold rolled or previously machined material, openings may also be square or hexagonal

or 'turret' is mounted on the near side of the cross slide; a toolholder with a parting off tool is often mounted on the opposite side, and another multi-sided turret (often hexagonal holding six tools and called the main turret), is mounted on a ram in place of the tailstock. These machines often operate automatically and are able to carry out multiple operations, such as turning, drilling, boring, screwcutting, facing, and parting off, on the same workpiece very quickly.

Another type of lathe used for very high volume work is the multi-spindle screw machine. Here rather than one spindle a number of hollow spindles are used, each being fed by long rods of material from a rod holder and feeder; there may be four, six, or eight spindles. Mounted on an endslide there will be a number of toolholders and tools equal to the number of spindles. This slide does not rotate but feeds the tools axially to the workpieces. There will also be tools mounted radially on cross slides. In this machine all tools cut simultaneously then withdraw to allow the spindles to index round to the next position. The cutting operations are therefore being carried out in parallel rather than in series. This means that a product can be produced every few seconds, the cycle time being governed by the longest cutting operation.

(b) The milling machine

Just as the lathe is the most used machine for producing rotational or cylindrical components, the most used machine for producing non-rotational or prismatic components is the milling machine. Again there are several types, but here the principles of operation can be examined by considering just two – the knee type horizontal and vertical mills, see Figure 9.10.

These machines have the following major components: a base, column, knee, saddle, worktable, overarm, milling head, spindle, and cutter. The base supports the other elements and therefore should be made of a material that has strong compressive strength and can absorb vibration, e.g. cast iron. The worktable rests on the saddle which is supported by the knee; this is a cantilever unit guided by slideways on the column. The saddle provides vertical adjustment and the saddle and the table allow

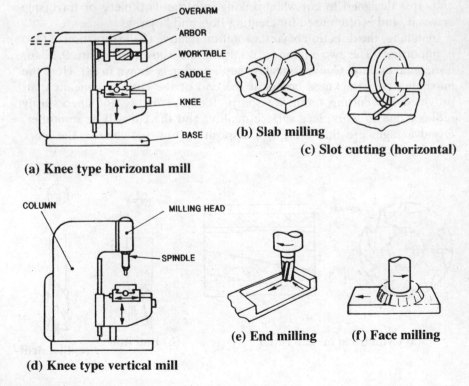

(a) Knee type horizontal mill

(b) Slab milling

(c) Slot cutting (horizontal)

(d) Knee type vertical mill

(e) End milling

(f) Face milling

Figure 9.10 Horizontal and vertical milling

mutually perpendicular horizontal axes' adjustment. The column contains the motors and gearing to drive the spindle. In the vertical type mill the spindle is vertical and is held in the milling head. In the horizontal machine the spindle is horizontal and drives an arbor which holds the cutting tools; an overarm is used to provide outboard bearing support.

Some milling cutters are shown in Figure 9.11. Figure 9.11(a) shows a light duty cylindrical, or slab, cutter for surface milling on a horizontal mill; in general, the heavier the duty the greater will be the helix angle relative to the axis and the fewer the number of teeth. The helical form allows each tooth to engage the work gradually and, since more than one tooth is usually in contact with the work at any moment, shock and chatter are reduced, thus producing a smoother surface. The keyway is to allow the cutter to be keyed to the arbor to prevent slippage. Many other types of cutter are used on the horizontal mill, most of them being disk shaped. For example there are slitting saws for cutting through the material, slotting cutters for producing slots of specified depth and thickness, and form cutters for producing any desired profile. Figures 9.11(b) and (c) show an end mill and slot drill respectively; these are used in vertical milling. The end mill has a number of teeth, e.g. four, on the circumference and one end. It is used for creating flat horizontal and vertical faces, and for profiling. The slot drill usually only has two teeth on the circumference and end. It is designed to cut while sinking into the workpiece or traversing across it, and is often used for creating slots and keyways.

In milling, the direction of cutter rotation relative to the direction of feed is important. The two methods of cutting are shown in Figure 9.12 for horizontal milling. Conventional, or 'up', milling is shown in (a). Here the maximum chip thickness occurs at the end of the cut. This means that, provided the cutting teeth are sharp, the tool life is not unecessarily reduced due to workpiece surface quality, and the cut will be smoother. Disadvantages are that there is a disposition towards chatter, the work

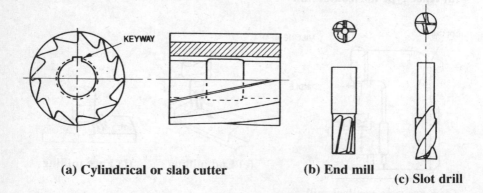

(a) Cylindrical or slab cutter   **(b) End mill**

(c) Slot drill

Figure 9.11   Some milling cutters

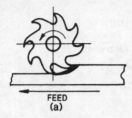 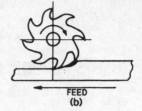

FEED
(a)

FEED
(b)

(a) Conventional or 'up' milling: max chip thickness at end of cut

(b) Climb 'down' milling: max chip thickness at beginning of cut

Figure 9.12   Methods of milling

tends to be pulled upward off the table thus making effective clamping essential, and the chips or cuttings are liable to pile up in front of the cutter, thus causing it to constantly have to cut its way through previously cut material. Figure (b) shows climb, or 'down', milling. Here the maximum chip thickness ocurs at the beginning of the cut. It has the advantages of tending to assist the clamping action by pushing the workpiece down onto its location; this makes it suitable for slender or flexible workpieces, also the chips are deposited behind the cutter, making the cutting process more efficient. Disadvantages are that due to the impact made by the cutter as it enters the work the surface should not have any surface scale as this will greatly reduce the tool life; also since the cutter tends to pull itself into the work backlash in the system must be reduced to a minimum; this is to avoid the cutter taking unpredictable 'bites' into the workpiece which would create shock loads causing damage to the tool and other parts of the machine.

(c) The drilling machine

Drilling is probably the most common operation in machining and although it is relatively simple it can present difficulties. These difficulties usually arise because the cutting tool, i.e. the drill, has a large length to diameter ratio and is therefore flexible. Also when drilling deep holes a build up of cuttings in the hole will cause the drill to jam and even break; provision must therefore be made to allow these cuttings to be removed. Drilling can be carried out on a lathe or vertical mill, but often a 'drilling machine' is used. The basic construction of a hand operated vertical drill press is shown in Figure 9.13; this type is also sometimes called a pillar or column drill. The work being drilled may be held in a 'drill jig', which is hand held and free to move in the horizontal plane, the drill being guided to the appropriate points by passing through drill bushes held in the drill jig. The horizontal compliance is necessary to prevent the drill being twisted due to slight positioning errors. This differs from a 'fixture' used in

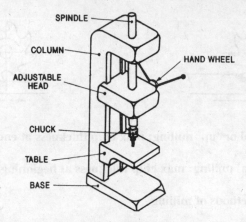

Figure 9.13   Hand operated vertical drill press

milling which clamps the workpiece rigidly to the milling table. Other types of drilling machines are: gang drilling machines which have a number of drilling heads in a line, the workpiece being passed from head to head for each required drilling operation; multiple spindle machines which can drill a number of holes in a component in one operation; radial drilling machines which have the drill head mounted on a radial arm which can rotate around the support column, these are used for large workpieces; turret drills which can have a number of drills mounted on an indexible turret, these are often numerically controlled.

The structure of the widely used twist drill is shown in Figure 9.14. It has three basic parts, the conical point, the body, and the shank. The shank is held in the drill spindle or chuck and may be tapered or parallel. The body has helical grooves, often two, called flutes along which the cuttings travel upwards and coolant can travel downwards. The remaining surface of the body is termed the 'land'. Immediately behind the cutting edge the full diameter of the drill is maintained for a short distance before the body diameter is reduced to provide the clearance necessary to minimise friction. This short distance may simply be termed the 'land' (British) or given the name 'margin' (US). At the point of the drill the lands terminate and where they meet with the leading edge of the flutes they form a cutting edge or lip. The core of the drill is termed the web; this provides strength to the drill and is really its backbone. Where the web meets the point a chisel edge is produced. When the drill is rotating the speed of the centre of this edge is virtually zero; this of course reduces the cutting efficiency and therefore increases thrust forces, causes deformation, and creates unwanted heat. When drilling large diameter holes the problem is removed by first drilling a small diameter pilot hole; otherwise the problem can be reduced only by making slight modifications to the shape of the web at the point.

Various other cutters are used in drilling machines, and some of these

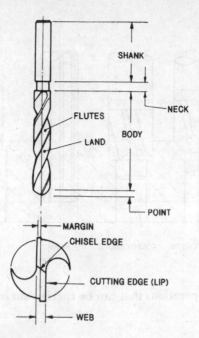

Figure 9.14   The twist drill

are shown in Figure 9.15. Combination centre and countersink drills provide starting points for subsequent drilling. They are also used for drilling workpieces that will subsequently be turned between centres in a centre lathe; the countersink provides protection for the edge of the centre hole. Countersinks provide chamfers on the edges of previously drilled holes; this removes the sharp edge and acts as a lead in for subsequent insertion of screw, bolts, etc. They are also used for providing recesses for countersunk head screws. Counterbores are used for increasing the diameter of the previously drilled hole a short distance below the surface; again the hole can be used for recessing bolts and screws. Reamers are used for removing very small amounts of material from a previously drilled hole; they leave a smooth straight surface of high dimensional and geometric precision. Taps are used for producing screw threads in holes; tapping is not a drilling operation but it is often carried out at slow speed in drilling machines.

9.5   Other cutting processes

There are many other machine tools, but those mentioned in the previous section serve to illustrate the basic principles involved. This section briefly discusses some of the other cutting processes available; Chapter 10 will also include comments on other means of 'metal removal'.

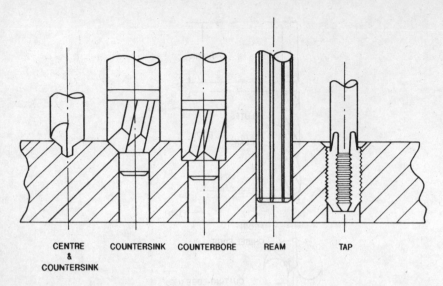

CENTRE   COUNTERSINK   COUNTERBORE   REAM   TAP
&
COUNTERSINK

Figure 9.15   Some operations that can be carried out on a drilling machine

(a) Thermal cutting processes

Processes that use heat to cut material include oxyfuel cutting, plasma arc cutting, and laser beam cutting.

- **Oxyfuel cutting** is very widely used for cutting ferrous and non-ferrous metals, the oxygen which supports combustion usually being mixed with another gas such as acetylene or propane to give the oxyacetylene and oxypropane cutting processes. For non-ferrous metals the material is melted by the flame produced by igniting the mixed gases, and blown away to form a cut known as the kerf. With ferrous materials the oxidation process is used. In order for the metal to be raised to a high enough temperature for oxidation, i.e. 'burning' to start, a gas-flame torch is used. This takes in oxygen and the fuel gas from separate supplies and mixes them to raise, for example, the temperature of steel to around 871°C. Once the combustion starts the oxygen required for the reaction continues to be supplied by the torch and theoretically no additional heat need be added. In practice, the fuel gas continues to be fed to compensate for heat lost by conduction, convection, and radiation. Handheld cutting torches are commonly used, but for large scale work, e.g. in cutting steel plate in ship production, numerically controlled machines are used. These machines have one or more cutting torches mounted on an overhead gantry which traverses the plate being cut. The process is used to cut profiled shapes in sheet and plate, and is also used to prepare edges of plate for subsequent welding. Accuracies of ±1mm are common although closer tolerances are possible under carefully controlled conditions. Cutting speeds are normally in the range of 100–2000mm/min.

- **Plasma arc** cutting differs from oxygen cutting in that plasma is not dependent on a chemical reaction with the material being cut, as in the oxidation of steel. In the basic process, an electric current in the form of an arc is passed between a tungsten electrode and the workpiece; this is called a 'transferred' arc. In addition to the arc, which provides the highly concentrated heat to melt the metal, a high velocity gas stream removes the metal from the kerf. The gas is supplied through a nozzle around the electrode. Thus whereas the oxygen cutting process is exothermic developing large amounts of thermal energy, the plasma cutting is endothermic, requiring large amounts of energy to be put into the process. This process provides extremely high temperatures, around 33,000°C, and is therefore ideal for cutting metals, in particular the high alloy or stainless steels and non-ferrous metals that are not so easily cut with the oxygen process. Cutting speeds of around 8m/min have been achieved in 6mm aluminium. The combination of high temperatures and the jetlike action of the plasma produces narrow kerfs and very smooth surfaces.

- **Laser cutting** utilises the fact that laser light can be focused to a very small focal point thus permitting very high power densities. The heat created at the point is used to melt or evaporate the material being cut. High power carbon dioxide lasers are now widely used in industrial applications. The laser is useful as a cutting tool only on materials that will absorb the laser light to a large extent. With the carbon dioxide laser wood and plastics cut easily; however, the absorption rate on mild and stainless steels is only 16–20%. For this reason a high pressure oxygen jet is usually used around the laser beam to assist oxidation of the material, the resulting temperature being in the region of 11,000°C. Laser cutting produces a high quality cut edge, with a very narrow cut width. The area around the cut is not adversely affected by heat and metal distortion is low.

(b) Water jet cutting

In this process, a jet of high pressure clean water from a waterjet gun is directed at the material being cut. The water pressure is very high at around 3500 bar and the jet narrow, between 0.2 and 2.5mm wide. The material being cut is usually lightweight glass reinforced plastic or carbon fibre a few millimetres thick. On materials such as these cutting speeds between 50mm/sec and 125mm/sec are achieved. It is used to trim excess material, or cut internal and external profiles, on three dimensional components such as crash helmets and car door and body panels. Because the jet is hazardous the process lends itself well to robotisation. The water jet gun is mounted on the wrist of an industrial robot which will probably have six degrees of freedom. The work is also sometimes mounted on a programmable computer controlled turntable to provide maximum manoeuvrability.

___ **Review Questions** ___

1 What is the most popular type of manufacturing process used in industry today? Give reasons why this is so.
2 Name **three** types of saw, and their uses.
3 What are the **two** essential qualities of a cutting tool?
4 What is the purpose of using materials other than tool steel for making cutting tools? Name **two** such materials.
5 Explain the **two** basic machining methods for producing shape.
6 Fully discuss the factors that influence how a material is machined; refer to the desired qualities of the finished component, and the cutting parameters.
7 Describe the basic components of a centre lathe, and their function.
8 Describe **three** methods of holding a workpiece in a lathe.
9 Name **one** type of lathe suitable for high volume production, and briefly describe its construction.
10 What are the basic components of a horizontal milling machine?
11 Name **three** types of milling cutter, and give examples of their use.
12 What are the differences between 'up' and 'down' milling?
13 Briefly, and by means of a sketch, describe the construction of a twist drill.
14 Apart from drilling, what other operations can be carried out on a drilling machine?
15 Describe the oxyfuel cutting process.
16 Describe the plasma arc cutting process.
17 Describe the laser cutting process.
18 Discuss the relative advantages and disadvantages of the three thermal cutting processes, and give examples of where each would be used.
19 Describe the water jet cutting process.
20 Discuss why you think water jet cutting is becoming more popular in modern manufacturing.

⬡⟨10⟩ **Other processes**

10.1 Introduction

As well as the processes mentioned in Chapters 6–9 there are a multitude of other manufacturing processes widely used in industry today. Some of these are briefly described in this chapter. It is not possible for anyone to be an expert on all manufacturing processes, there is simply too much to learn and too many developments occurring for an individual to be familiar with everything. This chapter is therefore simply intended to provide an introduction to some additional processes a good designer, manufacturing engineer, or industrial manager, should be **aware** of.

10.2 Pressworking

Presswork involves carrying out the processes of shearing, bending, and drawing in a press which usually holds a press tool. Presswork is the most economic method of mass producing components from sheet metal. Historically, the use of presses allowed the economic production of products so that they could be sold at affordable prices. Products such as clocks, cash registers, and adding machines were totally dependent on their components being produced in press tools. However although products utilising electronics have largely replaced the old mechanical and electro-mechanical designs, there is still a demand for components made from pressed steel, aluminium, and brass. The ubiquitous motor car would be far too expensive for wide ownership if it was not for the pressed steel panels from which its body is constructed. Chassis, electrical tags and connectors, and other sundry components within video recorders, televisions, computers, and other modern products are made from pressworked components. Frames and panels used for 'white goods' such as domestic washing machines, fridges, and cookers are again made in presses.

Presses are capable of very high production rates since the time to produce one component is simply the time for one up and down cycle of the ram carrying the press tool, and the time it takes to feed into the press a new portion of material. In fact, using tools with multiple dies can allow a number of components to be produced every second! Most press operations are carried out with the material in its cold state. The press itself consists of a machine frame (see Figure 10.1), supporting a bed and a ram, a mechanism to make the ram move at right angles to the bed, and a means of powering the mechanism. The power may come from electric motors or

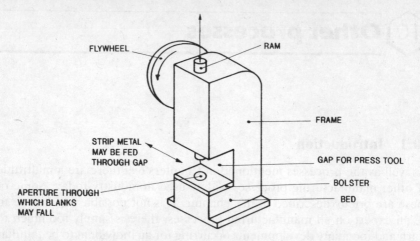

Figure 10.1   Basic configuration of a gap press

hydraulic rams. For fast operations such as punching, blanking, and trimming, a press that uses an electric motor to drive a large flywheel is ideal. The energy from this flywheel is transferred to the ram through mechanisms such as cranks, eccentrics, or gears. For slower operations such as those involved in squeezing or drawing hydraulic power is better.

For most products the press is fitted with a 'press tool' which is in two parts. The top part is fitted to the ram of the press and is therefore free to reciprocate vertically, it is often fitted with the 'punch'. The bottom part is fixed to the bed of the press and usually contains the 'die'; it may have a through hole to allow punched blanks or components to fall through the bed of the machine into a bin or conveyor belt. Assuming the press has adequate capacity it is easy to change from one product to another by simply changing the press tool. The tools themselves can be expensive depending on their complexity.

Some of the operations carried out by presswork are shown in Figure 10.2. In cropping, the material is sheared across its whole width. In blanking, an aperture is created by shearing, the material that is removed is the required part and it takes the dimensions of the die (there always needs to be clearance between the punch and the die). Holes in components are created by piercing, the dimension of the hole taking the dimensions of the punch. In bending, two dimensional deformation takes place, care being required in the tool design to prevent cracking and maintain dimensional accuracy. In drawing the material is stretched in three dimensions and careful design of the tooling is again required to prevent wrinkling or rupturing of the metal.

A simple press tool for producing a metal washer is shown in Figure 10.3. The strip of cold rolled material is fed through the stripper plate in the direction shown until it is midway between the piercing punch and the blanking punch. In this case the stripper plate, which pulls the material off

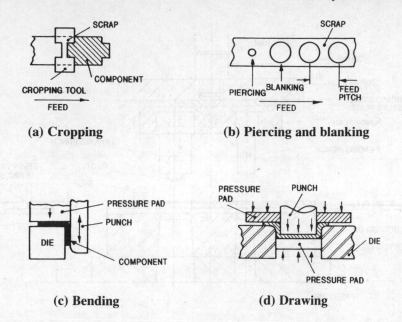

(a) Cropping (b) Piercing and blanking

(c) Bending (d) Drawing

Figure 10.2 Some pressworking operations

the punches, is fixed and integral with the strip guides. The material may be fed by hand, but usually an automatic feed is used. On the first downward movement of the top tool the piercing punch creates the central hole of the washer. When the tool has risen the material is then fed forward until it reaches the spring loaded stop. On the next downward movement of the tool the pilot on the blanking punch locates on the previously pierced hole before the punch comes down and punches out the finished washer. The purpose of the pilot is to ensure concentricity of the inner hole with the edge of the washer. The strip is then fed the pitch length shown between each stroke of the press. This is a two stage tool; much more complex multi-stage, or 'progression', tools are commonly used. These have multiple punches and a large number of steps through which the material is fed before the first component is produced; of course after the material has passed through the final stage each press stroke produces a component. Other tools, called 'combination' tools, combine a number of operations in the one stage, e.g. blanking and drawing.

10.3 Non-traditional machining processes

Non-traditional machining (NTM) processes are so termed because they are relatively new methods of machining compared to chip formation and other shearing processes. The introduction of harder, stronger, and more heat resistant materials, which are difficult to machine by conventional processes, has led to the introduction of NTM. These newer processes

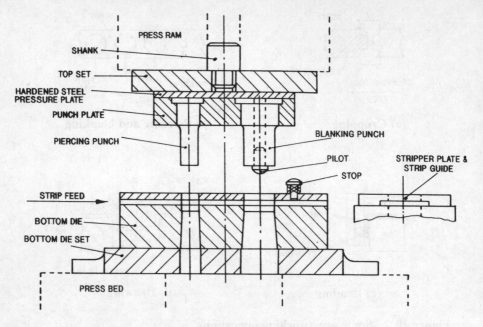

Figure 10.3 Simple piercing and blanking tool

usually do not operate by creating large chips. There are four basic types, defined by the major factor that produces the metal removal, i.e. thermal, electrochemical, chemical, and mechanical.

- One of the more popular of the thermal NTM processes is **electrodischarge machining** (EDM). The process is sometimes termed 'spark erosion', since it relies on the eroding effect of electric sparks crossing between two electrodes, one electrode being the tool and one the workpiece being machined. If both tool material and workpiece material are the same then the greater erosion occurs on the positive electrode; therefore to minimise tool wear and maximise metal removal rate, the workpiece is made positive. The principle of operation is shown in Figure 10.4. The electrodes are immersed in a dielectric fluid, i.e. a liquid that can sustain an electric field and act as an insulator, such as paraffin. The sparking occurs due to heavy electrical discharges across the gap between the electrodes. The interval between the sparks is around 0.0001 seconds, the sparks releasing their energy in the form of local heat. The local temperature is approximately 12,000°C causing the spark to melt the material and form a small crater. The dielectric fluid is pumped and therefore carries away the eroded metal particles. It is a very useful process since as long as the workpiece is electrically conductive it does not matter how hard, tough, brittle, or heat resistant it is. Very delicate work can be carried out as there is virtually no force between the tool and the workpiece. Since the shape of the machined

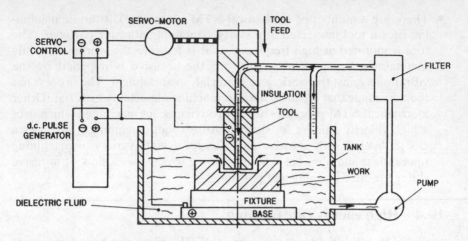

Figure 10.4 Electrodischarge machining

hole conforms exactly to the tool electrode, shapes of almost any cross section can be produced. A popular use is the production of dies for presswork.

- In **electrochemical machining**, or ECM, the tool is made the cathode (−ve or negative electrode) and the workpiece is made the anode (+ve or positive electrode). The process involves electrolysis, i.e. the workpiece is progressively dissolved by electrochemical action. An electric current is passed between the workpiece and the tool via an electrolyte which is pumped rapidly through or around the tool (this operation is actually the reverse of metal plating). The electrolyte is a conductive solution of an inorganic salt such as sodium nitrate. The tool is progressively fed into the workpiece creating an aperture which is the inverse shape of its own. The flowing electrolyte carries away the dissolved particles. Both the tool and workpiece need to be conductors of electricity, the tools often being made of brass, copper, or stainless steel. The process is used for mass production of complex shapes in conductive materials. It has the advantage that there is no wear on the tool and stress free machined surfaces are produced. The tooling, however, can be expensive due to development costs.
- In **chemical machining** no external electrical circuit is necessary. The material is 'machined' by chemical processes similar to those found in corrosion, e.g. etching is a chemical machining process. In chemical milling the workpiece is first cleaned, then the areas not to be etched are masked by a material impervious to the chemical reagent. The workpiece is then dipped in, or sprayed with, the chemical. After an appropriate time the workpiece is cleaned and the masking removed. This process is widely used for the production of integrated circuits, but can also be used for machining much larger workpieces.

- There are a number of **mechanical NTM** processes. Ultrasonic machining uses a tool immersed in a slurry containing abrasive particles. The tool is vibrated at high frequency as it is fed into the workpiece while maintaining a gap. Within this gap the abrasive is impelled by the vibration against the workpiece material, so abrading it. The process has the advantage that it can be used to machine almost any material. Other mechanical NTM processes are hydrodynamic jet machining which uses a high velocity fluid jet for slitting, abrasive jet machining which uses a gas jet loaded with abrasive particles for a wide variety of machining operations, and abrasive flow machining which uses a flow of abrasive slurry for edge finishing and polishing.

10.4   High energy rate forming

Included in high energy rate forming (HERF) are a number of processes that form components at a rapid rate by using the application of extremely high pressures at very high velocities. In explosive forming the high pressures resulting from the detonation of chemical explosives are used for forming sheet metal components. Figure 10.5 shows the principle. A die is made of concrete and lined with an epoxy resin; a facility is included to allow extraction of air from the cavity between the workpiece and the die. The workpiece of sheet, or plate, metal is clamped across the die so that an airtight seal is formed. The whole assembly is placed underwater and a shaped explosive charge placed in the water above the workpiece. Air is evacuated from under the workpiece, and the charge detonated. The shock wave passes through the water to the metal which is deformed by the rapid change in pressure, thus taking the form of the die. Explosive forming has many advantages. The size of equipment necessary for producing large workpieces is reduced, die costs are relatively low and explosives are also cheap. Materials difficult to shape by other methods can be deformed in this way, e.g. some high strength refractory metals too brittle for conventional techniques are found to respond well when subjected to high momentary stresses. Prototypes can be made without expensive tooling. The method is quick and capable of producing parts to tight tolerances. However, it also has some disadvantages, e.g. for very large components the dies are heavy and special lifting tackle needs to be on hand. The number of variables inherent in the process can also make development costs high, and due to the use of explosives and the need for safety it is often not possible to integrate the process into the production facility.

10.5   Powdered metal processes

These processes, sometimes simply termed 'powder metallurgy', involve pressing fine powders into a desired shape. This is usually carried out in a metal die under high pressure. The compact is then heated, i.e. 'sintered', for a specific period; the temperature at which this is carried out must be

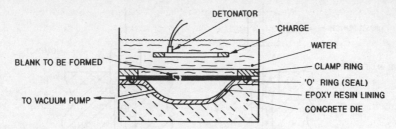

Figure 10.5   Explosive forming a steel hemisphere

below the melting point of the main metal involved. The combination of heat and pressure cause the major metallic constituents to weld together at their points of contact. This means that a porous component can be formed for use as (say) a filter, or different metallic or non-metallic constituents can be added to impart desired characteristics to the final product. For example, graphite is added to improve lubricating properties in sintered bearings. The principle of operation is shown in Figure 10.6.

Powdered metal may be obtained by any of the following methods. Machining, which produces coarse particles; crushing, for fine irregular particles; shotting, which involves pouring metal through a sieve and cooling it by allowing the sieved particles to drop into water, this produces spherical or pear shaped particles; atomisation, in which the metal is sprayed, thus producing particles of irregular shape which can be made to any size required by adjusting the spray. Iron and copper are the two main bases of the metals used, e.g. iron and brass are used for small machine parts and bronze is used for porous bearings.

In Chapter 9 cemented tungsten carbide cutting tools were mentioned. It is therefore worthwhile using them here as an example of the sintering process. (1) Tungsten is obtained from the mineral scheelite by chemical and mechanical treatment. (2) The tungsten is mixed with carbon powder and heated to form tungsten carbide; these are the hard particles of the tool. (3) Cobalt is mixed in; this is the binding material or cement; other additions may also be made such as carbides of titanium, tantalum, and niobium, to improve wear and crater resistance. This mixing is carried out during crushing in large mills. (4) The powder mixture is pressed into compacts which are presintered at 900°C in a protective atmosphere. (5) The compact is then sintered at 1300–1600°C. At this temperature the binding material has melted and dissolved part of the carbides; 10–50% of these are in a molten state. The cemented carbide shrinks some 20% linearly and 50% by volume and becomes non-porous.

The cemented carbide cutting tool is an example of how powder metallurgy is used to produce items from materials that are difficult to machine. Other types of products are as follows. Complex shapes that would otherwise require much machining, e.g. gears which can be produced accurately with a fine finish and can be impregnated with oil.

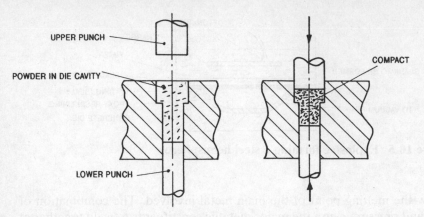

UPPER PUNCH

POWDER IN DIE CAVITY

COMPACT

LOWER PUNCH

Figure 10.6 Pressing or briquetting operation in powder metallurgy: two punches are used to maximise uniformity of density of compact

Products where combined properties of two materials are required, e.g. electrical contacts made with copper or silver to provide high conductivity, and tungsten, nickel, or molybdenum to provide resistance to fusion. Also electric motor brushes containing copper for high current carrying properties, and graphite for lubrication; or non-porous bearings made from soft tin held within a hard matrix of copper. A different product is the porous bearing made from powdered iron or bronze and containing oil 10–40% by volume, these bearings require no lubrication during their service life. As a final example porous metallic filters can be made with extremely fine pores constituting around 85% by volume.

Powder metallurgy has the advantages that: no scrap is produced, no machining is required, complex shapes can be produced, a variety of materials can be used with combinations of mix and structure, high production rates can be achieved, and only semi-skilled or unskilled labour is required for production. Disadvantages are that the cost of powder materials is high, the cost of dies is high, the strength of the component is usually less than a forged, cast, or machined component, and the design of the component is limited since constant density of the component is often difficult to achieve in components of complex shape.

10.6 Pipe and tube manufacture

This section is not concerned with a specific process, but rather a specific product. Pipe, or tube, manufacturing processes are briefly considered together for convenience. They involve a variety of processes, most of them already mentioned except for welding which is covered in Chapter 11.

Canes of bamboo joined together after having the internal diaphragms knocked out may have been the earliest form of pipe. The Aztecs and

Ancient Greeks used earthenware pipes to transport water and the Romans used lead piping for their water schemes. Today metal pipe is mostly made from strip metal or solid ingots; thick walled pipe is also made from plate.

Butt welded pipe is the most common; it is used for conveying gas, water, and wastes, and for structural applications. In the process, strip steel is heated in a furnace to welding temperature and passed through a series of forming rollers which bend it into a circular section. The edges of the strip are slightly bevelled to allow them to meet accurately when formed. In continuous butt welding the strip is supplied in coils, the ends of the coils being flash welded together to provide a constant unbroken flow of material through the rollers. A 'flying saw', i.e. a saw that travels linearly at the same rate of the pipe while cutting, ensures that the process is continuous while still allowing the pipe to be cut to length. Pipe is made by this method in sizes up to 75mm diameter.

In electric butt welding once again strip is made continuous by flash butt welding the beginning of one cold rolled coil to the end of the previous one. The strip is passed through rollers to form the tubular shape then finally passed through three centring rollers which hold the formed tube in position while two additional electrode rollers, located on either side of the seam, supply current to generate the heat of welding. Good quality tubes are produced by this process, good bore concentricity, precise control over wall thickness and accuracy of diameter are all obtained. Also the high quality surface reduces the possibility of pockets of corrosion forming when in use, making them suitable for boiler or pressure applications. Pipes up to 400mm diameter with wall thicknesses of from 3–13mm are made by this process. Larger diameter pipes are usually fabricated by forming plates to shape in special presses, then using the submerged arc welding process to join the seams. Pipes from 400–1200mm diameter and 6–15mm wall thickness are produced by this process.

Seamless pipe can be produced by centrifugal casting, extrusion, piercing, or rotary forging. Centrifugal casting was explained in section 7.5. The extrusion process was explained in section 8.4; for tube production direct extrusion is used but with a mandrel to shape the inside of the die. A billet is placed in the extrusion chamber, the mandrel is pushed through the centre of the billet, then the ram advances pushing the metal through the die and around the mandrel. Aluminium and plastic are simpler to extrude than steel which may be extruded up to about 75mm diameter.

In the piercing process a solid billet is centre punched then heated in a furnace to hot working temperature. It is then passed between two specially designed and oriented rolls that cause the billet to be squeezed in one direction as it is both rotated and advanced axially. This complex motion causes an aperture to open in its centre as it is forced over a piercing mandrel. While still at working temperature the billet, now in tubular form, is passed through grooved rollers and over a plug to bring it to the desired diameter and wall thickness. Seamless tubes up to 150mm diameter can be produced by this method, though further working can be used for pipes up to 610mm diameter. To produce even higher quality seamless pipe suitable for containing fluids at high pressures pierced billets are passed through the rotary forging process. This involves passing the tube over a mandrel, which maintains the internal diameter, while squeezing the material between forging rolls.

10.7   Metal finishing processes

After initial production, by whatever process, components usually need some form of finishing or surface treatment. Often the component will have to be cleaned in some way to remove residue created by the previous process, or rough edges or excess material will have to be removed. Then to protect the metal when exposed to atmosphere, or to provide an attractive appearance to the customer, a surface treatment of the metal will be necessary. A few examples of these finishing processes are given here.

- Components that have been sand cast often have sand particles stubbornly adhering to their surface. This spoils the appearance and also causes excessive wear on cutting tools if the component has to be machined. The sand is therefore removed by an abrasive cleaning process such as **shot blasting**. In this process, sand or steel shot is impelled against the component at high speed by utilising compressed air.
- After components have been hot worked their surfaces oxidise and a black scale is formed. This scale has to be removed before further work is carried out as it can lead to surface defects in the finished component. Scale removal is carried out by the process of **pickling**. This involves dipping the metal parts, which must have been cleaned to remove oil and dirt, in a bath of dilute acid. If controlled properly the result will be a smooth, clean, scale free component. Abrasive cleaning can also be used for removing scale.
- A process used for removing rough edges, after (say) machining or blanking and piercing, is **tumbling**. Here, components are placed in a specially designed barrel mounted on trunnions. Sometimes abrasive particles such as pellets of granite are added. As the barrel rotates the components, with which the barrel is almost filled, are drawn upwards before sliding down onto those below. This gentle tumbling action causes the component edges to be smoothed and rounded.
- Among the finishing processes **electroplating** is very popular. The process may be used to improve appearance, wear and corrosion resistance, or to add material for the purpose of increasing the size of the component. Most metals can be plated and even plastics if first coated with a conductive material. Figure 10.7 shows the principle of the process. The components to be plated are made the cathode and are suspended in a solution of dissolved salts of the metal to be deposited.

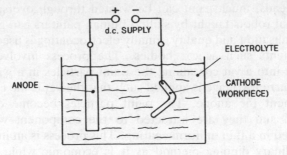

Figure 10.7 The electroplating process

Also suspended in the solution is a slab of the metal to be deposited, this is made the anode. A direct current voltage is applied and metallic ions migrate through the solution to the surface of the cathodic components. They then lose their charges and are deposited as a metal plating. Steel, aluminium, and die cast zinc components are all commonly plated with metals such as tin, chromium, copper, and for smaller components such as jewellery, with gold and platinum.

- **Anodising** provides a corrosion resistant surface which is also decorative. It is an oxidation process, that converts the component surfaces to a hard, porous oxide layer. In this process the components are made the anode and they are suspended in an acid bath; chemical adsorption of the oxygen from the bath results. A variety of surface colours can be obtained by the use of organic dyes, black, silver, gold, grey, red and bronze being popular. The process can also be used to provide a suitable base for painting. Anodised surfaces are particularly popular on aluminium products.

- The familiar process of **painting** is widely used for providing corrosion protection and an attractive appearance on many products. At least two coats are usually applied. The first coats have three tasks, to ensure paint adhesion, to enhance corrosion resistance, and to produce a smooth flat surface by filling in small cavities caused by surface imperfections. The final coats are more highly pigmented and provide attractive colours and textures. Three methods of paint application are normally employed. Small parts or components that require their entire surface coated in paint can be dipped. This process involves lowering the component into a vat of paint either manually or automatically while passing along a conveyor. Good surface finishes are difficult to achieve as the paint can leave wave marks as it runs off, and it is not economical where only thin coatings are required. A second method is spray painting. This can be done by hand, which is unhealthy and unpleasant for the painter and often inefficient. Automatic spray painting removes the health hazard, if carried out in an enclosed area. Only a thin coating of paint is usually applied at each coat to ensure a good finish. When using automation, if the components are simply passed through fixed spray heads, much paint can be wasted through overspray; however, industrial robots taught by skilled human painters can greatly improve paint utilisation and quality. Finally electrocoating is used to cover large components such as car bodies. The process involves dipping the product into a vat containing the paint particles in a water solvent. A direct current voltage is applied such that the vat is the cathode and the component the anode. The paint particles become electrostatically charged and they are attracted to the component where they are deposited in a thin uniform coating. This process is an improvement on the ordinary dipping method as it is economic while also providing better coverage of internal surfaces and a better finish which can be thinner and more evenly spread.

Review Questions

1 What process would you expect to be used for producing the following?

(i)   High quality seamless pipe 120mm diameter suitable for carrying chemicals at high pressure.

(ii)   Brass gear wheels 30mm diameter by 2mm thick at a production rate of one million per year.

(iii) 10 metre lengths of 200mm diameter steel pipe for low pressure liquid waste disposal.

(iv)   Two hemispherical pressure vessel end pieces made of steel 30mm thick and 3 metres in diameter.

(v)   One octagonal aperture in the die of a press tool; the die is to be of single piece construction.

(vi)   A decorative matt black finish on the aluminium casing for a microscope.

(vii) Porous metallic filters 20mm diameter by 20mm long at a rate of 500,000 per year.

2 State the reasons for the continuing popularity of presswork as a means of producing components.

3 Briefly hand sketch a simple press tool, and discuss the types of operation that may be carried out.

4 Briefly describe the EDM and ECM processes.

5 State **three** advantages and **three** disadvantages of explosive forming.

6 Describe the production of cemented tungsten carbide cutting tools.

7 Discuss the advantages and disadvantages of the powdered metal processes.

8 Briefly describe **five** different processes used for producing metal pipes and tubes.

9 Describe, with the aid of a sketch, the electroplating process, and discuss why it is used.
10 Discuss the differences between the basic paint dipping process and that of electrocoating.

11 Joining processes

11.1 Introduction

Consider almost any manufactured product: aircraft, motor cars, televisions, computers, or ships. All are really **composites** of a number of different elements. In previous chapters we have seen some of the means whereby the individual items and products can be produced; here we examine the methods used to **join** these elements together. The joining process is usually called 'assembly' if mechanical fastening is being used or a number of components and 'sub-assemblies' are being combined. If welding, especially fusion welding, is being used then 'fabrication' is normally the term applied.

This chapter looks at just some of the range of techniques for joining that are available to the manufacturing engineer. The choice of technique will depend on a variety of factors, for example bolted joints tend to absorb vibrations better than welded joints, but a welded construction would probably be cheaper. Adhesives are becoming a popular alternative to welding and riveting as they are simple to apply, they preserve the appearance of the material, and when metals are joined in this way they do not change their metallurgical properties. The choice of the joining process influences the cost of the product, aesthetic qualities, and the means of repair and maintenance. Figure 11.1 is a chart showing some examples of the joining processes used in manufacturing industry; it is these that are described in the following sections.

11.2 Mechanical fastening

These methods may be semi-permanent or permanent; some examples are shown in Figure 11.2. The semi-permanent methods using screws, spring clips, nuts and bolts, etc. allow easy dismantling of the assembly for repair and maintenance. For heavy duty applications bolted assemblies may be selected. For assemblies requiring medium strength and expected to be dismantled by skilled workers, cap screws with hexagonal or hexagonal socket heads are used. A castellated nut may be used in conjunction with a split pin to prevent rotation in situations where a low tightening torque has been applied to the nut. Self-tapping screws are used in light duty applications, often on plastics, where they make the expense of tapping the screw hole unnecessary. Self-locking plates can be used on thin metal

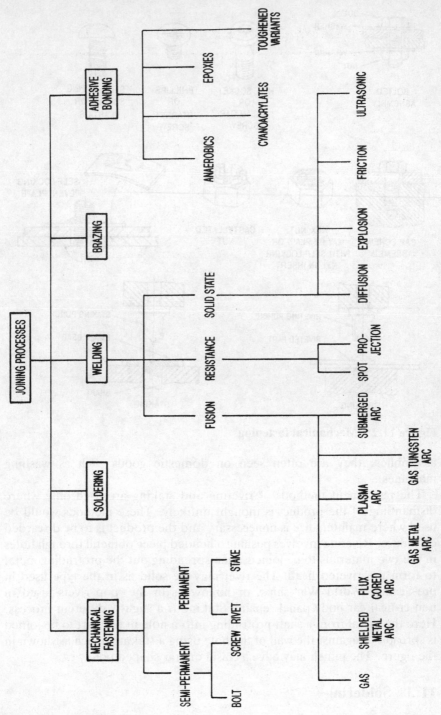

Figure 11.1 Chart showing some examples of the range of joining processes used in manufacturing industry

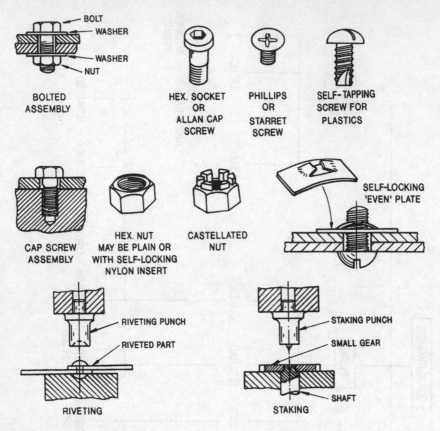

Figure 11.2 Mechanical fastening

assemblies; they are often seen on domestic goods such as washing machines.

The permanent methods of riveting and staking are used only where dismantling of the product is thought unlikely. These methods would be used where maintenance is unnecessary and the product is to be discarded on failure. Riveting involves pushing a headed piece of metal through holes in the two materials to be joined, then spreading out the protruding metal to form the riveted head. The rivet may be solid as in the type used in pre-Second World War ships, or hollow as in the 'pop rivets' used in non-critical car body panel repairs. Staking is a slightly different process. Here the metal from a shaft protruding into a hole in the part to be joined is spread out against the wall of the hole using a staking punch as shown in the figure. The punch may have a chisel or star shaped point.

11.3 Soldering

Soldering is a process that uses heat, solder, and flux, to form a joint between two metals (see Figure 11.3). Heat is applied to the joint and the

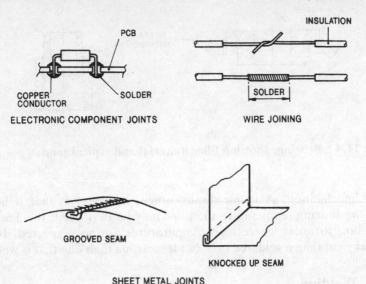

COPPER CONDUCTOR | PCB | SOLDER
ELECTRONIC COMPONENT JOINTS

INSULATION | SOLDER
WIRE JOINING

GROOVED SEAM

KNOCKED UP SEAM

SHEET METAL JOINTS

Figure 11.3 Soldering

solder. The solder is usually an alloy of lead (80–40%), tin, and a very small amount (under 0.5%) antimony; it has a melting point below 450°C. The solders with higher tin proportions are used only where higher fluidity and strength are required as tin is relatively expensive. The surfaces to be joined must be cleaned and dried before soldering takes place. Heat and flux is then applied. The flux further cleans the metal by dissolving oxides on the surface and preventing new oxides forming during heating; it also assists the solder to flow into the joint. The solder may be applied from a coil, and an electric soldering iron or gun used to apply heat. For large volumes of electronic components mounted on printed circuit boards wave soldering is commonly used. In all applications solder joints do not provide high strength and should therefore not be used in situations where they may be subjected to heavy mechanical loads.

11.4 Brazing

Brazing is similar to soldering in that the metals to be joined are not heated above their melting temperature. A non-ferrous filler material is used which has a melting temperature above 450°C. Since the parent metal is not melted the filler material must obviously be of a different composition, usually an alloy of copper, silver, or aluminium. A flux, or inert atmosphere, is used to help ensure a clean joint. The filler material is drawn into the space in the joints through capillary action, thus necessitating a good close fit between the components to be brazed (see Figure 11.4). Almost all metals can be joined by brazing; less heating is required when compared to welding, therefore less distortion of the workpiece occurs, and the process

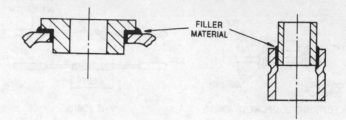

FILLER
MATERIAL

Figure 11.4   Brazing, showing filler material and typical joints

can be mechanised. A major disadvantage, however, is that if heated above the brazing temperature the joint may be destroyed; this limits its application to areas where high temperatures are not expected. It is a stronger joint than a soldered one, but less strong than one that is welded.

11.5   Welding

In welding, two materials are joined together by the use of temperature or pressure, or a combination of both. The materials are usually metal but some welding of plastics is also carried out. The descriptions which follow apply to the welding of metals unless otherwise stated. At the joint the material fuses together to form a solid structure. Figure 11.1 shows the three main weld groupings, i.e. fusion, resistance, and solid state.

- In fusion welding the metals to be joined are brought together and heat is applied to the joint. The edges of the parent metal are often prepared by machining, thus necessitating the use of additional 'filler' metal. The heat melts the parent and filler material at the interface, so allowing a strong homogeneous joint to be formed.
- In resistance welding the passage of an electric current across the joint interface causes local heating and melting; pressure is applied at the same time and a strong joint results.
- In solid state welding, pressure is often used in conjunction with appropriate metallurgical conditions; the parent metal is not melted.

(a)   Joints and welds

Four of the basic joints used in welding are shown in Figure 11.5, i.e. butt, corner, tee, and lap. There are various types of weld used to create these joints and Figure 11.5 shows the fillet and butt welds, which are the most common types.

- The structure and nomenclature of a **fillet weld** is shown in Figure 11.6. The edges of the material to be joined require no special preparation. The fusion zone, i.e. the area within which the metal is melted, consists mainly of the filler metal with a little of the parent metal. Fillet welds are

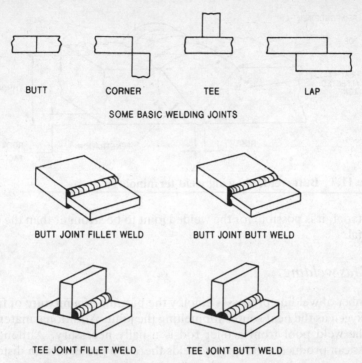

Figure 11.5 Some basic welding joints

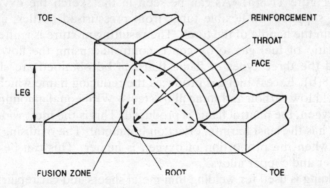

Figure 11.6 Fillet weld, showing weld terminology

often used to fill a corner and are very common in structural work, e.g. stiffening ribs for a ship's hull may be welded in this way.

• A **butt weld** is shown in Figure 11.7. Where maximum strength is required on thicker materials, some sort of edge preparation of the parent metal is usually necessary, Figure 11.7 shows a 'V' preparation. This preparation is created either by the torch used in originally cutting the plate, or by machining using a single point cutting tool in a planing machine. When welding mild steel, using mild steel for the filler

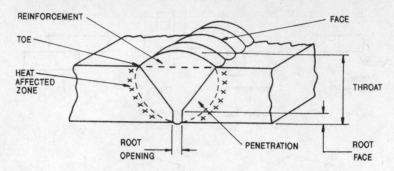

Figure 11.7   Butt weld, showing weld terminology

material, it is possible for the welded joint to be stronger than the parent metal.

(b) Gas welding

A number of welding processes employ the burning of a mixture of fuel gas and oxygen as the heat source for melting the joint. Additional material fed into the weld pool from a filler rod is usually necessary. Although this process can produce good quality welds there is a problem with distortion, and this prevents its widespread use in industry.

Acetylene is a common fuel gas used. An oxyacetylene welding torch is shown in Figure 11.8(a). As can be seen in the sketch the oxygen and acetylene, supplied via flexible tubes from pressurised bottles, are combined within the handle of the torch. The resulting mixture is ignited at the tip. The ratio of fuel gas to oxygen is controlled using the flow control valves and the three types of flame that can be obtained are shown in Figure 11.8(b). Excess fuel gas produces the reducing flame which can be used to weld low carbon and some alloy steels. With equal amounts of fuel gas and oxygen, the neutral flame is produced. This is the most widely used flame as it has the least harmful effect on hot metal. The oxidising flame is produced when the proportion of oxygen is higher. This can be used to weld copper and copper alloys.

Gas welding is used for welding thin metal sheets and car repairs. It can also be used for welding cast iron. The equipment is portable and relatively inexpensive.

(c) Shielded metal arc welding

Shielded metal arc, manual metal arc, or 'stick', welding are all different terms for the same process. Figure 11.9(a) shows the equipment necessary, and Figure 11.9(b) shows the operation of the process. Stick welding is a very common method of welding because of its portability, flexibility, and wide range of applications. In the process the heat created by an electric

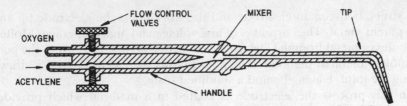

(a) Simplified section of oxyacetylene welding torch

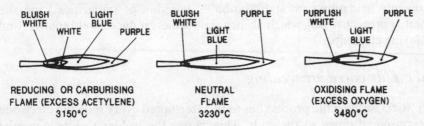

(b) Three types of oxyacetylene flame

Figure 11.8 Oxyacetylene welding

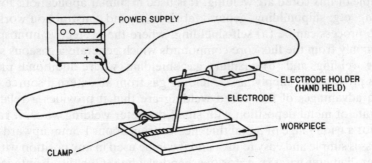

(a) Basic equipment for shielded metal arc or 'stick' welding

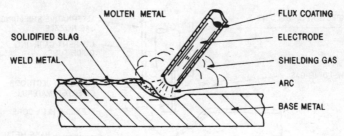

(b) The shielded metal arc process

Figure 11.9 Shielded metal arc welding

arc struck between an electrode and the work melts the electrode tip and the parent metal. The current is of low voltage and high amperage. Molten globules of metal from the electrode are carried across the arc into the pool of molten metal at the joint. The pool follows the electrode as it is drawn along the joint, leaving behind a solidified seam.

In this process the electrode is coated in a material which provides various functions. The electrode is often called the welding 'rod' or 'stick', and the coating 'flux'. The flux provides: a protective atmosphere which prevents oxidation, arc stabilisation, separation of impurities from the melt, a protective slag which absorbs impurities, reduced weld spatter, and alloying elements.

(d) Flux cored arc welding

In 'stick' welding the process has to be interrupted every time the electrode is consumed down to the stub. This causes the welder to lose potential production time as he replenishes his rod in the gripper. The problem could be overcome if the stick could become a length of wire which could be coiled and fed into the weld pool. This is not possible with the normal configuration as the outer coating of flux will crack when deformed. Thus the solution to the problem is to make the electrode a hollow wire containing flux internally in a powdered form. Figure 11.10 shows the principle of flux cored arc welding. It is used in similar applications to stick welding, e.g. shipbuilding, general fabrication, and construction work.

The process can be (a) self-shielding, where the protective atmosphere comes only from the flux core compounds which generate a gaseous shield during welding, and (b) auxiliary gas shielding, where additional protection is provided by supplying a shielding gas from an external source.

The advantages of flux cored welding are that it provides a relatively high rate of metal deposition with small diameter welding wires; it can be used for a wide range of metal thicknesses from about 1.5mm upwards; the process is simple and easy to use, and it can be used in any position with the smaller diameter wires, e.g. for overhead welding. One disadvantage with

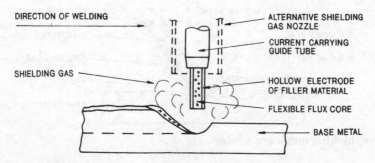

Figure 11.10 Flux cored arc welding

the process is that a considerable amount of welding fumes are emitted during operation. This means that additional equipment has to be provided for drawing off the fumes, especially when welding indoors.

(e) Gas metal arc welding

Another name for this is Metal Inert Gas, or 'MIG', welding. The process is shown in Figure 11.11. A bare continuous wire electrode is fed through the welding torch from a coil. The torch is water cooled. An inert gas is fed down the annulus of the torch to form a cloud around the arc and weld pool which protects the weld from atmospheric contamination. The gas is often carbon dioxide though other gases can be used. The process provides relatively high deposition rates. The fact that the wire can be fed, and the process monitored, automatically means that it is suitable for use in conjunction with industrial robots. In fact robotic arc welding is now one of the most popular applications for robots.

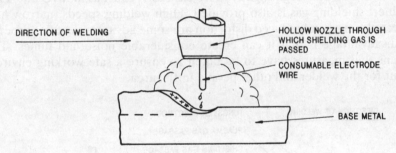

DIRECTION OF WELDING

HOLLOW NOZZLE THROUGH WHICH SHIELDING GAS IS PASSED

CONSUMABLE ELECTRODE WIRE

BASE METAL

Figure 11.11   Gas metal arc welding

(f) Gas tungsten arc welding

Tungsten Inert Gas, or 'TIG', welding are alternative names for this process. It is similar to MIG welding except that a non-consumable electrode is used, a hand fed filler rod usually being necessary to supply additional metal to the weld pool. The inert gas in this case is usually Argon or Helium. The process is shown in Figure 11.12. It can be used for welding a wide range of often difficult to weld materials such as cast iron, aluminium alloy, magnesium, titanium, and stainless steels, etc. The process is ideal for welding thinner sheets of metal under 1mm thick.

(g) Plasma arc welding

Deep and narrow welds in most metals, usually less than 6mm thick, can be produced by this process. Gas is heated to an extremely high temperature by an electric arc, then forced across to the weld area. The arc temperature can reach 33,000°C and the gas is ionised, i.e. it becomes a plasma. The

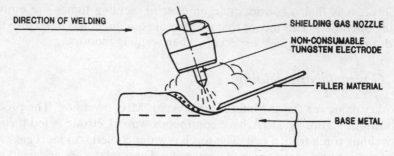

Figure 11.12   Gas tungsten arc welding

two methods of using this process are shown in Figure 11.13 (a) and (b). In (a) the arc is transferred across from the electrode to the workpiece, in (b) the arc occurs between the electrode and the nozzle, and it is the plasma gas alone that carries the heat across to the joint; this latter method is easier to control though slightly more expensive. Just as in MIG and TIG, an inert shielding gas is also provided. High welding speeds, narrow heat affected zones, and reduced distortion are some advantages of this process. A disadvantage is that it can create considerable noise and fumes. This means that measures have to be taken to ensure a safe working environment for the welder and other people in the area.

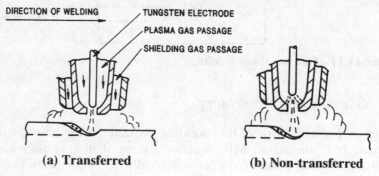

(a) Transferred　　　　**(b) Non-transferred**

Figure 11.13   Plasma arc welding

(h) Submerged arc welding

Operating in a similar manner to stick welding this process can be applied to much thicker materials. The joining of steel plates for ships' hulls is a typical example. The main differences in the process are that the electrode is continuous, the flux is supplied in a powder form through a dispensing tube, and the path of the arc is within the molten flux so preventing contamination from the atmosphere. Figure 11.14 shows the principle. The

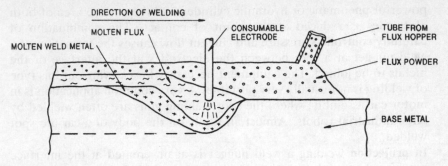

Figure 11.14 Submerged arc welding

process is often carried out automatically; the welding head is suspended from a gantry as it traverses the joint. Rate of welding, feed rate of the electrode wire, and flow of flux, are all controlled automatically. The welds produced are usually of high quality. A large metal deposition rate is possible but stronger joints are created if a number of smaller welding runs are made rather than a single large one.

(i) Resistance welding

The previous welding techniques were all fusion types in that the parent metals were melted along the joint. In resistance welding the flow of an electric current across the interface between the two metals to be joined creates the heat necessary for a localised coalescence. The metals to be joined are almost always thin sheet steel.

- In resistance **spot** welding, shown in Figure 11.15, the two overlapping pieces of metal to be welded are placed between two water cooled copper electrodes. The system is constructed so that one of the electrodes can be held steady while the other can exert downward pressure onto the joint, as shown in Figure 11.15. The pressure at the point of contact is high, as the moving electrode is actuated by a

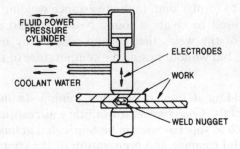

Figure 11.15 Spot welding

powerful pneumatic or hydraulic cylinder and the surface area of both electrodes is reduced at the point of contact. The combination of carefully controlled pressure and current flow causes the formation of a weld nugget at a spot between the electrodes at the interface of the metals to be joined. The equipment necessary for carrying out this type of welding is not usually very portable. A very common application is in motor car assembly, where the spot welding guns are often wielded by large industrial robots. Almost all joints on the body of a car are spot welded.

- In **projection** welding a weld nugget is again created at the interface between the metals to be joined. Again it is made by a combination of pressure and resistance heating from the flow of current across the interface. However in this case the small contact area across which the current flows is created by forming projections on one of the metal sheets to be joined. The principle is shown in Figure 11.16. The equipment is often mounted on a pedestal similar to some used in spot welding. The electrodes in projection welding are wide and flat, whereas those used in spot welding are narrow, with a small contact area. Strip and sheet metal components and wire mesh products such as supermarket trolleys are welded in this way (the small contact areas at the intersection of wires constitute projections).

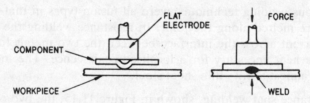

Figure 11.16 Projection welding

(j) Solid state welding

In solid state welding the material to be joined is not melted directly by an external heat source. For example, in the fusion welding processes only heat was added to form a joint, in the resistance welding methods heat **and** pressure were used to create a joint. Now, in solid state welding, we consider some of the welds that can be created by using pressure and sometimes heat, but without raising the temperature of the metal above its melting point.

- **Diffusion** welding is used mainly for joining dissimilar or relatively expensive metals. Components for military aircraft using the advanced materials, such as superalloys, can be fabricated in this way. The process involves careful cleaning and preparation of the contacting faces of the parts to be joined. The parts are then placed against each other and pressure is applied for a considerable length of time. Heat is also applied by carrying out the process in an oven; the temperature may be about half of the melting temperature of the material. During the process the weld is formed by the migration of atoms across the boundary at the interface between the two metals. This means that the process is slow and hence relatively expensive.

• **Explosive welding** is used mainly for cladding, i.e. joining sheets of metals with one type of property to those of another. For example armour plating, or thin sheets of corrosion resistant material, can be bonded to softer and cheaper structural plates of (say) mild steel in this way. The process is shown in Figure 11.17. An explosive charge is placed on top of the metals to be joined. The charge is usually of sheet form and is progressively detonated from one end. On detonation a stress wave is formed which compresses the metal sheets together as it travels along the length of material to be joined. The kinetic energy in the pressure wave is so intense that mechanical bonding takes place between the metals. The process is of course dangerous and must be carried out under carefully controlled conditions.

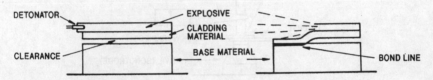

Figure 11.17 Explosive welding

• **Friction welding** is used for the rapid joining of two components where at least one has rotational symmetry. It also produces strong joints between dissimilar metals. The process is shown in Figure 11.18. One of the components to be joined is held in a chuck and rotated at high speed. The other component is then brought into contact with the spinning piece and an axial force applied. The friction created generates heat sufficient to cause fusion of the two metals at the area of contact. Typical

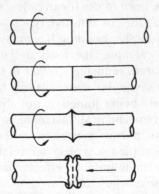

Figure 11.18 Friction welding

applications of the process are; joining of motor car transmission shaft elements, joining of bolt heads to bolt shanks, and construction of engine valves.

- **Ultrasonic welding** is used for joining thin sheets, foil, and wire of similar or dissimilar materials, and it is also used for joining plastics. The process is shown in Figure 11.19. The workpiece is subjected to a downward static force from the mass shown. It is also subjected to an oscillating lateral movement generated by the vibrating transducer which is operating at several kHz. The combination of movement and force at the interface of the materials creates a temperature of up to half the material melting point, and breaks up any layers of oxides or contaminants. Thus the combination of pressure and temperature allows the creation of a very strong bond.

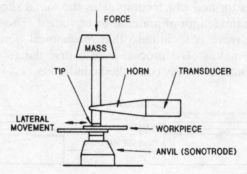

Figure 11.19 Ultrasonic welding

There are many other welding processes, but those that have been shown here should be adequate to convey an idea of the variety of applications.

11.6   Adhesive bonding

Although adhesives have been in use for decades, recent advances in their design have led to a wide range of adhesive types, and consequently a wide range of applications. Adhesive bonding has many advantages over other joining techniques. For example, the load at the joint interface can be distributed over a large area, reducing stresses in the joint. Adhesives are lightweight. Completely dissimilar materials can be joined together. The structure of the materials being joined is not disturbed in any way by having holes drilled for mechanical fastening, or being melted during welding. Thin, fragile, or porous materials can be easily joined. As the temperatures at which bonding takes place are relatively low, no distortion or, if metal, damaging metallurgical effects happen to the material. Adhesives are inexpensive when compared to other joining methods. Products joined by adhesives generally look better than those that have been welded or mechanically fastened. The disadvantages are that: the adhesive will fail if subjected to too high a temperature; surface preparation of the materials to be joined is critical, therefore this part of the process can be time consuming; the time to cure the joint may also be long; and some adhesives are unpleasant or dangerous to work with in an enclosed area.

(a) Joint loading and design

Figure 11.20 shows in (a) the loading conditions that may be experienced by an adhesive joint, and in (b) examples of different types of joint. As can be seen, adhesive joints that are subjected to compression loads have the best strength, those in tension and shear are acceptable, but those in cleavage or peel have poor strength. Therefore when designing a product adhesive joints should be positioned so that they experience compressive forces, and tension or shear if necessary, but cleavage and peel conditions should be avoided. The joint design itself should be such that as large a surface area of adhesive as possible is employed. Mechanical strengthening also helps, e.g. the use of a glued dowel adds considerable strength.

(b) Adhesive types

A wide variety of adhesive types exist, each one designed to be suitable for certain applications and materials. Four types are briefly noted here as typical examples.

- **Anaerobic** adhesives are used for making gaskets, thread locking on bolted or screwed components, and pipe sealing, etc. They are widely known as 'sealants' or 'locking compounds'. They increase the strength of mechanical joints, which should be close fitting as the adhesive cures in the presence of metal and the absence of air.
- **Cyanoacrylates** are used for the assembly of plastic and electronic components. They cure through reaction with moisture present on the surfaces of the materials being joined. Close fitting joints are necessary, but curing speed may be measured in seconds, and a high strength joint is obtainable.
- **Epoxies** are used for large joints and in tough applications such as the bonding of carbide tool tips. They are versatile and give strong hard joints with most materials. They are often in two parts, i.e. an epoxy resin and a hardener, which when mixed together produce the adhesive.
- **Toughened variants** are used in critical applications such as in aircraft construction. The anaerobics and cyanoacrylates are acrylic based, the epoxies are obviously epoxy based, and the toughened variants are acrylic and epoxy based. A rubber material is incorporated in the toughened variant material to provide high peel strength and shock resistance. They also have a fast cure rate.

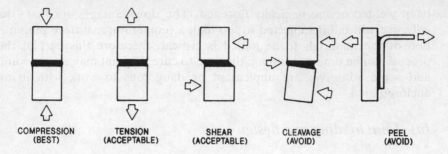

(a) Adhesive joint loading conditions

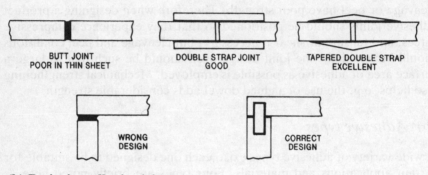

(b) Designing adhesive joints

Figure 11.20 Adhesive bonding

This chapter has shown the most popular methods of joining materials together to form sub-assemblies, assemblies, or complete products. The choice of the most suitable method for a particular task should take into account the aesthetics of the product, its functional performance, and the manufacturing processes available. This again illustrates the need for a team approach to decision making, the selection of the joining method possibly relying on input from, for example, an industrial designer, a mechanical engineer, and a manufacturing engineer.

Review Questions

1 Briefly list the **five** main categories of joining processes used in manufacturing, and state the general type of application to which each is suited.
2 What is 'welding', and what conditions are necessary for it to occur?

3 What is the difference between a fillet weld and a butt weld, and under what conditions would each be used?
4 Describe the welding process that is most likely to be used for making minor repairs to the sheet metal body of a car.
5 Why is 'stick' welding so widely used?
6 What advantage is gained by putting the flux in the core of the electrode in shielded metal arc welding?
7 What is gas metal arc welding, and why has it become so popular for automated welding installations?
8 Describe an arc welding process suitable for welding cast iron or aluminium alloy.
9 What are the advantages of the plasma arc welding process? Name **one** disadvantage.
10 Describe the process you would choose for welding together thick steel plates such as those used for ships' hulls.
11 Describe the welding process widely used in the car industry for fabricating car bodies.
12 What do diffusion, explosive, friction, and ultrasonic welding have in common? Name **one** application for each.
13 Why has adhesive bonding become popular as a joining process?
14 Name **one** type of adhesive, and a typical application.
15 Are joining processes necessary? What can be done to eliminate them?

168

⬡ 12 Plastics

12.1 Introduction

This chapter is concerned with the manufacturing processes used for making plastic components. Plastic materials were discussed in section 4.3, where their importance to modern technology was also noted. Plastics are mostly synthetic polymers, and they are produced today, along with synthetic rubbers, from petroleum products. However, although about 90% of the world's polymers come from petroleum, a brief description of the manufacture of the natural polymer, rubber, is first given.

Plantations of rubber trees are grown in a suitable climate; Malaysia, for example, is the world's largest producer. A helical cut is made around the trunk of the rubber tree and the watery sap, i.e. latex, which is a polymer of isoprene, is tapped off. This is then passed through filters to remove impurities. It is next coagulated into a relatively weak, soft, and inelastic solid by the use of acid and a squeeze drying process, or by centrifugal action. By further heating the rubber and mixing it with sulphur the rubber is cured, i.e. 'vulcanised'. In this process the sulphur atoms form cross links between the long polymer molecules, thus restricting their ability easily to slide over each other. This produces a harder, stronger rubber more suitable for engineering purposes. If the amount of sulphur is sufficiently large, then a hard rigid material called ebonite is produced.

Synthetic rubbers are mostly produced from petroleum industry products. For example, SBR or styrene butadiene rubber, which is used for tyres and transmission belts, etc. is a copolymer made from the monomers styrene and butadiene. The ability to control the chemical process allows a variety of rubbers to be made to suit various applications, e.g. for resistance to chemicals neoprene and nitrile rubbers are used, or silicon based types are produced which are resilient to extreme thermal cycling making them suitable for seals in aerospace products. Combinations of natural and synthetic rubbers may be used to obtain materials with any desired combination of properties.

12.2 The primary production of plastics

Just as in the primary production of metals, the initial stages of plastics production are carried out in large expensive complexes, in this case refineries for processing crude oil. The oil is composed of a mixture of hydrocarbons, i.e. compounds of hydrogen and carbon. These are separated into their components, called fractions, in a fractionating column (see Figure 12.1). Each hydrocarbon has its own boiling point; this means that the mixture can be separated by fractional distillation. In this process the oil is boiled by passing superheated steam through the column; the fractions condense and separate at different levels in the column; each is drawn off at the appropriate height. The bubble caps allow the vapour to rise freely through the column but prevent condensed material from running back down. As can be seen from the sketch the naphthas with boiling points around 120°C can be drawn off somewhere between the kerosene and petrol levels; it should be noted that all boiling points shown in Figure 12.1 are approximate.

Continuing with the example of the naphthas, the fractions can then be 'cracked' to produce the gases ethylene and propylene. 'Cracking' is the name given to the process of breaking down larger molecules into smaller ones. This is usually done with the assistance of a catalyst to accelerate the process. The ethylene is then polymerised to form polyethylene, the structure of which was shown in Figure 4.7(b), or PVC, polyester, or synthetic rubber. The propylene is polymerised to produce polypropylene, which is the basis for polyurethane, acrylic fibres, nylon, and some foam plastics. Chemicals other than the naphthas are also used to produce plastics, e.g. toluene is used to produce benzene which can be further processed to give a range of useful plastics.

Ethylene is also used to produce styrene, which polymerises to produce polystyrene. Figure 12.2 shows schematically the production of polystyrene; this serves as a typical example of the plastic production process. A

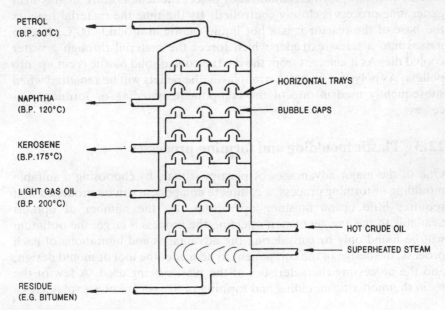

Figure 12.1 Schematic of a fractionating column

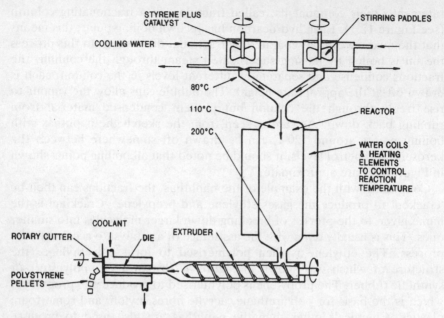

Figure 12.2 Manufacture of polystyrene

partial polymerisation by mixing the styrene with a catalyst in tanks begins the process. The valves to the preliminary mixing tanks can be opened and closed as necessary to maintain a continuous feed to the reactor. It is in the reactor that full polymerisation takes place, the temperature of this heat generating process is closely controlled. By the time the material reaches the base of the reactor it is a hot liquid plastic at around 200°C. It then passes into a screw extruder which forces the material through a water cooled die. As it emerges from the die the cooled solid plastic is cut up into pellets. As polystyrene is a thermoplastic the pellets will be remelted when subsequently used in one of the component moulding or forming processes.

12.3   Plastic moulding and forming processes

One of the major advantages of plastics is that, by chooosing a suitable moulding or forming process, a complete component can be produced that requires little or no finishing operations. As the number of options available to the engineer when selecting the process is large, the optimum will be found only by considering the advantages and limitations of each process, the design of the component to be made, the tool or mould design, and the processing characteristics of the plastic being used. A few of the main thermoplastic moulding and forming processes are now explained.

(a) Extrusion

This is a continuous process in which one or more Archimedian feeder screws are mounted within a cylinder (see Figure 12.3). This cylinder is heated, and as the screws rotate they plasticise and convey the plastic along their threads from the feeder hopper to a die. The section of this die determines the cross sectional shape of the extrusion. Extrusion machines come in a range of sizes with screws ranging in diameter from 25mm to 200mm.

Typical products are tubes, rods, sheets, and continuous lengths of almost any profile. By modifying the process it is possible to produce products with a combination of materials, e.g. by incorporating pressure rolls just after the die the extruded plastic can be bonded to a substrate of another material such as a fabric, paper, or metal. By modifications to the die it is possible to include metal sections or wire within the extrusion. In the dual extrusion process plastics of different properties can be combined so that, for example, an extruded strip may be produced, one side of which is rigid and suitable for attachment to (say) a refrigerator door, and the other side flexible, thus suitable for forming a seal. Extruded sections are important in providing the plastic in a suitable form for processes such as blow moulding and blown film production. Since extrusion is a relatively fast process, it is suitable for high volume production. To cut the material to length as it emerges from the extruder a flying saw is often used which travels with the material as it cuts. The range of size and sections able to be produced is wide, and component surface finish and precision is very good. The machines themselves are expensive, but once the initial investment is made a wide variety of sections can be produced by simply changing the die.

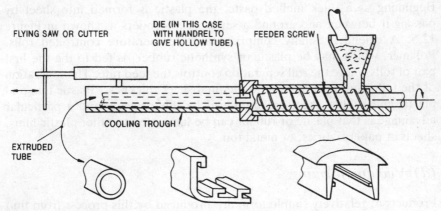

Figure 12.3 The extrusion process and typical plastic sections

(b) Blow moulding

Used to produce hollow products such as plastic bottles this process utilises short lengths of extruded tube called parisons as shown in Figure 12.4. After extrusion, while the plastic is still hot, an appropriate length of the parison is located in the mould. When the mould closes the bottom end of the parison is closed and compressed air is passed in through the open top. The parison inflates and adopts the shape of the mould cavity. By maintaining the air pressure the plastic is held in contact with the water cooled cavity surface until its shape is stable.

Bottles of a multitude of shapes, sizes, and transparent, translucent or opaque colours are produced by this method. Soft drinks, detergents, cosmetics, shampoos, etc. are all contained in blow moulded bottles. Many other lightweight hollow components are produced by this method, although the surface finish is not usually as good as that produced by injection moulding. However, relatively good quality products can be produced at high production rates.

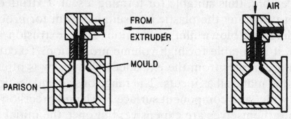

Figure 12.4   The blow moulding process

(c) Calendering

Continuous production of sheet and film plastic is obtained by this process. Beginning as a thick melted paste, the plastic is formed into sheet by passing it between and around a series of nip rollers as shown in Figure 12.5. A calender usually comprises four temperature controlled rolls. Polymer, which may be plastic or synthetic rubber, is fed to the the first pair of rolls where the roll separation controls the feed rate. The separation of the following rolls determine the final sheet thickness. Plastic film and plastic and rubber sheet are produced by this process, and a particular advantage is that plastic or rubber can be laminated to other plastic films, sheets of paper, fabrics, or metal foil.

(d) Vacuum forming

Products of relatively simple form are produced by this process from thin thermoplastic sheets (see Figure 12.6). The plastic is clamped in a support

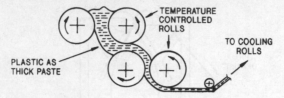

Figure 12.5 Calendering

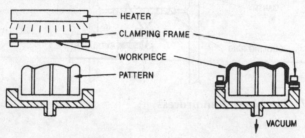

Figure 12.6 Vacuum forming

frame and exposed to radiant heat until it reaches a pliable state. The frame is then drawn down over a pattern and hermetically sealed to the chamber walls, as shown in Figure 12.6. A vacuum pump now withdraws air from between the pattern and the plastic, thus causing atmospheric pressure to force the plastic against the surface of the pattern. The combination of the vacuum and the mechanical action on the plastic as it is pulled over the pattern causes the plastic to adopt the shape of the pattern. The plastic, cooled rapidly by air, becomes rigid again, and the pattern is withdrawn.

Products such as margarine tubs, egg containers, disposable drinking cups, and larger items are produced by this method. Care has to be taken with pattern design as the stretching of the plastic tends to create thin walls at component corners.

(e) The blown film process

In this process a tube is extruded vertically while at the same time it is inflated by the introduction of compressed air (see Figure 12.7). The extrusion is drawn upwards and through nip rolls as shown, these rolls prevent the air escaping immediately. The air flow is controlled to produce a constant bubble size and wall thickness. The film is flattened by the rolls as it is drawn onto a wind up unit. Between the rolls and wind up unit there may be perforating blades, heat welding clamps, and handle cutting punches, these being used to produce the rolls of disposable 'plastic bags' widely found in supermarkets. Larger bags and sacks for refuse disposal and holding agricultural products are also produced by the process.

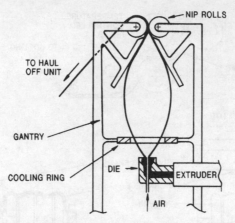

Figure 12.7   The blown film process

(f) Injection moulding

For high volume production injection moulding is the most widely used and economic of all the thermoplastic processes. Figure 12.8 shows the basic elements of an injection moulding machine, and Figure 12.9 shows the process schematically. The plastic, which is in powder or granular form, is loaded into the feed hopper. This may be done manually, or automatically via tube conveyors from bulk storage bins. The plastic falls from the hopper into the heated machine barrel; this barrel contains a rotating and reciprocating screw, which acts as both a plasticiser and an injection unit. As the plastic passes along the screw flight the root diameter of the screw increases, so compressing the plastic. The shearing action between the particles of plastic generates heat, thus changing the plastic to a semi-fluid state. Heat is also added in a controlled manner via the heater bands around the barrel. Immediately in front of the screw is a chamber for receiving the compressed plastic. As the chamber is filled, the screw is forced backwards until it trips a limit switch that signals the control system to cause the hydraulics to force the screw forward. This causes injection of the plastic into the cavity of the mould, the plastic being prevented from flowing back by a one way valve in the nozzle of the moulding machine.

The process is used to produce very large production quantities of components of widely ranging size. Production rates are also high and the components may have an excellent surface finish. With thermoplastic materials there is no waste since the runners and sprues can be regranulated and reused. Disadvantages are that the moulding tools and machines are expensive, closed containers cannot be made without additional assembly work, and complex shapes and re-entrant angles in a design further escalate the tooling costs.

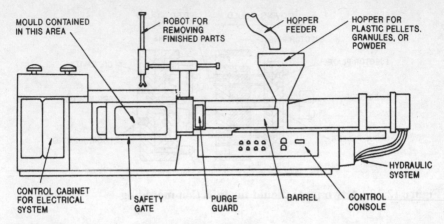

Figure 12.8   An injection moulding machine

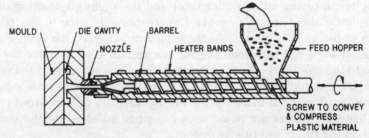

Figure 12.9   A reciprocating screw injection system

12.4   Injection moulding tool design

Due to the importance and widespread use of injection moulding in manufacturing, a little more detail is given here on the design of the moulding tools. The purpose of the tool is first to form the plastic to the desired shape and second to cool the formed product.

Figure 12.10 shows a simplified sectional sketch of a two plate injection moulding tool. The locating ring on the fixed half ensures that the mould is properly located relative to the moulding machine, and the guide pins ensure that both mould halves are kept in alignment with each other. The plastic is injected into the fixed half of the mould, the nozzle from the injection moulding machine barrel mating with the tool sprue bush. The other half of the tool is attached to the machine clamping system and can move in the directions shown. When the halves are clamped together the plastic flows into the mould cavities through a central sprue and runner system. The plastic then cools as water flows through internal channels in both mould halves.

After the cooling period is completed, the moving half is pulled back. The moulded components, together with sprue and runners, remain with

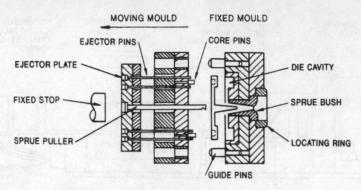

Figure 12.10 A two plate mould for injection moulding

the moving mould half. This is due to the plastic in the sprue having flowed into the notch of the sprue puller shaft and the slight contraction of the cooled plastic also tending to make the components stick to the convex surfaces of the moving mould. As the mould moves back the ejector plate hits against the fixed stop thus causing the ejector pins to move forward relative to the mould; this pushes the moulding forward and off the mould surface. The moulding may then be allowed to fall down into a bin or conveyor, or it may be lifted out of the machine by an industrial robot. These handling robots are sometimes equipped to separate the components from the sprue and runner system.

The example discussed refers to a multiple cavity mould. It is also possible to have single cavity moulds that do not require a runner system. The decision whether to use single or multiple cavity moulds is an economic one. Factors that influence this are: number of components to be produced and rate of production – multiple cavity moulds will be best where these factors are high; the precision required in each component; the type of plastic; the capacity of the moulding machine; and the position of the mould parting line.

The decision on where to place the parting line depends on a number of factors, including the shape of the article and the number of mould cavities. Components with re-entrant shapes that cannot be released in the normal direction of the mould opening require moulds with more than one parting line. To allow these components to be made facilities such as side or rotating cores may need to be used. Figure 12.11 shows a cam operated side core. As the mould opens right to left the slide rides up the pin shown in the right mould half. This causes the side core to be withdrawn from the moulded component, so allowing a hole to be created at right angles to the the normal direction of tool movement. Figure 12.12 shows one method of achieving internal screw threads in a component. As the mould moves linearly over the screw it causes rotation of gear A, which is internally threaded onto the fixed screw. This causes gear B, which is keyed to a shaft with the threaded core at one end, to rotate. The shaft is also threaded and

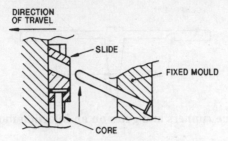

Figure 12.11   Method of achieving 'side' holes using side cores operated by cam action

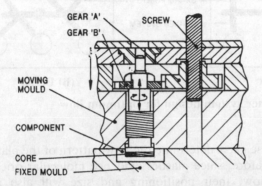

Figure 12.12   Method of achieving internal threads using a rotating core

runs in a screw threaded bore of the same pitch as the core. Thus movement of the mould causes rotation and extraction of the core.

The designer of the multi-cavity injection moulding tool must also carefully consider the layout of the sprue runner and gating system. The 'gate' is the small aperture where the material from the runner enters the mould cavity; it is also the point where the finished component is broken off from the runner. Figure 12.13 shows an end view of these elements. The runner system should be arranged in such a manner as to allow each cavity simultaneously to receive an equal amount of pressurised plastic at each injection. Thus the tool design should provide the shortest possible flow route for the plastic between the sprue and each cavity. Figure 12.14(a) shows a poor layout since the two cavities nearest the sprue will be filled first; this makes it almost impossible to produce mouldings of uniform quality, since these two cavities will receive extra pressure as the injection continues. Figure 12.14(b) shows a better layout, where each cavity receives an equal share of plastic simultaneously; also the cold slug wells at the end of the runners trap partly cooled polymer. Bad cavity layout should always be avoided since it can cause problems such as stress build up in a component, differences in component sizes, and mould release problems. It is also important to give close attention to the position and size of the

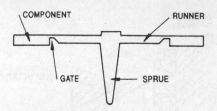

Figure 12.13   Sprue runners and gates on an injection moulding

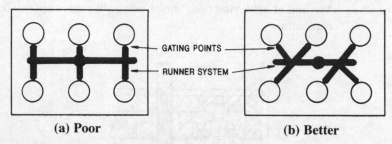

| (a) Poor | (b) Better |

Figure 12.14   Runner system design for optimum flow

gates. This is because gates determine the flow pattern of the plastic within the cavity and therefore, since plastics evidence molecular orientation in the direction of flow, their positioning and size will also affect the mechanical properties of the finished component.

The surface finish of the cavity should be created with great care since every scratch or mark on the surface will be transmitted to the component. Unless a textured surface is desired most mould cavities are highly polished – an expensive process.

12.5   Plastic component design for injection moulding

Just as with any component design functional requirements such as load bearing, resistance to adverse environmental conditions, dimensional constraints, service life, ergonomic, and aesthetic specifications must always be met. The designer of injection moulded components must also be familiar with the constraints and advantages of the polymer material being used, the capabilities and limitations of the injection moulding process, and the implications of the component design for the mould tool design. Additionally the plastic product designer should also consider the following points.

● Large flat surfaces should be avoided as they tend to warp. Corrugated, grooved, or curved surfaces are better. If flat surfaces must be used warping can be minimised and the surface strengthened by the use of ribs. Care needs to be taken when designing ribs, however, as they can cause light sink marks on the opposite surface to where they are located.

This is due to the rib creating an additional mass of material which contracts more than the surrounding thinner material. Sink marks can be minimised by ensuring that rib thicknesses do not exceed two thirds the thickness of the main wall and their height does not exceed three times the thickness.

- Corners should be rounded since as well as producing lower stress concentrations than sharp corners they also offer less flow resistance to the injected plastic.
- The component wall thickness should be kept constant as much as possible; where changes in section are necessary these should be made as gradual as possible.
- Consider that as the plastic in the mould cools it also contracts. Therefore should the sides of the component be made parallel in the direction of mould opening, it will be evident that the moulding will tend to shrink onto the convex portions of the mould and so make removal difficult. For this reason a slight taper, called 'draft' must always be provided in the component design. This is more apparent on large components as they require greater draft.
- Re-entrants, or undercuts, should also be avoided, or at least kept to a minimum, as they will add extra expense to the manufacture of the injection moulding tool. This is obvious from the earlier section (p.176) where it was shown that re-entrants often demand the use of cam operated side cores or complex rotational cores. Even small re-entrants such as engraved characters should be avoided and replaced with transfers.

Figure 12.15 shows a fictitious component exhibiting poor and improved design. The points mentioned above are included, along with some additional ones. For example, the rectangular hole in the back wall is expensive to make since it requires a rectangular cam operated side core. A circular opening would be cheaper, and changing the opening to a slot completely removes the need for a side core. Large masses of solid plastic, like the pillars in the sketch, cause sink marks – hollows are better. In the component on the right there is a threaded hole which is threaded right up to where the hole meets the surface. This causes a knife edge which is easily damaged; a recessed thread is better, and in this case the thread form has been rounded. Figure 12.16 shows the use of metal inserts in a plastic moulding. These are inserted into the component either by placing them in the moulding tool and allowing the plastic to flow around them before cooling, or by press fitting them into the previously moulded component. These allow high strength features to be added where necessary, although very large metal inserts should be avoided as differences in thermal expansion create stresses. In conclusion, as with any design, the simplest component design will be the best one.

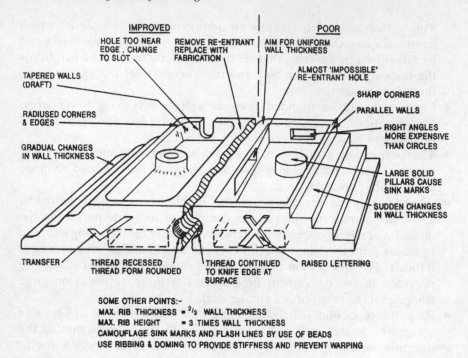

Figure 12.15   **Some aspects of plastic component design**

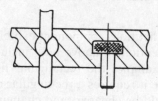

Figure 12.16   **The use of metal inserts**

Review Questions

1. Natural rubbers are vulcanised during their manufacturing process; briefly state what vulcanisation is, and why it is necessary.
2. What is the major source of the world's plastics and synthetic rubbers?
3. What is the purpose of a 'fractionating column', and how does it work?
4. Briefly describe how polystyrene is produced.
5. What **four** factors does an engineer need to consider to ensure that the optimum manufacturing process is selected for making a plastic component?
6. Describe the process used to produce continuous lengths of plastic product of constant cross section.

7 Describe the blow moulding process, and the type of product to which it is most suited.
8 What is the calendering process used for?
9 Describe the vacuum forming process, and give examples of typical products produced by it.
10 Describe the process used to produce disposable plastic bags and refuse sacks.
11 Why is the injection moulding process best suited to high volume production?
12 Explain how the injection moulding process works (no sketches are necessary).
13 Describe the basic construction of an injection moulding tool.
14 Why is it advisable to eliminate re-entrants in an injection moulding design?
15 Explain why the designer has to pay particular attention to the manner in which the plastic is transferred from the moulding machine nozzle to the mould cavity.
16 Why are ribs necessary in some plastic mouldings, and why are their width and height important?
17 What is the purpose of 'draft' in a plastic component?

⬡13 Manufacture in the electronics industry

13.1 Introduction

Almost every manufactured product we use today either contains electronic components, or has been designed and made by processes utilising electronics. The wordprocessor being used to write this sentence contains semiconductor based technology, the plastic for the keyboard was made by electronically controlled moulding processes, and the assembly of the individual components was done by microprocessor controlled machines. Motor cars are designed using electronic computers, they are assembled using microprocessor controlled robots, and often they contain such items as electronic ignition, instrumentation, and fuel management systems. Our complex and varied telecommunication systems utilising land lines, microwaves, and satellites, would not operate without electronics. To supply this ubiquitous hardware we rely on the electronics manufacturing industry.

At the beginning of the 20th century no electronics industry existed. Then in 1904 the thermionic valve was invented and this was followed in 1906 by the triode. These components made possible the construction of many of the electronic devices we know today, albeit in a relatively slow and cumbersome manner. For example, forty years after the invention of the triode the electronic computer ENIAC required approximately 1400m² of floor space, weighed around 30,500 kg and contained 18,000 vacuum tubes. However 1947 saw the invention of the transistor; this semiconductor technology was rapidly developed and by the 1960s many transistors, diodes, resistors, and capacitors could be produced on the one 'chip' of silicon material; these were called 'integrated circuits'. In 1970 an integrated circuit that could carry out many of the activities associated with computing was produced; this was the 'microprocessor'. By the middle of the 1980s a million components could be created on a single chip, i.e. very large scale integration or VLSI. Today we have computers that can sit in our laps or even fit in our pockets, whose power would amaze those who worked on ENIAC. The next stage of development will involve hundreds of millions of components on the one chip, this being termed giga scale integration or GSI. Difficulties arise with this since the line widths of the circuit need to be below the 1μm used today.

This chapter is concerned with the manufacturing processes used to produce semiconductor electronic components and the printed circuit boards on which they are assembled. The assembly process itself will also be briefly examined. Though not included here, other discrete components are found in electronic systems. For example, resistors may have a wound wire, conducting metal oxide film, or carbon powder construction, and capacitors can be made from sheets of metal foil and insulating material wound into a compact canned package. Also to be found may be components such as potentiometers, switches, and liquid crystal displays.

13.2 Semiconductor component manufacture

Semiconductor materials are so called because they have electrical properties that lie between those of conductors and insulators. However what makes them useful is that their electrical properties can be altered by adding carefully controlled amounts of impurity atoms, called dopants, to their crystal structure. There are two types of dopant – '*n*' type which makes the material electron rich, and '*p*' type which which makes the material electron deficient. A component is constructed on a crystal of semiconductor material by selective doping. For example by creating an *n*-type element in contact with a *p*-type element, a *p–n* junction is produced. This creates a diode junction since the configuration will conduct current only in one direction (see Figure 13.1).

Semiconductor components such as transistors and diodes can be manufactured as discrete items for use in a multitude of products such as radios and televisions. They are also used as discrete components in power handling applications where relatively large currents are being manipulated. However, although the basic technology is the same, the most complex conditions occur when large numbers of them are being created on a single chip, i.e. the integrated circuit (IC) mentioned in the previous section. It is this situation, the manufacture of an IC chip, that is considered here.

The chip manufacturing process comprises a number of steps; these are shown in simplified form in Figure 13.2.

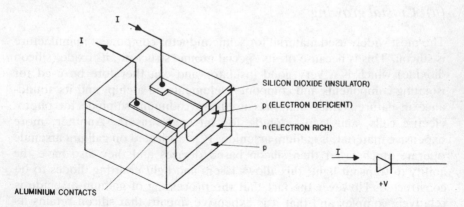

Figure 13.1   A semiconductor diode configuration

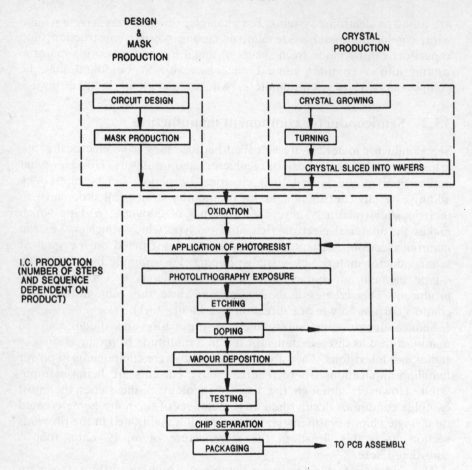

Figure 13.2   An integrated circuit manufacturing sequence

(a) Crystal growing

The most widely used material for semiconductor component manufacture is silicon. This is because of: its special atomic structure, its oxide (silicon dioxide) which is a very good insulator and can therefore be used for isolating components and component elements on a chip, and its abundance in nature. Other materials used are cadmium sulphide for photo-electric cells, and lead sulphide for infrared sensors. Another, more expensive material, is gallium arsenide. ICs fabricated on gallium arsenide operate much faster than silicon based devices and they also have the ability to transmit light; this allows lasers and light emitting diodes to be constructed. However the fact that the processing of gallium arsenide is relatively complex and that it is expensive, means that silicon retains its popularity as a substrate material.

Silicon occurs in quartzite sand, i.e. silicon dioxide. It must be purified before it becomes the flawless single crystal needed for chip manufacture. First it is heated with carbon, i.e. coal or coke, in an electric arc furnace to produce polycrystalline silicon which is about 97% pure. It is then further processed by heating, fractional distillation as a chloride, and vapour deposition, to eventually produce polycrystalline silicon which is virtually 100% pure. This is now melted in a quartz crucible; dopant material may also be added at this stage. A seed crystal of silicon is dipped into the melt and then withdrawn very slowly while also being rotated. The melt material solidifies onto the seed crystal so forming a larger crystal, called a 'boule', which is eventually about 0.15m diameter and 1m long. This crystal growing is called the 'Czochralski process'.

The boule is then inspected for flaws, its electrical properties tested, and defective parts removed. Since the crystal growing process does not allow tight control of the diameter size the boule is now turned and ground to produce a precise cylindrical shape between 50 and 150mm in diameter and 1m in length. It is then sliced into wafers about 0.5mm thick using a diamond saw. These are polished to a mirror finish and inspected to ensure that any damage caused by the sawing process has been removed. Crystal growing and wafer production is carried out by companies specialising in this work. Therefore the final stage is to pack the wafers and despatch them to the component manufacturer's factory.

(b) Integrated circuit production

Although the following steps are the basic ones used in IC production, it should be remembered that the actual manufacturing process will involve repetitive implementation of these steps to produce a number of different levels, doped regions, and electrical interconnections on the one chip (see Figure 13.3).

- **Photolithography**. None of the conventional machining processes are capable of producing the fine definition required to produce a million components on a one centimetre square chip of silicon. Resort has to be made to photographic techniques. Even here, ordinary light cannot be used as its wavelength, from about $0.4\mu m$ to just under $0.8\mu m$, is too coarse for the definition required in these circuits. For this reason ultraviolet light, around $0.1\mu m$, or electron beams with around $0.000001\mu m$ wavelength are used to provide very fine resolution.

  Photolithography involves printing patterns of the circuits and their elements onto a mask. Since each wafer of silicon is used to produce a large number of ICs the pattern is repeated many times on the one mask. The mask itself is produced photographically on glass from information produced by a computer aided design (CAD) system (see Chapter 21). An image of the patterns is projected from the mask onto the wafer, which will have been previously coated with a photosensitive

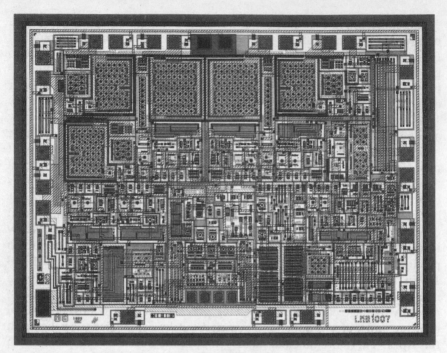

(a) Computer Aided Design-generated plot of an integrated circuit

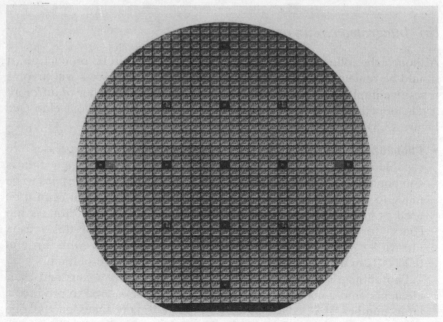

Source: Wafer provided by National Semiconductor (UK) Ltd

(b) 125mm diameter wafer of silicon with over 1000 integrated circuits ethced

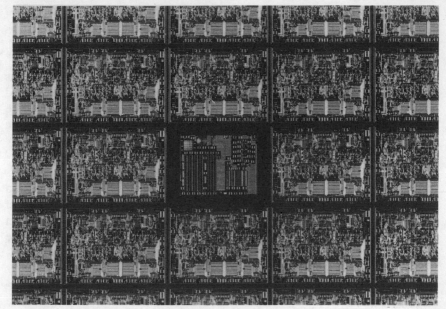

Source: National Semiconductor (UK) Ltd

(c) Enlarged section of the wafer in (b)

Figure 13.3 The integrated circuit

film. This film, called a photoresist, when exposed to ultraviolet light or
electron beams becomes either more ('positive resist') or less ('negative
resist') soluble to an etchant solution. Thus after exposure the wafer can
be treated with the etchant to leave the appropriate parts of its surface
exposed. Layer fabrication can now take place, these exposed surfaces
being subjected to processes such as oxidation, dopant diffusion, vapour
deposition, or further etching. The design of the IC will determine how
often, and in what order, these processes are carried out. Between each
step, the photolithography process will be used to produce new patterns.

- **Oxidation**. As noted earlier, silicon dioxide is an excellent insulator; it
  also effectively blocks the dopant diffusion process, adheres strongly to
  the silicon substrate, and is able to be removed by an etchant which does
  not attack the substrate. It is therefore used to create masks on the chip
  surface and to separate individual ICs on the wafer; it is also used as an
  integral part of the circuits and components themselves.

  To create an oxide pattern on a silicon substrate the following
  procedure is carried out. In 'dry oxidation' the silicon substrate is
  exposed to an oxygen rich atmosphere in a furnace at a temperature of
  between 900 and 1200°C. This simple process causes oxidation of the
  silicon surface. When carried out in an atmosphere containing steam the
  process is called 'wet oxidation'; this produces a higher oxide growth

rate but with lower density. Thus a combination of both the dry and wet processes are often used. After cleaning, the oxide surface is coated in a photoresist material which is then pre-baked in an oven at about 100°C. The photolithography process is now implemented as described earlier. Assuming that a positive resist has been used and the exposed resist has been removed by an etchant solution, the remaining resist is toughened by a post-baking operation. This now allows the uncovered oxides to be removed down to the substrate level by another etchant, thus creating the desired pattern. Finally the remaining photoresist is removed by dipping in a dissolving solution such as acetone.

- **Chemical vapour deposition and dopant diffusion**. This is the process that is used to create the *p*-type and *n*-type semiconductor regions on a substrate. It is carried out by placing the substrate in an atmosphere of chemical vapours which deposit the dopant. The process is carried out in a furnace at a temperature between 800 and 1200°C. While in the furnace, atoms from the dopant material diffuse into the silicon substrate, thus causing displacement of the silicon atoms.

- **Metal vapour deposition**. The devices produced by the foregoing processes all need to be interconnected by metal conductors to allow the IC to operate; vapour deposition is the process used to create these conductors. Normally aluminium or aluminium alloy is used, but for higher device densities tungsten may be necessary. Again photolithography and etching are used to create the connector paths. In vacuum deposition the wafer is placed in a vacuum where the metal to be deposited is melted. Under these vacuum conditions the metal boils and deposits itself on adjacent surfaces. The process is therefore so organised that the metal vapour which propagates out from the melt in a straight line coats the desired surfaces. Chemical vapour deposition is also used for depositing thin films of non-metallic materials onto a substrate.

After all these processes have been carried out on the wafer a number of times and the ICs have been created, they have to be tested, then separated. Testing is carried out automatically by needle probes contacting appropriate points on the circuits. Computer programs run the tests and flawed ICs are automatically marked with an ink dot. The ICs are then separated by either diamond sawing or scribing along lines between the ICs and snapping them off rather like tile cutting. At this stage in the process the ICs are usually called 'dies'.

(c) Packaging of integrated circuits

Since the individual dies are fragile and easily damaged they must be given a protective casing. They also need to be provided with connections of a practical size to enable them to be connected into circuits on printed circuit boards, etc. The die may be attached to its protective casing or package by metallising the back then soldering it onto a metal plate in the package, or it may simply be epoxied into place. The package will have metal leads to allow connection to the outside world. The die will have metallised contact pads created by the vapour deposition process mentioned earlier. These contact pads are connected to the package leads by pressure or ultrasonic bonding techniques. The package is then closed and sealed while ensuring that no moisture or contaminants are included (see Figure 13.4).

The package is now given its final tests. Those that must exhibit very high reliability, e.g. for aerospace and military use, are given high temperature, temperature cycling, vibration, and other tests to ensure that the circuits that would fail early in their service life are identified.

13.3   Clean rooms

With component dimensions in integrated circuits being in the region of 1μm it is apparent that contamination by foreign particles during manufacture could be a serious problem. For example human hair is between 30 and 100μm in diameter, bacteria between 0.3 and 30μm, and tobacco smoke between 0.01 and 1μm. To avoid contamination by foreign particles special rooms are built for semiconductor manufacture and other fine assembly work; these are called 'clean rooms', and incorporate a number of techniques for ensuring a clean environment.

To prevent contaminated air entering the room, air has to pass through high efficiency filters; these must be 99.97% efficient at removing particles over 0.3μm in size. Charcoal filters may also be used to remove chemical

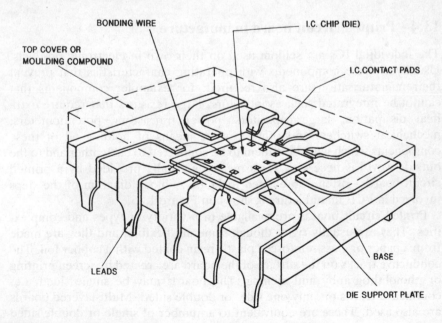

Figure 13.4 Integrated circuits in dual in line package

contaminants from the air. To make sure that only cleaned air is present in the room a positive air pressure differential is created between the room and the outside factory. This pressurisation ensures that air will only escape **from** the room and outside air can enter only through the filtering system.

Although air into the clean room can be filtered, humans inside the clean room present a major source of contaminants. Although eating, drinking and smoking are prohibited humans still constantly introduce contaminants from breathing, skin particles, hair, and clothing. To eliminate this contamination surgical masks, gloves, hair caps, and gowns are worn by operators. For ultra clean rooms the workers may be completely isolated from the environment by wearing one piece overalls and visored helmets that drape over the shoulders and are connected by tube to an external air supply. A differential air pressure is again created between the inside of the suit and the clean room to ensure that air travels from the room into the suit and not vice versa. Airlocks are used by the personnel when moving in or out of the clean room.

Normal air in the atmosphere contains more than 100,000 particles greater than $0.5\mu m$, per 3.5 litres. Clean rooms are classified by a number which indicates the number of particles greater than $0.5\mu m$, per 3.5 litres that are permitted. For fine assembly work clean rooms of class 1000 down to 100 may be used, but for rooms where device manufacture is taking place class 10 will be necessary. Temperature and relative humidity are also carefully controlled in clean rooms – usually at around 20°C and 40% respectively.

13.4   Printed circuit board manufacture

The individual ICs are seldom used on their own in electronic products. Usually discrete components with operating characteristics that prevent their miniaturisation are also required: for example, components that cannot be integrated such as inductors, large resistors that require extra heat dissipation, large capacitors, power transistors, potentiometers, mechanical switches, and other ICs. A means of holding all of these components which will allow them to be connected to each other and to the outside world is necessary. This means is usually provided by a printed circuit board – often abbreviated to PCB. A block diagram of the steps involved in PCB manufacture is shown in Figure 13.5.

Printed circuit boards are available in a variety of types and complexities. They are usually rigid, though some are flexible, and they are made from a paper or glass reinforced plastic resin coated with a copper foil. The conductive tracks on the surface of the board are created by screen printing or photolithography and etching. The boards may be single sided, i.e. conductive tracks on only one side, or double sided. Multi-layered boards are also used. These are equivalent to a number of single or double sided PCBs made into a sandwich, each layer being separated by glass reinforced

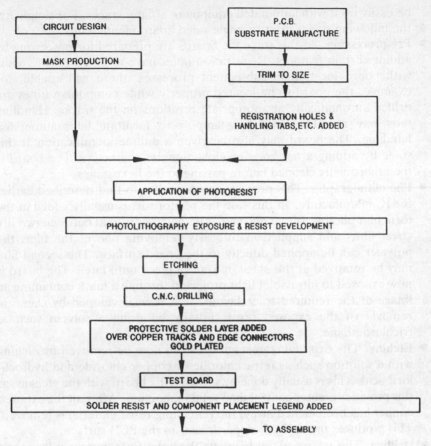

Figure 13.5   Single sided PCB manufacturing sequence

plastic and interconnected by conductive 'via' holes.

- **Substrate manufacture**. The board substrate is made under clean room conditions since any contaminants on the copper surfaces could prevent proper functioning of the board in service. For single and double sided boards the copper foil, usually produced by electroplating, is placed on the highly polished surface of a steel plate resting in a press. Assuming that a glass reinforced plastic substrate is being created, layers of glass cloth impregnated with an epoxy resin are placed in layers on top of the copper foil until the desired thickness is obtained. Finally either a release film is added for single sided boards or another sheet of copper foil for double sided boards. Another highly polished steel plate is attached to the press ram. By using high pressures and steam heating of the steel plates the boards are compressed and the resin cured. After cooling the boards are trimmed to remove excess resin. Usually one press has many plates and can therefore produce many boards at each pressing. Boards are usually produced in standard sizes to allow them to be easily used with automated equipment at later stages. For simplicity, the following stages refer to single sided board manufacture.

- **Pre-processing**. At this stage the boards are prepared for processing by adding certain features. Registration holes have to be created to assist with board location in subsequent processes; these will enable, for example, the board to be located properly while component holes are drilled automatically at appropriate positions on the tracks. Handling tabs may also be added by stamping to facilitate later automated handling. The board may also be given a unique identification at this stage by adding a bar code or alphanumeric characters. The board is then thoroughly cleaned before passing to the next stages.

- **Photolithography**. This process is very similar to that described earlier for IC manufacture. In this case the photoresist is usually added in the form of a photosensitive polymer. The polymer is held between two dry cover films and supplied in rolls. By removing one of the films the polymer can be applied directly to the board surface. The second film may be removed at this stage or kept in place until later. The board is now exposed to ultraviolet light projected through a mask containing an image of the required track layout. It is then developed by chemical removal of the exposed resist, usually by using a solvent such as trichloroethane.

- **Etching**. The exposed copper surfaces can now be removed by etching with a solution such as ferric chloride or copper chloride and hydrochloric acid. This is usually done by spraying the board with the etchant, as this provides greater control than total immersion. After all the exposed copper has been etched away, the remaining resist material is removed. This produces the desired copper tracks on the PCB surface.

- **Drilling**. This is carried out to create the holes for component leads and pins, and also for bolting and screwing holes to take larger components such as transformers and heat sinks. The precision with which these drill holes are located is extremely important since automated component insertion methods may be used. A number of boards may be drilled at the same time by creating a stack and drilling through. The drilling will probably be carried out by a CNC, i.e. computer numerical control, drilling machine (CNC is described in Chapter 21). These machines will automatically drill the required pattern of holes based on instructions received from the computer aided design (CAD) system used to design the board layout. Drilling is also used to create the 'via' holes in double sided and multi-layer boards. The boards are passed between abrasive rollers to remove the rough edges created around the drilled holes; this is referred to as deburring.

- **Board finishing.** The board now has bare copper tracks and 'lands' (these are the local areas where the track is widened around the lead holes or surface mounted device (SMD) contact points). To prevent the copper oxidising, which would give problems later at component assembly, it is given a coating of solder. This is done by plating or a process known as roller tinning. Edge connectors are usually gold plated for reliability. The board is then tested for continuity of the tracks and inspected for flaws. Finally the component locations are identified by means of a printed legend and, with the exception of the lands, the board is coated in solder resist.

13.5   Assembling components to printed circuit boards

Having considered electronic component and printed circuit board manufacture, we will now examine how they are assembled together to produce a finished 'populated' PCB. Component configuration and presentation are considered before looking at the final assembly process.

(a)   Component configurations

Electronic components can be classified as: (1) **leaded**, these may have axial, radial, or dual in line (DIP) leads; (2) **surface mounted**, these have no leads; and (3) **non-standard**. Sketches of these configurations are shown in Figure 13.6. Non-standard components may be edge connectors, switches, transformers, etc. Discrete resistors often have an axial lead configuration, transistors a radial, and integrated circuits a DIP. Components produced in leaded configurations can also be produced as surface mounted devices, i.e. SMDs. In comparison to leaded components. SMDs allow the production of more densely populated boards, i.e. boards can be made smaller yet perform the same functions; they have a physical construction ideally suited to automated PCB manufacture, they can be mounted on both sides of the PCB and therefore the only holes needed to be drilled in the board are 'via' holes for electrical connections between

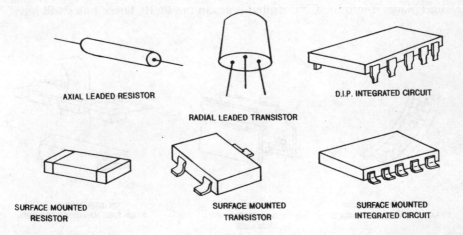

AXIAL LEADED RESISTOR

RADIAL LEADED TRANSISTOR

D.I.P. INTEGRATED CIRCUIT

SURFACE MOUNTED RESISTOR

SURFACE MOUNTED TRANSISTOR

SURFACE MOUNTED INTEGRATED CIRCUIT

Figure 13.6   Component configurations

each side. However they may be more expensive than the leaded type and difficult to assemble manually. Because of this and difficulties in making some leaded components in SMD form PCBs are usually populated by a mixture of leaded, SMD, and non-standard components.

Axial and radial leaded components are usually packaged in edge tape bandoliers or sprocket feedable tapes, DIPs in linear stick magazines, and SMDs in blister tapes or stick tubes. These are shown in Figure 13.7. In some systems many bandoliers, each carrying one type of component, are used automatically to create a new bandolier which will have all components sequenced in the correct order for automatic assembly in a special component insertion machine. DIPs can be provided in magazine packages. These can be mounted at the workstation in such a manner as to allow the DIPs to slide out of the magazine onto a rail where they can easily be picked up manually or automatically for assembly. For SMDs stick tubes are similarly used, or by peeling off a retaining tape, blister packages can be fed past the component pick up points at an assembly station.

(b) Assembly methods for leaded components

Electronic components are assembled to PCBs manually, automatically, or by a combination of manual and automatic methods.

Manual assembly methods are used for shorter production runs, or where relatively slow production rates of up to say 500 components per hour are to be placed, or where the components are difficult to assemble by other means. Leaded components need to have their leads cut to length and pre-formed before insertion (see Figure 13.8). In manual assembly this can be done by the operator using pliers or by using a special die (in automatic assembly the pre-forming is done automatically using special tooling). The operator lifts the component from a bin or presentation point and places it into the CNC drilled holes in the PCB. These holes will have

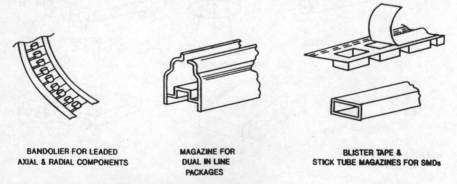

BANDOLIER FOR LEADED
AXIAL & RADIAL COMPONENTS

MAGAZINE FOR
DUAL IN LINE
PACKAGES

BLISTER TAPE &
STICK TUBE MAGAZINES FOR SMDs

Figure 13.7   Component delivery packages

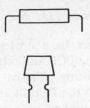

Figure 13.8   Preformed axial and radial leads

been marked at the PCB manufacturing stage with identification numbers to assist the operator. A further refinement is to use a machine which presents the components to the operator in a specific sequence; this is synchronised with a projector placed over the board. The projector is supplied with a roll of film which is indexed to allow the position of each component to be illuminated on the board as the operator carries out the insertion. For very small volumes the assembled PCB may have each component individually hand soldered, but it is more likely that the board will move on to an automated soldering process such as wave soldering.

Automated assembly is used for higher volume production. Typically industrial robots will be used where the demand is for around 1800 components per hour to be assembled, since robots can be easily reprogrammed to cope with changing production requirements. For higher production rates, say up to 30,000 per hour, dedicated automated assembly machines are used. Axial and radial leaded components are automatically removed from their bandoliers or sprocket feedable tapes, their leads are pre-formed, they are inserted, and then their leads are cropped and clinched ready for soldering. DIPs are gravity fed from their stick magazines to their appropriate pickup points.

After insertion the components must be soldered to provide the electrical connections between them and the PCB land areas (lands are the wider parts of the PCB tracks around the component holes). This operation requires the application of a flux to remove metal oxides and contaminants and to distribute the applied heat uniformly across the joint, and a molten solder. For large volumes, production techniques such as wave soldering are used. Here the boards are mounted on conveyor tracks which support them along two edges. The boards then have flux applied to them by one of three methods. They may pass through a bath of flux foam, or over a wave of flux created in a bath, or they may be sprayed with flux. They then pass through a pre-heating operation which raises their temperature to about 90°C and activates the flux. The board then passes over the surface of a bath of molten solder. A wave of solder is created in the bath as the board passes such that all exposed conducting surfaces are coated in solder.

(c) Assembly methods for SMDs

Since surface mounted devices have no leads, different techniques for holding them in position on the PCB and soldering are needed. Two main methods are used, the first being adhesive and wave soldering. In this method adhesive is applied to the PCB at appropriate points (see Figure 13.9). The adhesive can be applied by a screen printing process or by dispensing from a syringe. The SMD is then placed onto the board, probably using an automated pick and place unit, in such a manner as to ensure it is making contact with the PCB lands and the adhesive coated areas. The adhesives used are curable, and depending on type the adhesive is now cured by exposing it to ultraviolet light or heat. The components are finally soldered to the board using the flow solder process. This differs from the soldering of the leaded components in that the SMDs themselves have to pass through the solder wave, therefore particular care has to be taken to ensure proper adhesion of the components before soldering begins.

The second method is called the solder paste and reflow solder method. In this, the solder paste acts as both the adhesive and the conductor. The paste is actually a suspension of powdered solder particles in a flux. Just as in the previous technique the paste is applied by either screen printing or syringe. The SMDs are then inserted by automatic pick and place devices. It is apparent that one of the qualities of the solder paste must be that it has a high enough viscosity to ensure that components stay in their positions throughout the process. The boards are then passed through the reflow stage in which the solder is melted and cooled to form the finished conductive joint. Various methods of melting the solder are used, two of which are the infrared and vapour phase. In infrared reflow soldering the boards are carried on a conveyor past a series of infrared lamps or heaters. It is relatively inexpensive and can handle high quantities, but consistent quality is more difficult to maintain. In the vapour phase method a suitable inert liquid is heated and vaporised in a tank. The PCBs are then placed in the tank where the vapour condenses onto their surfaces. During condensation the latent heat of the vapour is transferred to the solder, causing it to melt. The process can be made continuous by passing the boards through the tank on a conveyor. This method produces good quality joints, but is relatively expensive and slow.

Figure 13.10 shows a special-purpose machine for populating PCBs.

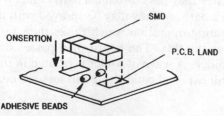

Figure 13.9   SMD insertion using adhesive

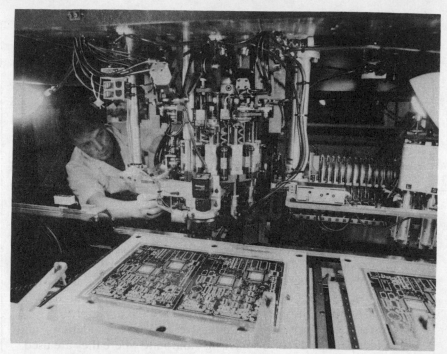

Source: Courtesy IBM

**Figure 13.10   A high speed component placement machine for populating
PCBs at IBM in Scotland**

13.6   Conclusion

The manufacture of electronic components and assemblies includes a wide
variety of processes that require inputs from many different disciplines in
science and engineering. The chapter is intended to provide only an
indication of the depth of the subject. For example, one area not covered
has been that of testing. Completed assemblies require to be tested in a
variety of ways, e.g. the operation of the individual components, the
continuity of the electric circuit, the positioning and polarity of the
components, and the functional performance of the complete assembly are
all factors to be considered. Special test rigs, artificial vision systems, and
chambers where the boards can be subjected to thermal cycling, high
humidity conditions, and vibration, etc. are all used to ensure that products
are up to the high quality demanded by international markets.

Review Questions

1 Discuss the significance of the invention of semiconductor technology.
2 What is an IC chip? Sketch a block diagram of the steps involved in its manufacture.
3 Briefly outline the Czochralski process.
4 Describe the process of photolithography, and discuss its use in the electronics industry.
5 Why is silicon dioxide an important material in IC manufacture; how is it obtained?
6 Briefly describe the processes of dopant diffusion and vapour deposition, and their use in IC manufacture.
7 Discuss why clean rooms are necessary in IC manufacture.
8 What do you understand by the term 'a class 10 clean room'?
9 By the use of a block diagram, briefly outline the steps involved in the manufacture of printed circuit boards (PCBs).
10 Describe the differences between leaded components and SMDs, and discuss why the latter are increasing in popularity.
11 Briefly outline the operations involved in PCB assembly.
12 Describe the processes of 'adhesive and wave soldering', and 'solder paste and reflow soldering', and state where they are used.

Further Reading

1 'Electronic Materials', by N. Braithwaite and A.G. Weaver. Published by Open University & Butterworths, 1990.
2 'Introduction to Semiconductor Microtechnology', by D.V. Morgan and A.K. Board. Published by John Wiley and Sons, 2nd ed. 1990.
3 'Printed Circuit Board Assembly', by P.J.W. Noble. Published by Open University Press, 1989.
4 'Printed Circuits Handbook', by C.F. Coombs. Published by McGraw Hill, 3rd ed. 1988.
5 'Surface Mount Assemblies', by J.F. Pawling. Published by Electromechanical Publications Ltd. 1987.
6 'Assembly of Discrete Electronic Components', by Ray Skipp. Published by McGraw Hill 1988.

Part IV
Manufacturing Management

⟨14⟩ Production planning

14.1 Introduction

In the previous chapters we examined the processes used to create products. But the creation of a product, especially a modern complex one comprising many elements, also necessitates careful planning and control of the production system. This section of the book considers how the resources of materials, machines, money, and manpower, are managed to produce competitive products for the world market.

Improvements in management techniques to increase efficiency are constantly appearing. As technology, markets, and society change so the methods employed by management change. At the time of writing current thinking on manufacturing management and organisation is reflected in concepts and techniques such as Simultaneous (or Concurrent) Engineering, Design For Manufacture (DFM), Manufacturing Resource Planning (MRPII), Just In Time manufacture (JIT), Optimised Production Technology (OPT), Total Quality Management (TQM), etc. most of these being referred to by their acronyms. Simultaneous Engineering and DFM were discussed in earlier chapters; the others will be examined in Chapters 15 and 18.

We begin this chapter by considering the geographic location of a manufacturing plant, then examining how the internal layout of the plant may be optimised for maximum efficiency. We next look at how to select the most suitable process to make a particular product, before going on to consider project and process planning. In the following chapters in Part IV we discuss some of the previously mentioned concepts and techniques used to help organise the flow of the work through the manufacturing system, ensure quality, and ensure that the manufacturing operation remains economically viable.

14.2 Plant location

Determining where to locate a manufacturing facility involves the consideration of a wide range of criteria. The relative importance attached to each criterion is dependent on the company involved. For example, a shipbuilding company will require proximity to a sea or river and possibly a steel plant for supply of steel plate, etc. However an electronics manufacturing company will be more concerned with the proximity to an inexpensive labour source for manual assembly tasks and skilled engineers for equipment design and maintenance. For larger companies, the decision will be made on a global basis. Criteria such as government incentives to attract foreign investment are important, for example many USA and Japanese companies have factories in the UK due to factors such as low rates for the use of land, special grants, and skilled local workforces. Also much foreign investment is made in the developing countries, where labour rates are still relatively low. Conversely, companies may decide to set up a manufacturing facility in an industrialised country simply to avoid trade barriers or the cost of exporting the complete product to it, e.g cars.

However, for smaller scale activities proximity to the end user is no longer of such importance. Companies must view the world as their market place, and take advantage of modern methods of transportation and communication. An experience of the author highlights this. A final year student, working with a company located close to Glasgow, required a small assembly fixture to be manufactured as part of her final year project. A local sub-contractor quoted £1000 for the work. She faxed a company she knew in Singapore who immediately quoted £200. The Singapore company got the work, the design was faxed to them and with the fixture being small and light it could be returned to Glasgow airport within a few days. This is the 'global village' in operation. Proximity to natural energy resources has also become of less importance; the success of Japan in manufacturing is evidence of this.

It is therefore apparent that the plant location problem is by no means trivial, and that the interrelationship of many criteria must be considered. The decision will be based on a combination of financial incentives offered by each country to invest in a specific locality, the land space available and building costs, and the infrastructure of the area, e.g. communication and transport links, skill level and cost of local labour, proximity to essential services and resources, and availability of local sub-contractors.

Figure 14.1 shows an example of a decision matrix that could be used to select a location for a new factory. A, B, C, D, and E, are possible sites. The criteria important to the company are listed down the left hand side of the matrix. Each criterion is allocated a weight between 0 and 10, proportionate to its desirability to the company. For example, this company needs a location close to a large pool of unskilled labour, the availability of skilled workers, the presence of financial incentives, and the space for eventual expansion. The boxes created by the rows and columns are split into two as shown. In the top left hand corner of each box a number betwen 0 and 5 is inserted, signifying the ability of the site heading the column to satisfy the relevant criterion. After all the corners have been filled, the multiple of each number and the criterion weight is entered in the bottom right hand of the box. The sum of the multiples for each column is now calculated. The site with the highest score at its column base is the one most likely to best satisfy all the needs and wants of the company.

CRITERION		WEIGHT	POSSIBLE FACTORY LOCATION				
			A	B	C	D	E
PROXIMITY TO:	SKILLED LABOUR	7	2 / 14	3 / 21	0 / 0	1 / 7	4 / 28
	LARGE POOL OF UNSKILLED LABOUR	8	5 / 40	2 / 16	0 / 0	4 / 32	2 / 16
	MOTORWAY	7	3 / 21	2 / 14	1 / 7	3 / 21	4 / 28
	AIRPORT	4	1 / 4	3 / 12	4 / 16	2 / 8	2 / 8
	SEA/RIVER	0	2 / 0	5 / 0	5 / 0	2 / 0	1 / 0
	HOUSING	5	4 / 20	3 / 15	0 / 0	3 / 15	4 / 20
	AMENITIES	5	3 / 15	2 / 10	0 / 0	2 / 10	3 / 15
POTENTIAL FOR EXPANSION		7	2 / 14	1 / 7	5 / 35	3 / 21	2 / 14
AVAILABILITY OF GRANTS/INCENTIVES		8	1 / 8	2 / 16	5 / 40	1 / 8	3 / 24
SAFETY		2	3 / 6	2 / 4	5 / 10	2 / 4	2 / 4
PLANNING CONSTRAINTS		5	2 / 10	3 / 15	5 / 25	4 / 20	2 / 10
ENVIRONMENTAL IMPACT		4	3 / 12	2 / 8	4 / 16	1 / 4	2 / 8
TOTAL			164	138	149	150	175

Figure 14.1 Decision matrix for plant location: site *E* is most desirable

14.3 Plant layout

First we will consider the classic patterns of plant layout which are still commonly found and are effective when used appropriately. We will then consider the use of component classification and coding which can be utilised to help construct what are called **cellular layouts**. This classification and coding of parts has implications for the whole manufacturing system, the overall concept being called **group technology** or GT. Group technology improves the overall efficiency of large manufacturing companies by identifying similarities in parts and grouping them into families. This produces benefits from the optimisation of equipment and tooling usage and the possibility of realising many of the benefits of standardisation.

Proper layout of a manufacturing facility is essential since it will determine the work and material flow throughout the factory. Some of the benefits of good layout design will be to: maximise productivity, ensure best possible use of floor space, simplify handling of work and materials,

improve equipment and labour utilisation, reduce throughput time, minimise product damage, improve safety and working conditions, reduce
travel times for personnel and materials, and simplify production control.

(a) Classic plant layout patterns

The problem of laying out a work area occurs in many situations, e.g. a
garage, a hospital, a laboratory, and even the domestic kitchen. Our
concern is with the manufacturing area of a factory. The traditional layouts
can be identified as follows.

1 **Random layout.** Likely to be very inefficient; this type of layout may be
   found in small factory units where the production volume and production variety has gradually grown. This may be seen in the initial stages of
   the evolution of a 'start up' manufacturing company.
2 **Functional layout.** This is a common but relatively inefficient type of
   layout. It is often used where the production of a large variety of
   products in batch volumes is required, e.g. the components for large
   water pumps for ships or desalination plants, and components for
   sub-assemblies for the aerospace industry such as radar equipment or jet
   engines. Similar processes are grouped together, thus creating **physical
   areas** such as drilling, turning, milling, injection moulding, and casting
   departments (see Figure 14.2(a)). The reasons the method is inefficient
   are that the material transport routes are long since material is transferred from department to department; work in progress is high; and in a
   large plant the tracking and control of individual orders can be difficult.
   The advantages are that specialist supervision and labour can be
   employed, and there is flexibility in the processing of the work as it can
   be transferred from department to department any number of times and
   in any sequence. The reasons for grouping together common specialised
   equipment such as injection moulding machines or foundry equipment
   are obvious; however, the advantages of grouping together the machin-

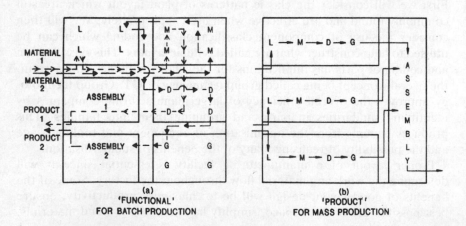

(a)
'FUNCTIONAL'
FOR BATCH PRODUCTION

(b)
'PRODUCT'
FOR MASS PRODUCTION

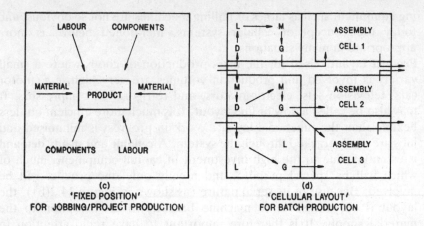

(c)
'FIXED POSITION'
FOR JOBBING/PROJECT PRODUCTION

(d)
'CELLULAR LAYOUT'
FOR BATCH PRODUCTION

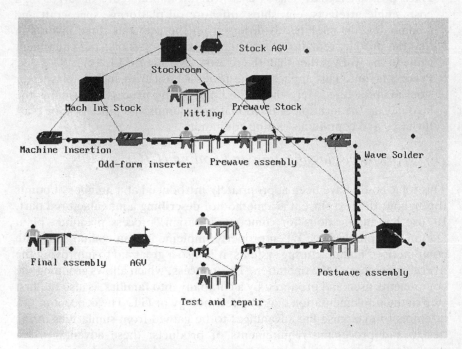

Source: Courtesy CACI Product Division

(e) A computer display from a factory planning package 'Simfactory II.5'. This allows various factory systems to be created and variables such as layout, manpower levels, and work in progress to be manipulated until an optimum plant layout is obtained. The display shows part of an electronics factory layout

Figure 14.2   Plant layout patterns

ing equipment such as lathes or milling machines are not so obvious, and today the concept of cellular systems, mentioned below, is more appropriate in many situations.

3 **Product layout.** Used for the mass production of goods where a small variety is involved and production volumes are very high, e.g. motor cars, television sets, electric motors, and refrigeration compressors. It may also be called a flow or line layout. It is much more efficient but less flexible than the functional layout. Work in progress is minimised and jobs are easily tracked through the system. A **reliable and steady demand** is essential, due to the high investment in capital equipment, much of which will be special purpose, and ideally only one product will be involved. Because of its serial nature (as shown in Figure 14.2(b)), the layout is very sensitive to machine breakdown or disruption to the material supply. It is therefore important to have rapid attention to breakdowns and reliable material deliveries.

4 **Fixed position layout.** This is used for the manufacture of large, high cost, single artefacts, e.g. ships, offshore oil platforms, spacecraft and communication satellites. It differs from the previous three layouts in that the product remains static while the workers, tools, and equipment **come to the work** rather than the reverse (see Figure 14.2(c)).

5 **Process layout.** This applies in the process industries such as plastics or steel manufacture. Here the technology of the **process** determines the layout, e.g. the location of fractionating columns and pipework, or blast furnaces and continuous casting equipment.

(b) Workpiece classification and coding (C/C)

This topic could have been appropriately introduced at a number of points throughout the text since it is a method of **describing** a manufactured part. Its use has implications for component design, process planning, plant layout, and purchasing. When properly implemented in conjunction with computerised manufacturing systems, it is also a great aid to improving the overall efficiency of the operation. This process, which allows grouping the components used and produced by a company into **families**, is also the first step in the implementation of group technology or GT. The concept of GT attempts to maximise the advantages to be gained from similarities in the design and processing requirements of products; these advantages are particularly important in large companies producing and using many thousands of parts.

Both design and manufacturing attributes can be used as a basis for the classification. Similarities in features of the component design such as the shape, dimensions, tolerances, surface finish, holes or re-entrant angles, and length to width or length to diameter ratio, are used as classification criteria. Similarities in manufacturing features such as the type of process used, the sequence of operations, the equipment employed, and the production volumes and rates required, can all be used to identify families of components. It should be noted that many of the design and manufacturing criteria are interrelated, e.g. the tolerance and surface finish obtainable is dependent on the process used.

The actual code used to define the part may be devised by the user company themselves to suit their own particular circumstances, or an 'off the shelf' industrial coding system may be purchased and tailored to suit. Each alphanumeric character in the code defines an **attribute** of the part, and although the code should be as simple and easily understood as possible, the number of characters can be large. The 'MultiClass' system, for example uses up to thirty digits. However, once allocated, the part code can be stored in a computer along with the codes for all other company parts. The computer is then used to sort the parts into families according to their codes.

Once the part families have been determined, it should be possible to manufacture all the parts from one family by using a group of **common processes or machines**. A grouping of machines like this is called a manufacturing 'cell'.

(c) Cellular layout

A manufacturing cell is the means of creating the products identified by the C/C process as belonging to a single family. The cell is an autonomous manufacturing unit which can produce a finished part, and it will contain one or more machines. This aspect of group technology is most commonly applied to machined parts, the cells usually containing numerically controlled machine tools, which will be described in Chapter 21, such as machining centres, lathes, and milling machines (see Figure 14.2(d)). Thus a company that has employed GT throughout its operations will often have a large number of these cells within its factory. The cells may be manned with one operator tending a number of machines, but they are often computer controlled and utilise robots for material handling. Consequently productivity and quality are maximised, and throughput times and work in progress can be kept to a minimum. Due to its flexibility the cell layout system is particularly suited to the manufacture of products in batches and where design changes often occur.

(d) Other considerations

Once the general type of layout has been decided, more detailed planning needs to be done. Space requirements for equipment, materials, and personnel must be allocated. Material handling methods will be considered, e.g. whether to use bulk transfer means such as conveyors, or to use discrete load transporters such as fork lift trucks or automated guided vehicles. Safety is obviously very important and aisles of adequate size must be available to provide safe access to all work areas; aisles must be clearly marked, usually by white painted lines, and kept clear at all times. Provision must be made for services such as electricity for lighting and machine power, data transfer links, compressed air, water, and possibly automatic removal of swarf from machining installations. Storage space for materials and tools will be made, but it should be remembered that in a modern factory work in progress must be kept to a minimum; this means that large storage areas on the shop floor for it should not be necessary.

The detailed layout will also be determined by carrying out studies to ensure minimisation of material flow, personnel movement, and work handling. Many techniques exist to aid this process, for example the use of scale drawings, three dimensional models, string diagrams, and computer simulation (see Figure 14.2(e)), are all common. Their description and use cannot be covered fully here, but some of the techniques are also used in method study and these are described in Chapter 16 on Work Study.

14.4   Material and process selection

The importance of an integrated approach to all aspects of manufacturing is emphasised here at the process selection stage. To select an appropriate process for a product, due consideration must be given to the material used. Conversely, the design engineer when considering the material for his product must also consider the processes that will be used to form the product. We will therefore, at this interface between product design and product manufacture, briefly consider material selection as well as process selection.

Figure 14.3 shows the factors to be considered when carrying out the material selection and process selection activities; it also indicates their close interrelationship. When selecting a material for a product the designer will try to permutate the material attributes shown in Figure 14.3 to achieve an optimum solution. For example, the material will require specific mechanical properties, it will need to possess certain minimum shear, compressive, and tensile strengths, or it may have to exhibit high elasticity, toughness, or wear resistance. Physical properties may also be important, e.g thermal and electrical conductivity, optical characteristics, or magnetic properties. The designer's choice of material will also be influenced by the expected lifetime of the product, the implications of product failure, and the type of environments in which the product will be used. The 'manufacturability' of the material is obviously of extreme importance, and will possibly cause the designer to modify his specifications in other areas; for example, if a material possesses particularly high compressive strength and is hard, then it may be impossible to produce the product by some manufacturing processes such as forging or extrusion. Thus terms may be coined such as 'weldability', 'castability', 'formability', and 'machinability' to describe how easily the material can be used in the manufacturing system.

Considerations common to both the material and process selection

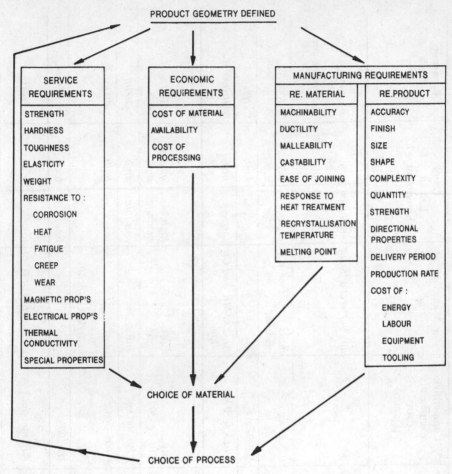

PRODUCT GEOMETRY DEFINED

SERVICE REQUIREMENTS	ECONOMIC REQUIREMENTS	MANUFACTURING REQUIREMENTS	
		RE. MATERIAL	RE. PRODUCT
STRENGTH	COST OF MATERIAL	MACHINABILITY	ACCURACY
HARDNESS	AVAILABILITY	DUCTILITY	FINISH
TOUGHNESS	COST OF PROCESSING	MALLEABILITY	SIZE
ELASTICITY		CASTABILITY	SHAPE
WEIGHT		EASE OF JOINING	COMPLEXITY
RESISTANCE TO :		RESPONSE TO HEAT TREATMENT	QUANTITY
CORROSION			STRENGTH
HEAT		RECRYSTALLISATION TEMPERATURE	DIRECTIONAL PROPERTIES
FATIGUE		MELTING POINT	DELIVERY PERIOD
CREEP			PRODUCTION RATE
WEAR			COST OF :
MAGNETIC PROP'S			ENERGY
ELECTRICAL PROP'S			LABOUR
THERMAL CONDUCTIVITY			EQUIPMENT
SPECIAL PROPERTIES			TOOLING

CHOICE OF MATERIAL

CHOICE OF PROCESS

Figure 14.3   Material and process selection factors

decisions are the number of components to be made, their size, their weight, the precision required, their surface finish, and their appearance. The possibility of making the product out of one part as opposed to a number of parts requiring joining is also a combined material and process selection problem; for example, selecting a thermoplastic to make a high volume product may allow it to be made in one piece using the injection moulding process.

Thus the type of material selected has a strong influence on the manufacturing process to be used. Figure 14.4 shows a sample of a number of processes with their capabilities. The manufacturing engineer's decision on which process to use will be based on the above mentioned factors, plus some further economic considerations. As well as the production volume, the rate at which the components are to be produced has a strong influence on the process; the costs of labour and equipment must also be considered.

Process	Typical tolerance (size dependent) (mm)	Surface texture (μmRa)	Competitive component size (kg/mm)	Materials	Costs Labour = L Equipment = E		Economic batch size
					L	E	
Casting Sand	±1.5	5.0 → 25.0	any	any but steel difficult	medium to high	low, high if automated	manual <100, automated any quantity
Shell	±0.1	1.0–3.0	0.1–15 kg	most medium	high	high	>100
Investment	±0.05	0.3–3.0	>0.5 kg	any	high	high	>100
Die	±0.05	1.0–2.0	0.01 kg–10 kg	Al, Zn, Mn, and Cu alloys	low	high	>10 000
Deformation Hot forging Open die	±5.0	1.0–25.0	any	most	high	medium	1–100
Impression	±0.5	1.0 → 25.0	0.01 kg–100 kg	most	medium	high	>100
Hot extrusion	±0.5	1.0–25.0	1 kg–500 kg	most	medium	high	>100m
Cold forging and extrusion	±0.1	0.4–4.0	0.001–50 kg	most (but stronger materials difficult)	low	high	>1000
Rolling	±0.5	1.0–25.0	10–1000 kg	most	low	high	>50 000m
Pressworking Blanking	±0.02–±0.4	0.1–6.0	<10 mm thick	usually steel or Al or Cu alloy	low	high	>1000

211

Process							
Bending	±0.2	0.2–0.8	<100 mm thick	usually steel or Al or Cu alloy	low	medium	>1000
Drawing	±0.1	0.2–0.8	<10 mm thick	usually steel or Al or Cu alloy	low	medium–high	>1000
Machining Drilling	±0.05	0.8–6.0	<100 mm diameter	most unhardened materials especially free machining and excluding ceramics	medium	low	1+
Turning	±0.03	0.4–12.0	<3000 mm diameter	most unhardened materials especially free machining and excluding ceramics	high–medium	medium	1+
Milling	±0.1	0.3–12.0	<1000 mm^2	most unhardened materials especially free machining and excluding ceramics	high–medium	medium	1+
Grinding	±0.008	0.2–3.0	<1000 mm^2	most	medium	medium	1+
Honing Lapping	±0.005	0.03–0.2	<1 mm^2	most	medium	medium	1+
Powder metallurgy	±0.3	0.4–1.5	<1 kg	any	low	high	>1000
E.D.M.	±0.02–±0.1	0.2–6.0	<300 mm diameter	any conductive	medium	medium–high	1–100
Injection moulding	±0.1	any	<5 kg	most thermoplastics and thermosets	low	high	>1000

Figure 14.4 Process selection: a table illustrating some of the relevant factors, guidelines may be modified according to conditions

Usually processes suited to high production volumes are also suitable for high rates of production; they also usually have high equipment costs and relatively low labour costs. Conversely, if lower volumes are required the equipment does not need to be so specialised but workers of a higher, and hence more expensive, skill level are required. The equipment cost in Figure 14.4 is only intended as a rough guide, since it really comprises two elements, the machine and the tooling. For high volume production, tooling is generally expensive, e.g. injection moulding, die casting, and closed impression die forging tools.

14.5   Project planning

As a scenario for this section we will assume that a small manufacturing company has decided on a location for its plant and has in fact selected a ready made building on an industrial estate. We will further assume that the manufacturing processes to be used have been selected and that the plant layout is being designed. Concurrent with the layout design, the necessary machines and equipment will be ordered and their installation planned. This is the project planning stage and certain techniques have been developed to assist the planner carry out the task efficiently and allow progress to be monitored. Here we briefly consider three aids for the project manager, i.e. the Gantt chart, Critical Path Analysis, and the Work Schedule chart. These can be used for any type of work where a large number of items or activities have to be drawn together to produce a finished product or task. Activities may be carried out in parallel to each other, in which case they are independent, or they may be dependent and have to be carried out in series. In this type of planning the activities are usually long term and measured in days, weeks, or months. This occurs in the jobbing type production noted in Chapter 1 where the task might be the building of a submarine, spacecraft, or offshore oil platform. These aids are also applied to projects such as the construction of a bridge, power station, house, the organisation of a trade exhibition and conference, or the installation of a new machine or layout in a factory.

Using the last type of activity as our example, we will assume that a robotic installation is being planned. The installation will comprise a conveyor line which will deliver boxed items to a pick up point. An industrial robot arm will pick up the boxes and stack them on a wooden pallet which, when full, will be removed by a fork lift truck. The robot and pick up point at the end of the conveyor are to be surrounded by a safety cage. The full installation is to be controlled by a PC type computer. We can therefore now identify a number of activities that must take place for the installation to be completed. The conveyor, robot, and computer must be ordered and delivered. It is assumed that the safety cage is already on site awaiting installation. The work area must be marked out and a foundation prepared for the robot. These items must all be installed, mains electricity connected, and the computer interfaced to the robot, conveyor, and safety cage.

Having defined the project we can now list the activities and allocate an estimated duration to each. We can also specify what activities need to take place **before others can begin**. For example, the foundation preparation cannot take place until the work area has been marked out, the robot cannot be installed until it is delivered and the foundation prepared, and the safety cage cannot be erected until the installation of the robot and conveyor is complete. Mains electricity cannot be connected until the conveyor, robot, and cage are installed. The computer can be installed any time after its delivery but cannot be interfaced to the rest of the equipment until the mains electricity has been connected. These activities and their expected durations can now be listed as shown in Table 14.1

Table 14.1

Activity		Duration (days)	Immediate predecessors
A	Mark out work area	2	Start
B	Prepare foundation	5	A
C	Delivery of conveyor	8	Start
D	Delivery of robot	10	Start
E	Delivery of computer	7	Start
F	Install robot	3	B, D
G	Install conveyor	3	C
H	Install computer	1	E
I	Install safety cage	3	F, G
J	Connect mains supply	4	I
K	Interface all equipment	5	H, J

The simplest technique to use to represent this data is the basic Gantt chart. This is shown in Figure 14.5. The major project activities are listed down the left hand side of the chart and the days represented by columns; calendar dates would probably be used in a real world application. Completed activities are shown as broad bars, activities not yet started or incomplete are shown as thick lines. The thick vertical line joining the two pointers is the present time indicator, the situation at the end of day 9 is shown in the chart. The main advantage of the Gantt chart is immediately apparent, i.e. it is easy to obtain a quick impression of the state of the individual project activities at the present time. It can be seen quickly that activities **A**, **B**, **C**, and **E** have all been completed on schedule, that activity **G** has been completed ahead of schedule, and that activities **D** and **H** are behind schedule. It also shows that the project activities are all expected to be completed by day 25.

Although the Gantt chart is quick and easy to read regarding the

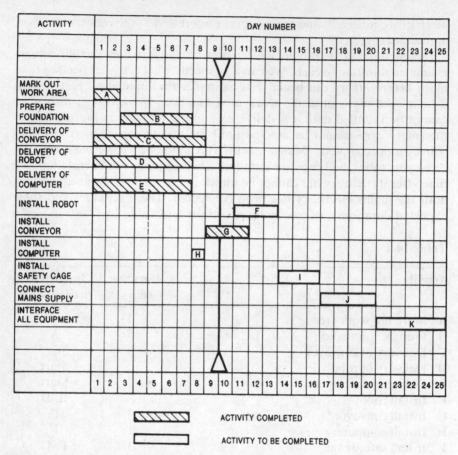

Figure 14.5   The Gantt chart

progress of the project, it does have some disadvantages for use as a planning aid and for obtaining more detailed progress information. For example, it does not make it obvious that although activity **H** is behind schedule by two days it will not interfere with the overall completion time of the project, whereas the two day delay on element **D** will probably also delay the project completion by two days. As well as not giving a clear indication of the **interdependence** of the various activities, it also does not allow the planner to see what activities must be completed on schedule to ensure that the project is completed as planned. Neither does it allow the planner to see how much an activity may be delayed without influencing the start of other activities; this difference between the earliest and latest activity start time is termed 'float'. A knowledge of activity interdependence and float is essential to the planner, as it can allow scarce resources to be applied where and when they will be most effective. This is particularly important where a large number of items and work elements are involved: in a real project these may number thousands. Network planning techniques have been developed to provide this necessary information, the most popular of them being Critical Path Analysis (CPA) and the Program Evaluation Review Technique (PERT) both developed in the USA in the 1950s. We will briefly examine the Critical Path Analysis method here.

The first four steps in the CPA technique have already been carried out, i.e. the project has been defined, the activities of which the project will be comprised have been listed, precedence relationships have been established, and estimates of the activity durations have been made. The next stage is to construct a network of nodes and arrows. The convention we will use involves representing an **activity** by an **arrow**, and representing an **event**, i.e. the beginning or end of an activity, by a **node**. Thus the arrows represent a period of time whereas the nodes represent a point in time. Figure 14.6 shows the network for our project. As can be seen, it provides all the information we need regarding precedence relationships and start and end times for each activity; it is constructed as follows:

- Using the previously compiled list of activities and precedence statements the **start node** is identified; in this case it may be assumed to be the point at which final approval is given for immediate commencement of the project. From this node arrows are drawn for each activity that can begin immediately the project starts. Each node is shown as a circle. The top half of the circle shows the node number; these are in multiples of ten to allow the addition of extra nodes should this be found necessary. The bottom half of the node circle is split into two; the reason for this is explained later. For example, in Figure 14.6, node 10 is the start point for activities 'A', 'C', 'D', and 'E'; and node 40 is the finish point for activity 'C'. Node 40 is also the start of activity 'G' and node 60 its finish; the logic of the network is such that activity 'G' cannot start until activity 'C' is finished. If we now look at node 60 we see that two arrows enter this representing activities 'F' and 'G'; this shows us that activity 'I' cannot commence until both activities 'F' and 'G' are completed. Using the arrows and nodes in this way, the network can be constructed. Further refinements are often necessary, such as the insertion of 'dummy' activities to allow precedence relationships to be represented that would otherwise be difficult to show.
- The next stage is to carry out a **forward pass** through the network to determine the **earliest event time** for each node. For example, node 10 marking the start of the project is assumed to be day zero although a calendar date would probably be inserted here in practice. Activity 'A' takes 2 days, thus the earliest time for node 20 is after 2 days; the number 2 is therefore entered in the bottom left of the node circle. Node 30, however, represents the completion of both activities 'B' and 'D'. This means that it cannot exist until both of these activities have been completed. We must therefore insert into the bottom left space the maximum event time elapsed at that point. Since activity 'B' takes 5 days, a total of 7 days will have elapsed by the time 'B' is completed.

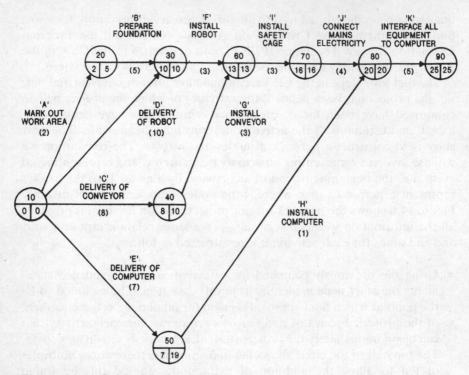

Figure 14.6   Critical path analysis

However, since activity 'D' takes 10 days it is this value that must be inserted into the node as the earliest event time. This process is carried out throughout the network until the earliest completion date for the project can be entered into the final node. Examination of Figure 14.6 shows that this earliest completion date is 25 days after the project start.

- Next a **backward pass** is carried out to determine the **latest event time** for each node. This will show the planner the latest each activity can be completed yet still maintain the earliest completion date. It follows logically that this process should also highlight those activities that must be completed according to schedule. The backward pass is carried out in a similar manner to the forward one, except that this time the activity durations are progressively **subtracted**, and the results entered into the bottom right hand sector of the node circle. The difference in value between the right and left hand numbers represents the 'float' available at that point. For example, the computer may arrive any time between day 7 and day 19 without affecting the earliest completion date of the project – i.e. activity 'E', the delivery of the computer, has a float of 12 days.

- The backward pass will also show up those activities with **zero float**. These activities meet at nodes where the earliest and latest node event times are identical. The network path created by these activities is termed the **Critical Path**, and all activities on this path must be completed on time if the project is to finish on schedule. The Critical Path for our project passes from node 10, through nodes 30, 60, 70, and 80, to node 90.

- Using this information the planner will now create a **schedule** for the project. Usually each event will be scheduled to start at the earliest possible time to provide maximum float; this may be modified if two parallel activities demand the same resources, e.g. specialised labour. To monitor the progress of the project the planner may also construct a work schedule chart. This is a variation on the Gantt chart and it is illustrated in Figure 14.7. The situation at the end of day 12 is shown, and all work to date has been completed to plan. However, since the critical path is shown along the top of the chart, the planner or project manager will immediately recognise a serious delay should one occur on these activities. The float available on the other activities is also shown as broken lines; therefore as long as the block showing the activity duration does not move beyond the broken lines the project may still be completed according to schedule.

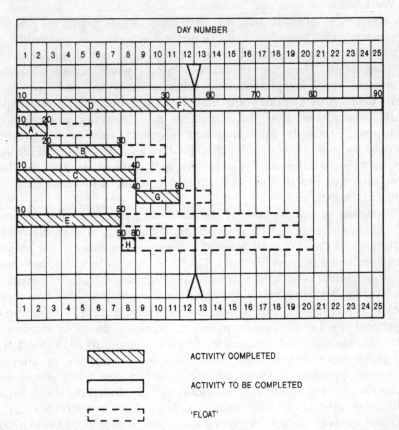

Figure 14.7 The work schedule chart

14.6   Process planning

In order to make a component by any production process it is necessary first to create a plan of how the component will be made. The selection of which process to use has already been covered in section 14.4; here we consider the means used to plan the detail of manufacture. Some processes require a smaller number of operations than others to make a component. For example, the process planning for making a component by injection moulding is simple, i.e. inject the plastic into the mould, remove component from mould when cool, trim excess material, place component on pallet. However the sequence of operations is often more complex, and this is particularly apparent when producing components by machining. As well as planning the manufacture of individual components, the assembly of these components into a finished product must also be planned; this requires the use of slightly different planning techniques. Process planning also allows labour and capacity requirements to be studied and an accurate estimate to be made of the time taken to produce the component or complete product. These aspects are considered more fully in Chapter 16 on Work Study.

Various types of charts may be constructed as aids to process planning. 'Assembly charts' are used to show the sequence of assembly and relationships between manufactured and bought out components and sub-assemblies. They are particularly useful when complex products comprising many components and sub-assemblies are being produced. More detailed descriptions are then produced by creating 'operations charts' which now show the individual manufacturing and inspection operations, processes, and equipment required. Further refinement is obtained by using 'flow process charts' which include additional information on transportation and storage. An indication of the type of charts being discussed can be seen in Figure 16.4, where a process chart for a product is shown.

Production of components by the machining processes often provides the most challenging aspects of this type of planning; despite the relative inefficiency of the process it remains a common problem for the planner. Computer aided process planning, CAPP, is used in industry, but due to the large number of variables, complexity, and general need for experiential decisions, some amount of human input is usually required. The type of machines and the skill of the labour involved have a great influence on the length and detail of the process plan. For example, the use of numerically controlled machine tools reduces the amount of handling of the workpiece and the number of times the tooling has to be changed or adjusted, inspection operations are reduced, and apart from relatively simple work holding devices jigs and fixtures are not required. Skilled craftsmen such as toolmakers do not require such detailed planning instruction as do unskilled workers. In fact, an experienced toolmaker will be able to make a component or product by simply working from the engineering drawings, whereas an unskilled production worker will require detailed instructions on what material and machines to use, and the sequence of operations to be followed. Naturally if a computer controlled process is being used such as a numerically controlled machine, the required information is held in the machine program and the machine operator simply has to load the material and unload the finished component.

To conclude this section a simplified example of an 'operation layout sheet' is shown in Figure 14.8 for a clevis rod (the clevis assembly is shown in Figure 16.4). For more complex machined components there are general

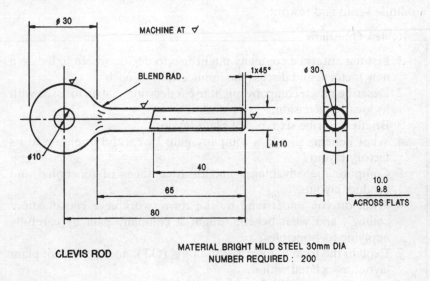

CLEVIS ROD

MATERIAL BRIGHT MILD STEEL 30mm DIA
NUMBER REQUIRED : 200

OPERATION NUMBER	DESCRIPTION	MACHINE
10	FEED 70mm LENGTH THROUGH COLLET & TIGHTEN TO CLAMP	LATHE 1
20	ROUGH TURN ø 10mm SHANK, TURN 1×45° CHAMFER, FACE END	LATHE 1
30	FINISH TURN ø 10mm SHANK SCREWCUT M10 THREAD	LATHE 1
40	UNCLAMP COLLET, WITHDRAW MATERIAL TO ALLOW PARTING OFF TO LENGTH	LATHE 1
50	RECLAMP COLLET, PART OFF TO LENGTH + 1mm	LATHE 1
60	CLAMP SHANK IN COLLET, USING FORM TOOL TURN 30mm DIA SPHERE	LATHE 2
70	INSPECT	BENCH
80	CLAMP IN FIXTURE AND MILL BOTH FLATS	MILL
90	REMOVE RAGGED EDGES WITH FILE	BENCH
100	PLACE IN JIG & DRILL 10mm DIA HOLE & DEBURR	DRILL
110	INSPECT	BENCH

Figure 14.8 Operation layout sheet

guidelines that should be followed when preparing the operation layout. For example, at least one datum surface should be established as soon as machining commences. This datum will be used as a reference surface for all subsequent operations. To maximise accuracy as many surfaces as possible should be created at the same setting, i.e. without unclamping the workpiece in the machine. The use of surfaces as secondary references other than the original datum should be avoided as long as possible. Precision operations or those producing a smooth finished surface should be created last in order to reduce the possibility of damage. Finally inspection operations should be included at appropriate intervals to minimise scrap and rework.

___ **Review Questions** _____

1 List **ten** criteria a company might use to decide where to locate a new factory, and discuss the implications of each.
2 Describe how a company might use a decision matrix to assist with its location decision.
3 Briefly describe **six** types of plant layout.
4 What benefits should a company gain by careful attention to its factory layout?
5 Compare the advantages and disadvantages of functional and product layouts.
6 What do you understand by the term 'workpiece classification/ coding', and what benefits might a company gain by carefully applying its principles?
7 Explain the term 'Group Technology' (GT), and the type of plant layout associated with it.
8 Apart from material flow, list and discuss some of the things that should be given careful consideration when making decisions on plant layout.
9 Fully discuss the relationship between material and process selection; include comments on the questions that should be asked by the planner as the decisions are made.
10 What is a 'Gantt Chart', how is it used, and what are its limitations for project planning?
11 Identify and list the steps to be followed in carrying out a Critical Path Analysis (CPA) of a project.
12 What is meant by the terms 'activity', 'node', 'activity inter-dependence', 'float', and 'critical path' in CPA?
13 Consider the following project information (St = start).

Activity	A	B	C	D	E		F	G
Duration	4	6	4	2	8		6	12
Predecessor	St	A	St	St	B, C		E	D

Activity	H	I	J	K	L
Duration	4	4	12	4	4
Predecessor	G	D	I	J	F, H, K

Construct the network for this, identify the float for each activity, and show the critical path.

14 Describe the function of the 'work schedule chart', and explain how it is an improvement on the basic Gantt chart.

15 What is the purpose of 'process planning', and how might the type of machinery and labour in use in a factory influence the process planning operation?

16 What is the purpose of an 'operation layout sheet', and what sort of guidelines should be followed by the planner as he or she constructs it?

Further Reading

1 'Production and Operations Management', by A. Muhlemann, J. Oakland, and K. Lockyer. 6th Edition. Published by Pitman, 1992.

2 'Operations Management', by Howard Barnett. Published by Macmillan, 1992.

3 'Material Handling Systems Design', by J.M. Apple. Published by Ronald Press, 1972.

4 'Production Flow Analysis', by J.L. Burbidge. Published by Oxford Science Publications, 1989.

5 'Systematic Layout Planning', by R. Muther. Published by Cahers (Boston), 1973.

6 'Critical Path Analysis and Other Network Techniques', by K. Lockyer. Published by Pitman, 1984.

7 'A Revolution in Manufacturing: the SMED System', by S. Shingo. Published by Productivity Plan (Cambridge, Mass.) 1985.

8 'Japanese Manufacturing Techniques: Nine Hidden Rules in Simplicity', by R. Schonberger. Published by The Free Press, 1982.

9 'A Management Guide to PERT/CPM', by J.D.L. Weist and F.K. Levy. Published by Prentice-Hall, 1980.

10 'The Shingo Production Management System', by Shigeo Shingo. Published by the Productivity Press Inc. 1992.

(N.B. The Further Reading at the end of Chapter 15 is also relevant).

⬡15 Production control

15.1 Introduction

Having considered the techniques used for planning a production system, we now need to examine how this production can be **controlled**. Strictly speaking the problems and techniques discussed here include planning as well as control; however, we use the term 'production control' to emphasise that it is the **ongoing** operation we are considering rather than 'one off' planning activities. This chapter concerns itself mainly with the flow of work and material through a factory; other chapters will deal with the control of quality, costs, and labour.

It should be noted that the content of this chapter, and indeed much of this section of the book, is part of the domain of 'Production and Operations Management' (POM). The principles and techniques of POM can be applied to almost any organised human activity, e.g. the planning and control of a hospital, fast food chain, air terminal, or manufacturing plant.

Efficient management of any operation demands a constant supply of up-to-date information; the means by which this is obtained is often termed a 'Management Information System' or MIS. Within a large modern manufacturing facility computers permeate the fabric of the organisation. It is through the use of these computers that Management Information Systems have gained the ability to become proficient at providing topical information when needed. Thus although the use of computers is considered more fully in Part V of the book, it should be assumed here that much of the information gathered and distributed is often handled electronically by computer systems. This allows management to monitor and control the current manufacturing operation and also to make informed decisions concerning the future. The core of the MIS is the 'data base'. This acts as a common store for all the data required for the efficient operation of the company. Ideally all the data, textual and graphical, should be computer accessible and stored in a logical form to facilitate access. The importance of the common data base is that changes made by one department are instantly recognisable by others, e.g. a component design change by engineering can be immediately acted upon by purchasing and production.

This chapter begins by looking at the basic elements of production and material control. However the concepts and techniques used broaden in scope until by the end of the chapter the implications of their use can be seen to include the whole structure and organisation of the company.

15.2 Elements of production control

Here we are primarily concerned with the ongoing monitoring and control of production within the manufacturing facility.

- Systems need to be in place that allow answers to questions such as those that follow. When should the material for product A be issued, and how much? Where is job B at this moment, and is it where it should be? Why is job C in the machining cell when it should be at assembly? How many of product D can be made by next Friday? What jobs are not running to schedule, and why? The tasks of production control are therefore, to schedule production based on sales orders or forecasts, to determine work priorities, to control stock levels, successfully to achieve production programmes, i.e. on time delivery, and to obtain optimum production equipment utilisation.
- The achievement of these tasks involves finding some way to determine: what job should be done, how many items should be made, when the work should be done, and where it should be done. In a large company this production control problem is an extremely complex one. Consider a product comprising hundreds or even thousands of parts being made in the one factory. The task of making sure each piece of material or part arrives at the correct process or assembly point at the correct time is notoriously difficult. Attempts to schedule the work must be made but it must also be realised that in all probability the schedule will be disrupted to some extent. Disruptions occur due to random events such as failure of a supplier to deliver material on time, machine breakdowns, labour problems, or a host of other problems almost impossible to anticipate. It is for this reason that no one materials management or production control system is absolutely foolproof. Also the type of production, i.e. process, mass, batch, or jobbing, will determine the most suitable type of system to adopt.
- Whatever system is used, before the scheduling of the work within the factory can commence it is necessary to know the sales demands which must be satisfied. This information may be contained in a document called the '**Master Production Schedule**' (MPS). This MPS provides the input to our system; it shows the quantities of the end product that are required, and when they are to be made. It is derived from placed customer orders or forecast sales.
- Also essential is a full '**Bill of Materials**' (BOM). The BOM is a document, or computer file, which contains information on all the materials, components, and sub-assemblies required to produce a product. This information may also be amplified to show how the product is manufactured, the quantity of each component and sub-assembly required for each product unit, and the actual manufacturing facilities to be used to produce the components and assemblies. The BOM is produced from information supplied by the design and manufacturing engineering departments. As a simple example the basic bill of

materials for a toy car is shown in Figure 15.1; as can be seen this also communicates the product structure.

- Other prerequisites for a successful system are operation layouts for each part, a thorough knowledge of the **work in progress** (WIP) within the factory, and a record of all material, components, and finished products held in stock.
- All items paid for by the company that are destined to become part of the finished product are classed as '**inventory**'. Thus we may have inventory, (a) held in stores waiting to enter the production system, (b) somewhere in the system at various stages of completion – this is WIP inventory, and (c) finished products or spares awaiting delivery to customers. The aim of all company personnel, and specifically the materials or production control manager, is to reduce inventory levels to the minimum necessary for smooth production. Inventory costs the company money, which will not be recovered until the stock is transformed into a sold product. This is why the '**inventory turnover ratio**' is so important. The ratio is obtained by dividing the cost of goods sold during a year by the average cost of the inventory held during that period. The actual ratio depends on the type of manufacturing business. For example a figure of 10 would be excellent for a company engaged in the manufacture of high value added products like machine tools, and a ratio of 100 would make a producer of consumer durables, such as televisions or cars, top of the league of world class manufacturers.
- The sequence of events is therefore as follows. The sales department informs the manufacturing facility of specific customer orders plus forecasted orders which may be statistically derived. From this an MPS

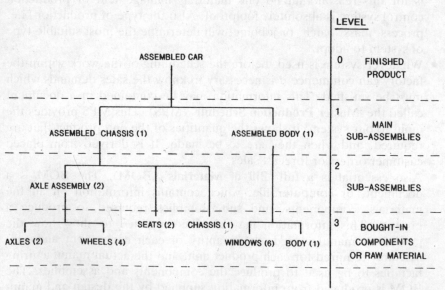

Figure 15.1 BOM structure for a toy car

is compiled. This MPS is used as authorisation to allow production of BOMs and subsequently the creation of production schedules. Information derived from the BOMs will also be used by the purchasing department to order the necessary raw material and bought out components. These detailed production schedules should take into account the capacity and availability of machines within the facility and the probable labour requirements. Areas should be identified where machines will be in high demand and where it might be necessary to find extra labour capacity by running overtime, extra shifts, hiring additional workers, or contracting out work to other factories. The production control department will also determine priorities, i.e. the sequence in which jobs should be done, and in the case of conflicting demands will make a decision on which job should be done first.

- Depending on the type of system being used a '**works order**' or its equivalent will be issued. This contains detailed information on what has to be done, and how it is to be done; the information to produce this will be found in the full BOM. The individual documents contained in the works order provide instructions, allow progress records to be logged and inspection reports to be recorded, and will allow cost reports to be compiled. In some cases, for example car manufacture, inspection records and other information can be held electronically in a microchip 'tag' which accompanies the car through the manufacturing process. The tag can be 'written' to and 'read' using a radio transmitter and receiver.

- **Progressing** work through a factory is often necessary. Ideally, especially with computerised production control systems, 'progress chasing' should be a thing of the past. Factories producing large numbers of complex products composed of many machined components, each of which has to go through a series of many different operations in many different departments, have always employed people as 'progress chasers'. This job is not completely obsolete since no system ever operates perfectly; this individual will make sure that the appropriate jobs are being worked on and not simply those that will allow the production department to produce good productivity statistics. This 'chaser', sometimes called an expediter, will also be sensitive to the implications of machine breakdowns, scrapped work, and the late arrival of raw materials; he or she will be sufficiently knowledgeable on sales requirements and production schedules to make appropriate decisions as to what alternative actions should be taken. The progress chaser can therefore carry out on-the-spot investigations and should have the ability to anticipate, rather than 'fire fight', production control problems. Continuously up-dated progress reports can be provided by the use of coloured Gantt-type wall charts, textual printouts from the computer system, or graphic displays on a computer terminal screen.

- Assuming a large factory with a wide variety of products and associated components, there will be a number of conflicting **criteria** that could be used to make **priority decisions**. One common criterion needs to be chosen to enable a consistent workable scheduling system to be established. For example it has been mentioned that WIP inventory costs money; a valid criterion on which to make priority decisions might therefore appear to be the minimisation of WIP. Alternatively, since machines cost money and indeed continue to cost money whether working productively or standing idle, then maximum machine utilisation could be a possible criterion to use. This ensures that the equipment is seen to be 'earning its keep'. Taking this idea further, maximum labour utilisation would also seem to be a criterion. However, it is **making what the customer wants** that keeps a company alive and competitive: that is to say the basis on which the work schedules are created should be simply on time delivery of the finished product to the customer. This implies that if a machine cannot be used to produce a component for which there is a known sale then there is no point in utilising it on unnecessary work, no matter how much the machine initially cost.

As well as the scheduling activity and progress monitoring, the production control system, as part of the factory management information system, also allows collection of other useful data. For example, quality records are obtained, logged, and analysed; labour reporting data such as time spent on particular jobs or time spent on reworking bad parts can be gathered; and the maintenance of stock records on raw materials, WIP, and finished components, sub-assemblies, and products can be achieved. Having considered the elements that comprise the production control function and the problems associated with it, there now follows a brief discussion on some current concepts and techniques associated with the subject.

15.3   Materials Requirements Planning

This technique, in common with other contemporary methods, fully utilises the power of computers to manipulate large amounts of data that would be impractical to handle manually. It was originally developed in the USA during the 1960s by Oliver Wight and George Plossl to overcome the problems associated with the traditional methods of inventory and production control then in use. It has been much refined and developed since then and is used in a variety of forms all over the world. We will first consider the basic materials requirements planning (MRP) technique, then see how the capacity of the facility can be taken into account by incorporating Capacity Requirements Planning or CRP; the concept is then further developed by examining Manufacturing Resource Planning or MRP II.

- MRP is a technique for handling the planning and control of the inventories required to satisfy the dependent demand. In this case the demand for materials and components is dependent on the number of products to be produced; this number is derived from the MPS. Thus the input to an MRP system will be the MPS based on customer demands,

BOMs for the product, and a record of existing inventory (see Figure 15.2). The output from the system will be a report which provides: purchasing with a schedule for buying raw material and components, materials control with a schedule for controlling the inventories, and manufacturing with a schedule for actually making the parts.

- As a simple illustration of the benefits of fine control of inventory, look at Figure 15.3. In (a) we see a chart showing the finished product inventory level for a product which is sold at a constant rate. The product is made in batches, production of a batch begins at point **X** and continues to point **Y**. Due to sales the inventory level decreases at a constant rate represented by the gradient between point **Y** and point **Z**. At **Z** the production of a new batch is started. (b) shows the inventory levels for the purchased materials and parts used to manufacture the product, obtained when using a simple reordering system. In (b) it can be seen that the stock of raw material and bought in parts steadily decreases from point **X**, when production begins, to point **Y**, when production ends. It then remains low until a new order of stock arrives at the factory for the next manufacturing cycle. The order for the raw material and parts is placed at point **A** in (b) and they are actually delivered to the factory at point **B**. The time between **A** and **B** is called the 'lead time', and although this is undesirable there will always be some elapsed time between ordering and receiving goods.

  (b) shows that between times **B** and **Z** the inventory of raw materials and purchased components within the factory remains constantly high until manufacturing begins again. This inventory and the storage space it occupies costs the company money; it therefore follows that costs could be reduced if the time between inventory delivery and inventory use could be reduced. This approaches a minimum when the lead time for the inventory elapses just as production begins; this is shown in (c). Of course the absolute minimum inventory cost will occur if each piece of raw material or purchased part arrives in the factory just as it is actually

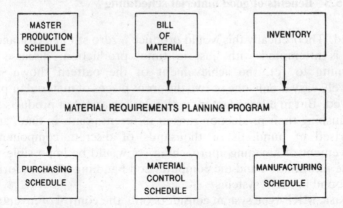

Figure 15.2 Basic MRP system

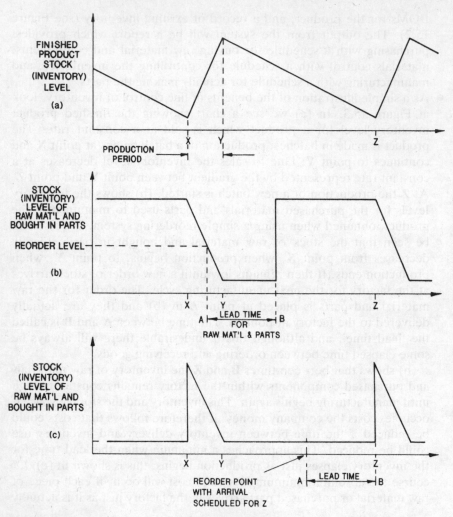

Figure 15.3 Benefits of good material scheduling

needed. Theoretically this would produce a zero storage cost and this is what is attempted with 'just in time' production, discussed later. Returning to (c), the achievement of the pattern shown may be relatively easy if only one or two different pieces of material or parts are involved. But in a large factory with a large variety of products starting and finishing their production runs at different points in time, and each comprised of hundreds or thousands of discrete components, the achievement of anything approaching (c) would be impossible without precise information and the computerised handling of this information, as is found in MRP systems.

• The basic MRP-type system considers only the control of inventory and scheduling of work. However to ensure that the decisions made are valid there must be some account taken of the **capacity** of the manufacturing facility to ensure that the schedules can actually be achieved. This check can be carried out at two levels. Initially a preliminary MPS is made, followed by a rough estimate of whether the capacity available is adequate to achieve the schedule. This is called Rough Cut Capacity Planning, and it basically uses as its input the resources available and equates this with the resources required; existing inventory is not included at this stage. If the capacity is not adequate, and alternatives such as contracting out work are not possible, then the preliminary MPS is adjusted accordingly. Using the **attainable MPS** the MRP program can be used to obtain a schedule. This schedule is then used as an input to the detailed capacity analysis stage; this is Capacity Requirements Planning (CRP). This provides much more detail than the rough cut capacity planning stage. Inputs here are individual machine and work centre capabilities, labour hours available, existing production commitments, existing inventories, and standard times. This information may be accessed from the previously mentioned data base or, if a comprehensive one does not exist, from records and reports from all the relevant departments. The steps in the overall process are shown in simplified form in Figure 15.4; this is sometimes called Closed Loop MRP since the outputs from the capacity planning stages are looped back and used as feedback to the MPSs.

- The three functions of MRP – the control of inventory levels, the specification of priorities, and the determination of detailed capacity requirements – are all immensely useful and assist the company in maximising its efficiency. However as mentioned earlier many large companies have a variety of computer systems in use, e.g. financial, labour reporting, quality reporting, and design. It has also been shown that an MRP system has the ability to make use of the data produced by these systems. Thus if we take the closed loop MRP system and expand it to incorporate the information from all other information generators and users within the factory, we obtain a very powerful tool for actually running the whole factory operation; this tool is MRP II

15.4 Manufacturing Resource Planning

Oliver Wight, one of the designers of MRP, coined the term 'Manufacturing Resource Planning', or MRP II. The term imitated MRP since MRP II is really based on MRP with CRP plus input from other computer systems within the organisation. MRP II broadens the scope of MRP to allow financial and production planning to be carried out at a strategic level by being able to use simulation to answer 'what if' type questions. Various possible scenarios can be created to analyse alternative business strategies, the effect of changes to the MPS, and consideration of the implications of machine breakdowns and material shortages.

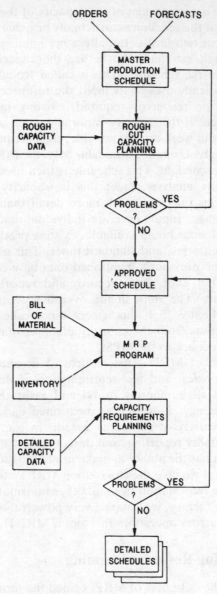

Figure 15.4   Closed loop MRP

- MRP II when fully implemented constitutes a management information system, or MIS, as described earlier. It allows efficient management of such diverse aspects as finance and personnel, consumables and tooling used on the shop floor, and the effects of design changes. It requires a reliable data base from which to draw its data. The old computer adage of 'garbage in – garbage out' is obviously applicable here. The integrity of all the data used by the system must be extremely high since even a small error might have large repercussions – just like the 'butterfly wing' effect in chaos theory where the aerodynamic effects of the flap of a butterfly wing in, say, Australia, can lead to the creation of a hurricane over Florida. This implies a regular and ongoing **sampling audit** for verification of inventory accuracy to ensure that up-to-date information is being used.

- The system should be flexible and easily modified and expanded to cope with changing business conditions at strategic and tactical levels. Modularity of the system is common to allow various modules to be introduced; this allows the system to be built up progressively. Examples of modules might be materials requirements planning, capacity requirements planning, payroll, sales analysis, accounts payable and receivable, financial analysis and forecasting. The system should be able to operate satisfactorily as each module is added; this allows the company to introduce full MRP II in a gradual step-by-step manner. This enables the users of the system to be trained, and it also spreads the system cost. Full systems are very expensive since as well as the hardware and software costs there is the cost of tailoring the software to suit the individual company; however, the expense is usually justified on the basis of estimates of reduced inventory costs, and increased profit. The time to install a full MRP II system may be as long as one–two years depending on the size of the company and the complexity of the operation.
- Finally, adequate training of all personnel is important since once the formal system is installed no informal systems or 'shortage lists' should be necessary; use of these would only corrupt the integrity of the formal system. To facilitate this the system must be 'user friendly' and interactive, i.e. it should be able to be interrogated easily and provide up-to-date information in a clearly presented manner.

15.5 Optimised Production Technology

Optimised production technology (OPT) is an approach to production planning and scheduling developed by a company called Creative Output and based on work by the two founders of the company E. Goldratt and I. Pazgal in the late 1970s and early 1980s. Although used for production scheduling the broad philosophy of OPT is valid for other aspects of manufacturing such as costing, investing, and measuring performance. A major difference between OPT and MRP is that it states that since it is the **constraints** within the manufacturing system that determine what can be produced and when, then the MPS should not be based on the schedule for the end products, but rather the schedule for the **constraining resources**.

- OPT assumes that valid production schedules are essential for any manufacturing system to be successful. It further defines 'success' as how well a company achieves its primary goal, this being the one noted in the introductory chapter of this book, i.e. **to make money**. All other goals are really sub-goals that help the company towards success. The financial criteria chosen to quantify the goal are, Net Profit (NP) which is an absolute measure how much money is made, Return on Investment (ROI) which is a relative measure of how much money has been made in relation to the money invested, and Cash Flow (CF) which is really the life blood of the company. The goal of the company implies that these three measures need to be maximised simultaneously.

- As was mentioned in **3.3(b)** above, when discussing Management by Objectives, goals and objectives have to be translated into concepts that can be easily recognised by those responsible for achieving them. Thus in manufacturing management the efficiency with which the the production scheduling system contributes towards achieving NP, ROI, and CF can be measured by looking at throughput, inventory, and operating expenses. OPT defines these as follows. **Throughput** – the rate at which money is generated by the system through sales; it should be noted that a finished product cannot increase throughput until the day it is sold and paid for. **Inventory** – this is all the money the system has invested in purchasing things which it intends to sell; thus inventory value is the purchase price of materials only. **Operating expenses** – all the money that the system spends in order to turn 'inventory' into 'throughput'; this means that the cost of carrying inventory is part of the operating expense. Thus the goal of the manufacturing manager is now simultaneously to increase throughput and decrease inventory and operating expense. By doing this NP, ROI, and CF will all be simultaneously increased, and money is made.

- Crucial to the OPT concept therefore is the identification of the critical **constraints** of marketing, capacity, batch size, and time. Again, these should all be considered simultaneously. The marketing constraint relates to what should be produced and when, capacity relates to the capacity of the production process or machine, batch size relates to the number of components to be processed at each operation, and time relates to the time consumed in carrying out the work and when it can be done. OPT's principal concern is with the identification of production resources whose capacity is less than or equal to market demands; these are termed '**bottlenecks**'. For example, assume a batch of material to be processed has to pass sequentially through three machines **A**, **B**, and **C**. Further assume that these machines have the capacity to produce 200, 100, and 125 parts per hour respectively. If the production schedule demands 100 parts per hour then operation **B** is the bottleneck. Machine B is also the only machine that can be 100% utilised unless work for other jobs that do not require machine **B** can be scheduled through **A** and **C**. It is these bottleneck operations that OPT says must be identified and used as the basis for creating the production schedule.

15.6 Just in Time manufacture

MRP was initiated in the USA, OPT in Israel, and JIT ('Just in Time') in Japan. 'Just in Time' manufacture is a phrase used to describe the concept of having zero inventory, i.e. having material arrive in the factory just in time to make the product. Basically the JIT philosophy is to achieve **zero** inventory, lead times, set up times, and breakdowns, and to be able to handle batch sizes of one economically. It is therefore used as a material and production control system and as a productivity improvement system. Best operation is obtained where the product variety is relatively limited and most of the parts are repetitively manufactured, e.g a car assembly plant. As in Japan it is also beneficial to have suppliers of parts in close physical proximity to the customer plant. The system has as its goal the production of parts, or purchase of material, in **just enough** quantities to produce one finished product at any one time.

To obtain this JIT style of manufacture a number of enabling concepts and techniqes need to be used. The ones noted here concern; the factory type, the factory layout type, operation set up time, schedule smoothing, and the Kanban production control system.

- **The focused factory concept.** Throughout the first half of the twentieth century the big manufacturing companies had large factories employing many thousands of people in the one plant. These massive manufacturing complexes would usually have many different types of production existing in close proximity, e.g. mass, batch, and jobbing. Since the work produced by these areas was interrelated and the skills and management techniques required by each were very different from each other, control of the factory was very difficult.

  Today the advantages of smaller factories employing fewer people and specialising in one type of activity are recognised. The range of labour skills required is reduced and management can utilise standard methods of control throughout the plant. Also this idea conforms with the modular design philosophy mentioned in **5.11** above, with factories producing common modules that can be used by a range of different customers. These factories are termed 'focused factories' since they focus on one type of product and production system, thus gaining the advantages that accompany specialisation and standardisation. Disc drives for computers are a good example of this; one factory may produce disc drive modules that are bought by a number of different customers for use in the assembly of their own company's computers. Other advantages are that the span of control and the number of hierarchical levels in the management structure are decreased, production and material control becomes simpler, and the productivity of the factory is maximised. A focused factory also generally provides the right conditions for the low variety and repetitive manufacture necessary for JIT.

- **Line and cell layout.** Within the factory a smooth flow of material is absolutely necessary. Thus, of the layouts described in Chapter 14, either a line layout for mass production or a cellular layout formed from using group technology for batch production must be used. The functional type of layout is not suitable as it produces too much WIP, material handling routes that are too long, and difficulties with control etc.

- **Set up times.** It has already been mentioned that JIT manufacture should be able to be used economically for batches of one. This would imply that as this batch quantity is even approached there will be frequent changes in the set up of machine tools. These changeover times from one type of product to another must be minimised by approaches such as the use of reprogrammable equipment, quick change tooling, analysis of the operation by method study techniques, storing all required tooling close to the machine or work area, and use of conveyors to move tooling as well as workpiece material.
- **Smoothing of the master production schedule.** Although the MPS may be constructed for a forward period of up to three months an attempt should be made to smooth this out so that an equal quantity of parts is required each day. This minimises expediting and reduces delays to produce a smooth flow of parts through the factory.
- **Kanban.** The proper coordination of production operations is the foundation upon which the whole JIT concept rests. In conventional systems it is very difficult to schedule the production of work for a factory manufacturing a product that consists of thousands of discrete components. If the production consists of a sequential series of activities then it is very easy for parts to be made at one operation yet not be able to move on to the next in series because of other part shortages, machine breakdowns, or temporary lack of capacity, thus creating a rapid build up of costly WIP inventory. This scheduling and production uses 'inventory pushing'. In JIT the opposite concept is adopted, i.e. parts are not made at one operation until they are requested by the following operation. This 'inventory pulling' method reduces WIP and when applied to bought in components and material removes the need for large in plant stores. The technique is also suited to the repetitive manufacture of a limited variety of products and to a smooth unchanging production schedule.

The method developed in Japan to achieve this inventory pulling is called **Kanban**, the word itself simply meaning 'card' since the system utilises cards to control the flow of work. It operates as follows. First a daily production rate is established and frozen for a period of, say, one month. Although the contributing departments and vendors are informed of this production rate they are not given a detailed production schedule; this is given only to the final assembly department. Components are held in containers in the raw material and finished goods stores of each manufacturing unit. Within each container is a card (Kanban).

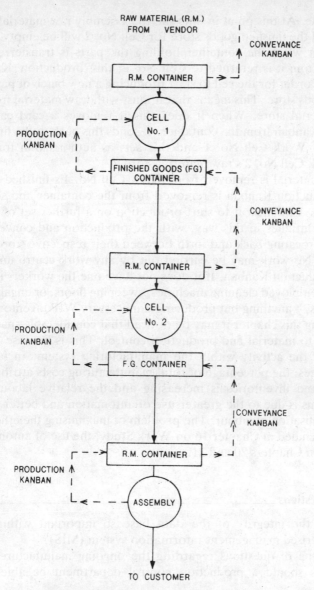

RAW MATERIAL (R.M.)
FROM VENDOR

CONVEYANCE
KANBAN

R.M. CONTAINER

CELL
No. 1

PRODUCTION
KANBAN

FINISHED GOODS (FG)
CONTAINER

CONVEYANCE
KANBAN

R.M. CONTAINER

CELL
No. 2

PRODUCTION
KANBAN

F.G. CONTAINER

CONVEYANCE
KANBAN

R.M. CONTAINER

PRODUCTION
KANBAN

ASSEMBLY

TO CUSTOMER

Figure 15.5 JIT manufacture using Kanban system

The method of operation is shown in simplified form in Figure 15.5. The assembly department initiates the work flow of the system by requesting parts from a supplier work cell or outside vendor; in Figure 15.5 we consider Work Cell No. 2 as the supplier. These parts are held in a container in the supplier's finished goods store and are transferred to the assembly's raw material store. The number of components in the container should be as small as practically possible, say constituting an hour or less of production time. At this point in time the the assembly raw material store will be full and the finished goods store for Cell No. 2 will be empty.

At the point when the container holding the parts is transferred the Kanban card from it is returned to Cell No. 2; this 'production' Kanban constitutes the order for the cell to start producing a new batch of parts for its finished goods store. This means that it must withdraw material from its own raw material store. When it does this it removes a card called a 'conveyance' Kanban from the container. It sends this back to the finished goods store of Work Cell No. 1 and this acts as authorisation for it to replenish Work Cell No. 2's raw material store.

When the material is removed from Work Cell No. 1's finished goods store the production Kanban is removed from the container and sent to Work Cell No. 1 to allow it to start production on a further set of parts. The process continues in this way, with the production and conveyance Kanbans reciprocating back and forth between their respective stores and work centres. No work may be carried out by any work centre unless it receives a production Kanban. If it does not have one the workers in that centre can be employed cleaning machines, sweeping floors, or engaging in Quality Circles, – anything but producing unnecessary WIP inventory!

In concluding this chapter it may be noticed that considerable space has been devoted to material and production control. This is because of the importance of the activity within the manufacturing system. In fact, in modern factories, the percentage of total manufacturing costs attributable to materials and inventories is increasing and the relative labour cost decreasing. This is due to the greater use of automation and better, more efficient, organisation of labour. The problem of maximising the efficiency of labour is included in Chapter 16 on Work Study; the use of automation is considered in Chapters 20 and 21.

Review Questions

1 Why is the integrity of the data base so important within a computerised management information system (MIS)?

2 What type of questions regarding the ongoing manufacture of products should a production control department be able to answer?

3 'Manufacturing schedules may become disrupted for various reasons': list some of the most common disruptive events.

4 What do you understand by the terms, Master Production Schedule (MPS) and Bill of Material (BOM)?

5 The Inventory Turnover Ratio is one indicator as to the health of a company; how is this ratio obtained and why is it useful?

6 What is the purpose of a 'works order'?

7 Progress chasers are still necessary in many factories; what is their function?

8 What is the prime criterion a company should use when creating a work schedule? What other criteria might additionally be used?
9 What are the basic inputs to, and outputs from, an MRP system?
10 What financial benefits might accrue from careful consideration of raw material reorder points?
11 Closed loop MRP systems are necessary to produce practical schedules; why is this so, and how do the closed loop systems operate?
12 How does MRP II differ from closed loop MRP?
13 What is the essential difference in the basis used for constructing the work schedule between MRP and OPT?
14 When using OPT, what are the sub-goals used by manufacturing to ensure they are achieving simultaneous maximisation of net profit, return on investment (ROI), and cash flow?
15 What is the essential philosophy of JIT?
16 How does JIT differ from MRP in the way the flow of inventory is controlled?
17 Under what type of production does JIT manufacture work best?
18 Explain the 'focused factory' concept.
19 Why are set up times of particular importance in a JIT type environment?
20 Explain the operation of the Kanban system.
21 Why is the importance of tight material and production control increasing?

Further Reading

1 'International Handbook of Production Operations Management', Edited by Ray Wild. Published by Cassell Education Ltd. 1989.
2 'Applied Production and Operations Management', by J.R. Evans et al. Published by West, 1987.
3 'Operations Management: Strategy and Analysis', by L.J. Krajewski and L.P. Litzman. Published by Addison Wesley, 1987.
4 'The Principles of Production Control', by J.L. Burbridge. 3rd ed. Published by MacDonald and Evans, 1971.
5 'Manufacturing Resource Planning: Making it Happen', by Thomas F. Wallace. Published by Oliver Wight Publications, 1985.
6 'Materials Requirements Planning', by J. Orlicky. Published by McGraw Hill, 1975.
7 'The Goal – Excellence in Manufacturing', by E.M. Goldratt and E. Fox. Published by North Riverside Press, 1985.

8 'The Haystack Syndrome', by E.M. Goldratt. Published by North Riverside Press, 1990.
9 'MRP, Kanban, or OPT – What's Best?', by R.E. Fox. Published in journal, Production and Inventory Management APICS Vol2 No4, 1982.
10 'Just in Time', by David Hutchins. Published by Gower, 1988.
(N.B. The Further Reading at the end of Chapter 14 is also relevant).

16 Work Study

16.1 Introduction

Although modern manufacturing systems are not as labour intensive as they were some years ago, the efficient use of the human resources of energy, skill, and intelligence remains very important. This applies not only to manufacturing but to all other industries where labour is employed. The techniques used to ensure efficiency and measure human work are the subject of this chapter. They are generally considered under the term 'Work Study'; this is a rational discipline in that the techniques ensure a systematic investigation of any situation examined. The two main components of Work Study are Method Study and Work Measurement.

Generally regarded as the basic tool necessary for increasing productivity, Work Study as a concept has probably been around informally since work began, though the scientific methods really saw the greatest period of improvement around the beginning of the 20th century. These major developments are widely conceded to be mostly attributable to four people, Frederick Winslow Taylor, Frank and Lillian Gilbreth, and Charles Bedeaux.

F.W. Taylor was concerned principally with the **time factor** in work. He realised that the overall times for jobs were of little value as standards of performance and that times for 'elements' of jobs were more appropriate if methods were to be examined. Frank and Lillian Gilbreth applied themselves to the **methods** by which jobs were done. Frank Gilbreth was responsible for defining the 17 fundamental movements by which all manual work could be described. Together the Gilbreths developed the 'principles of motion economy' by which optimum work methods could be developed. Charles Bedeaux was responsible for introducing the concept of **rating**. This is used to determine how actual observed times differ from the times which should be required. Bedeaux attempted to construct an objective system of time study by which work methods could be compared and on which incentive schemes could be based. In Bedeaux's system a common unit was used to describe work on any particular job. This time unit also included rest and relaxation allowances.

Work Study (British terminology), or Motion and Time Study (MTS) (American terminology), remains primarily concerned with discovering the **best ways of doing jobs**, and with establishing **standards** based upon such methods. It also considers the 'human element' and that individuals differ in performance potential. Factors such as sex, age, health, physical size, strength, aptitude, training attitudes, response to motivation, and other psychological factors, have a direct bearing on output. Workers also dislike being treated as machines, therefore careful consideration must always be given by the Work Study practitioner to worker contact and the interrelationship of both to management.

The relationship to each other of Method Study and Work Measurement, and their essential components, are shown in Figure 16.1. Although shown apparently in parallel, it is important to note that Work Measurement should not be carried out unless a proper Method Study has already been undertaken. If this is not the case then it is quite possible that

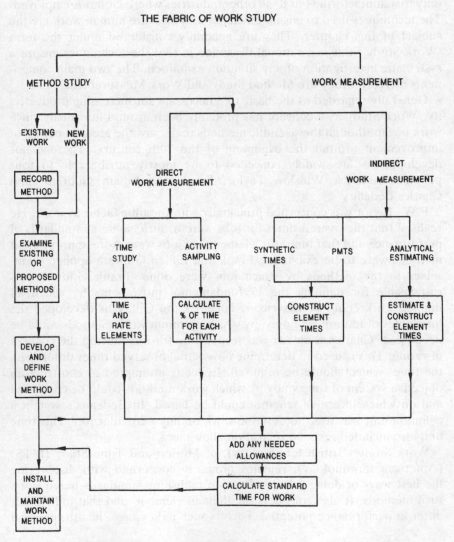

Figure 16.1   The fabric of work study

erroneous times will be applied to jobs, thus making all subsequent costing and estimating exercises worthless.

16.2 Method Study

Method Study involves recording and analysing all factors relating to the manner in which a piece of work is carried out. The work may either be existing or proposed. The aim of the study is to make the job easier, maximise efficiency, and minimise costs.

Method Study therefore provides a thorough, step by step approach to achieve the goal of the 'best' way of carrying out a work task. The procedure to be followed is widely recognised as that now shown, and although the steps apply to a job already in existence the general concept also applies when initiating a completely new job.

- **1st Step** *Select* the work to be studied.
- **2nd Step** *Record* the existing work method and all relevant data.
- **3rd Step** *Examine* the record obtained in the previous step.
- **4th Step** *Develop* the most efficient or optimum method of work.
- **5th Step** *Install* this method and adopt as standard practice.
- **6th Step** *Maintain* this practice.

These six steps are now considered in more detail.

(a) Select

To ensure maximum benefits from the effort put into the Method Study exercise, it is important to select appropriate situations. For example, there would be little benefit in conducting an extensive work study investigation in a situation where there was very little manual work and production was dependent mostly on the design of machines. Similarly if the manual work was temporary or for any reason expected to be short lived, it may be impractical to carry out a full work study. However situations where the duration of the work is short but repetitive, e.g. maintenance work, will be suitable for work study. The economic results of the study, whether they are increases in output, reductions in scrap, improved safety, reductions in training time, or better use of equipment or labour, should always outweigh the cost of the investigation. This maximum cost benefit should not only be sought after by looking at direct costs, but should also be looked for in the **indirect cost** areas. The human factor should always be considered; thus not only areas where there is apparent wasted time should be studied, but also areas where there is high labour turnover and absenteeism.

(b) Record

There are many recording techniques available for the modern work study practitioner. Factors that influence the choice of technique are the rapidity with which the record has to be taken, and the amount of detail desired. When first investigating a situation, one of the broad rapid techniques might be used, but as the necessity for examining the detail of the job becomes more important a more time consuming technique may be necessary. Tools such as video cameras are ideal for making permanent records of work for future analysis. Integral digital time displays assist the practitioner to determine durations of work elements. High speed and time lapse photography can also be used.

To change the visual record of a job into a form suitable for further analysis, techniques using charts and tables are used. Examples of some industrial problems and their relevant recording techniques are now briefly described.

- The techniques associated with **plant layout**, such as Flow and String Diagrams, Templates, 3 Dimensional Models, and Travel Charts. Some of these are illustrated in Figure 16.2. They are suitable where large scale movements and areas are being examined without requiring detail to be analysed.
- When the activities of one or more **men and/or machines** are being examined, then Multiple Activity Charts, Activity Analysis, or Man and Machine Charts can be used (see Figure 16.3).
- **Process Charts.** There are many variations of these, e.g. the Outline Process Chart, the Flow Process Chart, and the Two Handed or Operator Process Chart. These are the most common of the method study recording techniques, the sequence of events being represented by a series of symbols which are basically the same for each type of chart (see Figure 16.4).
- Where **long or irregular work cycle times** occur, and where studies of groups of workers are required, then Memo-motion Photography or

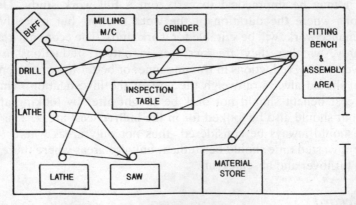

Figure 16.2   Templates, pins, and string used to plot the movements of a toolmaker in a small machine shop

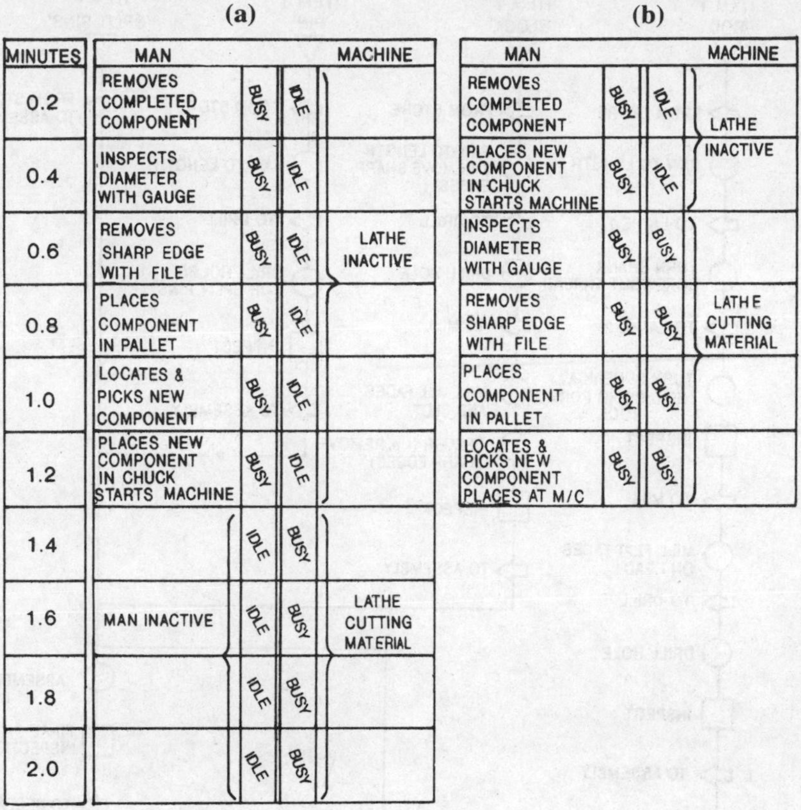

(a)

MINUTES	MAN			MACHINE
0.2	REMOVES COMPLETED COMPONENT	BUSY	IDLE	
0.4	INSPECTS DIAMETER WITH GAUGE	BUSY	IDLE	
0.6	REMOVES SHARP EDGE WITH FILE	BUSY	IDLE	LATHE INACTIVE
0.8	PLACES COMPONENT IN PALLET	BUSY	IDLE	
1.0	LOCATES & PICKS NEW COMPONENT	BUSY	IDLE	
1.2	PLACES NEW COMPONENT IN CHUCK STARTS MACHINE	BUSY	IDLE	
1.4		IDLE	BUSY	
1.6	MAN INACTIVE	IDLE	BUSY	LATHE CUTTING MATERIAL
1.8		IDLE	BUSY	
2.0		IDLE	BUSY	

(b)

MAN			MACHINE
REMOVES COMPLETED COMPONENT	BUSY	IDLE	LATHE INACTIVE
PLACES NEW COMPONENT IN CHUCK STARTS MACHINE	BUSY	IDLE	
INSPECTS DIAMETER WITH GAUGE	BUSY	BUSY	
REMOVES SHARP EDGE WITH FILE	BUSY	BUSY	LATHE CUTTING MATERIAL
PLACES COMPONENT IN PALLET	BUSY	BUSY	
LOCATES & PICKS NEW COMPONENT PLACES AT M/C	BUSY	BUSY	

Figure 16.3 **Man and machine activity chart: analysis of the method in (a) allows the more efficient method in (b) to be constructed; an amount of rest time would have to be given to the man at appropriate intervals**

Work Sampling may be employed. In this technique movements are recorded using a video or cine camera designed to take pictures at longer than normal intervals. It is therefore a method of **sampling**, as activities are observed at regular intervals rather than continuously. When the recording is played back at normal viewing speed, patterns of movement unnoticed in real time often become apparent. Passenger movements in airports and rail stations, the movement of ships in rivers, and the flow of customers in large shops or post offices are typical applications of this technique.

- **Cyclegraphs** are recordings of the paths followed by moving objects obtained by attaching light sources to the objects and photographing the scene using a time exposure camera. The effect is observed by taking a time exposure at night of a city traffic junction. The paths taken by the vehicles using the junction are observed as continuous paths of light on the final print. This effect is utilised by attaching lights to operators'

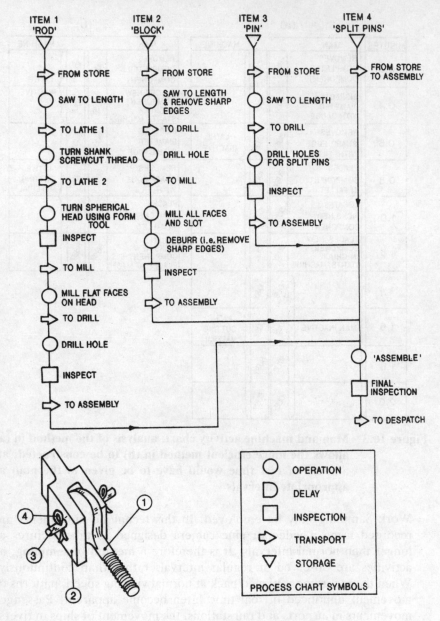

Figure 16.4 Clevis assembly: process chart

wrists and observing the paths travelled during a particular piece of work, e.g. folding a shirt in the garment trade. By rapidly pulsing the lights on and off for specific periods the resulting traces will show up as broken lines. These are known as Chronocyclegraphs, and by counting the pulses the length of time for each movement can be found.

- When the work movements to be recorded are so **complex** or **fast** that the other techniques are inadequate, then SIMO (Simultaneous Motion Cycle) Charts are often used (see Figure 16.5). To facilitate the detailed study required, the fundamental movements which together constitute all types of manual work are classified and identified by the use of 'Therbligs', (the name 'Gilbreth' reversed, see Figure 16.6). The use of these 'Therbligs' in conjunction with SIMO Charts is referred to as 'Micromotion Study'. By using high speed video or cine techniques, complex and intricate finger and hand movements can be filmed and observed in slow motion, or frame by frame, and from these observations the SIMO chart can be drawn.

(c) Examine

In this stage, the information recorded is constructively analysed by systematically questioning each activity observed. Assuming that here we are concerned with a manufacturing task, then the recorded activities will fall naturally into two main categories: (1) Those in which the material or workpiece is being worked upon, moved, or examined, and (2) those in which it is not touched, as it is either in storage or at a standstill owing to a delay. The activities in category (1) may be further subdivided into three groups: (i) 'Make Ready' activities, (ii) 'Do' operations, and (iii) 'Put Away' activities. Thus while 'Make Ready' and 'Put Away' activities can be represented by 'transport' and 'inspection' symbols, 'Do' operations can be represented only by 'operation' symbols. The object of the exercise must be to achieve as high a proportion of 'Do' operations as possible, since these are the only ones that carry the product forward in its progress from raw material to completed product. These are 'productive' activities and 'add value' to the product; all others, however necessary, may be considered as 'non-productive'.

There is a well established questioning sequence which examines the purpose, place, sequence, person, and means of the activities. This has the aim of eliminating, combining, rearranging, or simplifying them. The questioning technique can be set out as follows.

- **WHAT** is done? Why is it done? What else might be done? What should be done?
- **WHERE** is it done? Why is it done there? Where else might it be done? Where should it be done?
- **WHEN** is it done? Why is it done then? When might it be done? When should it be done?

- **WHO** does it? Why does that person do it? Who else might do it? Who should do it?
- **HOW** is it done? Why is it done that way? How else might it be done? How should it be done?

These questions are the basis of a successful method study, and should be asked, in sequence, **every time** a study is undertaken.

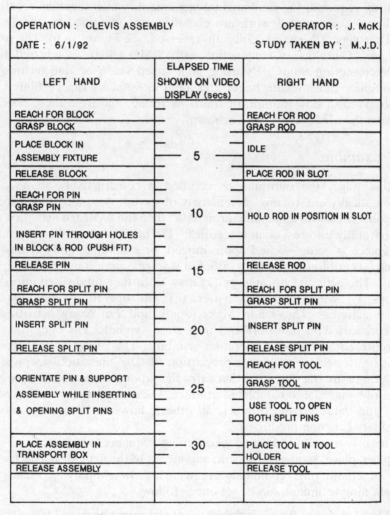

LEFT HAND	ELAPSED TIME SHOWN ON VIDEO DISPLAY (secs)	RIGHT HAND
OPERATION : CLEVIS ASSEMBLY		OPERATOR : J. McK.
DATE : 6/1/92		STUDY TAKEN BY : M.J.D.
REACH FOR BLOCK		REACH FOR ROD
GRASP BLOCK		GRASP ROD
PLACE BLOCK IN ASSEMBLY FIXTURE	5	IDLE
RELEASE BLOCK		PLACE ROD IN SLOT
REACH FOR PIN		
GRASP PIN	10	HOLD ROD IN POSITION IN SLOT
INSERT PIN THROUGH HOLES IN BLOCK & ROD (PUSH FIT)		
RELEASE PIN	15	RELEASE ROD
REACH FOR SPLIT PIN		REACH FOR SPLIT PIN
GRASP SPLIT PIN		GRASP SPLIT PIN
INSERT SPLIT PIN	20	INSERT SPLIT PIN
RELEASE SPLIT PIN		RELEASE SPLIT PIN
		REACH FOR TOOL
ORIENTATE PIN & SUPPORT ASSEMBLY WHILE INSERTING & OPENING SPLIT PINS	25	GRASP TOOL
		USE TOOL TO OPEN BOTH SPLIT PINS
PLACE ASSEMBLY IN TRANSPORT BOX	30	PLACE TOOL IN TOOL HOLDER
RELEASE ASSEMBLY		RELEASE TOOL

Figure 16.5   SIMO (simultaneous motion) chart for 'assemble' operation in Figure 16.4

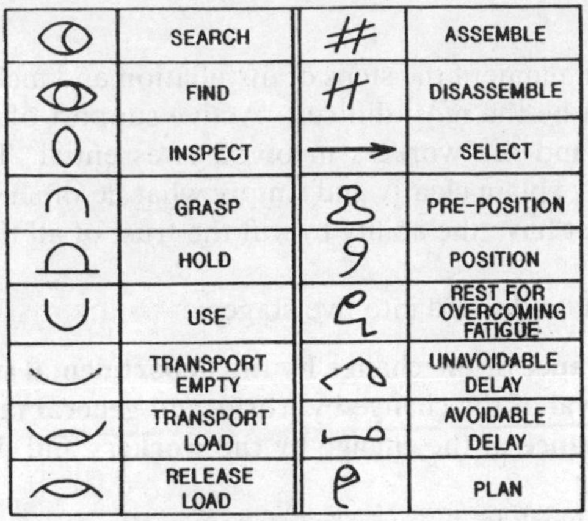

◎	SEARCH	#	ASSEMBLE
◉	FIND	H	DISASSEMBLE
○	INSPECT	→	SELECT
∩	GRASP	⌇	PRE-POSITION
⌂	HOLD	9	POSITION
∪	USE	⌇	REST FOR OVERCOMING FATIGUE
◡	TRANSPORT EMPTY	⌃	UNAVOIDABLE DELAY
◠	TRANSPORT LOAD	⌐○	AVOIDABLE DELAY
◠	RELEASE LOAD	℮	PLAN

Figure 16.6 'Therbligs'

(d) Develop

Just as in the 'Examine' stage, there is a methodology for implementing the 'Develop' stage. It consists of four steps: eliminate, combine, sequence, and simplify. It is applied to each separate activity in the job, i.e. each meaningful group of work elements.

The total **elimination** of unnecessary actions is obviously the first and most important step towards an improved work method. These redundant activities can arise due to changes that have occurred in the product or bad work practices that have gradually been adopted. Once the possibilities of elimination have been exhausted the **combination** of actions must be considered, e.g. parting off a component in a lathe and facing the following component simultaneously. Next, the opportunities for changing the **sequence** of actions must be examined, with a view to subsequent further elimination and combination. Finally, if additional improvements are still required then the more costly **simplification** of the activity may be necessary. This can be done by reducing the number of operations and optimising delays, storage, and transportation.

To facilitate simplification, the 'Principles of Motion Economy' can be used. These are rules, originally formulated by the Gilbreths, that help ensure that a job will be carried out with the minimum of effort and the maximum achievement. Essentially, they state that work should be designed so that movements are minimised, simultaneous and symmetrical (e.g. two hands working in unison at an assembly task), rhythmical, habitual, and continuous.

Once the steps of elimination, combination, sequencing, and simplification have been completed, some additional experimental and practical adjustments will probably have to be made. When the practitioner is finally satisfied with the method the last two steps can be implemented.

(e) Install

Due to the human element the steps of installation and maintenance of the method can often be the most difficult. Active support of the practitioner by management and the workers involved is essential. The practitioner should be able to explain clearly and simply what he or she is trying to do, and he or she must have the ability to win the trust of all those affected by the study.

Installation can be divided into five stages:

- Gaining **acceptance** of the change by the **departmental supervision**.
- Gaining **approval** of the change by **works** and **general management**.
- Gaining **acceptance** of the change by the **workers** and their **representatives**.
- **Retraining** the workers to operate the new methods.
- Maintaining **close contact** with the progress of the job until satisfied that it is running as intended.

(f) Maintain

To ensure the new method is maintained it should be monitored by the work study department. This is because human nature is such that a drift away from the method will probably occur if there is no check. Many disputes over time standards arise because the method being followed is not the one for which the time was specified: foreign elements have crept in. If the method is properly maintained, this cannot happen. If it is found that an improvement can be made in the method, then this should be incorporated officially, a new specification drawn up and new time standards set.

Now that the most appropriate method for doing the work has been established, it is necessary to establish the times required to complete the work elements.

16.3　Work Measurement

Work Measurement is the application of one or more of a number of techniques used to determine the time required to carry out a specific piece of work. The principal work measurement techniques are as follows.

- First, there are the **direct** methods of Time Study and Activity Sampling. In these techniques, the work study practitioner directly observes the work being measured.
- Secondly there are the **indirect** techniques which can be implemented without the physical presence of the work. These are: Synthesis, Predetermined Motion Time Systems (PMTS), Estimating, Analytical Estimating, and Comparative Estimating.

The measurement of work is not just desirable but is absolutely essential for both the planning and the control of production. Without work measurement data, it would not be possible to determine what output can be achieved from existing facilities, quote delivery dates and costs, measure the efficiency with which the existing equipment or labour is being used, operate incentive schemes, use standard costs for budget control, or determine what extra equipment and labour will be required to achieve a certain output. It may be said that where method study is the principal technique for reducing work by eliminating unnecessary movement, work measurement is concerned with investigating, reducing, and subsequently eliminating **ineffective time**. It should be recognised that method study and work measurement are complementary to each other, one aiding the other to attain the desired organisational goal.

(a) Basic procedure

As with Method Study so also with Work Measurement a systematic approach is necessary. The steps of this are as follows:

- *Select* the work to be measured.
- *Define* the methods to be used. Break the job down into elements. Critically examine the recorded data, and the detailed breakdown. This will ensure that the most effective method is being used, and that unproductive elements are separated from those that are productive.
- *Measure* the quantity of work involved in each element, in terms of time, using the appropriate direct or indirect work measurement technique.
- *Obtain* the total work content plus any allowances.
- *Establish* the standard time for the operation, which will include the time allowances to cover relaxation, personal needs, contingencies, etc. It must be ensured that the series of activities and methods for which the time has been compiled, is defined. Finally the time will be issued as **standard** for the activities and methods specified.

(b) The standard unit of work

The concept of using a unit for measuring work is founded on the notion that the human work content of many different types of job can be expressed quantitively in terms of a common unit. Some terms used by work study practitioners in connection with this concept are given below

- *Standard Performance*: This is the rate of output which qualified workers will naturally achieve without overexertion as an average over the working day or shift, provided they adhere to the specified method and provided they are motivated to apply themselves to their work.
- *Standard Unit of Work*: This is composed of both work and relaxation,

the proportion of each varying with the nature of the job. In the British scale, 60 of these units would be created in one hour of unrestricted work at standard performance (standard performance is explained under the section 'rating' below).

- *Work Content*: This comprises the basic time and relaxation allowance plus any other allowance for additional work.
- *Standard Time*: This is the total time that should be required to complete a job at the Standard Performance. This will be composed of the total Work Content plus allowances, plus any other time that may have to be added for delays and other unoccupied time.

Thus, because the unit of work represents a specific amount of work plus allowances, it has no absolute time value. However since it must be given some relevant dimension, a figure of 60 units of work per hour at Standard Performance may be adopted. These units are called 'standard minutes', so that if one unit of work is carried out at standard performance then it will be completed in one minute of time.

(c) Time Study

Time Study is normally required when there has been a change in the nature of an existing job, or a new job has been started: remember that Time Study should not be attempted until a proper Method Study has been carried out. Time Study is a work measurement technique used for recording the times taken, and the rates of working, under specified conditions. It can then be used to establish the Standard Time for the job.

Time scales used when conducting the study may be seconds or decimal fractions of a minute, the latter being the more common and precise. Other time scales, e.g. decimal hours, can be used but only in special circumstances.

Traditional Time Study equipment includes a stopwatch, a time study board and forms, and a calculator. Today's practitioner can add to this electronic recording boards with integral digital stopwatches (see Figure 16.7), and video equipment with precise digital clocks playing back on the video recording to enable precise separation of work elements and establishment of their times.

- *Rating*: The real object of work measurement and time study is to determine not how long it actually takes to perform a job, but how long it **should take**. It is therefore necessary to compare the actual rate of working of the operator with a standard rate of working, so that the observed times can be converted into basic times, i.e. the time required to carry out an element of work at Standard Performance. This performance rating is the comparison of an actual rate of working against a defined concept of a standard rate of working. This standard rate corresponds to the rate that workers would naturally adopt when working, assuming that they know and follow the specified method, and

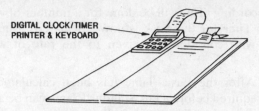

DIGITAL CLOCK/TIMER
PRINTER & KEYBOARD

Figure 16.7 Electronic recording board

that they are motivated. On the British Standard performance scale, standard rating is equal to 100. Thus if a worker was rated at 50 he would be working at half the expected standard rate and the time observed would be halved by the practitioner and used as the basis for further calculations. Some practical examples help to create an idea of a standard rate. For example, British Standard 100 is considered to be equivalent to a walking speed of a constant 4 miles per hour, or to dealing a pack of cards into four hands in 22.5 secs. We therefore have a scale with the standard rate at 100 and complete inactivity at 0. The practitioner is trained to be able to recognise the conditions of the standard rate of working, and to assess to the nearest 5 points the degree to which a worker's observed speed and effectiveness varies from the 100 standard. The procedure in which the practitioner carries out this assessment, while recording the observed time, is known as **rating**. The rating is used to find the basic time for a job or an element as shown below:

Basic Time = (Observed Time) × (Rating/Standard Rating), e.g. if an operator is rated as being very fast and is allocated a rate of 125, and the observed time was 0.2 minutes, then the Basic Time = $0.2 \times (125/100) = 0.25$ minutes.

- *Procedure*: The procedure for implementing a Time Study is shown below.

  1 First everyone that will be involved in the study should be **notified**; they should be told the reasons for the study and how it will be conducted.
  2 **Collect** and **record** all relevant information. The conditions under which the work being studied is being done must be recorded; this will provide useful information for the future when estimating times for similar jobs. The record will also be useful if disputes arise at a future date concerning the time established for the job, for example the method of the tooling may have changed from that in the initial study.
  3 The work being studied is divided by the practitioner into **elements**. This facilitates the analysis of the work.
  4 The elements are **timed** using a stopwatch or from the digital clock on

a video recording. This will be done for a number of work cycles.

5 The **Basic Time** for the work is now calculated, using the gathered data and with consideration given to the rate of working of the operator.

- *Allowances*: After the Basic Time has been calculated there is one further step required before a fair Standard Time can be allocated to the job. This involves the allocation of allowances to compensate for the operator fatigue, delays and interruptions that are unavoidable in every work situation. These allowances are composed of the following elements. (a) A **Relaxation Allowance** to allow the operator to attend to personal needs and to recover physically and mentally from exertion; this may add 10–30% onto the Basic Time, depending on the nature of the work. (b) **Unoccupied Time**, which occurs when the worker is unavoidably prevented from doing productive work; this should obviously be minimised if it cannot be eliminated. (c) A **Contingency Allowance** to cater for occasional interruptions, and adjustments to equipment, etc.

It is now possible to devise the Standard Time for the job, which, as mentioned previously, is the total time in which a job should be completed at standard performance; it is shown schematically in Figure 16.8.

The foregoing sections have shown how it is possible to use Method Study to determine the most efficient way of carrying out a job, and then to use the Work Measurement technique of Time Study to establish the Work Content and Standard Time.

There are other techniques used in Work Measurement. Another direct measurement technique is **Activity Sampling**. Here the work is not

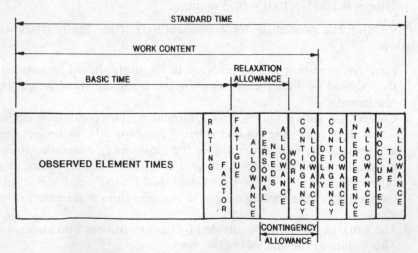

Figure 16.8   Build up of standard time

measured using a timepiece; it is sampled. Activity Sampling is used in situations where it is desired to measure the work of large amounts of people, say in an office. Over a period of time a large number of individual observations are made. At each observation a record is made of what is happening at that moment, and the percentage of the observations recorded for a particular activity is taken as representing the actual time during which that activity occurs.

Indirect Work Study techniques include Estimating and Predetermined Motion Time Systems (PMTS). Estimating is a technique used for determining the time required to carry out a job by using knowledge and experience of similar work done previously. PMTS is a technique that uses times previously established for basic human motions. This synthetic method allows times for jobs to be built up even before the work has started. There are many varieties, but one of the most popular is Methods Time Measurement or MTM which has been developed at three levels. MTM 1 is the most accurate and detailed; it will also take the longest time to implement. MTM 2 is used where the detail of MTM 1 would economically prevent its use. MTM 3 is intended to be used in work situations where at the expense of some accuracy times are required as soon as possible.

16.4 Work Study as a service to management

To keep any system in control, e.g. an aircraft in flight, an industrial robot, or a factory, **feedback** on the state of that system is required to the system controller. In an industrial organisation the controller is management. Feedback from the shop floor is therefore necessary in the form of quantitive and objective information that can be used to monitor the effectiveness of the labour force. Work Study is the means whereby this information can be produced. The information can also be used by the management for **forward planning**, e.g. to estimate how many man hours will be required to satisfy future customer orders, and to estimate future costs.

(a) Labour control and reporting

The information coming from the shop floor to the management must be sufficiently detailed to identify specific areas of poor performance, unproductive work, or excessive cost. How this is done is best understood by following the process through progressively.'

- Throughout the day the shop floor workers will spend their time either directly on work for which there is a standard time, or on diverted work such as repairs, or on waiting for material or equipment. Only the direct work is productive and adds value to the product. The operators will record, by writing on report sheets or keying into a computer, how they have spent their time each day. This record will show what products and operations were worked on, how many were produced, and how much time was spent on direct and diverted work. It should be noted at this stage that although terminology varies between countries and even factories, the concepts remain the same. Indirect workers such as labourers will also submit reports detailing how they have occupied their time during the day.

- From these reports the data processing department will be able to compare the times the operator spent on specific operations against their previously devised standard times. It will then be possible to provide management with information on the performance of the direct operators, the performance of a department excluding the indirect workers, and the overall performance which will include all the workers on the shop floor. A breakdown of how the unproductive time was spent will also be supplied; this will enable problem areas to be pinpointed.
- The performance figures will probably be supplied in a similar manner to the following:

  OPERATOR PERFORMANCE = (Total Standard Times produced/ Total time spent directly producing work for which there is a Standard Time) × 100

  DEPARTMENTAL PERFORMANCE = (Total Standard Times produced/Total attendance time minus time spent on indirect work) × 100

  OVERALL PERFORMANCE = (Total Standard Times produced/ Total attendance time) × 100

  A short example illustrates the use of these indices.
  During a 5 day week a department reports the following information.

Total standard time produced	= 450 hours
Time spent on direct work	= 500 hours
Time spent on indirect work	= 80 hours
Number of operators	= 20
Number of hours available per day	= 7.5

  Calculate the overall performance, the departmental performance, and the operator performance.
  Total Attendance Time = 7.5 × 5 × 20 = 750 hours.
  Therefore:

		%
Overall Performance	= (450/750) × 100	= 60
Departmental Performance	= (450/(750 − 80)) × 100	= 67
Operator Performance	= (450/500) × 100	= 90

- A detailed report on performance is therefore provided to management and supervision. This would normally be supplied to shop floor supervision, e.g. foremen, on a daily basis on the day following that on which the work took place; this will enable prompt corrective action to be taken. The supervisor will receive a full report on each individual operator, and a composite report for the performance and time utilisation for his department as a whole. Reports will probably be summarised on a weekly basis for line management, and factory management will probably receive weekly or monthly reports as appropriate. Action should be taken immediately on the reports, e.g. low operator performance needs prompt investigation, as also do instances of high rework or other diverted time. Communicating productivity data to the shop floor is also important. Charts showing various performances for each department can be erected in prominent locations. Charts of quality, e.g. reject rates and costs of scrap, are also useful.

(b) Payment by Results (PBR)

In this type of payment system the workforce is usually paid a basic rate plus an amount proportional to performance. This may be on an individual or a group basis. It is apparent that the type of performance indices shown in section (a) provide useful data on which to base such systems.

(c) Planning

Since Work study provides a data base of information on how long specific operations should take, the total time required to build products, and the methods and equipment required to produce specific quantities of a product, it can be used to predict **future** manpower and capacity requirements based on anticipated product sales volumes. The total standard times involved in a product can simply be multiplied by the anticipated weekly production target to find the total standard times required per week. This can then be related to the the overall performance the factory or departments are achieving to arrive at a total time required for the anticipated production volumes. Knowing the total man hours available per week, this total time can then be used to determine the required manpower.

Review Questions

1. What is 'Work Study', and what is its purpose?
2. What is the principal aim of method study?
3. Explain the **six** basic steps that must be taken to complete a successful method study.
4. What types of work are particularly suitable for method study?
5. Describe **three** techniques used in method study for recording how work is done.
6. What type of questions should be asked when examining the record of how work is done?

7 Discuss the **four** steps necessary for developing a new work method.

8 What personal characteristics should the person responsible for implementing a new work method possess?

9 What is the principal aim of work measurement?

10 Work measurement can be carried out directly or indirectly. Discuss the important differences between these two methods, and name **two** techniques associated with each.

11 Discuss the important uses of the information obtained from work measurement.

12 Describe the basic procedure for carrying out a work measurement exercise.

13 Explain the concept of the 'standard unit of work'.

14 What is the purpose of 'rating' in a Time Study exercise?

15 List the steps to be followed in conducting a Time Study exercise.

16 What is meant by the 'Standard Time' for a job? State what elements contribute to its value.

17 What is PMTS, and under what conditions might it be used in preference to Time Study?

18 Discuss how the information obtained from Work Study can be used to analyse the performance of workers on the factory floor.

19 Discuss how Work Study can provide information useful for planning future operations.

Further Reading

1 'Productivity Measurement and Improvement' by Lawrence S. Aft. Published by Prentice-Hall Inc., 1992.

2 'Introduction to Work Study' Published by the International Labour Office (ILO), 1979.

3 'Work Study' by R.M. Currie. Published by Pitman Publishing Corporation, 1967.

4 'Productivity and Quality Improvement' by J.A. Edosomwan. Published by IFS Publications, 1988.

5 'How to Improve Human Performance' by Thomas K. Connellan. Published by Harper and Row, 1978.

6 'Reinventing the Factor' by Roy L. Harmone and L.D. Peterson. Published by Free Press Publishing, 1990.

7 'Handbook of Industrial Engineering'. Edited by G. Salvendy. 2nd Edition. Published by Wiley, 1992.

8 'Work Study' (monthly journal) Published by Sawell Publications.

17 Manufacturing accounting

17.1 Introduction

(a) The purpose of accounting in manufacturing

The financial aspects of manufacturing cover such a broad range of activities that to explain them in one chapter is impossible. What is therefore attempted here is an outline of some of the financial features involved in running a manufacturing organisation. Most of what is discussed comes under the classification of 'Management Accounting', a term widely used to describe those accounting procedures used as an aid to management.

Within a manufacturing company the finance department utilises accounting information for three basic purposes. The first is **decision making**; here, information on probable costs and increases or decreases in profits associated with alternative courses of action are analysed. Secondly, information is provided to assist with efficient **control** of the manufacturing system; included here will be the preparation of budgets and the subsequent analysis of costs incurred against those planned. Finally the information is used for **reporting** and **recording**; this involves the compilation and updating of financial records and reports, not only for management, but also for shareholders who will be interested in profit and loss accounts, etc. and for the government who will need the information for tax purposes. We will limit our concern here to the decision making and control activities.

(b) The composition of manufacturing costs

Figure 17.1 shows the approximate distribution of costs within a manufacturing organisation, and how they contribute to the selling price of the finished product. The ratios of each cost will vary considerably between companies. For example, a company producing complex products incorporating state of the art technology might have a higher proportion of the selling price composed of research, development and engineering costs. A company trying to sell in a highly competitive consumer goods market might spend a higher proportion on sales, advertising, and marketing. Within the manufacturing costs themselves it can be seen why much attention is given to the control of **inventory**: parts and materials can constitute around 50% of the total. This again will vary depending on the

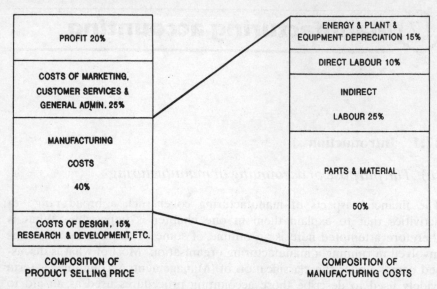

Figure 17.1   Distribution of costs for a manufacturing company

type of production; for example, compare the mass production of steel bolts to the one off construction of a communications satellite. In the former, material costs would be high and labour costs low; in the latter, the ratio is reversed. Two types of labour are shown in Figure 17.1. Direct labour is composed of the cost of those who work directly on the product, for example machine operators and component assemblers. Indirect labour is composed of the cost of all those whose work indirectly contributes to the production of an individual product, for example labourers, material handlers, and storemen.

From what has been said it is apparent that **manufacturing costs** are essentially composed of the three main elements with which this book is concerned, i.e. **manpower**, **machines**, and **materials**. These costs represent resources that must be used **effectively** and **efficiently** if the company is to survive. The effectiveness of their use is easily determined by observing results, i.e. was the product produced at the right quality, at the right time and at the right cost? However, the efficiency with which the resources were used involves some calculation, and the resulting figure is termed **productivity.**

(c) Productivity

The efficiency of any system is represented by the ratio of the value of outputs from the system to the value of inputs to the system. For example, the efficiency of a machine is measured by the value of the energy output to the value of the energy input; this can never be greater than unity – otherwise 'perpetual motion' would be possible. In the case of our manufacturing system we do not use units of energy but units of money, whether they be pounds, dollars, yen, or ecu. Thus the efficiency, or productivity, of our system is represented by the ratio:

$$\text{Overall Productivity} = \frac{\text{Total output in monetary terms}}{\text{Total input in monetary terms}}$$

This measure of efficiency differs from that of the previously mentioned machine in that the **overall** productivity must be greater than unity. That is, in the manufacturing system money is being used to create even more money, while in the engine energy is being 'lost' due to friction, heat, etc. in the process of producing work. The output from the manufacturing system is the market value of the goods produced; the input is the total cost of the manufacturing operation. The overall productivity ratio is the true indicator of the company's efficiency, but it is difficult to calculate in absolute terms. In practice, it is often split into three different efficiency measures by looking at how the three major manufacturing resources are utilised. Thus we get Labour Productivity, Capital Productivity, and Material Productivity. These ratios are usually used for comparison purposes, e.g. a company might compare its labour productivity from one year to the next, or make a comparison with similar companies in other countries to determine its own competitiveness.

Labour productivity is the one most often quoted by the media. This is the ratio of the value of goods produced to the cost of the labour used to produce the goods. The value and costs would be taken over a specific period of time, e.g. per hour, day, or year. Capital productivity compares the value of goods produced with the cost of the machines, equipment, and buildings used to produce the goods. Material productivity compares the value of goods produced with the costs of the materials and energy required to produce the goods. It can be seen, therefore, that if a company invests in a great deal of automated equipment it will require less labour, and therefore its labour productivity will increase. However, due to its investment in capital equipment its capital productivity may have decreased. Also if the company discards old, inefficient equipment and purchases new machines it might find its capital productivity decreased in the short term, but its material productivity increased due to less scrap being produced and more efficient use of energy, e.g. electricity, gas, etc. It is for these reasons that although the individual ratios are good for comparison purposes it is their **net result**, i.e. the overall company productivity, that is of prime importance.

Now that we have considered the way in which costs can be used to indicate the health of a manufacturing company, let us take a different perspective and consider how the company might use cost information for the purposes mentioned earlier, i.e. decision making and control.

17.2 Costs for decision making

(a) Risk

Before embarking on any project involving the outlay of money it should be acknowledged that there will be some amount of risk present. This risk can either be ignored, which is extremely unwise, or analysed in depth mathematically, which is extremely difficult. Here, we are simply acknowledging its presence. The 'riskiness' of a project is determined by the possible variation in the future returns from the investment. For example, it is generally riskier to invest money in helping a new manufacturing company start up than it is to deposit the money in a reputable bank. The investor will therefore look for a much higher potential return on the investment if it is put into the manufacturing company.

It is worth noting that in times of recession the risk is greatly increased, thus making it more unlikely that the 'capitalist' with money to use will look to industry as a profitable place to invest. This is because most people are 'risk averters' rather than 'risk seekers'. This creates a downward economic spiral difficult to change since, as we noted in Chapter 1, manufacturing industry is the main **creator** of wealth and therefore a major aid for pulling out of recession. Only a few risk seeking entrepreneurs will go for the industrial investment; the potential rewards are high, but so also is the risk.

A distinction can be made between 'risk' and 'uncertainty'. Uncertainty occurs where there is insufficient evidence to evaluate the riskiness of a situation. Risk, however, occurs when enough information is known about a situation to allow a probability of achieving certain results from the investment to be estimated. Naturally the further into the future one looks the more uncertainty there will be, and so the riskiness will also increase. This will be evidenced by a broader range of possible outcomes from the investment. This concept is shown in Figure 17.2 in the form of probability distributions. In Figure 17.2 the broader the distribution, the greater the standard deviation, and hence the greater the risk. A tight distribution signifies low risk.

Risk analysis is not normally carried out by the management accountant, or an engineering manager trying to appraise a potential capital investment, but the concept of the presence of risk and the possibility of including it rationally in decision making should be remembered.

(b) The 'make or buy' decision

A manufactured product is made up of various parts and sub-assemblies; these may either be bought in as completed items or made in the factory. The decision on whether to make or buy the product will be determined by a number of factors, for example a comparison between the cost of making the item using existing equipment and labour compared with

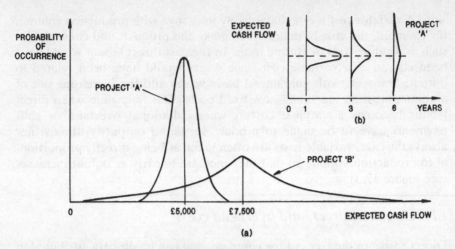

(a) SHOWS PROBABILITY OF OCCURRENCE OF EXPECTED CASH FLOW FOR TO PROJECTS 'A' & 'B'
THERE IS A HIGH PROBABILITY 'A' WILL ACHIEVE THE £5,000 CASH FLOW EXPECTED WHEREAS
PROJECT 'B' COULD ACHIEVE A HIGHER CASH FLOW BUT IS MUCH 'RISKIER!

(b) SHOWS HOW 'RISKINESS' OF PROJECTS INCREASES WITH TIME.

Figure 17.2   'Risk' represented by probability curves

buying it. If the company has the capacity, the proper equipment, and
appropriately skilled labour, then it will probably be better to make it on
site. However, if the plant is already working to capacity a comparison of
costs should be made including the costs of possibly renting or purchasing
more space, buying more equipment, and hiring and training new labour.
In this case it may be found that it is cheaper to purchase, say sub-
assemblies for a PC computer, from a local sub-contractor or from a
country abroad where there are cheaper labour rates. The supplier should
be reliable and fully committed to company quality standards, and more
than one source per item is often necessary to avoid suppliers developing
monopolies. The economics of the 'focused factory' mentioned earlier in
the book will also be important here, i.e. control of all aspects of
manufacture including costs is easier in smaller factories with a focused
activity.

(c) Fixed and variable costs

To enable costs to be used for decision making it is helpful to classify them
under the terms 'fixed' and 'variable' costs. The conditions under which the
classification is made should be understood since changing conditions can
alter the nature of the costs; for example, a cost which is 'fixed' in the short
term may become 'variable' in the long term. A **fixed cost** is one that is
unlikely to change with production volume: for example, depreciation on a
machine, the cost of special equipment, or the cost of shop floor supervi-

sion. A **variable cost** is one that is likely to change with production volume: for example, the cost of materials to make the product, and consumables such as welding rods or cutting tools. In the past direct labour would have been classed as a variable cost since wages would have been related to output; however, with guaranteed basic wages and the increasing use of automation these are really now fixed costs. The only time when direct labour becomes a variable cost is when additional overtime or shift payments have to be made to produce increased output. Although not always the case, variable costs are often taken as being directly proportional to production volume so that they increase linearly as output increases (see Figure 17.3).

(d) Direct, indirect, and overhead costs

Direct costs are the costs of the company that can be directly attributed to the manufacture of a specific product; they comprise direct material and direct labour costs. **Direct material** is all the material purchased and used in the finished product, including any scrap incurred. This cost is the cost of material required per unit multiplied by the number of units produced. **Direct labour** is all the labour used to work directly on the product. This cost is the direct worker's wage rate multiplied by the time spent working on the product. This cost therefore comprises both variable and fixed cost.

Indirect costs are those costs that can be only indirectly attributed to the manufacture of a specific product. They are also called overhead costs.

Overhead costs include rent and rates, the cost of heating, lighting, office staff, general labourers, storemen, computer systems, telephones, fire insurance, management, maintenance, and depreciation on machines and other equipment, etc. Although most are fixed costs in that they exist irrespective of the quantity of product manufactured, there are also some that vary depending on volume produced.

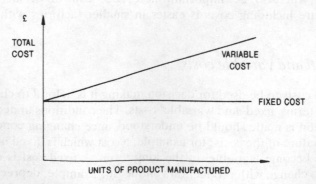

Figure 17.3   Fixed and variable costs

(e) Break even charts

Although subject to certain limitations, the simplest and clearest method of illustrating the relationship between cost, volume, and profit, is the break even chart. A typical break even chart is shown in Figure 17.4. It demonstrates that for a particular project, with the associated fixed and variable costs shown, the company must obtain sales to allow $X\%$ of capacity output to be achieved before a profit can be made. Charts like these can be constructed to assist the company in deciding the level of investment it should make in manufacturing facilities in order to satisfy perceived market needs.

The break even chart can also be used to decide which project or process to adopt for the manufacture of an anticipated annual component volume. Fixed and variable costs for each alternative should be determined and a chart similar to that shown in Figure 17.5 constructed. This will indicate which one to choose for a specific production volume (cf. Figure 14.4).

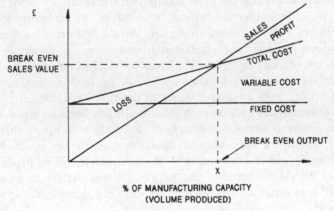

Figure 17.4   Cost–volume–profit break even chart

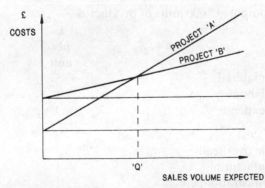

Figure 17.5   Break even chart for project selection: if sales volume expected is less than 'Q', then project 'A' should be adopted; if greater, then project 'B' should be selected

(f) Marginal and differential costing

This type of costing is suited to decision making, it is also known as 'direct' costing. At any given production volume, the marginal cost is the amount by which the total costs are changed if the production volume is increased or decreased by one unit. Fixed costs are therefore excluded from the calculation. It is basically a simple technique and relates costs to production volume rather than time. It is therefore useful for providing information for decisions related to the volume and type of production to be adopted.

The marginal cost of one product, at a specific level of output, is shown in Figure 17.6. It is shown as the sum of the variable costs per unit. If the company produces a number of products, then the difference between their marginal costs and their selling prices is called their **contribution** towards fixed costs and profit. Assuming the company has ample capacity (remember the significance of bottlenecks noted in section 15.5.), then the effect of additional orders for each product on the company profit is shown in Figure 17.7. This information can be used by the company to decide which products it should concentrate on, should resources be scarce, i.e. which products provide the highest contribution.

The concept of using differences in costs for decision making is also used in **differential** costing. Differential costs allow projects, or any alternative courses of action, to be ranked in order of desirability. Differential costing does not concern itself with costs that have already been incurred, or costs that are common to all courses of action, but only with future differential costs. For example, supposing a decision has to be made between producing components by process A in department B, or process X in department Y. Assuming that the processes and departments are well established, and other factors such as process capability and capacity are

Level of output = 1000 units of product A

Cost source	£ per unit	
Direct material	5	
Direct labour	1	
Direct expense	2	
'Prime' cost	8	
Variable overheads:		
Manufacturing	1	
Administration, etc.	1	
Marginal cost	10	(cost/unit)

Figure 17.6   Marginal cost of a project

Product	Selling price per unit	Marginal cost/unit	'Contribution' per unit	Additional units	Additional profit
A	15	10	5	500	2500
B	12	8	4	800	3200
C	16	11	5	400	2000
D	14	12	2	600	1200
					8900

Figure 17.7   Effect of increased production on a company's profit

equal, then the decision should simply be based on the future differential costs for each process. This would include the anticipated costs of materials, labour, process energy and consumable costs. Any other costs should be ignored for the purposes of decision making.

17.3   Investment apppraisal

(a) The payback period

Assume a company has the opportunity to invest in either a single project that will generate a cash inflow, or select one project from a number of alternatives. One of the simplest and quickest ways of gauging the project's worth or comparing alternative projects is to use the **payback** method. In this method of appraisal, the time required to recoup the cost of the initial investment is calculated. This involves estimating the cash inflows resulting from the project, for each year of the project's life. These cash inflows could be increases in cash flows or simply estimates of net cost savings as a result of the investment. When the cumulative sum of these inflows equals the original investment, then the **payback period** is said to have elapsed. The calculation is shown in Figure 17.8 for three alternative projects. As can be seen, it does show quickly that the investment can be recouped from either project **A** or **B** in 3 years, but it does not take into account the fact that project **B** gives returns much earlier than project **A**. Also project **C** is potentially very profitable in later years but using the payback method this project would be discarded in favour of projects with a shorter payback period. The method is therefore only a rough guide, and really suitable only where high risk makes future anticipated cash flows uncertain.

(b) Decision criteria

A major problem of the payback method is that it gives no indication or comparison of the profitability of projects. Since the company is likely to be in business to make a profit this must be its prime criterion. Now the

Investment	Project A 60 000	Project B 60 000	Project C 60 000
Year Cash flows			
1	10 000	40 000	10 000
2	20 000	15 000	10 000
3	30 000	5 000	20 000
4	–	–	20 000
5	–	–	20 000
6	–	–	20 000
Payback period	3yrs	3yrs	4yrs

Figure 17.8   Problem with the 'payback' method of investment appraisal

company's funds that it uses for investment have a cost associated with them, e.g. if it borrows money it will have to pay interest on the loan. If the company was to fund itself by loans that cost 15% and made profits of only 10%, then it would soon be out of business! This means that the company should not invest in projects that produce less than a 15% return on investment. In this case, the company therefore has a **marginal investment rate** of 15%, and any investment should produce a return at least as high as this. Thus an investment appraisal method must be found that takes into account this marginal investment rate, sometimes called the **minimum profitability criterion**. This will ensure that the company does not enter into investments or projects that are unprofitable.

A full investment appraisal calculation should therefore take into account: (i) the marginal investment rate, (ii) the amount of capital to be tied up in the project, (iii) the net cash flows resulting from the investment, and (iv) the timing of these cash flows. It should use this information to produce a **net present value** (NPV) for the project. If produced for a number of projects, their NPVs may then be compared to determine the one that is the most attractive. Calculating NPVs involves using the **Discounted Cash Flow** (DCF) technique.

(c) Discounted cash flow (DCF)

In DCF all inflows and outflows of cash are related to a base year, usually called 'year 0'. Cash flows in years after the base year are transformed into their present value by 'discounting' them. This is done because it is recognised that one unit of money today is worth more than the same unit one year hence. This can be explained by assuming that if we have £10 today; we can either spend it on goods or services worth £10 or invest it in, say, a bank account. If it is invested the money will, in one year's time, be worth £10 plus the interest earned, e.g. at 10% it would be worth £11. Conversely, £11 income one year in the future is worth only £10 today. In fact, if offered the choice we would accept the £10 now as there is some risk involved in obtaining the £11 in the future. For the purposes of investment appraisal calculations, the rate at which anticipated future cash flows will be discounted will be the company's marginal rate of return. This rate will be determined by current interest rates and the company's business risk and financial structure. The actual discounting calculation is quite simple since tables of 'discount factors' for different rates are readily available. The present value of the future cash flows is found by multiplying them by the appropriate discount factor from the tables.

The NPV for the project is found by taking the present value of expected cash inflows and deducting the present value of expected cash outflows. For example, if the present value of expected returns from the project is £15,000, and the net cost of the project is £10,000, then the net present value will be £5,000.

As an example, assume that a company is considering the purchase of a machine tool in year 0 at a total capital cost of £140,000. Because of the cost of spares and other costs directly associated with the project the company will require an additional £10,000 working capital which will become available to the company again at the end of the project's life. There are no cash inflows expected to be received from the project until the end of year 1 when they should be £40,000. In each following year the cash inflows should be £70,000; £60,000; £40,000; and £30,000. These cash inflows will probably have been estimated by using the previously mentioned marginal costing techniques. The tax system at the time will allow the machine to be depreciated at 25% of the reducing balance each year; this means that the government recognises that, due to use and increasing obsolescence, the value of the company's machine is decreasing every year. The amount of this depreciation is called the Capital Allowance and the government permits this to be used as a tax allowance, thus reducing the amount of tax to be paid in any year. For the duration of the project we will assume the corporation tax on profits to be 35%. The company is aided in its financing of the project by the availability of £20,000 in grants towards the purchase of the machine tool. The marginal investment rate of the company is 16%. The question the company must now ask itself is: what is the NPV of this project?

Figure 17.9 shows the calculation made to determine this NPV. First the net cash investment made in year zero is calculated; this is the sum of the costs to the company less any incentives, grants, etc. available. Column (1) of the calculation shows the year in which the cash flows take place; column (2) shows the increase in cash inflows expected by the end of each year; column (3) shows the tax to be paid on the previous year's profits; column (4) shows the capital allowances or depreciation allowed on the machine; column (5) shows the tax saved because of these allowances (it is assumed the company is paying tax from profits on other investments allowing tax to be saved in year 1); column (6) shows the net cash flow at the end of that year; column (7) shows the discount factors found from tables used to

Net Cash Investment (in year 0);

		£
New machine tool		140,000
Additional working capital required		10,000
		150,000
Subtract value of grant		20,000
		130,000

Cash Flows;

(1) Year	(2) Cash inflows	(3) Tax (35%)	(4) Capital allowances	(5) Tax saved	(6) Cash flow	(7) PV factor	(8) PV
1	40 000	–	35 000	12 250	52 250	0.862	45 040
2	70 000	14 000	26 250	9 188	65 188	0.743	48 434
3	60 000	24 500	19 688	6 890	42 390	0.641	27 136
4	40 000	21 000	14 766	5 168	24 168	0.552	13 340
5	30 000	14 000	11 174	3 876	19 876	0.476	9 460
6		10 500			(10 500)	0.410	(4 306)

Total 139 104

Residual values;

Machine tool	32 200
Working capital	10 000
	43,000

multiplied by PV of 0.410 =   17 712

Grand total   156 816

Net Present Value = £156 816 − £130 000
                  = £26 816

Figure 17.9   Investment appraisal using DCF

discount the future cash flows to a year 0 value; and column (8) shows the resulting present value of the cash flows. When the project is finished the machinery and other equipment used will still retain some second hand value. This contributes to what is called the 'residual value' of the project. This expected residual value is discounted at the appropriate rate and added to the total of the present value column; this provides the grand total of the NPV of the investment. The NPV is now calculated as described earlier. In this example the NPV of the project is £26,816. It should be noted that although this type of calculation seems very precise it is in fact based on estimates. It should therefore be used more as an indication of the quality of the investment rather than a precise quantitive analysis.

If the NPV of the project is greater than zero then the project will be profitable, and a worthwhile investment. If a number of alternative projects are evaluated in this way then their NPVs can be compared and the most attractive selected.

17.4 Cost analysis and control

(a) Absorption costing

In order to determine the cost of producing a product we need to take into account not just the direct costs but also the overhead costs. That is, the selling price of the product must be such that the overhead costs are recouped, otherwise the company will be unprofitable. The problem is to find a realistic way to apportion the costs to the product. This must be done carefully since serious problems have resulted in the past with accountants allocating costs to departments and eventually to products that make them artificially expensive.

In absorption costing **cost centres** are identified within the factory. These centres are seen to be composed of **cost elements**, i.e. material cost, labour cost, and expenses. These elements may themselves be composed of direct and indirect costs. The direct costs are incurred within the cost centre, and are therefore easily allocated. However, the indirect costs are incurred both within the centre and apportioned from the overhead costs incurred by the manufacturing operation in general, e.g. the costs of maintenance, rent and rates, administration, finance and power. The most important aspect of absorption costing is the selection of **appropriate** criteria on which to base the apportionment of costs. An example of how overhead cost might be allocated, i.e 'absorbed' by a cost centre, is shown in Figure 17.10. This indicates how an hourly overhead rate can be obtained for a department. Should the number of operating hours change the overhead rate would have to be recognised as being flexible and be adjusted accordingly.

The 'Chunky Chip' and 'Crunchy Crisp' Factory

Cost	£	Classification
Potatoes	140 000	Direct material
Operator wages	15 000	Direct labour
Maintenance wages	16 000	Indirect labour
Rent and rates	100 000	Indirect expense
Electricity	200 000	Indirect expense

Notes:
Floor area of chip making machine department = $15m^2$
Floor area of crisp making machine department = $35m^2$

Breakdowns on chip machine = 300 hours
Breakdowns on crisp machine = 500 hours
Chip machine power rating = 100 kW
Crisp machine power rating = 300 kW
Production time for chip machine = 36 000 hours
Production time for crisp machine = 36 000 hours

Overhead analysis:

Expense	Basis	Total	Chip department	Crisp department
Maintenance wages	Breakdown time	16 000	6 000	10 000
Rent and rates	Floor area	100 000	30 000	70 000
Electricity	Machine power rating	200 000	50 000	150 000
	Totals		86 000	230 000

∴ Overhead rate for chip machine department = 86 000/36 000 = £2.4/hr

Overhead rate for crisp machine department = 230 000/36 000 = £6.4/hr

Figure 17.10   Allocation of costs to cost centres (chip and crisp departments) using absorption costing

(b) Historical and standard costs

In a manufacturing environment costs may be either **historical** or **standard**. In an historical costing system the costs are analysed after operations have occurred whereas in a standard system the costs are estimated or calculated before the costs have been incurred. Both systems are usually employed together, i.e. standard costs are prepared, then after the event they are compared with the actual historical costs incurred. The difference between the the actual and the standard cost is called the **variance**, which may be 'favourable' or 'adverse'; these variances can be analysed to 'home in' on problem areas. It should be noted that these variances need to be made available to managers almost immediately. It is no use trying to control an operation by using information that is provided perhaps a week or even a month after the event.

17.5 Conclusion

This chapter has highlighted some of the financial aspects of the running of a manufacturing operation. The subject is extremely wide and only a sample of the most relevant aspects has been presented, e.g. the different ways in which a company might finance its operation and the construction of annual reports and statements to shareholders have not been included.

However this does not imply that accounting techniques and practices are unimportant to the manufacturing engineer or manager. In fact manufacturing engineers and managers should be thoroughly familiar with the techniques and practices to ensure that the company accountants allocate costs realistically and make sound decisions based on **real** costs, and not on those that have been artificially derived.

Decisions concerning the manufacturing operation should not be made for the expediency of producing short term cost savings or creating cost reports that simply look good. The long term outlook should always be adopted to ensure growth and ongoing profitability. Poor costing practices can lead to work being unnecessarily sent out to sub-contractors because their labour rates seem lower, when in fact most of the company's costs are in overheads which will increase if sub-contracting is adopted due to the extra administration involved. In the worst case, the accountants might prevent a product being manufactured because it is thought that it would be too expensive to make in comparison to a similar one supplied by a competitor. This could be disastrous for a company since if it is not making products, it is not creating wealth and so it will simply fade away, whereas the competitor will have no competition and will thrive! While costs must be measured, controlled, and used with finesse, it must always be remembered that a manufacturing company is in business to make money by making **products**!

Review Questions

1 For what **three** basic purposes does the financial department in a manufacturing organisation use accounting information?
2 Discuss the distribution of costs within a manufacturing company.
3 What is 'productivity', and how might it be measured?
4 Why is it important to consider risk when making an investment decision?
5 What factors should be considered when making the 'make or buy' decision?
6 What are 'fixed' and 'variable' costs?
7 What are 'direct' and 'indirect' costs?
8 What is a 'break even chart', and how might it be used?
9 Why is marginal costing a useful accounting technique for manufacturing companies?
10 What is the 'payback' method of investment appraisal, when might it be used, and what are its deficiencies?
11 What is a company's 'marginal investment rate'?
12 What factors should be included in a full investment appraisal calculation?
13 In DCF, why are future cash flows discounted back to year 0?
14 What is the significance of the net present value (NPV) of a project?

15 What is 'depreciation'?
16 What is 'absorption costing', and what is its purpose?
17 What are 'historical' and 'standard' costs, and how are they used?
18 Present a reasoned argument stating why a manufacturing manager should be familiar with management accounting practices.

Further Reading

1 'Costing: An Introduction' by Colin Drury. Published by Chapman and Hall, 2nd edition 1990.
2 'The Essence of Management Accounting' by Leslie Chadwick. Published by Prentice-Hall, 1991.
3 'Management and Cost Accounting' by Colin Drury. Published by Chapman and Hall, 1991.
4 'Cost and Management Accounting' by Roger Hussey. Published by Macmillan, 1989.
5 'Relevance Lost; The Rise and Fall of Cost Accounting', by R.S. Kaplan. Published by Harvard Business Press, 1988.

18 Quality

18.1 Introduction

(a) Defining Quality

What is 'Quality'? We often use the word 'quality' to imply that something is the 'best' of its kind, e.g. a Rolls Royce is a quality car or a luxury cruise liner provides a quality holiday, but this is a rather vague use of the term. Consider that today we, as consumers, all expect that whatever we spend our money on should be of 'good quality'. This means that the producer of the goods, or supplier of the services, has to find a more specific definition of 'quality' against which the standard of the product can be measured. Now, since we cannot all afford Rolls Royces or luxury cruises, yet we say we expect our purchases to be of good quality, we probably mean that we perceive a product or service to be of good quality if it provides what we believe to be **good value for money**. Thus we see that quality defines how well the product conforms to our expectations. In turn, our expectations are based on how much we paid for the item and the specification supplied by the provider. We, the customer, have the responsibility of deciding how much money we are willing to pay, and the supplier has the responsibility of ensuring that whatever is supplied conforms to specification. We can therefore, for our purposes, define quality as **how well a supplied product or service conforms to the customers' expectations and the suppliers' specifications**. Implied in this definition is the principle that the customers' expectations are related to **price** and the suppliers' specifications related to **cost**.

This concept suggests that there is a certain minimum level of quality acceptable; this is usually embodied in consumer protection regulations approved by government. For example, in the UK any goods which are sold must be 'fit for the purpose intended'. Many countries now have 'product liability' laws which hold the designer and manufacturer of goods responsible for their safe design and construction.

The purpose of this chapter is to examine how a manufacturing company can ensure that it produces good quality products, i.e. products that conform to specification, are fit to use for the purpose intended by the consumer, and are safe. We will therefore be considering the philosophy of 'total quality' and some of its aspects and elements.

(b) Total quality management

There are two terms in common usage today implying the same concept; these are Total Quality Management (TQM) and Total Quality Control (TQC). The latter term, TQC, was originally developed by an American, A.V. Feigenbaum, and the concepts embodied in his book *Total Quality Control* (1961). These concepts and techniques were introduced to Japan and became an essential part of the Japanese way of thinking in their manufacturing industry. Today TQC is an integral component in their 'Just In Time' (JIT) manufacturing systems. More recently the term 'Total Quality Management' has become popular in the USA and Europe; it means the same thing as TQC but since the word 'control' has been replaced by 'management' the phrase does convey more of the breadth of the subject.

The environment of TQM is shown in Figure 18.1. An awareness of 'Quality' should permeate the whole structure of the manufacturing organisation. Senior management have the responsibility of taking the lead in establishing a climate which fosters a dedication to quality.

An important aspect is that to ensure quality standards are being met some sort of **quantitive** or **qualitative targets** have to be set. These need to be quantifiable so that actual performance can be compared against that planned. Methods such as 'management by objectives', noted in Chapter 3, can be used to assist in this. For example, market research people must ensure they make quality judgements regarding the price and specification criteria acceptable to the consumer; feedback on this will be available only when consumer reports on the product begin to return from the market. The design department must create a quality design based on conformance to marketing, manufacturing, material, and cost constraints. Vendors, selected by the company, must be fully aware of the company's expectations regarding conformance to stated specifications. This applies whether the vendor is supplying components that must conform to dimensional specifications, material that must conform to metallurgical specifications, or a service such as cleaning, catering, or transport, which will have their own specifications determined after consultation between the vendor and the company.

Figure 18.1 also makes it apparent that within the manufacturing operation itself physical work areas can be considered for allocation of quality targets to be achieved, these being monitored, reported, and analysed by techniques such as statistical quality control (SQC). However, to ensure that the personnel within these areas are capable of achieving the targets, appropriate training must be given to operators and supervisors, etc. Once the product is packed and despatched the company must still consider the quality of transport used to deliver the product, specifications regarding the handling and storage of the goods must be created and adherence to these ensured. With some products, the installation may also be part of the supplier's liability; again specifications and customers'

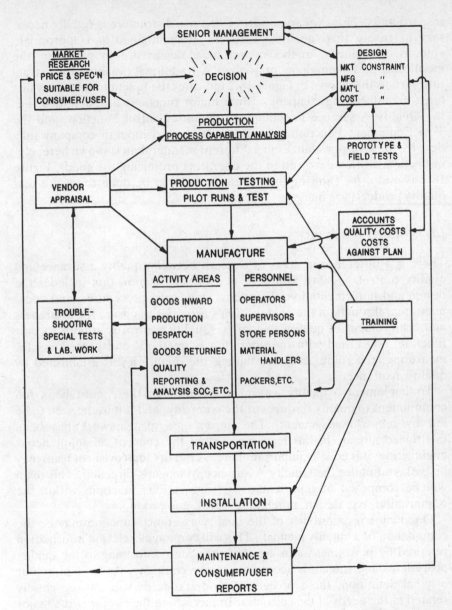

Figure 18.1 The 'total quality' environment for a manufacturing company

expectations need consideration. The customer closes the loop by feeding back information directly through complaints or returned questionnaires, or indirectly by increasing or decreasing purchases.

18.2 Organisation for quality

Throughout the company the responsibility for quality is everyone's responsibility. However some sort of organised structure is usually necessary to ensure that 'quality awareness' is maintained and appropriate systems, techniques, methods, and technologies are in place for the monitoring and maintaining of quality. A traditional organisational structure such as that shown in Figure 18.2 indicates the functions necessary in a large manufacturing company. Three major functions are identified, i.e. the Quality Assurance Function, the Quality Control Function, and the Test Equipment Function. Therefore although a modern company may devolve these responsibilities in a different manner than is shown here, e.g. inspection is often devolved to the operators producing the goods, Figure 18.2 is useful for showing the necessary tasks to be done to ensure that quality products are made.

(a) Quality assurance

There is a difference in areas of concern between quality **assurance** and quality **control**. Quality assurance is a broad function that includes the design and implementation of systems, standards, procedures, and documentation throughout the organisation's activities to ensure the awareness and achievement of quality standards. Quality control is a more specific function, concerned with the operation of methods and procedures for measuring, recording, and maintaining the quality levels established by quality assurance.

To implement a quality assurance programme there must be a full commitment to quality throughout the company, and it must be seen to be led by senior management. The importance of teamwork has been mentioned already in this text, e.g. within the concept of simultaneous engineering; it is equally important here. A **quality improvement team** may be gathered under the Quality Assurance Manager's direction. This team will be composed of representatives from various functions within the organisation, e.g. design, purchasing, sales, and production.

One major responsibility of the quality assurance function may be the compilation of a 'quality manual'. This will contain all relevant information required by personnel to ensure that they are conforming to the quality procedures and standards acceptable to the company. As implied by our original definition, these procedures and standards will also be closely related to the needs of the customer. In fact where the customer is a major client, such as the armed forces or a nuclear power generating company, then it is the client who often specifies the procedures and standards to be followed. The client will also wish to carry out on site inspections of the manufacturer's premises to verify this conformance.

International standards have been developed to indicate which companies have in place quality practices that are of a specific grade. For example the International Standards Office ISO 9000, equivalent to the British Standard BS 5750, lays down for manufacturers and suppliers exactly what is required of a total quality system. By adopting this

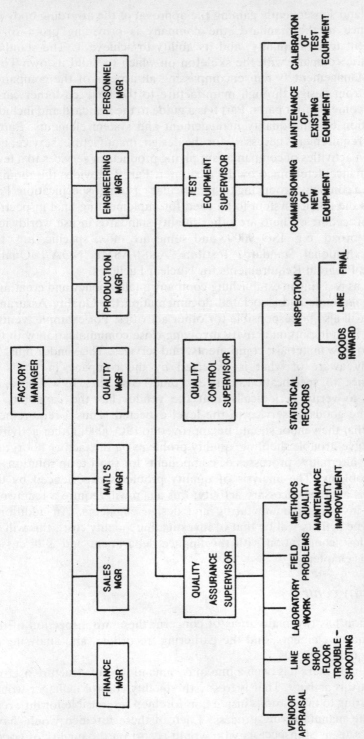

Figure 18.2 Traditional structure of a quality department

standard, and subsequently gaining the approval of the awarding body for conformance to the standard, the company is providing proof of its commitment to total quality, and its ability to achieve it. The standard provides the company with the skeleton on which to build its own Total Quality Management system encompassing all aspects of the company's activities from design through manufacture to the final 'customer care'. ISO 9000 comes in four parts. Part 0 is a guide to the standard and includes a description of total quality management and system elements. Part 1 states the requirements necessary for the design, manufacture, service, and installation activities of companies supplying products or services to a level of performance determined by the customer. Part 2 provides the requirements for a company producing to a particular customer specification. Part 3 specifies the quality system to be used for implementing final inspection and test procedures. There are other quality standards in use worldwide; some are broad, e.g. ISO 9000, and some are more specific, e.g. the American National Standards Institute ANSI/ASME NQA.1 Quality Assurance Program Requirements for Nuclear Facilities.

As well as assisting in establishing company quality policy and creating a quality programme and associated documentation the Quality Assurance Manager will also be responsible for other activities. For example 'vendor appraisal' is an important activity involving close communication with the suppliers of raw materials, components, and services. The vendor must be made fully aware of what is expected by the company in terms of conformance to specification, delivery time, cost, etc. It will also be necessary to verify periodically that the vendor has the capability to produce the goods or service to the level expected. Thus a requirement might be that the vendor should be approved to ISO 9000. Other activities might involve 'trouble shooting' quality problems on the factory floor, e.g. suggesting alternative processes or components for short term solutions to urgent problems. The analysis of quality problems experienced by the customer is another necessary activity; this again will require a teamwork approach involving manufacturing and design engineers. An additional analysis type activity will be that of investigating 'quality cost'; this will be done in close cooperation with the finance department and is discussed later in this chapter.

(b) Quality control

This function has two main areas of concern; these are inspection of the product and its elements, and the gathering, recording, and analysing of statistical quality records.

Traditionally there has been a line of command type of structure used to implement this activity. That is to say the quality control manager would have reporting to him various inspection foremen responsible for different parts of the manufacturing process. Each of these foremen would have control of a team of inspectors who would report on the quality of goods being processed in their area. For example, an inspection team of inspectors and foreman would be responsible for checking vendor's material arriving into the factory; this would be called 'goods inward' inspection. Each department or work cell on the shop floor would have its own inspection team, and teams of inspectors would be employed at the final assembly, packing, and despatch areas. These inspection teams would require thorough knowledge of the product and production processes to allow them to make intelligent decisions on the acceptability or otherwise of what was being inspected.

However in today's manufacturing environment the armies of inspectors and a tiered quality control hierarchy are often no longer required. The increasing use of automated machinery with built in inspection systems is one reason for this. Automated machines can incorporate automatic inspection devices that can check the product quality at each operation before the component leaves the machine; this allows 100% inspection and the potential for 'zero defects'. Another feature of many factories is that where manual operations are still required, the responsibility for inspecting the product quality is devolved to the operators themselves. In this case the operators are also responsible for the rectification of their own work, thus giving them a greater incentive to produce good parts first time. Finally the JIT manufacturing concept means that when material arrives at a work centre it is assumed to be already inspected and ready for use. This means that the 'goods inward' inspection function is much reduced and a greater responsibility put onto the vendor to ensure that his product arrives on time and already quality approved for immediate use. This principle has developed to such an extent that, although absolute perfection is not attainable, the number of defects supplied should now be measured in parts per million rather than parts per thousand.

The second activity in this function is that of Statistical Quality Control (SQC). Although it was mentioned that automated equipment can be used to achieve 100% inspection, this is by no means widespread or indeed possible in every situation. There is therefore still a need for statistical sampling of incoming goods to the factory, work in process, and finished products. Even where automation is used, data can be gathered by electronic means and analysed by computer to monitor quality and rapidly identify any worrying trends that may eventually lead to bad products. This function of gathering, recording, and analysing the information produced by the inspection function remains important. The results of the analyses should be communicated rapidly to all relevant areas of the factory to enable any necessary action(s) to be taken. It is worth noting that in fully automated systems this communication may be virtually instantaneous with the records and analyses being able to be viewed by interrogating a networked computer terminal. Owing to its importance we will consider SQC a little more fully later.

(c) Test equipment

The third function within the quality organisation is that of the acquisition and maintenance of all the quality 'hardware' needed for inspection and testing throughout the manufacturing process. The actual equipment involved will be dependent on the type of product being produced and the manufacturing processes used. For example, simple handheld gauges may be required to inspect a manual machining operation, an artificial vision system may be used for inspecting component positions on a PCB, or a complex environmental chamber might be used for testing the performance of a product under various humidity and temperature conditions. All inspection and test equipment has to be regularly and systematically checked for wear and drift and appropriate adjustments made.

18.3   The cost of quality

(a) The importance of quality costs

It has been mentioned more than once in this text that the primary goal of a manufacturing company is to make money. This means that to express ideas and events in the lowest common denominator, monetary terms have to be used. Therefore we try to find some way of identifying the costs of quality, just as we identify costs associated with raw material or labour. There is of course an ethical limit to this. For example no-one should attempt to compare the cost of an added safety feature with the probable costs of lawsuits for injuries resulting from the absence of that feature. Safety is a quality cost that has to be accepted; some manufacturers will spend more on this than others, but the cost will ultimately be reflected in the selling price of the finished product.

The determination of quality costs will provide the company with additional information for control purposes and allow the identification of opportunities for reducing these costs. This is important since the cost of quality is increasing due to the growth in products that require high reliability and longer working lives, e.g. in the nuclear, chemical, aerospace, and off shore oil industries. Consumers also expect high performance and reliability from their cars, washing machines, and audio and video equipment. This means higher precision in the mechanical elements from which they are constructed and hence higher quality costs to enable this precision to be achieved. Our reliance in industrialised countries on technology is now considerable, e.g. drawing money from an automatic cash dispenser at the bank, buying a frozen meal from a refrigerated display, driving home in a car, then using a microwave cooker to heat the meal before watching a video, an entire sequence of events that relies on millions of manufactured parts operating according to specification.

(b) Classifying quality costs

We briefly consider two ways of grouping quality costs. The older method is to split costs into **prevention, appraisal**, and **defects/failure costs**. The more recent grouping by the American Society for Quality Control (ASQC), separates quality costs into two components, i.e. **Price of Conformance or POC**, and **Price of Non-Conformance or PONC**. We will first examine the elements of the traditional three component structure.

- **Costs of prevention.** These are the costs associated with preventing the appearance of poor quality work, scrap, and rework. This group includes the costs of planning and implementing the quality assurance programme, the construction of the quality manual, development of procedures, and the costs of training personnel to use the quality system and meet the quality standards. Also included are the costs associated with gathering, analysing, and reporting quality data, the costs of implementing quality improvement projects, and the costs of evaluating the quality of new·product designs and the quality aspects associated with their introduction.
- **Costs of appraisal.** Included here are the costs of vendor appraisal, all inspection and test costs, calibration and maintenance of inspection and test equipment, and the costs of products used for destructive testing and consumables such as X-ray film and dyes used for non-destructive testing.
- **Costs of defects.** These are the costs associated with failure to conform to the prescribed quality standards; they can be considered under internal and external failure costs. Internal failure costs include: the loss in labour and material in producing scrap, the cost of reworking poor work, the cost of reinspection and retest, the cost of the resulting under-utilisation of equipment, and the cost of the time involved in deciding what to do with non-conforming material and components. External failure costs include: replacing of defective products returned by the customer, investigation of complaints and associated compensation to the customer, services provided to the customer while the product is under warranty, and the cost of concessions to allow downgraded products to be sold as 'seconds'.

Using the other grouping system in which the Cost of Quality is found by summing the **Price of Conformance** and the **Price of Non-Conformance**, we see that COQ = POC + PONC. In fact the POC is comprised of the above mentioned prevention and appraisal costs, these being classified under the headings of prevention, training and quality education, reviews and evaluations, procedure verifications and quality appraisals, inspection, and preventive maintenance. The PONC represents the costs associated with labour, machines, and materials incurred when work is not up to quality specifications at the first attempt. This is similar to the previously mentioned failure cost. It includes the costs of rework, rescheduling work due to non-availability of the failed parts or products, additional inventory, servicing, handling customer complaints and compensation demands, replacements and repairs made under warranty, machine downtime, etc. It is claimed that allocating costs to the two groups of POC and PONC is simpler than using the older three grouping system, and that it makes standardisation of the process easier, thus allowing interfirm comparisons.

(c) Obtaining costs of quality

Obtaining accurate quantitive values for these costs is difficult and expensive if appropriate accounting and cost reporting systems are not in place within the organisation. Methods of monitoring and controlling manufacturing costs were discussed in Chapter 17. However it may be said here that the calculation can be based on one or more of the following: (a) The labour costs of personnel involved in any quality activity; (b) the whole costs associated with a department whose sole responsibility is some aspect of quality; (c) the cost to process one quality 'unit' multiplied by the number of units – e.g. the cost of quality training for one person multiplied by the number of people trained or the cost of handling one customer complaint multiplied by the number of complaints; (d) the deviation cost – i.e. the difference between the costs involved in producing a good product first time and one that has been reworked or made as a replacement for one that was scrap. Should appropriate cost control structures not be in place within the company it is possible to use costs based on intelligent estimates. These will suffice as a short term measure until proper procedures are established.

(d) The optimum quality level

There are essentially two different views of what constitutes the optimum quality level, and how the different quality costs are related. These views are shown graphically in Figure 18.3. The horizontal axis in each graph shows the quality level, represented by the number of defective products produced as a percentage of the total production. The vertical axis indicates the quality costs involved in achieving the corresponding quality levels.

Figure 18.3(a) shows the traditional view. Here it is assumed that to achieve zero defects the costs of appraisal and prevention approach infinity, thus making the company uncompetitive. Conversely as the number of defects produced increases past a certain point, due to appraisal and prevention costs being reduced, then the cost of these defects approaches infinity since the company loses all credibility in the market place and has to cease trading. Between these two extremes there is some optimum point where the costs of failure equal the costs of appraisal and prevention; this is the optimum point where the total quality cost is minimised.

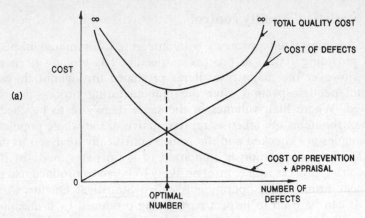

(a) Traditional perception of quality costs

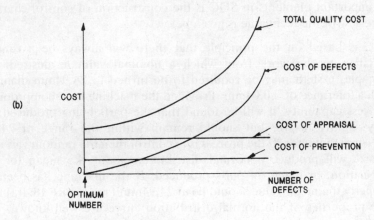

(b) Alternative perception of quality costs

Figure 18.3   Cost behaviour curves

Figure 18.3(b) shows a more recent view, in which the optimum number of defects is zero. This perception comes from the belief that, once their most effective level has been found, appraisal and prevention costs should remain constant. If quality consciousness pervades the company then the awareness of every individual within the organisation ensures that they assume responsibility for the quality of their work. This results in an ongoing reduction in the number of defects. At zero defects there are no failure costs, e.g. rework, scrap, customer returns, and warranty repairs. Also as defects approach zero the company's credibility increases, thus leading to an increased market share.

In practice, the truth probably lies somewhere between both of these perceptions, i.e. a zero defect situation is ideal but the appraisal and prevention costs increase as absolute zero is approached.

18.4   Statistical quality control

The use of automated processes with integrated automated inspection devices providing 100% 'in process' inspection has already been mentioned. However the majority of items produced throughout the world today still need inspection after the manufacturing process has been completed. Where high volumes of the same items are to be checked, **samples** of the items are taken as representative of the whole population. These samples are checked and the results statistically analysed to determine, (a) if the population is composed of good parts, and (b) if the manufacturing process is in control or likely to begin to produce bad parts in the near future. This operation is called Statistical Quality Control (SQC). It can be used to inspect parts being produced by a machine or incoming goods to a factory that have been supplied by a vendor. SQC can be implemented using manual or computerised methods. Since one of the more important elements in SQC is the construction of control charts, a brief review of the technique is given below.

- SQC is based on the principle that there will always be a **random variation** in the work from which a nominal value is desired. For example, a shaft may be required to be turned to 24.94mm diameter with a tolerance of ±0.04mm. Provided the machine has an appropriate 'process capability' it will be found that the parts being produced will vary slightly in size but should remain within the range of 24.90–24.98mm diameter. If the process is in control then the random variation in size will produce a normal distribution about the mean for any population, or batch, of parts produced. If the machine has been set properly the mean value should lie at 24.94mm (see Figure 18.4(a)).
- The properties of the normal distribution curve are well known. It is therefore possible to use these to assist with the ongoing control of our turning operation. The properties of the curve are shown in Figure 18.4(b). This shows that if we set points A and A' at 1.96 standard deviations above and below the mean, then it will be found that 95% of all items produced will have their sizes between these two points. Also if we set points B and B' at 3.09 standard deviations above and below the mean, then 99.8% of parts will lie between them. This principle is used to construct control charts.
- We can take the normal distribution curve that we would expect to obtain from the item population produced by our process and turn it through 90°, as shown in Figure 18.4(c). If the tolerance band is now superimposed on the curve it can be seen that, in this case, the process is in control and producing 100% good parts. The actual control charts for the process are constructed by setting 'Warning Limits' and 'Action Limits' at the 1.96 and 3.09 standard deviation levels respectively (see Figure 18.4(d)). This is based on the principle that there is a 1 in 40 chance of the mean of any sample withdrawn from the process being

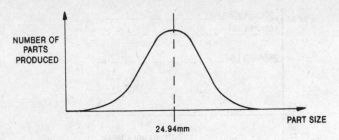

(a) Distribution of part sizes produced by turning

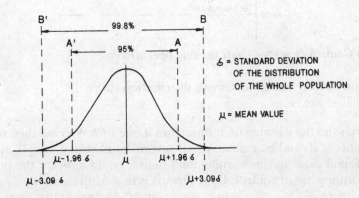

(b) Properties of the normal distribution curve

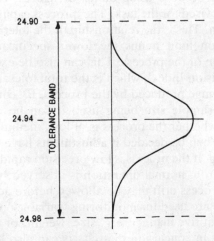

(c) Size distribution in relation to tolerance

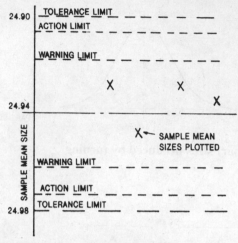

(d) Control chart for shaft turning operation

Figure 18.4   Using the normal distribution curve

beyond the warning limit; therefore if one such is found then subsequent checks should be made. Also if several consecutive sample means were found close to the warning limit then it could indicate the process was drifting out of control. If the process is in control there is only a 1 in 1000 chance of a sample mean being beyond the action limits; therefore if one sample mean is found to be in this region, the process should be stopped for checking.

- Control charts are in practice constructed by taking samples from the process when it is known to be working satisfactorily and following a straightforward procedure using tables of figures, or computer programs, specially devised for the task. The 'process capability' is also taken into consideration. This is the relationship of the **tolerance band**, i.e. the upper specification limit minus the lower specification limit, to the standard deviation of the process. This can also be expressed as an RPI or 'Relative Precision Index', which is the total tolerance divided by the average sample range produced by the process. By comparing the ratios obtained to the sample size being used it can be determined, from standard tables, whether the process is of low, medium, or high relative precision. It can then be decided if adjustments have to be made to the control charts, e.g. if the process is low precision rapid action is essential if any deviation from normal operation is observed, whereas with high precision more process drift may be allowed before action is necessary.
- The above charts are used for monitoring 'variables' which are measurable in some quantitive manner, e.g. size, weight, or volume. However it is worth noting in conclusion that charts can also be constructed for monitoring 'attributes' which are either acceptable or not acceptable,

e.g. painted surfaces, flawed bottles, or 'good' or 'bad' sweets on a conveyor belt.

18.5   Quality measurement

(a) Specification and tolerancing

To ensure that quality standards are being met, the actual quality achieved must be measured. In order to do this, the quality levels must be clearly specified in such a way that measurement is possible.

For example, it is not good enough to say that the internal diameter of a shaft bearing is to be 25mm and the shaft that fits into it has also to be 25mm diameter. This is wrong because it is impossible to make anything 'exactly' to size except by a very low probability chance, and even if something was made exactly to size it would be impossible to measure that it had been achieved. Also in the example if the shaft was made slightly larger than 25mm diameter or the bearing internal diameter slightly less, then the two would not be able to fit. Historically 'making to suit' was the normal method of manufacturing this type of assembly, i.e. each component of a product was individually crafted to fit together to form the whole. However the mass production systems of today demand interchangeability of components; this is also necessary for replacement parts. For this reason **tolerancing** must be used. A third method, called 'selective assembly' is sometimes used in special cases. This applies where the clearance between components must be held to such a tight tolerance that the process capability is not able to produce sufficiently precise components. In this case the components are very accurately measured and graded into various size groupings, subsequently suitable components are matched with each other. This happens with some precision shaft and bearing assemblies and in the manufacture of ball race assemblies (these are bearing assemblies using ball bearings).

A tolerance is a permissible deviation from the desired specification. Tolerancing is most frequently associated with dimensional tolerancing and geometric tolerancing of parts, but it can also apply to any specified parameter such as weight, temperature, time, current, voltage, strength, hardness, metallurgical composition, number of blemishes in a paint finish, etc. In our example of the shaft and bearing, the designer could state that the shaft diameter could be 24.98–24.90mm and that the bearing could be 25.00–25.08mm internal diameter. Thus the clearance between the shaft and the bearing could vary between 0.02 and 0.18mm, depending on the machining operation (see Figure 18.5). This is only an illustration in practice tables of **limits and fits** are used to determine the tolerances to be used. Usually these are given for different types of fits, the two most common being (a) **clearance** fits and (b) **interference** fits, in which the shaft is a press fit in the hole. In order to verify that tolerances have been

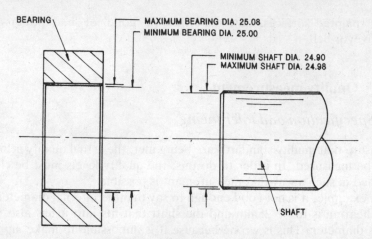

Figure 18.5   Dimensional tolerancing applied to a bearing and shaft to ensure a clearance fit

achieved it is necessary to carry out some form of measurement, therefore before concluding this chapter we will briefly consider some aspects of this.

(b) Metrology

'Metrology' is the science of measurement; it is based on the fundamental measures of **length**, **time**, **mass**, and **temperature**. These, together with the **Ampere** for electric current and the **Candela** for luminous intensity, form the six basic international units of measurement. All other units are in some way derived from these. Here we will restrict our concern to the measurement of length.

- In 1960 the worldwide standard for the fundamental unit of length, i.e. the **international metre**, was defined as 1,650,763.73 vacuum wavelengths of the orange red light given off by the electrically excited isotope Krypton 86 (Krypton is a rare gas from the atmosphere). Most industrialised countries now use the metric system, with the notable exception of the USA which uses the old imperial units where one inch is equivalent to 0.0254 metres.
- In practical terms within the factory, various methods are used to check the sizes of manufactured components. These methods can be separated into measurement, comparison, and gauging.
- Measuring instruments can be either direct or indirect. **Direct** instruments allow a reading of size directly from a lined scale. **Indirect** instruments do not contain line scales and are used to transfer dimensions to a direct instrument; this increases the opportunity for error, therefore direct methods should be used wherever possible. Examples of direct measuring instruments used for measuring lengths up to a few

centimetres are: the steel rule which can be used with skill to measure to a maximum precision of around 0.25mm, the micrometer for a precision of 0.01mm, and the toolmaker's microscope for a precision of 0.001mm. For slightly greater distances, say over a metre or so, laser interferometry can be used to achieve accurate measurements down to ±0.0002mm.

- Comparators, or deviation type instruments, do not measure an absolute length but instead amplify and measure variations in the distance between two surfaces. For example, dial indicator gauges translate the vertical linear movement of a spindle into a scale reading on an indicator. The means of translation may be mechanical, mechanical/optical, or electrical. To describe the operation assume the height of a surface is to be measured. The dial indicator, the item having the reference height, and the item whose height is to be measured are all placed on a flat smooth metal, or granite, table called a 'surface table'. The indicater spindle is allowed to come into contact with the reference surface and the reading on the indicator dial is noted or set to zero. The spindle is now lowered into contact with the item to be measured and the difference in dial reading noted. The height of the measured item will therefore be the height of the reference ± the dial indicator reading. Accuracies of ±0.0003mm are obtained using this type of technique.
- An important means of obtaining reference lengths, e.g. the reference height quoted above, is the use of gauge blocks, sometimes called slip gauges or Johansson blocks. These are used as the standard references within companies and are obtainable in various grades. They are purchased as boxed sets containing a carefully devised range of blocks. The individual blocks can be 'wrung' together to create any desired length. The blocks are made from heat treated and stress relieved alloy steels made flat and parallel to within a range of 0.00002–0.00012mm depending on the grade.
- Gauges used for production purposes are the simplest, quickest, and cheapest means of inspecting the size of components. They are usually in the form of GO and NOT GO gauges. For example, when checking a hole a cylindrical gauge will be used such that the GO end should be able to enter the hole while the NOT GO end of the gauge should not enter. It is apparent that the tolerances to which both ends of the gauge are to be made must be much tighter, normally by a factor of ten, than those of the component being checked.

18.6 Quality circles

This chapter began by emphasising the need for a 'total quality' awareness by an organisation; it then considered the detail of how the system could be made to work before finally examining some of the actual techniques and hardware used to measure the conformance of the manufactured parts. In conclusion we now look at the concept of 'quality circles' (QCs) which are a means of integrating and encouraging the efforts of individuals towards improving the effectiveness of the company.

Quality circles originated in Japan and have to some extent been implemented in other countries. In some factories in the west, where worker and management relationships were good, similar activities have often occurred, though not called by the same name. Essentially QCs are groups of workers that form together at regular intervals, say weekly, to discuss quality problems related to their own sphere of influence within the company. It is a participatory problem solving system that also stimulates an ongoing quality awareness in those involved.

The circle members may apply recognised problem solving techniques. For example, Pareto analysis is a method based on the rule that 80% of effect is caused by 20% of the population. In quality terms this could mean constructing a histogram of all the different defects found from a problem process or operation. Examination of the histogram should show which defect is causing the most trouble; this should lead to identification of the problem source. A similar approach can be used very effectively for analysing quality costs. Other techniques involve the construction of 'cause and effect' diagrams which require the writing down of the problem or effect, then working backwards so forming a tree, or fishbone, in which all possible causes are listed. Analysis of the diagram by systematically eliminating the possible causes should highlight the problem source. Finally if a problem suddenly arises where none existed before the simple question: 'What has changed?', should be asked. This may identify that a new batch of material has been used, or Maintenance has just finished working on a machine, or a new operator has began work; changes like these often prove to be problem sources.

The concluding remarks to this chapter must therefore be that quality is everyone's responsibility and that on it, in today's intensely competitive environment, will rest the success or failure of the company.

Review Questions

1 Why is it important to be able to define 'quality'?
2 Discuss, briefly, what you understand by the term 'Total Quality Management'.
3 Show the type of functions that may be classified as quality related activities by sketching the organisational structure for a traditional quality department.
4 Discuss the type of activities that would normally be classified under the heading 'Quality Assurance'.
5 What is the purpose of ISO 9000?
6 Why is vendor appraisal such an essential activity for the modern manufacturing organisation?
7 Discuss the type of activities that would normally be classified under the heading 'Quality Control'.
8 Why should there be few full time inspectors in a modern factory?

9 What is the purpose of SQC?

10 Describe **two** methods of classifying the cost of quality in an organisation.

11 Why is the identification of quality costs of increasing importance to manufacturing organisations?

12 List the types of costs that would be included within each of the **three** more traditional cost groups.

13 Why has the POC and PONC cost grouping been introduced?

14 State whether you agree or disagree with the statement that 'minimum quality costs occur with zero defects'. Explain your reasoning.

15 What is the significance of the normal distribution curve in SQC?

16 What are control charts, and why are they particularly useful in large volume production?

17 Why is it important to know the RPI of a process when setting up control charts?

18 Why is tolerancing necessary when manufacturing components?

19 What are the **six** basic international units of measurement?

20 What are the **three** basic methods used for checking the size of manufactured components, and how do they differ from each other?

21 Slip gauges are an essential possession for a manufacturing company; why is this so?

22 What are Quality Circles, and what benefits do they bring to a company?

Further Reading

1 'Total Quality Control' by A.V. Feigenbaum. 3rd ed. Published by McGraw Hill, 1983.

2 'What is Total Quality Control' by Kaoru Ishikawa. Published by Prentice-Hall, 1985.

3 'Quality is Free' by Philip B. Crosby. Published by McGraw Hill 1979.

4 'Lets Talk Quality' by Philip B. Crosby. Published by McGraw Hill, 1989.

5 'Juran on Quality By Design' by J.M. Juran. Published by Free Press, 1992.

6 'Juran's Quality Control Handbook'. 4th ed. McGraw Hill, 1988.

7 BS 5750 (ISO 9000) 'Quality Management and Quality Assurance Standards'. Published by the British Standards Institution, 1987.

8 'Metrology for Engineers' by J.F.W. Galyer and C.R. Shotbolt. 5th ed. Cassell, 1991.

⟨19⟩ Human factors

19.1 Introduction

Manufacturing is about **people** just as much as it is about technology and organisation. As well as creating products **for** people to use, manufacturing involves the use **of** people in the creation process. Some of the factors that relate to these people are considered in this chapter.

Within the manufacturing system people should be able to enjoy their work and carry it out efficiently in a pleasant, healthy, and safe environment. Here we will examine how these criteria are met by looking at the areas of job satisfaction, health and safety, and ergonomics.

19.2 Job satisfaction

Before people can enjoy their work and gain satisfaction from what they are doing they must feel motivated to carry out that work in the first place. In 1943 Abraham Maslow proposed a 'Theory of Human Motivation' which included a hierarchy of needs composed of five levels (see Figure 19.1). He said that needs would appear in **ascending** order only. For example, a physiological need would be the satisfaction of hunger and thirst, and the need for safety would be of secondary importance until these essentials of life had been acquired. In our industrialised societies with advanced economies the physiological needs are usually satisfied for most members of society. Similarly on a general level safety needs are satisfied except in specific cases where, for example, accidents or criminal acts might occur. The social needs at level 3 will be satisfied through the personal life of the individual, though work will also serve a useful function here. However most people look to work to help them satisfy the needs suggested at levels 4 and 5, i.e. esteem needs and self-actualisation. This work may be that of a mother, or father, who works full time at home raising a young family, or a volunteer worker with a charity, or someone who is self-employed. In this chapter, we are mostly concerned with the manufacturing employee working in a traditional factory environment.

In Chapter 16, Work Study was examined as a means of improving the efficiency and ease with which a job could be completed; however additional factors should also be taken into account when designing a job for a worker. **Psychological** factors should be considered to ensure that the worker is able to experience fulfilment of levels 4 and 5 on the Maslow scale. It may be argued that in most cases this is unnecessary, and that

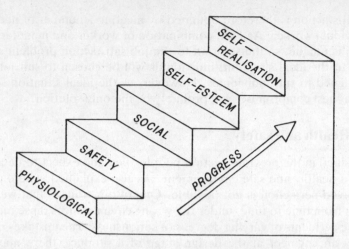

Figure 19.1 Maslow's scale of the hierarchy of needs

many people will be willing to do a particular job simply for the pay alone. This is all very well, but it should be remembered that it is the **best** performance we are looking for from a worker, not one that is mediocre or barely adequate.

Factors such as monotony of movements and boredom should be minimised. This appears contrary to the principle of specialisation and division of labour where simple repetitive tasks are used to produce high labour productivity. But, as in everything involving human beings as individuals, there is no perfect solution to any problem. There is evidence that some individuals actually prefer to have a rigidly defined, repetitive work cycle, while others benefit from variety and flexibility in how they are allowed to tackle a job. For example, the traditional way to assemble mass produced items such as motor cars or typewriters is to use an assembly line. Here, the manual workers have to work at the same speed as associated machinery and at a rate governed by the speed of, say, a conveyor belt. In this case, each worker completes a simple operation and repeats this many hundreds or thousands of times per day. Monotony, boredom, and fatigue can easily occur in these situations and this leads to poor quality products, absenteeism, and high labour turnover rates. It has been found that by changing the job so that the individual workers can each build a larger part of the finished product, for example a complete typewriter, then work satisfaction can improve. This leads to a greater pride in the job and better quality. Absenteeism and labour turnover also reduces, and this lowers the costs involved in lost time and in training new workers. Naturally the actual production rates will be slower as the benefits of labour specialisation are lost; this loss in production rate generally is so important that most mass production factories today still adhere to the production line system, though the needs of the individual will still be recognised and satisfied where possible.

Job satisfaction is therefore obtained by meeting a number of needs for the individual worker. As each combination of worker and manufacturing situation is unique, so the solution to the job satisfaction problem will be unique. In the ideal situation, individuals will be chosen to suit jobs and jobs designed to suit individuals. However, as the ideal situation seldom occurs, a 'best compromise' will probably be the only solution.

19.3   Health and safety

As explained in the previous section people need and expect to be able to work in a healthy and safe environment. As also explained, where people are involved perfection is not possible. One of our traits is that we make mistakes from time to time; under the wrong circumstances these mistakes can cause accidents of varying degrees of seriousness. The mistakes may be made by an engineer at the design stage of a product, there may be a mistake made by someone preparing a procedure to be followed in operating a process plant, or someone may make a simple mistake such as pushing the wrong button or carelessly walking too near moving machinery. Each of these mistakes could cause an accident, and it is estimated that hundreds of people are injured or killed every day throughout the world due to industrial accidents alone. Another aspect that must be considered is the health of the individual within the manufacturing system. Again due to human error and commercial pressure, conditions detrimental to health may appear. In this section we will look at the provisions that should be made to make work both healthy and safe.

(a) Legislation

In most countries today there exists law to provide a minimum standard of health and safety within industry. For example in the UK there is the Factories Act 1961 and the Health and Safety at Work (etc.) Act 1974. There are also further Regulations and Codes of Practice approved from time to time to suit new and changing situations, e.g. COSHH (Control of Substances Hazardous to Health Regulations). Copies of extracts of these publications, relevant to the particular industry concerned, must be displayed in prominent positions in work areas. This ensures that all employees have access to a general knowledge of the law as it relates to their own situation. Adherence to the law is ensured through inspection visits by the Health and Safety Executive in the UK. It is an offence to obstruct an inspector during the course of his duties, and he has the power to inspect a factory at any time of the day or night. Each country has its own system of law but the broad scope and content of regulations are, by necessity, very similar. We are concerned here with manufacturing industry and the subject will be considered under the headings of health, safety, and welfare.

(b) Health

- Within the factory the working conditions should be such that no hazard to health exists. There should be no fumes or particles in the atmosphere that could cause harm in the short or long term. If such particles do exist, then protective clothing and breathing equipment or filters should be provided and worn. For example particles of fibreglass or asbestos are particularly dangerous and the best way of dealing with this type of hazard is to remove it at source. Substitute materials should be found, or an alternative process that does not produce these particles, or effective filters at the point of particle creation should be used. Grinding operations, handling sacks of powder material such as flour, and paint spraying are all tasks that involve the possibility of inhaling harmful material. A method of removing the human element in these jobs is to automate them using industrial robots, and this is in fact common practice, with large productivity gains being experienced, particularly in paint spraying applications.

- More general considerations include the following. There should be a high standard of cleanliness in factories, and this applies not only to foodstuff and electronics manufacturing. The floors, walls, and ceilings should be regularly cleaned, washed, and redecorated at reasonable intervals. Refuse bins and other rubbish should be cleared daily; this improves hygiene and also reduces the risk of fire. Workers themselves should also ensure their clothing is kept clean as very serious skin disorders can occur due to prolonged contact with oily clothes. There should be no overcrowding and around $12m^3$ per person should be regarded as a minimum, though this will obviously increase greatly if material handling is required and large machines are present. Food should also not be consumed where there is a possibility of absorbing poisonous fumes or dust.

- Lighting must be adequate in every part of the factory to prevent accidents and avoid eye fatigue. Noise levels should be kept to a minimum and adequate hearing protection worn where necessary. Work areas should be well ventilated. Suitable temperatures should be maintained and the heating methods used should not in themselves be harmful. These factors will be considered again in section 19.4 on ergonomics below.

(c) Safety

- **The cost of accidents.** Within industry about 50% of all accidents are caused by either handling and lifting, or machinery. Apart from the personal discomfort and distress experienced by the victim and his family, there is also the financial cost of accidents to be considered. These costs arise due to lost production, loss of earnings of the individual, cost of benefit paid to the worker if injury results, and cost of compensation and or legal costs if legal action is taken by the victim in pursuit of a claim. The cost of production time lost may be considerable; this arises due to the lost time of the injured employee; the lost time of other employees who stop work to give assistance or are curious, sympathetic, or shocked; the lost time of foremen and managers who have to investigate and report on the accident; the cost of retraining someone to do the injured person's work; the cost of repairing damage that may have resulted to equipment, and so on.

The loss of earnings to the employee involved in the accident may cause anxiety to himself and his family. This can be offset by compensation payments though these will probably not be immediate and cannot of course ever totally compensate for pain and suffering.

Thus the cost to government, industry, and individuals is considerable and in the UK runs into millions of pounds per year with comparable figures in other countries.

- **The causes of accidents.** Accidents occur due to unsafe acts or unsafe conditions, or both. The unsafe act might be one of the following; someone operating a machine without authority or proper training; someone disabling a safety device in order to improve their rate of work; working from an unsafe position or adopting an unsafe posture. Examples of unsafe conditions are: inadequate lighting, oil on floor, overcrowded work areas, and dangerous work arrangements. These and other unsafe acts and conditions are termed 'hazards'. They occur everywhere people are present and they eventually cause accidents. Hazards are caused by **people**: sometimes the human error occurs very early on in a chain of events and the accident is separated widely in time from the unsafe act. An example of this would be a faulty weld on a ship's hull which becomes apparent as an accident only months later when a crack appears and propagates catastrophically. Often there is very little time between the unsafe act and the accident. An example of this would be an operator ducking under a guard rail to get at a piece of equipment and being hit by, say, the moving arm of an industrial robot located behind the rail.

- **The prevention of accidents.** This can be considered under four areas: the original design of equipment and machinery used, the physical layout of the work area, the training adopted by the factory personnel, and the safety devices and procedures in place.

1 First, equipment and machinery should be designed by qualified engineers and all materials and components to be used clearly and unambiguously specified. Quality components should be incorporated, they should have a minimum of moving parts and be solid state where appropriate. If possible, the type of components used should already have proven their reliability in other applications. The equipment and machinery should be manufactured under well supervised conditions, and to specification. Records should be kept of how the work was done,

who did it, and the result of any inspection operations or tests carried out.

2 Having ensured that the equipment used has been designed and manufactured to satisfactory safety standards, the next stage is to install the equipment so that it can be operated in a safe manner.

3 All personnel within a factory or other industrial environment should receive basic safety training. This will inform them of unsafe practices, the need for tidiness and cleanliness, and any hazards particularly associated with their work. For example 'substances hazardous to health' have to be carefully controlled regarding their use and storage, and all personnel likely to come into contact with them should be made aware of any special precautions to be taken. Those who operate machinery and other equipment must receive specialised training regarding their work. This training is essential if safe working conditions are to prevail. The supplier of the equipment being used could provide the training and should also ensure that the equipment has been installed safely. It may be necessary to compile a 'safety manual' to be read by all who are going to operate the equipment. In a particularly dangerous area a 'permit to work' might be issued to the relevant personnel, and access denied to those with no need to be there.

4 Hazardous equipment and machinery should be guarded. This can take many forms and some of these are now noted.

Fencing. This may vary from a simple handrail about one metre high, to a complete cage using two metre high steel mesh or toughened perspex. The caging would be used in most areas where large pieces of moving machinery are present (see Figure 19.2(a)). The space between the

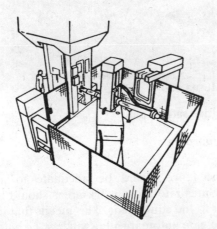

Source: MTTA

(a) A robot safeguarded with fixed and interlocking guards; the robot is removing material from an induction furnace and loading an upsetting press

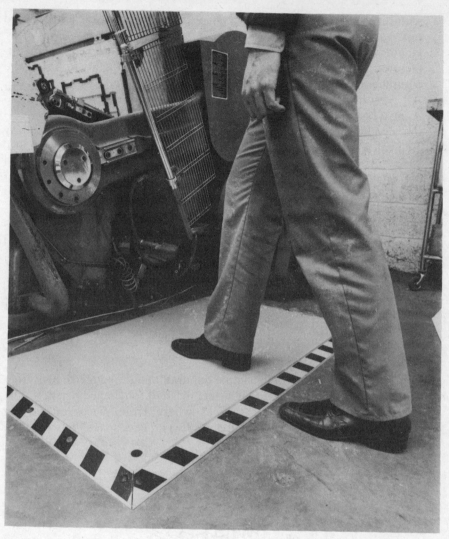

Source: Courtesy Herga Ltd

(b) A pressure sensitive safety mat

Figure 19.2   Safeguarding

equipment and the fence would be adequate to allow maintenance personnel access. Gates into these work areas should be interlocked into the electrical power to the equipment. This means that if a gate is opened a switch built into the gate automatically switches the equipment off.

Light curtains. Instead of building a physical barrier it is possible to use light beams. In these systems an array of light emitting diodes passes light across a gap of a few metres to an array of photosensors. When someone passes through the gap, the beam is broken and the equipment is switched off.

Pressure sensitive mats. These are used either at entrances to work areas or around the hazardous machinery. Should someone step on the mat a switch is closed, so stopping the equipment. These mats are pneumatically or electrically operated (see Figure 19.2(b)).

Guards. Guards actually on the machinery are common. These usually open to allow the machine operator access while the machine is at a safe part of its cycle. They are also interlocked to ensure that the dangerous parts of the machine cannot move until the operator withdraws from the danger area and closes the guard.

Safety equipment. All workers should wear appropriate safety equipment. In almost all workshops it is necessary to wear protective goggles. These will prevent damage to the eye from flying particles such as may be present during grinding and cutting operations. Because of the harmful radiation given off when electric arc welding, welders must use protective face shields with tinted viewing windows. Protective helmets, or 'hard hats', should be worn where there is any overhead working taking place.

Fire Precautions. There are regulations regarding the number and position of fire exits within a building. Exits should be easily accessible, easily opened from the inside and never locked. Personnel should be conversant with the procedure to be followed in case of fire. They should also be aware of the different types of fire extinguisher, what they are used for, and their locations which should be prominent. Flammable materials should be clearly marked and stored carefully; there are special regulations for explosive materials such as pressurised gas.

(d) Welfare

Welfare is an aspect of health and safety in which the more general concerns of the well-being of the individual are considered.

- Employers are bound by law to provide adequate facilities for the welfare of their employees. For example, drinking water must be provided in ample quantity and of good quality. Clean drinking vessels or drinking fountains should be available.
- Clean, well maintained washing facilities should be available and supplied with soap and towels.
- There should be facilities for the drying and storing of clothes not worn during working hours.
- A first aid box should be easily accessible and it should contain an appropriate range of materials for the type of work being undertaken in the local area. The box should be in the charge of a responsible person.

This section has shown that health and safety is everyone's responsibility. The designer, manufacturer, and supplier of the equipment to be used in the factory have an obligation to ensure that it is safe to operate and that a clear instruction manual is provided. The employer has to ensure that his premises and procedures conform to the appropriate laws, regulations, and codes of practice. He must ensure that adequate training and appropriate safety equipment is provided to the employee. The employee has the responsibility to make himself familiar with the hazards that are likely to occur in his job, and to take advantage of any safety training, advice, and equipment offered. The next section will consider ergonomic aspects which will combine methods to improve productivity with methods to make work safer and more enjoyable.

19.4   Ergonomics

'Ergonomics' is the study of the worker's relationship to the surrounding environment with intent to improve efficiency and work satisfaction. The word is composed from the Greek 'ergon' meaning work and 'economics'. Other terms used for ergonomics are 'human engineering' and 'human factors engineering'. An ergonomist receives and analyses input from both the engineering and the human sciences, e.g. materials selection, functional design, statistics, mechanical engineering, etc. and from anatomy, physiology, and psychology (see Figure 19.3).

When a worker is carrying out a job, he is operating in a 'closed loop' system. By this we mean that he observes a situation, he analyses what is happening and what subsequently needs to happen, he takes action to cause the required change to occur, he observes the result of his action on the situation, and so on. This is shown in Figure 19.4. This will occur in any task where a human is actively participating in a process, e.g. assembling a

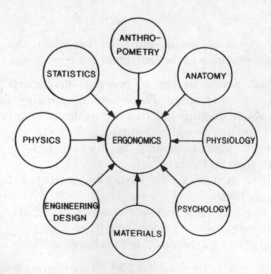

Figure 19.3   Some of the engineering and human sciences contributing to the study of ergonomics

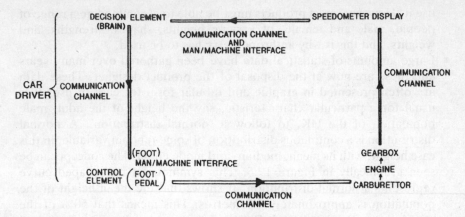

Figure 19.4   Closed loop system: a human driver controlling the speed of a car

product, controlling a chemical plant, or even driving a car. All the elements involved in this control loop must perform at their optimum. Here we are concerned with the efficiency of the human operator, how well he can observe the situation, and how well he can effect the necessary changes. Ergonomics therefore includes consideration of the design of the equipment and workplace, and the general environment surrounding the worker. These two aspects will now be considered in more detail.

(a) Equipment and workspace design.

As mentioned in Chapter 1, products may be classed as consumer or as producer goods. In the first category, we have items such as cameras and motor cars. Increasingly these products are being designed with an emphasis on ergonomics, and this is often a factor used to attract customers. The 'ergonomically' designed camera, for example, has its body contoured to fit comfortably into the hand, it is not too heavy, it is balanced for comfortable handling, controls are easily accessible even when looking through the viewfinder, and non-slip rubberised surfaces are used where appropriate. In motor cars, gear levers are located for fast and easy shifting, the windscreen is designed for maximum visibility, and the fascia panel, containing displays and controls, is easily seen through the non-slip optimum diameter steering wheel. The principles employed in the design and layout of these consumer products also apply to producer goods, and these are now considered.

- To ensure that the product design will suit the largest number of people anthropometry, i.e. the measurement of people, is used. If a single item is being made, say a made to measure suit or a seat for a racing car, then it can be designed to fit exactly the person that is intending to wear or use it. However, most products must be able to accommodate a range of people, male and female, of varying heights, shapes, strengths, and weights, and this is why anthropometry has to be used.

- Large amounts of statistical data have been gathered over many years and these are now at the disposal of the product designer. These data are often presented in graphic and tabular form for ease of use. It is usual for a particular characteristic, say the height of the adult male population of the UK, to follow a 'normal distribution'. A normal distribution is a continuous distribution of some random variable, in this case height, with its mean, median, and mode equal. The concept can be seen graphically in Figure 19.5. This symmetrical bell shaped curve represents a normal distribution. It shows that the mean height of the population is approximately 1.7 metres. This means that 50% of the population are above and 50% below this height. The 'standard deviation' is a numerical factor used to indicate scatter. From the curve it can be seen that one standard deviation from the mean includes about 34% of the population. Two standard deviations above and below the mean enclose about 90% of the population. Thus if a piece of equipment was designed so that people of between 1.6 metres and 1.9 metres tall could use it, then the designer would be confident of his design suiting 90% of the adult male population of the UK.
- The anthropometric data can be used to construct models of typical members of the population. These models can be used in graphic computer simulations to assist with design, or two dimensional cardboard mannikins can be made if the relatively expensive computerised methods are unavailable. Figure 19.6 shows examples of these models alongside the design for a lathe. Figure 19.7 shows a plan view of an

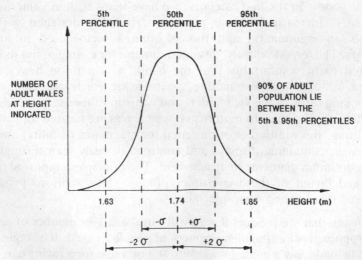

Figure 19.5   Distribution of heights of adult male population

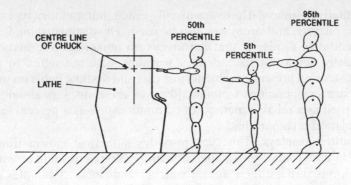

Figure 19.6   Use of two dimensional models to assist with lathe design

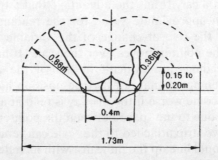

Figure 19.7   **Plan view of operator and typical dimensions to assist in workplace design for an assembly operation**

operator together with suggested dimensions for a group of adult males using a seated workplace. Seats should be designed to be comfortable and provide proper back support. If the operator is working at a bench doing assembly work then components and tools should be stored at specific locations within easy reach. This will ensure that the operator can develop habitual movements without the need for the eyes to direct the hands.

• As well as considering the dimensions of the equipment and workplace, the designer should consider the instrument displays and control elements that might be used. Displays should convey information to the worker in the simplest manner possible. No unnecessary information should be presented as this could create confusion. This principle is now employed in the pilot's workspace, i.e. the cockpit, of modern aircraft. Here computer screens display the essential information required by the pilot as the need arises. This reduces the proliferation of confusing dials and indicators that would otherwise be necessary. In the industrial situation the number of displays required is usually much less and conventional displays are the norm. These displays are of three main types, qualitative, quantive, and representational.

1 **Qualitative displays.** These are usually visual, but auditory types such as bells, buzzers, and sirens can also be used. The distinguishing feature of a qualitative display is that it conveys no numerical information. It is normally employed to convey a warning, e.g. red lights to indicate ignition or oil pressure problems in a car, and flashing lights on machines that are in operation. Colour coding of these displays should not be regarded as a reliable method of communication as a percentage of the population is colour blind.
2 **Quantitive displays.** This type provides numerical information to the user in either analogue or digital form. Everyone is familiar with these two forms through their use on watches and clocks. Examples of these instruments are shown in Figure 19.8. The analogue display shows a reading on a scale analogous to the value it represents, for example the speedometer on a car. It has the advantage that a quick glance will tell the observer an approximate value for the reading. It is also advantageous in that the rate of change of the variable being monitored is easily seen as the pointer moves over the scale. It has the disadvantage that precise readings are difficult in that if the pointer is between graduations, then an estimate of its true position has to be made. This problem can become worse if the display is read at an angle, as parallax error can occur due to the space between the pointer and the scale. The use of a reflective strip attached to the scale can remove this problem as the observer should line up the indicator with its reflection before noting the reading (see Figure 19.9).

Digital displays show the numerical information directly as a number, for example the mileometer on a car. This has the advantage that a reading to any accuracy desired can be made, provided enough numerals are on the indicator. Some digital displays are mechanical but most today are electronic, liquid crystal or light emitting diode displays. This fact leads to another advantage, i.e. they are relatively easily integrated with electronic and electrical control systems. One disadvantage is that if

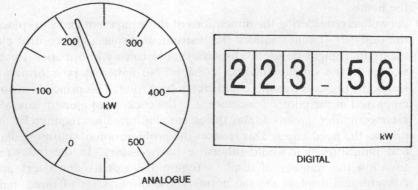

Figure 19.8   Quantitative displays

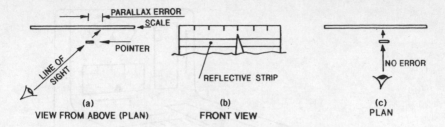

Figure 19.9   Use of reflective strip to reduce parallax error

the value is rapidly changing or fluctuating, then a quick glance may not be enough to determine the actual value, or direction and rate of change. In some instances when the advantages of both types of display are required then they are combined into the one instrument.

3 **Representational displays.** A representational display provides a pictorial diagram or working model of a process. This must be kept as simple as possible to keep extraneous information to a minimum. Such displays would be found, for example, in large process plants, railway control rooms, and electricity distribution centres. Computer screens can be used and simulation programs could be incorporated to show possible future events.

There is a wide variety of controls available for the designer to select for any piece of equipment. Knobs, buttons, horizontal and vertical levers, joysticks, and handwheels are only a sample. Factors to be considered when selecting a means of control are the force required to be exerted, the speed with which this force is to be applied, and the accuracy with which the process has to be controlled. For example, for delicate control a large diameter knob will allow fine, precise movements, but it will be unsuitable for rapid movements or the application of high forces. At the other extreme a large vertical lever will allow the rapid application of a large force but would be most unsuitable for precision movements.

When designing integrated display and control elements it is important, for safety reasons, to adhere as far as possible to the conventions recognised in the country in which the equipment is used. Simple examples are: pushing a switch downward usually means 'on', rotating a switch clockwise also means 'on', but turning a water tap clockwise usually means 'off'. If an operator rotates a control clockwise or moves a cursor from left to right, he will expect an increase in whatever value is being adjusted. A composite of some of these control and display conventions is shown in Figure 19.10 for increasing values.

(b) The working environment

Environmental conditions have a strong effect on the efficiency, comfort,

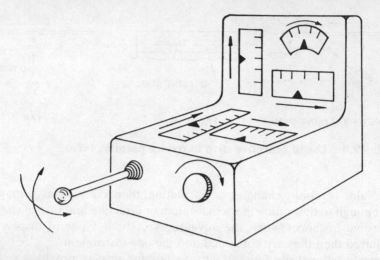

Figure 19.10 Controls and display conventions

and health of the worker. We will consider them under three main headings: lighting, noise, and heating and ventilation.

- **Lighting.** The minimum amount of light recommended by the Chartered Institution of Building Services (CIBS) for a continuously occupied working space is 200 lux (SI units) or 200 lumens per m². This represents the minimum illumination which should be apparent throughout a factory for safety purposes. Much more light than this is needed to avoid eye strain when carrying out activities involving detailed tasks. In practice levels of 1000 lux or higher are often necessary. A table showing lighting recommendations extracted from the CIBS Code 1984 for Interior Lighting is shown in Figure 19.11. These lighting levels can be measured quickly and simply by using easily purchased light meters. Light sources should be chosen carefully. There are various types available, e.g. tungsten filament, fluorescent tube, mercury discharge, etc. The range of sources available all have different characteristics regarding cost, power consumption, colour, and amount of light produced.

    The **amount** of light is only one factor. Other considerations should be the **distribution** of the light, e.g. daylight coming in from side windows may only one illuminate side of the factory while the other is in deep shadow; supplementary artificial lighting will be required here. Glare is another problem. Light reflected from shiny work surfaces or instrument glasses can cause strain and fatigue. This can be avoided by proper design of surfaces and careful positioning of light sources. For instance the need to choose light sources carefully to avoid 'veiling reflections' on visual display units, is of particular importance within the office environment.

- **Noise.** Noise is created by vibrations and movements which cause a rapid rise and fall in the pressure of the air surrounding the vibrating or moving source. These pressure changes are propagated through the air in the form of 'sound waves' which we hear when they impinge on our ear drum. These sounds can be pleasant, as in soft music; they can convey information, as in speech; they can be annoying, as produced by a motorbike with a poor silencer; or they can be harmful, such as those experienced at close proximity to a jet engine. In the working environment noise is often described as 'unwanted sound', and it constitutes one of the most widespread and frequently encountered industrial hazards. The effect of noise can be both psychological and physiological. It can lead to a decrease in working efficiency and in some cases can present a safety risk. The most significant danger from noise is its ability to damage one of our most important senses – the sense of hearing.

We recognise noise as being composed of two elements, these are the **frequency** and the **amplitude** of the sound wave. The frequency is measured in Hertz (Hz) which is cycles per second. Low frequency sound produces low notes and high frequency produces high notes. Humans can usually hear sound between 20Hz and 15000Hz, although this range decreases with age. The amplitude of the sound is measured in Decibels (dB) and this is an indication of intensity or volume. The higher the decibel number the louder the sound. A logarithmic scale is used for measuring decibels so that a ten times increase in intensity is measured by 10dB. This means that if a whisper at the threshold of hearing is 0dB, and the noise of a large machining centre is 90dB, then the machining centre is 1000 million times as intense as the whisper.

While the ear can hear from 20–15,000Hz, it is not equally sensitive to all frequencies, e.g. 65dB at 100Hz does not seem as loud as 65dB at 1000Hz. Overall sound pressure level in dB does not therefore provide a good measure of 'loudness'. In order to modify objective measurements to correspond to the response of the human ear, weighting networks are used which discriminate against frequencies at which the ear is less responsive. The most commonly used network is the A-weighting, and sound pressure levels measured on this basis are denoted dB(A). All UK and International criteria related to industrial noise exposure are based on measurements of dB(A). It is thought that industrial noise first causes hearing loss to occur in the 4000Hz region, with most annoying noise occurring between 1000 and 4000Hz. Figure 19.12 shows values for typical sounds in dB(A). Equipment is available to measure noise levels in dB as well as dB(A), and to isolate and measure individual frequency components.

The risk of hearing loss due to exposure to noise depends on both the level of noise and the duration of exposure. If the noise is steady, then a direct A-weighted sound pressure level provides an adequate basis for assuming exposure. Where the noise fluctuates, as occurs in most industrial situations, the concept of the 'Equivalent Continuous Sound Level' or

Standard Service Illuminance (lx)	Characteristics of the activity/interior	Representative activities/interiors
50	Interiors visited rarely with visual tasks confined to movement and casual seeing without perception of detail.	Cable tunnels, indoor storage tanks, walkways.
100	Interiors visited occasionally with visual tasks confined to movement and casual seeing calling for only limited perception of detail.	Corridors, changing rooms, bulk stores.
150	Interiors visited occasionally with visual tasks requiring some perception of detail or involving some risk to people, plant or product.	Loading bays, medical stores, switchrooms.
200	Continuously occupied interiors, visual tasks not requiring any perception or detail.	Monitoring automatic processes in manufacture, casting concrete, turbine halls.
300	Continuously occupied interiors, visual tasks moderately easy, i.e. large details >10 min arc and/or high contrast.	Packing goods, rough core making in foundries, rough sawing.

500	Visual tasks moderately difficult, i.e. details to be seen are of moderate size (5–10 min arc) and may be of low contrast. Also colour judgement may be required.	General offices, engine assembly, painting and spraying.
750	Visual tasks difficult, i.e. details to be seen are small (3–5 min arc) and of low contrast, also good colour judgements may be required.	Drawing offices, ceramic decoration, meat inspection.
1000	Visual tasks very difficult, i.e. details to be seen are very small (2–3 min arc) and can be of very low contrast. Also accurate colour judgements may be required.	Electronic component assembly, gauge and tool rooms, retouching paintwork.
1500	Visual tasks extremely difficult, i.e. details to be seen extremely small (1–2 min arc) and of low contrast. Visual aids may be of advantage.	Inspection of graphic reproduction, hand tailoring, fine die sinking.
2000	Visual tasks exceptionally difficult, i.e. details to be seen exceptionally small (<1 min arc) with very low contrasts. Visual aids will be of advantage.	Assembly of minute mechanisms, finished fabric inspection.

Source: CIBS Code (1984) Reproduced from the CIBSE Code for interior lighting 1984 by permission of the Chartered Institution of Building Services Engineers

Figure 19.11   Examples of activities/interiors appropriate for each standard service illuminance

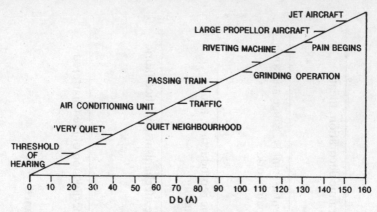

Figure 19.12   Db(A) values of typical sounds

'Leq' is used. This is the notional continuous level which, if experienced over the exposure period, would cause the same A-weighted energy dose to be received by the ear as that due to the actual sound. Values of Leq must be qualified by stating the exposure period to which the level relates. The European Community Directive 86/188/EC, embodied within the UK *Noise at Work Regulations 1989*, uses the equivalent continuous sound level over a standard 8 hour working shift as the basis for specifying limits of exposure. In the regulations this 8 hour Leq is termed the 'Daily Personal Noise Exposure, LEP,d'.

Where the working day is different from 8 hours it is standard practice to normalise the actual Leq value to an 8 hour exposure. For example, the following combinations of noise level and exposure period are equivalent to an LEP,d of 90dB(A):

108dB(A) for 7.5 minutes
96dB(A) for 2 hours
93dB(A) for 4 hours
89dB(A) for 10 hours

The regulations clearly state that the employer in all cases has a statutory duty to reduce the risk of hearing damage to employees to 'the lowest level normally practicable'. Three 'action levels' are described in the regulations as:

First Action Level   LEP,d of 85dB(A)
Second Action Level   LEP,d of 90dB(A)
Peak Action Level   Peak Sound Pressure of 200Pa (140dB)
                          (Impulse Noise)

For exposures at or above the first or peak action levels a **noise assessment** must be carried out by a competent person to identify which employees are so exposed. Where employees are likely to be exposed between the first and second action levels the employer must provide hearing protection if requested by the employee. Where exposure is at or above the second action level or peak action level, exposure must be reduced to the lowest level reasonably practicable other than by the provision of personal ear protectors. If exposure is still at or above the second or peak action levels then the employer must provide suitable personal ear protectors and ensure that they are worn. Such areas of high exposure must be clearly identified as **Ear Protection Zones**.

The problem of minimising industrial noise should, however, begin at the equipment **design** stage. Machines and process equipment should be designed for quiet running with minimum vibration. The next level is to ensure that machinery is properly **maintained**, e.g. bearings lubricated frequently and replaced promptly when necessary. After this comes **containment** of the noise within the machine's immediate vicinity. This can be carried out by using acoustic mufflers; these are soundproofed boxes which fit around the noise source. Finally, if the noise levels are still too high, personal protection will need to be worn by the workers in the local area. This takes the form of ear plugs or ear muffs. One reason that these are used only as a last resort is that they remove the ability to hear normal noises in the work area. This can be a safety hazard; for example a warning shout from a colleague or an approaching vehicle may not be heard. Special frequency selective hearing defenders are available to reduce this problem, but they are more expensive.

- **Heating and ventilation.** As mentioned earlier in this chapter, harmful atmospheric contaminants, such as paint particles, dust, and gases, must be extracted from the work area or protective equipment supplied to the workers. In addition, heating and ventilation should be maintained in the workplace at such a level as to ensure physical comfort for the workers.

The Factories Act requires a 'reasonable' temperature to be maintained in any working space. Where work is sedentary and there is little physical effort 'reasonable' is often interpreted as a temperature of at least 15.5°C after the first hour of occupation. The definition and assessment of 'comfort' is complex, however, and depends on variables that are both personal, such as activity and clothing, and environmental. For example, if some workers are physically active in operating machines or lifting material in the same area as others are sitting at a bench carrying out assembly work, then what is too warm for the first group may be comfortable for the second.

'Thermal comfort' therefore relates to the ease with which the body's internal energy production can be balanced by its energy loss to its surroundings. This energy loss will depend on heat transfer by evaporation of moisture from the skin to the air, and by radiation and convection of heat from the body to the surrounding environment. The required environmental conditions for comfort under different work activities have been studied by many researchers, notably Fanger (see Further Reading), and his co-workers. Fanger identifies the following environmental variables which will influence comfort perceptions:

1 **Air temperature.** This affects the amount of heat loss by convection from the body and is a very important factor for thermal comfort assessment. A wide variety of thermometric devices are available to measure air temperature, but the mercury in glass thermometer is probably still the most convenient instrument. In cases where there is likely to be a significant difference between the air and mean radiant temperatures, a radiation shield, which may simply be a piece of aluminium foil on a frame, can be placed around the bulb of the instrument.
2 **Air speed.** Air speed affects convection as well as moisture evaporation from the body surface. The average air speed may be measured by a variety of instruments, the most commonly used at present being the hot wire anemometer. An air flow of around 0.15m/s is suitable for most situations provided the air and mean radiant temperatures are acceptable. Normally at about 0.5m/s people will complain of draughts, but at less than 0.1m/s of staleness.
3 **Mean radiant temperature.** This controls the loss of energy from the body by radiation. The traditional instrument for measurement of mean radiant temperature is the Globe thermometer which consists of a 150mm diameter hollow blackened sphere, normally of copper. The temperature sensor is usually a mercury in glass thermometer with its bulb located at the centre of the sphere. To assess the mean radiant temperature simultaneous readings of the Globe and air temperature and the air speed are required. An alternative to the Globe instrument is a blackened sphere of 100mm diameter which gives a reading of 'dry resultant' temperature.
4 **Relative humidity.** This affects the degree of evaporation from the surface and is therefore of much greater importance when heavy work is being carried out and the individual is sweating. It is normally uniform throughout a space, therefore readings are required only at one position. The normal method of measurement involves using wet and dry bulb thermometers. Relative humidity is expressed as a percentage, with values between 35% and 70% considered acceptable for most situations. Below 35% static electricity build up can cause difficulties and above 70% building fabric condensation may occur.

Thermal indices are used to express thermal comfort in terms of a single number which is often an index temperature. Examples are air temperature (a poor thermal index when used alone), Globe temperature and dry resultant temperature. Most indices of this kind are convenient to use when assessing the suitability of environments in terms of thermal comfort. Dry resultant temperature is the index which is recommended for use in the UK. This index does not take into account relative humidity, which might also have to be measured depending on the work situation. For comfort conditions to exist it is recommended that the dry resultant temperature should lie between 19 and 23°C.

19.5 Conclusion

This chapter has indicated some of the human factors that must be considered by the engineer or manager in a manufacturing organisation. One whole area of concern that is not investigated here is that of 'industrial relations'. Industrial relations is the study of **social relationships** within an industrial context and it involves 'workers', i.e. non-management personnel, management, and the government. The interrelationship of these three groups can be very complex and all are involved in creating the terms and conditions within which work takes place. The character of industrial relations differs widely not only between countries but also between industries and individual companies. For example, the management style in a traditional heavy engineering company is often quite different from that in a new electronics company; this will produce different worker–management relationships and hence different types of industrial relations problems. In conclusion, it can be said that while broadly following the scale of needs mentioned at the beginning of the chapter, the aspirations of individuals within an organisation will never be exactly the same. This often leads to disagreement and conflict; it is the job of a good manufacturing manager to ensure that this conflict is constructive rather than destructive. This approach can be facilitated by also ensuring that all the human factors mentioned in the chapter have been carefully considered.

Review Questions

1 Do people really need to work? Give a reasoned basis for your answer.
2 Give examples of the type of work situation that should be avoided to ensure that a factory worker is psychologically satisfied.
3 How might job dissatisfaction be manifested in an employee's behaviour and performance?
4 What is the purpose of legislation such as the 'Health and Safety at Work Act'?
5 List typical factors that should be considered to ensure the health of factory workers.
6 'All accidents are caused by someone!' Do you agree with this statement? Why?
7 Discuss where accident costs are incurred.
8 Within the factory situation, what are the **three** broad areas that can be considered for accident prevention?
9 List **three** types of guarding that can be employed to improve safety when machinery is being used.

10 Who has the responsibility for safety within a factory? Discuss the functions of the personnel you describe.
11 Describe the work of an ergonomist.
12 Discuss how anthropometrics can be used to assist in the design of healthy, safe, and easy to use equipment.
13 Describe the **three** main types of display used in industrial equipment, and explain the type of application to which each is suited.
14 What is the 'control convention' in integrated display and control elements?
15 Name **three** aspects of lighting that should be considered to ensure worker efficiency in the factory or office environment.
16 Why is it extremely important to give attention to the noise levels in a work area?
17 Describe the **two** elements of which noise is composed, and discuss their relevance to the employer and the employee.
18 Discuss what is meant by the 'Equivalent Continuous Sound Level' (Leq) experienced by workers.
19 At what **four** levels should machinery created noise problems be tackled in an industrial situation?
20 Discuss fully the factors that contribute to the thermal comfort of a worker; include in your answer comments on how they are measured.

Further Reading

1 'Applied Ergonomics Handbook'. Edited by Ian Galer. Published by Butterworths, 1989.
2 'The Control of Substances Hazardous to Health Regulations 1988 (COSHH)' by Health and Safety Executive. Published by HMSO, 1988.
3 'Lighting' by D.C. Pritchard. 3rd edition. Published by Longman, 1985.
4 'CIBS Code 1984 For Interior Lighting'. Published by the Chartered Institution of Building Services, 1984.
5 'Noise at Work – Guidance on Regulations (The Noise at Work Regulations 1989)' by the Health and Safety Executive. Published by HMSO, 1989.
6 'The Effects of Noise on Man' by Karl D. Kryter. Published by Academic Press, 1970.
7 'Acoustics and Noise Control' by B.J. Smith, R.J. Peters and S. Owen. Published by Longman, 1982.
8 'Sound Analysis and Noise Control' by John Foreman. Published by Von Nostrand, 1990.

9 'Thermal Comfort' by P.O. Fanger. Published by McGraw Hill, 1972.
10 'Environmental Ergonomics' by I.B. Mekjavic, E.W. Banister and J.B. Morrison. Published by Taylor and Francis, 1988.
11 'Ergonomics – Standards and Guidelines for Designers' by Stephen Pleasant. Published by BSI, 1987.
12 'Technological Change at Work', by I. McLoughlin and John Clark. Published by the Open University Press, 1988.
13 'Computers, Jobs, and Skills – The Industrial Relations of Technological Change' by Christopher Baldry. Published by Plenum Press, 1988.

Part V
Manufacturing Automation

⟨20⟩ Elements of automation

20.1 Introduction

(a) The origins of 'automation'

At the beginning of this book the increasing use of **mechanisation** during the industrial revolution was noted. The word 'mechanisation' has its origins in the Greek 'mekhane' which means 'machine', and was first used in English in the word 'mechanic' during the 14th century. Mechanisation refers to the application of machinery to do work previously done by humans, horses, oxen, etc. The term **automation** however, implies the concept of mechanisation with the added feature of automatic **control**. The word 'automatic', used first in the 18th century, was derived from the Greek 'automatos' meaning 'acting independently'. James Watt's governor (1788) was used to control the speed of a steam engine automatically, the Jacquard Loom (1804) used punched cards to control the pattern woven in cloth automatically, and in 1873 Christopher Spencer produced a fully automatic lathe with drum cams to control the movements of the cutting tools. The term 'automation' came into common usage in the 1940s in the motor car industry as a general description of the methods used to control processes automatically. The concept of the 'automatic factory' became popular about this time, the interest being evidenced by 'Project Tinkertoy' in 1954; this was previously discussed in Chapter 2. Here we will use the term 'factory automation' to encompass the equipment and techniques used either to eliminate the need for human work, as with industrial robots, or to assist humans, as in computer aided design (CAD; see also Chapter 21).

(b) The advantages of automation

Why use automation? It is generally accepted that unemployment, or at least the absence of the opportunity to earn money by working, is a bad thing. Why, then, use a system that eliminates the need for human work? There are many reasons and a number of them are noted here.

● It should first be noted that automation, when applied properly, will increase the **wealth creation** ability of a company, and therefore make the jobs of its existing workforce more secure and better paid. The creation of this wealth will be passed on to the nation through taxes and the spending power of the workforce. Thus the government obtains more money to pay for public services, and the suppliers of goods to the workers from the successful company obtain additional sales. Also the suppliers of the automated equipment will require engineers, technicians, and craftsmen to build the equipment. This means that increasing automation does not necessarily mean increasing unemployment. In fact the opposite is usually the case; the countries using the most automation and modern manufacturing techniques have the lowest unemployment rates.

- The various types of productivity were discussed in Chapter 17; from that discussion it should be self-evident that the use of automation must improve **labour productivity**, i.e. the cost of labour is reduced while the value of goods produced either remains constant or increases. However, if improvements in total productivity are to be gained then the investment in the automatic equipment must be made wisely, with realistic expectations of the equipment's capabilities. The car industry has the most notable examples of productivity improvements through automation, and comparisons of the number of cars produced per worker are regularly made between manufacturers in different countries. Broadly speaking automation also improves the efficiency of companies by providing the following advantages:

1 **Quality** is improved by removing the human element. People become tired while working, and in repetitive jobs bored; they are therefore prone to mistakes. Products produced by manual work also vary in quality due to differences in personal skills. Once automatic equipment is set up to produce good parts it will continue to produce good parts. Any tendency to deviate from the standards set can be monitored using statistical quality control (SQC) techniques and the process modified as required. With modern automated equipment in-process automatic inspection can allow 100% inspection of the product as it is being made, thus aiding the achievement of 'zero defects'.

2 **Production rates** are increased over those possible by manual methods. Where the work is repetitive and can be broken down into a sequence of simple movements automatic production rates can be many times those of human workers, e.g. consider the speed of operation of an automatic bottling plant, newspaper printing press, or a special purpose machine for the population of printed circuit boards. Production rates are also increased in areas such as design and drawing offices where computer aided design (CAD) techniques are applied.

3 **Working conditions** are improved where automation displaces human workers from tasks which are dangerous, hazardous to health, unpleasant, or tedious. For example, the handling of radioactive materials, spray painting, situations where heat and humidity conditions are high, and monotonous assembly work. In each of these areas it is expensive to employ humans as health and safety legislastion has to be satisfied. Also, if the work is unpleasant or boring, high labour turnover will mean

constant hiring and training of new workers to replace those that leave. Thus, as well as being ethical and humane, automation often saves money in these applications.

4 The predictability and consistency of automation means that the **flow of work** through the factory can be more easily monitored and controlled. Consequently this means faster throughput times and reductions of work in progress; this makes the factory more competitive by reducing costs and the time between order receipt and delivery of goods.

These, then, are some of the advantages of automation and the reasons for its increasing use. It does have some disadvantages, however. For example its implementation usually requires large capital expenditures by the company; these will be justified using the investment appraisal techniques mentioned earlier in the book. Also, depending on whether 'hard' or 'soft' automation is used, the flexibility of the company to cope with changes in product demand or design may be limited.

(c) 'Hard' and 'soft' automation

This was previously noted in section 3.6 above. 'Hard' automation refers to the type of equipment built to carry out a process or make a product using 'dedicated' or 'special purpose' machines for mass production quantities of, say, over 100,000. These are purpose built to make a specific product and their structure and control cannot be easily changed to produce any other products.

'Soft' automation refers to automatic processes or equipment that can be easily reprogrammed to cope with changes in products or tasks. Soft automation is becoming more popular due to the shorter life cycles of products and the need to satisfy a wide range of different customer demands. This type of automation usually makes use of computer or microprocessor based control techniques. Manufacturing equipment such as industrial robots and numerical controlled machine tools (see Chapter 21) come into this category. The application of computer controlled machines in factories is generally termed Computer Aided Manufacture, or CAM. The use of computers to aid the design process is called Computer Aided Design, or CAD. Finally the integration of CAD, CAM, and other systems such as computer based Management Information Systems, or MIS (noted in Chapter 15) is called Computer Integrated Manufacturing, or CIM.

A graph showing the interrelationship between volume and the cost per unit is shown in Figure 20.1. for manual work and hard and soft automation.

20.2   The building blocks of automated systems

Automated manufacturing systems are constructed of sub-systems which in

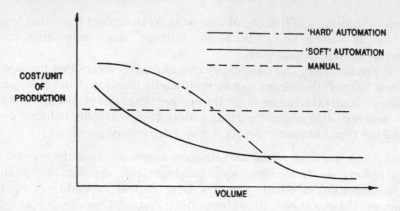

COST/UNIT OF PRODUCTION

VOLUME

— · — · — · —   'HARD' AUTOMATION
— — — — — —   'SOFT' AUTOMATION
— — — —   MANUAL

Figure 20.1   Interrelationship between volume and cost per unit for manual methods and hard and soft automation

turn are constructed from basic components. Here we will consider just some of these components, and how some of them are combined to form functioning sub-systems.

(a) Mechanical devices

- **Cams.** Probably one of the earliest control devices, these are used to control the movements of cam followers, which are in turn connected to linkages. These linkages are used to move cutting tools, pick and place devices, or inspection probes, etc. Three types of cam are shown in Figure 20.2. The cam profile is machined into the surface of the cam which is usually made of steel; it is the profile of the rotating cam which determines the movement of the follower. Cams are not now widely used since it has become easier and in some cases cheaper to control movements by computer controlled systems using feedback control.
- **Geneva Mechanism.** This is used to produce a rotary indexing movement in, for example, a worktable or toolhead of a turret lathe. Its principle of operation is shown in Figure 20.3. The slotted geneva plate has

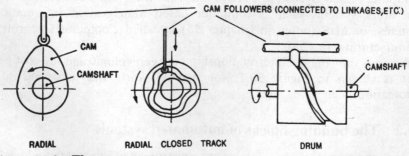

CAM FOLLOWERS (CONNECTED TO LINKAGES, ETC.)

CAM

CAMSHAFT

CAMSHAFT

RADIAL   RADIAL CLOSED TRACK   DRUM

Figure 20.2   Three types of cam

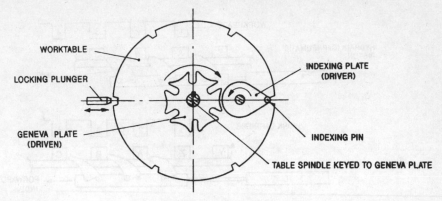

Figure 20.3 **Geneva mechanism for rotary indexing: view from underside of indexing worktable**

equispaced radial slots. An indexing plate has a fixed pin which engages with the slots as it rotates. Since the geneva plate in Figure 20.3 has six slots one revolution of the indexing plate will cause the geneva plate to rotate one sixth of a revolution, i.e. 60°. After each index the locking plunger will hold the mechanism in position until the rotating pin engages again. The number of steps per revolution is determined by the number of slots in the geneva plate. The indexing plate is driven via an electric motor.

- **Pawl linear transfer system.** This is used to produce a linear indexing movement; the principle of operation is shown in Figure 20.4. Reciprocation of the transfer bar is effected by a fluid power piston. Since the movement is equal to the spacing of the workheads, the work carriers will be indexed the desired distance along the line with reciprocation.

- **Conveyors.** These come in many forms. For example, roller conveyors are popular for transporting individual units such as boxes or components; the rollers may be powered by electric motors or free running. For bulk material, small components, and foodstuffs, powered belt conveyors are often used.

- **Limit switches.** These are simple electromechanical devices found in almost all automatic systems. They are made in various configurations, and two are shown in Figure 20.5. They incorporate a small microswitch operated by a mechanical plunger. This plunger is caused to move by a variety of means depending on the application. When the switch is operated it sends an electrical signal to the system controller to initiate some action. These switches are used in many applications, for example to limit the travel of a handling device, sense the presence of components on a conveyor line, or detect the opening of a safety barrier.

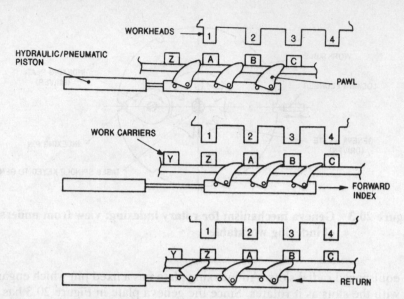

Figure 20.4   **Principle of Pawl linear transfer system**

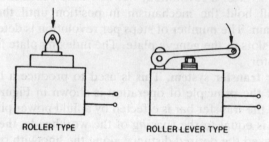

Figure 20.5   **Examples of limit switches**

(b) Fluid power devices and systems

Pneumatic devices which use compressed air between 1 and 7 bar pressure, and hydraulic devices which use hydraulic fluid pressurised to between 70 and 170 bar are used to drive many automatic systems; for example, hydraulic or pneumatic actuators would be used to operate the pawl mechanism mentioned earlier. Hydraulics are useful where very high loads have to be moved or sudden shock loads are experienced, but due to the problems associated with the high pressures and the possibility of leakages hydraulic machines are now less common in manufacturing systems. Pneumatics, however, are very popular. These devices are cheap, fast, clean, safe, and easy to work with. Almost all factories have an air compressor and compressed air system installed (they are even now found outside industry for powering 'animatronic' displays of characters and dinosaurs, etc.).

Pneumatic and hydraulic devices work on the same principle, i.e. a pressurised fluid is forced through connecting tubes to an actuator which does the work. The fluid is pressurised by a compressor in the case of air and a pump in the case of hydraulics. The flow of the fluid is controlled in both cases by valves. In automatic systems these valves incorporate electromagnets called solenoids which allow the valves to be opened or closed by electrical signals from a controller. With hydraulic systems much more complex control of speeds and forces can be obtained by using servo-valves which regulate the flow of fluid based on instructions from an electronic control system. The reason hydraulics allow better control is that hydraulic fluid is incompressible while air is not; this means that pneumatic actuators are used for simple movements where the load or actuator can be pushed against a fixed stop. A sketch of some pneumatic components is shown in Figure 20.6 and a simple system is shown in Figure 20.7.

(c) Electric motors for automation

For powering applications that require a continuously running motor with simple on–off control, then we may simply note that a motor will be used of suitable power and size. However for more complex control of automated machines, such as numerically controlled machine tools or industrial robots, specialised motors are used. These are called servo-motors because they incorporate some sort of 'feedback' device which sends a signal back to the controller indicating the actual response of the motor to a command signal. Two types of servo-motors are common, i.e. the permanent magnet direct current motor, and the brushless motor. Electric motors operate on the principle of passing an electric current through conductors in a magnetic field and so producing a torque. In servo-motors the magnetic field is produced by the permanent magnets, and the conductors are created by the motor coils; schematic sections of them are shown in Figure 20.8. The PM DC motor has been the most common due to relatively simple control; however, brushless motors are now gaining in popularity as the cost of their control decreases. Brushless motors do not have brushes to wear and so replacement costs and downtime due to maintenance are reduced; they also dissipate heat better, and are simpler in construction. These motors are usually controlled by a method called 'pulse width modulation'; this allows control of the current passed to the motor coils. This means that the motor torque is controlled, and hence the speed of rotation.

For moving light loads non-servoed stepper motors are used; these do not need feedback devices. They 'step' round one increment, say 1.8 degrees, for every pulse received from the motor controller. Thus if the controller counts the number of pulses sent to the motor the angle of the motor shaft will be known at any point in time; also by monitoring the rate at which the pulses are sent the speed of the motor may be calculated.

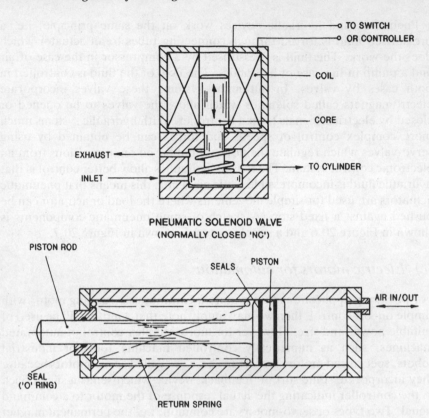

PNEUMATIC SOLENOID VALVE
(NORMALLY CLOSED 'NC')

SINGLE ACTING PNEUMATIC CYLINDER
FORWARD ACTION PNEUMATICALLY POWERED
RETURN ACTION BY SPRING

Figure 20.6   Pneumatic solenoid control valve and cylinder

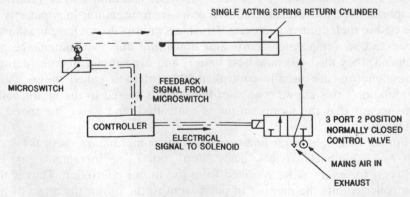

Figure 20.7   Simple pneumatic circuit utilising elements shown in Figures 20.5 and 20.6 (two states of control valve are shown symbolically)

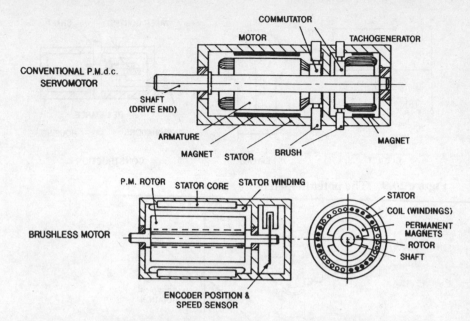

Figure 20.8   Sectional view of servo-motors used in automated systems

(d) Feedback devices

These devices, used widely in soft automation systems, provide feedback information on displacement and speed to the controller. There are a wide range of types; we will consider just three here: the potentiometer and the tachogenerator, both analogue devices, and the digital optical shaft encoder. Analogue devices produce an infinitely variable signal proportionate to the quantity being measured, whereas digital devices produce a series of discrete pulses whose rate or pattern provides the necessary control information.

- A **potentiometer** is used to provide information on angular displacement. It is essentially a rotary variable resistor, its principle of operation being shown in Figure 20.9. A direct current supply of V volts is applied across a resistance R. The output voltage is measured by tapping over a distance r. The distance r, and hence the output voltage v, will vary depending on the angular displacement of the wiper arm as it rotates about the central shaft. The shaft is usually attached to the part of the automatic device whose movement is being measured.
- A **tachogenerator** operates as a motor in reverse, i.e. it generates a current when its coils are rotated in a magnetic field. When made integral with a motor by mounting it on the same shaft, as shown in Figure 20.8, it produces a voltage signal proportionate to the speed of rotation (see Figure 20.10).

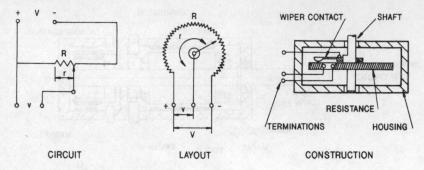

CIRCUIT   LAYOUT   CONSTRUCTION

Figure 20.9   The potentiometer

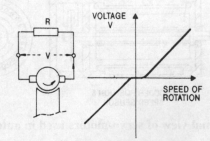

Figure 20.10   Tachogenerator circuit and voltage graph

- The **optical shaft encoder** is now a very popular means of obtaining feedback information. Its principle of operation is shown in Figure 20.11. It is composed of a glass disc which may be transparent with opaque sections, or opaque with transparent apertures. The disc is mounted on a shaft, e.g. the shaft of an electric motor. A lamp, light emitting diode (LED), or array of LEDs is located on one side of the disc while a light detecting sensor, or array of sensors, is located on the other. These photosensors produce a voltage when exposed to light. As the sections or apertures pass the light source(s) so the sensor(s) register the pulses of light by creating corresponding voltage pulses which are sent to the controller. Since the pattern of sections or apertures is known, e.g. say 360 apertures per revolution, by counting the number of pulses the angle of the shaft will be known. By noting the number of pulses per second the speed of the shaft will be known, and by noting the change in speed with respect to time the acceleration or deceleration of the shaft can be determined.

A microprocessor based controller is usually used with these devices. Encoders are of two types, the incremental encoder and the absolute encoder. The incremental type simply sends a train of pulses to the controller; this means that if power is removed from the system, even for a short time, then the encoder will not know where it is in absolute terms when power is restored. This means that when, for example, they are used

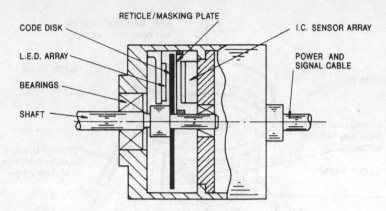

RETICLE/MASKING PLATE

CODE DISK

I.C. SENSOR ARRAY

L.E.D. ARRAY

POWER AND
SIGNAL CABLE

BEARINGS

SHAFT

Figure 20.11   Section through an optical shaft encoder

on industrial robots the robot has to be taken to a 'home' or reference point every time power is restored to it. Absolute encoders do not have this problem; they have a coded pattern of sections or apertures that uniquely defines the angular displacement of the disc. Thus if power is lost then restored, the unique pattern of signals from the photocell array will inform the controller of the exact position of the shaft.

(e) The vibratory bowl feeder

This is the most popular part holding and feeding device for automated systems, being found in almost every factory engaged in assembly work. Its construction is shown in Figure 20.12. It basically comprises a cylindrical bowl with a slightly convex base and a helical track running from the base of the bowl up around the internal wall to the rim, where it meets a delivery chute. The bowl is supported on three leaf springs inclined at an angle as shown in Figure 20.12; these springs are fixed to a heavy base. Between the bowl and the base is a powerful electromagnet. In operation, the bowl is partially filled with the parts that are to be fed. When power is supplied the electromagnet is switched on and off at high frequency. During each instant that the magnet is on it pulls the bowl downward in a twisting action caused by the inclined springs. Thus as the bowl vibrates at high frequency the parts in the bowl are shaken down the convex base to the bowl wall, where some will rest on the helical track. The high frequency vibratory twisting action causes the parts on the track to be left momentarily suspended in air; they then drop down onto the surface of the track at a point slightly ahead of where they left it. In this way, the parts move up the track to the delivery chute. Once they reach the chute they slide down to the work station under the force of gravity. Careful design of the bowl track can ensure that only parts at the desired orientation are fed to the delivery chute (see Figure 20.13 for an example).

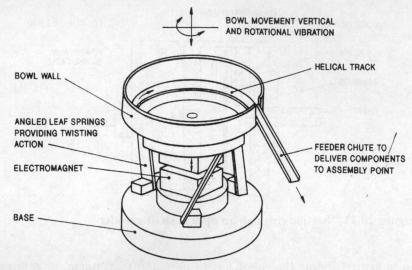

Figure 20.12   Vibratory bowl feeder

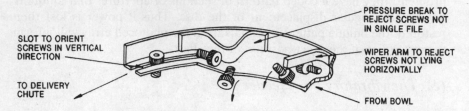

Figure 20.13   Example of methods used to orient components as they are fed up the bowl feeder track

20.3   Transfer systems

Transfer of parts between workstations in an automated system is effected by rotary or linear transfer machines and linear transfer lines. The workstations themselves may involve machining, handling, assembly, or inspection operations. Linear systems can be used for any number of workstations, but rotary machines are limited to applications where only a small number of operations are involved. Examples of rotary and linear transfer systems are shown in Figure 20.14. The heads of these systems are constructed from basic elements such as those mentioned earlier, e.g. pneumatic and hydraulic actuators with grippers or inspection probes attached, or cutting tools driven by electric motors. The rotary or linear movement of the parts can be effected by a variety of means such as the geneva indexing mechanism for rotary machines, or the pawl type linear transfer system; there are in fact a wide range of transporting methods, e.g. chain pullers, overhead conveyors, linear motors, and conveyors. These configurations are often found in hard automation systems, where each

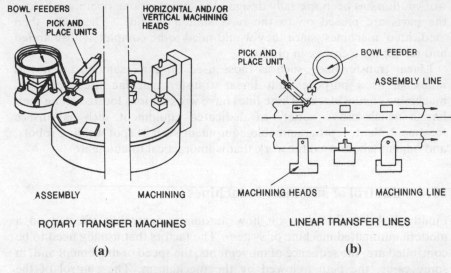

ROTARY TRANSFER MACHINES

(a)

LINEAR TRANSFER LINES

(b)

Source: Courtesy IBM

(c) A linear assembly line with reprogrammable industrial robots. A SCARA type robot can be seen in the centre: bowl feeders on the left are feeding keyboard buttons down chutes for assembly to the keyboards on the right

Figure 20.14   Rotary and linear transfer systems

workstation has been specially designed to carry out one operation before the parts are passed on to the next station in 'line'. These are then 'dedicated' machines, since they would need to be completely dismantled and rebuilt for a change in product.

Linear transfer lines, such as those used for car assembly, are not as inflexible as a purpose built linear transfer machine used for, say, machining engine blocks. These lines have workstations located along their length which use a variety of dedicated equipment such as surface treatment plant, reprogrammable equipment such as spot welding robots, and human labour used for work that is impractical to automate.

20.4 Control of automated machines

Finally, a brief discussion on how automatic control is effected on a modern automated machine or system. The factors that usually need to be controlled are: the sequence of movements, the speed of movement and, in some cases, the path followed by the mechanism. The control of the sequence of movements can be obtained by sending **trigger signals** from a microprocessor system, such as a computer or a programmable logic controller, to the control valves or motors of the machine. However, speed and path control is more complex and usually involves control of electric current to a motor for electrically powered systems, or to a valve which subsequently regulates the flow of fluid in systems that are fluid powered. Terms that are used to describe the type of control system used are: **open loop**, **closed loop**, **feedback**, and **servo-control**.

- **Open loop control** is the type of control found, for example, on cam operated machines or machines under computer control that are subjected to small loads. In this type of control, the machine is expected to operate exactly as commanded by the system controller and no automatic verification is made. This can be used only where light loads are involved and there is a high degree of confidence that the desired action will take place; the concept is shown in Figure 20.15.

- **Closed loop control** is the type used in almost all computer or microprocessor controlled machines. It is found in numerical controlled machine tools, industrial robots, and automated guided vehicles; outside the factory it is found in such things as advanced SLR cameras, car

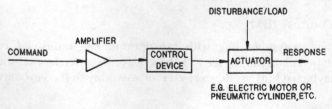

Figure 20.15   An open loop system

fuel management systems, and aircraft autopilots. All of these artifacts have a common attribute – they are '**mechatronic**' devices. A mechatronic device is one that is composed of mechanical, electrical, and electronic elements under the control of a microprocessor.

- Implicit in the term 'closed loop control' is the concept of '**feedback**'; this signifies that a signal is sent back from the device being controlled to the controller. This signal contains information on how the device is responding to the controller's commands; the controller can then use this information to modify its commands to ensure that the device performs as required. For example, assume that the controller sends a signal to an amplifier to send a specific current to an electric motor which should cause the motor to rotate at a desired speed. The feedback device on the motor, e.g. a shaft encoder, sends a signal back to the controller that the motor is moving too slowly. The controller will then modify its output signal to cause the current to the motor to be increased; the concept is shown in Figure 20.16.
- This type of control is often called '**servo-control**'. Essentially, servo-control implies a system that involves amplification of a control signal, e.g. the braking system in a car where the manual force applied to the brake pedal is amplified by the brake servo-system to produce a larger force at the brake pads. In the types of machines we are concerned with, this type of control is always present since the low power command signal is usually a low voltage signal from the controller. However in industrial applications servo-control is usually synonymous with feedback and closed loop control.

This concludes our discussion on the elements of factory automation; Chapter 21 will consider soft automation in the form of Computer Aided Manufacturing (CAM), which utilises many of the elements that have been discussed here.

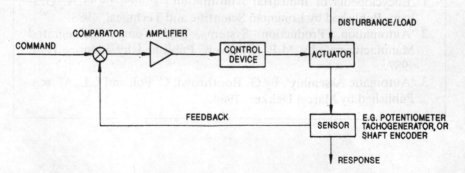

Figure 20.16 A closed loop system

Review Questions

1 What is the difference betwen 'mechanisation' and 'automation'?
2 'Automation causes unemployment!' Discuss fully why you agree, or disagree, with this statement.
3 Give **five** advantages of automation.
4 How might production volume affect the decision to use manual workers or hard or soft automation?
5 Why is 'soft' automation gaining in popularity?
6 How does a cam control the movements of a machine member?
7 What is a geneva mechanism, and how does it operate?
8 What is a limit switch, and what is its use?
9 Compare the advantages and disadvantages of using hydraulic and pneumatic power for automation equipment.
10 What is a servo-motor? Describe the two most common types used in factory automation.
11 What is the difference between an analogue and a digital feedback device?
12 Describe the operation of a feedback device that could be used to provide information for the control of angular displacement and speed.
13 Describe how a vibratory bowl feeder operates, and why it is so commonly found in factories.
14 Explain the terms 'open loop' and 'closed loop' control.
15 What is a 'mechatronic' device? Give an example of one used in a factory.

Further Reading

1 'Encyclopedia of Industrial Automation', Edited by G.A. Graham. Published by Longman Scientific and Technical, 1988.
2 'Automation, Production Systems, and Computer-Integrated Manufacturing', by M.P. Groover. Published by Prentice-Hall, 1987.
3 'Automatic Assembly', by G. Boothroyd, C. Poli and L.E. Murch. Published by Marcel Dekker, 1984.

21 Computer Integrated Manufacture

21.1 Introduction

Computer Integrated Manufacture (CIM) is the concept of a totally automated factory in which all the elements of manufacture previously described in this book are controlled by computer in an integrated manner. Although the cost of such a totally automated system is still unacceptably high, some companies have made considerable steps toward CIM with the goal of gaining a competitive advantage in the world market place. It should be noted at this stage that it is not just the use of computers that is significant; rather it is the skill with which the company's operations are **planned** and **integrated** together with the judicious application of computers that brings success. No single aspect of manufacturing is a panacea or guarantee of success, especially computerisation; it is the manner in which the company operates as a **homogeneous unit** that is important.

The following elements are the essential ingredients of a CIM system. Most of them can be implemented individually, thus allowing CIM to be approached in a step by step manner; however, their individual benefits must be shared with the rest of the factory so that they do not become isolated islands of automation.

- **Computer Aided Design** (CAD) involves the use of computers to create and analyse engineering designs. These designs can then be produced as drawings or the information used as direct input to the manufacturing equipment to produce the actual product.
- **Computer Aided Manufacture** (CAM) is a general term used to describe the manufacture of parts and products by equipment and systems controlled by computer. Individual pieces of equipment that can be computer controlled are: CNC machine tools such as lathes, milling machines, and machining centres; industrial robots; automated guided vehicles; automated identification and material tracking systems; and automated inspection equipment such as artificial vision systems. These can all be combined to form flexible manufacturing cells (FMCs) and flexible manufacturing systems (FMSs). Some of this equipment can be controlled by programmable logic controllers (PLCs).

Ideally the advantages of CAD and CAM can be optimised when combined with other elements such as automated storage and retrieval of parts (ASRS), computer aided process planning (CAPP), manufacturing resource planning (MRP II) and management information systems (MIS).

When this is done efficiently in conjunction with a common computerised data base and electronic data interchange, then the CIM concept is achieved.

We will now consider these elements in more detail before returning to CIM in general.

21.2   Computer Aided Design

(a) The advantages of CAD

The use of computers in design was initially restricted to the production of drawings; this was basically computer aided draughting. Today, CAD allows a designer to work interactively with a computer to create designs of components, products, or systems, observe how these designs respond to simulated influences, then modify the design accordingly. CAD systems vary in size and complexity from the very large that use costly computers, to the simple but relatively powerful that utilise the ubiquitous personal computer (PC). The following are some of the advantages of CAD.

- The time between receiving a request for a design and completion, i.e. the '**lead time**', is **reduced**.
- The designer can produce **more designs in less time**, i.e. **productivity** is increased.
- The **quality** of the design is improved, because the designer can act interactively with the system and use simulation techniques to arrive at the optimum design for various operating conditions.
- The product **cost** can be minimised, since the designer can use the computer to access the company's database to check for standard or existing components rather design new ones.
- Conversely, any designs created on the CAD system can be directly fed into the central database and used by **other departments** such as manufacturing and purchasing. This facility also ensures that everyone throughout the factory is working to the same issue number of drawing, i.e. any drawing modifications are instantly made known to all interested departments.
- If drawings are to be produced they will be clear and conform to a **standard presentation**.
- CAD systems with the ability to display the design three dimensionally (3D) with colour rendering and animation, help the designer to **visualise** the completed product.
- Finally, though not commonly implemented, the potential of integration can be maximised by transmitting the information held digitally in the CAD system, via a postprocessor, to the **machine tools** used for actual manufacture. This removes the need for drawings and the associated potential for human communication and interpretation problems.

(b) The elements of CAD

- A CAD system is composed of two major elements, its **hardware** and its **software**. Figure 21.1. shows the hardware of a typical CAD system.
- The **hardware** necessary for a basic CAD system comprises (i) a computer, (ii) mass storage mediums, (iii) a graphics screen, (iv) input devices, and (v) output devices.
- Important aspects of the computer used are the processor, the random access memory or RAM, and components that allow high quality graphics to be displayed and various forms of engineering analysis to be carried out. At the personal computer level these latter facilities are made possible by providing the computer with graphics cards and maths co-processor cards. Larger computer systems have specialised hardware that allows the software to run complex programs very quickly. The **processor** speed is critical in determining the overall performance of the system although the compatibility of related factors such as the width of the data path is also important.
- **Mass storage mediums** take many forms. Information can be held on optical disks, hard disks, floppy disks, and tapes. The actual memory used by the computer for temporary storage of information – the RAM mentioned previously – is also important, since it determines the size of packages that can be run, and the speed at which they operate.
- **Graphics screens** have the ability to display the high definition pictures required by some packages, especially those used to produce graphics for non-manufacturing applications such as pop videos and television programme introductions. Important considerations here are the screen size and resolution, what colours are available, and what high speed 'locally computed' functions are available such as 3D rotation and area colour filling.
- The most common **input** device is the **keyboard**; however, for CAD other means of inputting information to the system are often more appropriate. Many systems use menus from which commands and actions can be selected by moving a screen pointer via a 'mouse'. As well as selecting textual instructions the mouse can be used for drawing, i.e. the movements of the mouse on the mouse pad allow points to be defined which can be joined by lines and components can be rotated,

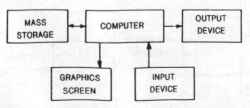

Figure 21.1   Hardware of a CAD system

etc. Other input devices are light pens, touch sensitive screens, joysticks, and electronic pads and pens. It is also possible to add old drawings into the CAD system by using a device called a digitiser. This device uses a sensor electronically to scan the drawing in a manner similar to a fax machine, thus 'digitising' the drawing.

- A wide variety of **output** devices are available, such as laser printers, ink jet printers, dot matrix printers, pen or electrostastic plotters, and special devices such as computer output to microfilm or 35mm slide units. Choice of device will be dependent on the production rate and quality of print required, the money available, and the size of print to be produced. The user would examine all of these parameters from the supplier's specification sheets before making a purchasing decision.

- The **software** required for a CAD system can be envisaged as comprising four elements (see Figure 21.2). These are the operating system, the graphics software, the applications software, and the applications database. Although hardware is important, it is the choice of software that is critical to the success of any CAD installation. The software must be reliable and suited to the needs of the company, and since some software is relatively expensive, it should be selected with consideration of its potential for future, possibly more demanding, projects.

- The **operating system** is the basic set of programs used to control the operation of the computer and its peripherals. Examples of operating systems are DOS and UNIX. The operating system used will affect the performance of the CAD system at a basic level; for example, it will determine if the system can carry out more than one task in parallel, i.e. multi-tasking, and if more than one designer can use the system at the same time, i.e. can more than one workstation be used?

- At the next level we have the CAD system **graphics software**. These are the programs that allow the user to create, display and modify product geometry. There are three basic ways of representing an object in a CAD system, i.e. a 'wire frame' structure, 'surface modelling', or 'solid modelling'; the last requires most computing power. Wire frame structures can be either 2D or 3D although most systems today will have 3D capability. Wire frame representations of designs can be enhanced by removing hidden lines from the display and representing the surfaces of the object by colour shading. Surface modelling has an added advantage in that it recognises and displays the blending and intersecting of 3D

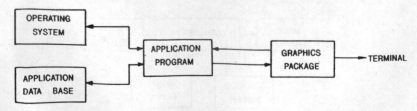

Figure 21.2   CAD software elements

faces. Solid modelling of objects involves different representation techniques, e.g. in constructional representation the software uses small solid geometrical shapes called primitives to construct the object. This allows more detailed engineering analysis of design to be carried out. For example the mass and volume of the object can be considered in calculations involving the centre of gravity and moments of inertia of the design.

- At the applications software level we find the **application specific packages** purchased by the designer in order to construct and evaluate particular designs and solve specific problems. The range of packages available spans all of the engineering disciplines. For example, a mechanical engineer may wish to use a powerful Finite Element Analysis package which will allow analysis of the behaviour of a design when subjected to forces. An electronics engineer may use a suite of packages which would allow an electronic circuit to be designed and then translate this into a printed circuit board layout diagram; this information could then be used as input to the controller of an automated PCB population machine. A construction engineer may use a package that facilitates routeing of pipework in a new building. As a final example a manufacturing engineer may design a series of components on the CAD system and, after further processing, use this digital information as input to a numerically controlled machine tool to create the finished parts. The manufacturing engineer may also use CAD to help with factory layout design and create animated simulations of work flow or kinematic devices such as industrial robots.
- Finally there is the **applications database**, which contains libraries of standard parts, symbols, and routines that will facilitate the design process. This can be linked into other data bases within the company, as mentioned earlier, to ensure that updated information on design is available throughout the organisation.

21.3 Computer Aided Manufacture

(a) Advantages of CAM

- CAM is intended to enable the cost benefits obtainable with automated mass production to be achieved at the batch production level. One of the reasons it can do this is the reprogrammable nature of the equipment. This means that, unlike hard automation, CAM equipment is able to respond rapidly to product design changes, and can be relatively quickly reprogrammed to suit new products as market demand changes. It therefore takes much longer to become obsolete, thus allowing the cost of investment to be recouped over a longer period. CAM also enables a company to tackle the manufacture of relatively low quantity specialised designs to suit particular market niches.

When used to replace people, CAM provides the following advantages:

- **Continuous working** is possible 24 hours per day, and 7 days per week. Interruptions are necessary only to allow access of maintenance personnel and for reprogramming when the product is changed. Contrast this with the use of people who require rest, refreshment, and lunch breaks. Also if 24 hour working is required, three 8 hour shifts are usually necessary, thus tripling the wage bill.

- **Consistent quality** is obtained by using CAM, and scrap and rework costs are reduced. This is because once a machine is programmed to carry out a task correctly it will continue to do so until either a random fault develops or a progressive deterioration such as cutting tool wear occurs. In either case automatic inspection systems can be used to monitor quality and send warning signals as appropriate. Contrast this with the use of people who become fatigued, ill, distracted, or bored with their work; when this happens mistakes are made and product quality drops. Hence in the motor industry cars with unacceptably high levels of faults are sometimes labelled 'Monday morning' or 'Friday afternoon' cars, since they are made by workers either unhappy about starting another week or with their thoughts on the approaching weekend.

- CAM systems, such as industrial robots, can be used in areas either **unpleasant** or **hazardous** to people. This removes the problems of absenteeism through boredom or dissatisfaction with the work, and it also allows health and safety regulations to be more easily complied with, e.g. paint spraying robots can operate in a room isolated from the rest of the factory thus removing the costs of protective clothing, ventilation, rest periods, etc. necessary for a human worker.

- **Less wasted material** is produced by CAM than with labour intensive methods; this is again a result of the consistency of operation.

- The cost of paying **wages** to people increases every year, whereas the investment in CAM is a once only payment. This makes it an attractive decision where long term manufacturing strategies are being planned.

- The costs of computerised equipment in relation to the costs of labour are **decreasing**. This is due to the reducing cost of the computing and electronic elements as they become more efficient and powerful for their size and are manufactured in higher volumes. The cost of the other machine elements, however, does not necessarily become less expensive; this is due to the fact that they often require a considerable labour input for their manufacture and the economics of volume are not so evident.

- Finally CAM allows much better general **control** of the manufacturing system, thus reducing lead times, work in progress, and stock. Increased productivity results, with quicker response times to customer requests and punctual delivery of orders.

Some of the essential components of CAM are now examined.

(b) The control of CAM equipment

- Elements of CAM systems such as numerically controlled machine tools, industrial robots, and automated guided vehicles, are controlled by **microprocessor based systems**. Most equipment is today electrically powered and it is the control of this that we will consider. However, before looking at how this is effected consider that these CAM machines have a number of axes to be powered and hence controlled. These are shown in Figure 21.3 for one type of machine tool and one type of robot configuration. Each axis that the machine has adds to its ability to machine complex parts in the case of a machine tool or increases its dexterity in the case of a robot.

- These elements usually use **closed loop control** systems as described in Chapter 20. Figure 21.4 shows the configuration of the hardware used to drive one axis of each of the machines shown in Figure 21.3. The control system sends out a command to drive the axis motor. If the motor was a stepper motor, this would be a train of voltage pulses to a power unit which would send out a corresponding train of high power pulses to step the motor round the required angular displacement. If the motor was of the direct current or brushless type, the signals from the controller would be amplified, using techniques such as pulse width modulation, to provide an appropriate current to the motor. Pulse width modulation operates by rapidly switching on and off sets of power transistors, thus allowing current to be passed to the motors in a controlled manner.

- To translate the rotary movement of the motor into the desired movement of the machine axis a variety of **transmission systems** can be used. Figure 21.4(a) shows a screw-nut system; in this type of transmission, the rotary movement of the motor rotates the screw which runs inside a nut containing ball or roller bearings. Since the nut is fixed to

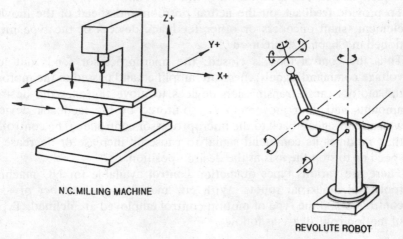

Figure 21.3   Machine axes

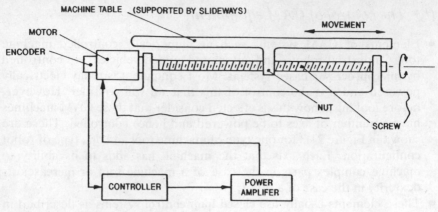

(a) Screw–nut system

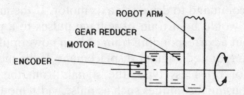

(b) Motor and gear reducer system

Figure 21.4   Transmission systems

the table, rotation of the motor results in a linear movement of the
table. In Figure 21.4(b) the motor shaft acts as the input shaft to a
geared speed reducer. Compact reducers such as harmonic and cycloidal
drives are common on industrial robots; these allow very large speed
reductions between the motor and the robot axis.

- To provide **feedback** on the actual position and speed of the moving
  element, shaft encoders or other feedback devices of the type mentioned in Chapter 20 are used.

- Thus the control loop is closed; the microprocessor sends out low
  voltage command signals; these are amplified and passed to the motors,
  the motors cause transmission devices to move the axes the desired
  amounts and their movement is monitored by the feedback devices
  which send signals back to the microprocessor controller. The controller
  then modifies its command signal to cause an increase or decrease in
  speed or to stop the axis at the desired position.

- There are various types of **motion control** available for NC machine
  tools and industrial robots. With NC machines the number of axes
  controlled and the type of motion control employed are defined. Types
  of motion control are as follows.

1 **Point to point** (P) – this causes movement of the axes of the machine such

that the relative movement of the machine cutting tool is from one point to another without regard to the speed of movement or the path taken.

2 **Linear** (L) – this involves control of one axis of the machine such that speed of movement is controlled.

3 **Contouring** (C) – this involves the simultaneous control of a number of axes, enabling them to operate in a coordinated manner to produce complex shapes, angles, and curves. Thus a 2CL machine can contour on two axes but has only linear movement on a third; this could therefore produce profiled plate shapes such as cams, whereas a 3C machine would have the ability to produce three dimensional contoured shapes, e.g. a hemisphere or cone shape.

Industrial robots have a similar variety of controls.

1 **Point to point** (PTP) control indicates that the end effector of the robot arm can be programmed to move from one point to another, but no consideration will be given by the controller as to the route followed between points; this type of control might be used for assembly work.

2 **Point to point with coordinated path** (PTPCP) control indicates that the robot will move its end effector between points, but will move its joints in a coordinated manner. This allows straight lines, circles, and curves to be followed. This type of control is useful for arc welding.

3 **Continuous path** control involves the robot duplicating a series of continuous movements originally made by the operator moving the arm, or a duplicate slave arm, through a complex series of three dimensional movements. This is the type of control necessary in spray painting.

4 Robots used for spot welding in the car industry use a system of control known as **point to point with line tracking**. Here, the robots are taught the points on a static car that are to be spot welded. When production actually starts the cars move past the robots in a continuous movement as they pass along the assembly line. The robot controller therefore takes information from a sensor, e.g. a shaft encoder, on the speed of the body movement, then compensates for this by altering the instructions to the robot to enable it to put the spot welds in the appropriate points on the car body as it moves through the robot's work envelope.

(c) Numerical Controlled (NC) machine tools

- NC machine tools were first produced commercially in 1952. Early machines operated by transferring the machining data, prepared by a 'part programmer', to punched paper tapes, then used these tapes to produce multi-channel magnetic tapes which were read by the machine tool control system. Today machines may be classed as NC, or CNC – computer numerical control. In a company manufacturing large batches of components with a constant demand for new designs the part programs may be prepared in a central programming area. The program information would be held on punched paper tape which would then be sent to control the appropriate NC machine. For small batches and batches of one, CNC machines would be used; they have their own microprocessor based programming and control system alongside or integral with their structure. With CNC the operator can create the part program on site by using manual data input (MDI) programming. The program can then be modified as necessary and after the requisite number of parts have been produced it can be stored on magnetic tape or floppy disc for future repeat orders.

- In programming the machine the programmer obtains the necessary geometric and dimensional information from the component drawing, possibly prepared on a CAD system. Information on the speeds and feeds to be used by the machine are either decided directly by the programmer or obtained from process planning or operation layout sheets. This information is then translated into instructions for the machine controller by creating a punched paper tape or by typing in commands via a keyboard alongside the machine. These instructions adhere to a standard ISO format code. This standardisation has been adopted to allow the same 'language' to be used for programming NC machines made by many manufacturers.

- CNC machines also have the capability of **interfacing** with other machines and transferring data between them. Thus they can be used to take the data from a CAD system and use this to machine the designed components without human intervention. When NC machines are networked together under the control of a large supervisory computer, which may also control other equipment such as industrial robots and automated guided vehicles, the term DNC, i.e. direct, or distributed, numerical control, is used.

- Figure 21.5 shows a typical CNC machine tool; in this case, it is a machining centre. This is a machine tool that is able to carry out a variety of machining operations each normally limited to one machine, e.g. it may be able to carry out milling, drilling, tapping, and boring. Machining centres also have the ability to change tools automatically and interface with computer controlled material handling equipment so that they can load raw material and unload finished components automatically. As well as NC lathes, milling machines, drills, and machining centres, the thermal cutting processes such as the oxyfuel and laser processes are also often controlled in this way.

- NC machine tools provide high precision, high production rates, and high machine utilisation due to less idle time for set ups, etc. Tooling costs are less than those for manually operated machines since fewer, and simpler, jigs and fixtures are required to hold and orientate the work. Since smaller batches of parts can be run economically inventory is reduced. Productivity is increased; this also results in less floor space required. Using NC machines with a number of axes it is possible to create components of complex geometry that are not easily obtained using manually controlled machines or hard automation.

- Finally it can be said that NC machines realise the benefits of CAM generally, as noted at the beginning of this section.
- An apparent disadvantage of NC machines is their high cost relative to manual machines. However, provided they are well utilised, this initial investment is usually recouped within an acceptable period of time. This particularly applies when the benefits that are more difficult to quantify, such as improvements in quality, reduced inventory, and more rapid response to customer requests, are included.

(d) Industrial robots

- An industrial robot is essentially a reprogrammable manipulator of parts, tools, or materials. It can therefore be used for a great variety of tasks, and it is this **flexibility** of use that has led to its wide application in industry. The first robotic manipulators were used in the 1960s but it was not until 1973 when microprocessor controlled robots appeared that their popularity rapidly expanded. As computing hardware and software decreased in cost and increased in power so the expectations of what robots could do exponentially increased. This led to a period in the early to mid-1980s where, aided by much media 'hype', robots were being expected to do far more than they were capable of; they were also being used unwisely – often in work where humans or hard automation would have been better. This led to disappointed users, and many robot companies went out of business. Today the industrial robot is seen as

Source: Beaver Engineering Group plc

(a) A CNC horizontal machining centre

(b) Components being machined in a CNC horizontal machining centre

Figure 21.5   A machining centre

simply another tool that can provide many benefits, provided it is wisely employed.

- Industrial robots are normally driven by electric dc or brushless motors. A few using hydraulic power may still be found in environments where heavy shock loads are experienced or high voltage electricity is not allowed due to fire risks. At the other extreme a few pneumatic robots are used where simple high speed operations are required. Figure 21.6 shows the major elements of an industrial robot. The **arm** is the part that carries out the physical work; there are a number of configurations available and the one shown is of the revolute type. The arm has three major rotational axes allowing it to sweep out, and work within, a spherical work envelope. In this particular robot the wrist also has three

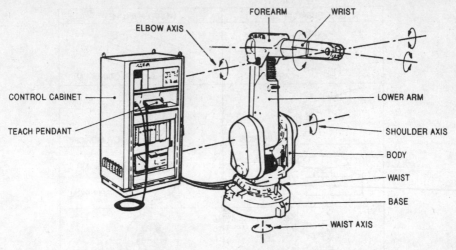

Source: ABB robotics AB

Figure 21.6   Major elements of an industrial robot

axes which allow orientation of the wrist about any point to which the arm has moved. The relative positions of these six joints provide this robot with six degrees of freedom. Six degrees of freedom are not always necessary, however; for example, the assembly of a properly designed product should not need a robot with more than four degrees of freedom. As well as the arm a **control unit** will be necessary. For an electric robot this will probably be in two sections, one low voltage and one high voltage. The low voltage section will contain the microprocessors for overall system control, individual axes control, and handling of analogue and digital input and output signals to and from the robot and other parts of the working environment, e.g. signals from safety sensors. This section will also contain the memory, disc drives, and the input and output ports, etc. The high voltage section will contain the power amplifiers and controllers for the motors; this will supply the current to the motors based on signals from the low voltage section.

- There are a variety of configurations of industrial robots produced, and Figure 21.7 shows the most popular types and their work envelopes. The anthropomorphic is the most flexible and can be adapted to a wide range of tasks, though it is most suitable for those that fully utilise its flexibility, such as spot and arc welding and spray painting. Because of its geometry it is not ideal for straight line movements such as those involved in assembly. Robots with a cylindrical work envelope are able to sweep out a large volume and have a linear vertical axis. They are suitable for material handling, palletising, machine tool servicing, and assembly tasks. The SCARA (Selective Compliance Assembly Robot Arm) has been specially designed for assembly. It has four axes; two of

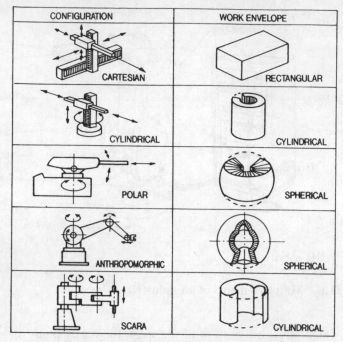

Source: Industrial Robotics – Mair

Figure 21.7   Most common robot configurations

these axes allow it to position its gripper anywhere within its cylindrical work envelope, the linear axis allows a straight downward movement for insertion, and a rotational axis on the wrist allows the gripper to orientate the component it is holding before insertion. The arm is designed to have **lateral compliance**, i.e. the ability to move slightly in the horizontal plane, to allow insertion of components to take place even if slightly out of alignment. The robots with linear axes are the easiest to control, and they can be given very large work envelopes by increasing axis lengths. For example, in gantry configuration they can be used for material handling of heavy components, or they can be mounted to run along the length of a bench for assembly work.

● Control of industrial robots was mentioned earlier; however it is worth noting here that the method of **programming** is closely related to the **motion control system** being used. For PTP control and PTPCP control, a 'teach pendant' is used for programming. Here the programmer teaches the robot by using a **handheld pendant** which contains one or more of the following components:

1 A small **keyboard** and **alphanumeric LED or LCD display**; this can be used for inputing simple instructions.

2 A **joystick** or array of buttons and knobs; these are used to cause the arm to move to desired points in space.
3 A **start button**, usually recessed for safety, an **emergency stop button** with an easily hit protruding mushroom shaped surface, and a **speed control**. For safety, this speed control, even at maximum, will not allow the arm to move at dangerously high speeds while programming is taking place.

Using the pendant, the robot is taken to each point that it will be required to move to in the actual production operation. At each point the operator uses the keyboard to put the coordinates of that point into the controller memory. The controller knows the point by reading the signals from the robot's internal position sensors, e.g. shaft encoders. Thus a 'point file' is built up in memory. Next the programmer types in instructions as to what the robot should do between and at these points, e.g. move from point *A* to point *B* at a speed of xmm/sec, at point *B* open gripper, and so on. In this way an 'instruction file' is built up. The robot controller integrates these files to create the full program. Teach pendant programming is used for programming robots engaged in welding, assembly, and material handling tasks.

Another method of programming is called **'teach by lead through'**. This involves physically leading the arm through its task. This is done with robots that use continuous path control. For example, a spray painter can program the robot by attaching a spray paint gun with a special pistol grip to the end of the robot arm. By holding the grip the programmer then carries out the desired spray painting operation; since the arm is attached to the grip it carries out the necessary movements to duplicate the operation. While the arm is moving, the positional information from the joint sensors is constantly fed back to the controller memory. The trigger on the spray gun provides the on/off signal for paint flow. Under production conditions, the controller simply causes the arm to duplicate the movements recorded during programming.

Both of the above methods are **'on line'** programming, i.e. the robot needs to be physically involved in the programming operation. This has the advantages that any problems likely to be encountered during production are easily identified; it is relatively simple to learn, and the precision of the robot can be verified as programming is taking place. However, the method has disadvantages in that the robot is taken out of production while programming, and complex programs with branching, sub-routines, and the ability to respond to external sensory input are difficult to create. For these and other reasons **'off line'** programming was developed. This allows robot programs to be written, using a high level language, at a site remote from the production area. The use of graphical **simulation** packages have made this method of programming much more reliable, since the movements can be observed on a graphics screen. These packages allow collisions to be detected and provide estimates of cycle times. Many of them also have libraries of commercially available robots to allow the best robot to be selected for a particular application and layout before actually embarking on the large capital investment of the robot itself (see Figure 21.8).

● Industrial robots are used in preference to people since they produce a constant level of quality, they can work in areas that are hazardous or dangerous for humans, boring, tiring or stressful jobs do not exist for robots, they are stronger than humans, and after the initial investment they do not need yearly salary increases or incur additional costs for insurance, etc. They are used in preference to special purpose dedicated equipment since they are easily reprogrammed to cope with new products or changes in the design of existing products; this means that they take much longer to become obsolete.

(e) Automated and autonomous guided vehicles

● AGVs have long been in use in warehouses and factories. However it is with the advent of CAM that they have been able to realise their full potential; examples of AGVs are shown in Figure 21.9. Within a Flexible Manufacturing System they are primary material handling

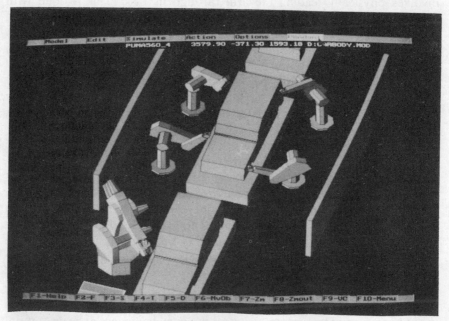

Source: Courtesy Robot Simulations

Figure 21.8   Simulation of industrial robots on a car assembly line; the simulation is being carried out on a personal computer using 'Workspace'

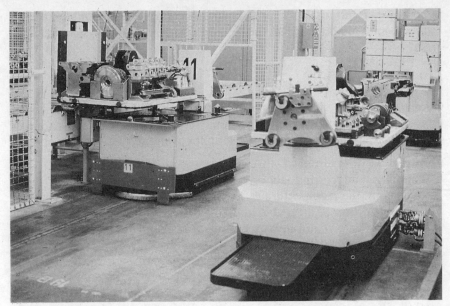

Source: Jungheinrich (GB) Ltd

Figure 21.9   AGVs being used to transport engine components

devices used to transport parts, tools, and materials to the appropriate machine tool where they are then transferred into the machine using a secondary handling device such as an industrial robot. AGVs can be programmed for automatic routeing and positioning, and many can be fully integrated into the manufacturing system by operating under the control of a supervisory computer. The simplest types follow slots in the floor in which chains move; guide pins in the base of the AGV locate the slots and hook into the chain. The chain then acts as a towline, pulling the vehicle along the slot track. These types are relatively inflexible; better systems can use self-propelled AGVs that use inductive sensors to follow hidden cable embedded in the factory floor.

- Even more flexibility is obtainable from autonomous guided vehicles. They operate under their own power, are free ranging, and use their own 'on board' guidance systems. Although still uncommon on the shop floor there are a variety of guidance systems available, and a combination of them can be employed. Internal sensor monitoring can be used as in industrial robots, e.g. the number of revolutions of each wheel, and changes in wheel orientation, can be monitored, and if the wheel diameter is known then the position of the AGV at any time can be calculated. However this is prone to error due to skidding or individual wheels losing contact with the floor. Other techniques for absolute positioning involve: inertial guidance systems incorporating gyroscopes; position reference beacons located throughout the factory with appropriate infrared or laser transmitters and receivers mounted on the AGV; and, although still at the research stage, on board vision systems.

(f) Vision systems

Computer vision systems are becoming more widely used in industry as their capabilities increase and the time they require to process images decreases. The following are some examples of where they can be applied.

- **Inspection.** It is estimated that visual inspection comprises at least 10% of total manufacturing labour costs; in some industries, such as those involved in the manufacture of PCBs, this is considerably higher. Thus the introduction of a reliable and consistent vision system to replace a human inspector naturally susceptible to fatigue and distraction can be very cost effective. The inspection may be qualitative, e.g. checking for flaws in glass bottles, checking for cracks in castings, and verifying if PCBs are completely populated with the correct components, or quantitive, e.g. measuring the dimension of a turned part or checking the width of a steel strip emerging from a rolling mill.
- **Component orientation.** Here the vision system is used to check the orientation of components before or after an operation. A typical example is that of orienting surface mounted electronic components on a PCB; some component insertion machines have integral vision systems for this purpose.
- **Identification.** A variety of applications are found under this heading, one of the earliest being character recognition where the vision system is used to read alphanumeric characters on mail or packaging. The system may also be used to identify individual components on a bench or pallet prior to assembly.
- **Guidance.** As noted earlier, vision systems can be used to guide AGVs; however, the most common guidance application is that of seam tracking in arc welding. Here a specially designed vision system is used to provide information on the weld joint immediately in front of the welding arc to allow a welding robot to follow the correct path precisely.

The basic elements of a vision system are shown in Figure 21.10. First a camera is required to acquire an image. These are usually now of the solid state type. A solid state camera is simply a tube with a lens at one end and an integrated circuit containing an array of photosensitive cells at the other. The associated power supply and signal amplification circuitry need not be actually in the tube; this therefore allows the image acquisition part of these cameras to be extremely small, light, and rugged. The density of the photosensitive cells determines the definition of the image acquired. A very cheap camera may only have a 32 by 32 array providing a picture containing only 1024 picture elements or 'pixels', whereas an expensive high resolution camera may have a 1000 by 1000 array providing an

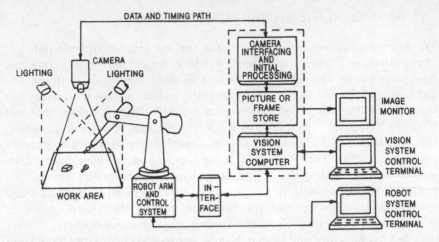

Source: *Industrial Robotics* – Mair

Figure 21.10 Elements of a robot vision system

extremely high definition picture of 1 million pixels. However, to allow the vision system computer to handle the image data in real time a resolution of somewhere between these two extremes is usually chosen. Colour is seldom used in industrial vision systems, to minimise the amount of data that needs to be handled. The amount of data can be further reduced by using the minimum amount of grey levels required in the picture. For example, if an object is dark and it is resting on a light background then to identify the object a silhouette type of image is all that is necessary; this is called a binary image, since each pixel needs only to be black or white, i.e. only one 'bit' is required to define the light intensity. However if the component is a casting that is to be examined for cracks, then a range of grey levels will have to be used. This will increase the data to be handled, e.g. if 64 grey levels are required then each pixel will require to be defined by a six bit 'word'.

The image from the camera, which is in the form of voltage signals from the photocells, is digitised and then held in a 'frame store'. This is a specially designed piece of electronic circuitry that allows one frame of the picture being looked at to be held static for a short interval while it is examined. This data is now further processed to allow features of the scene to be analysed. For example, if the vision system is being used to select one component from a number of different items lying on a table, then it will use its program to check various features. For each item it may check area, perimeter length, and the number of holes present. If the system has already been taught the features associated with the desired component, it will now be able to carry out the selection process. If the vision system was interfaced to a robot this information could now be used to signal the robot to pick up the selected component.

(g) Automatic identification (ID) systems

We have considered how components can be machined, manipulated, transported, and inspected within a CAM system. This section considers how parts can be identified and tracked automatically through the manufacturing process. Auto ID ensures that the systems within the factory are using up to the minute information on which to base decisions that will affect ordering, the scheduling of work, the amount of work in progress, the amount of stocks held, and the on time delivery to the customer. By using Auto ID to track materials, components, and products from goods inward through to despatch, information on progress, quality, production history, and destination is all available instantaneously. In fact, some manufacturers of consumer products are linking their own computer systems with those of their major supermarket chain customers, so that they can manufacture and despatch their product to ensure that a constant supply is available at the supermarket. This would be extremely difficult if it was not for Auto ID systems in the form of bar codes.

- **Bar coding** is the most widely used and familiar method, due to its versatility. In this type of system numeric or alpha-numeric information is represented as a series of bars of varying thickness and separations. They are quite ubiquitous and you will see them on sweet wrappers, newspapers, pre-packed food, drink cans, and even the cover of this book. There have been various symbologies developed for different applications. The bars are read by a scanner which shines a light, commonly a low power laser, at the bar code and monitors the amount of light reflected onto a sensor. This provides a series of binary voltage levels which are decoded to provide the identification data. Within the factory, bar codes can be attached to components or their containers as they pass through the manufacturing system; the information on them is transmitted to the supervisory computer at appropriate intervals.

- Another method is the **magnetic strip**. These are strips of material containing information in the form of electromagnetic charges, such as are found on credit and identification cards. They can be used in factories for product identification or operator time attendance cards. The band is read by a decoder which may be a hand held wand or wall mounted.

- **Optical character recognition** (OCR) involves using a scanner to examine stylised alphanumeric characters that can also be easily read by people. As mentioned earlier, vision systems can be used for this with a camera scanning the characters and the computer analysing the image.

- Finally **radio frequency** identification (RFID) has advantages in some areas. It is possible to read and write information to a small transponder or 'tag' attached to the component or product being tracked. The tag contains a custom made programmable integrated circuit and a long life battery. Consider one of these attached under the wheel arch of a motor car in an assembly plant. As the car moves along the production line the tag comes within the range of a fixed position transmitter and receiver. This transmitter emits an interrogation signal which the tag responds to by sending out a unique train of radio pulses; these act as an identification signature. The receiver decodes this information then transmits it to the supervisory computer. Radio frequency identification is ideal where there is no direct line of sight between the identifier and the reader, where the environment is dirty or dusty, or where the identifier is covered up by the process, e.g. painting a car body.

(h) Programmable logic controllers

Automatic control of valves, motors, and switches, etc. is a necessary part of a CAM system.

- For this type of control programmable logic controllers, i.e. PLCs, have been developed. Both PLCs and 'personal computers' (PCs) are used for similar purposes on the factory shop floor. However PLCs are usually designed to be built up in a **modular manner** to suit a variety of control tasks, whereas PCs are designed more for business use and require the addition of special control boards for interfacing to manufacturing equipment. A good comprehensive definition of a PLC is that of the National Electrical Manufacturer's Association in the USA which states that a PLC is, 'a digitally operating electrical apparatus which uses a programmable memory for the internal storage of instructions for implementing specific functions such as logic, sequencing, timing, counting, and arithmetic to control machines or processes through digital or analog input or output modules'. PLCs can be used to coordinate the actions of a number of machines in a machining cell, or to synchronise the operation of machining heads or assembly stations on transfer lines.
- The basic components of a PLC are shown in Figure 21.11. The keyboard and display allow programming and interrogation of the PLC. The power supply provides noise free power to the controller and the output signals. The memory contains the program instructions on how the PLC is to control the external equipment, and what it is to do with incoming data. The central processor or CPU is the microprocessor system which provides the logic, decision making, and mathematical functions. It also supervises the handling of all the input and output signals through the interfaces. These input and output interfaces provide a simple means of communicating with the equipment being controlled and monitored. The input and output signals may be analogue or digital. PLCs can be programmed by preparing a 'ladder logic' diagram; however, for more complex tasks high level languages similar to those used in personal computers may be used.

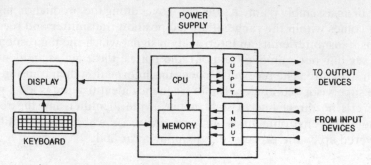

Source: Industrial Robotics – Mair

Figure 21.11   Programmable controller: major components

(i) Flexible manufacturing systems

CAM elements such as NC machine tools, industrial robots, AGVs, and PLCs can be integrated to form Flexible Manufacturing Systems which are controlled by a supervisory computer (see Figure 21.12). Most of these are at present flexible machining systems, but there are also some flexible assembly systems (FAS) in existence. Their purpose is to allow complete manufacture of small batches of components on customer demand, i.e. with very short lead times and little work in progress. This concept can be adopted on a small scale within a conventional factory by creating flexible manufacturing cells (FMCs). For example, a cell may comprise two or three machine tools serviced by one or more robots; it may also have an automated inspection station, possibly using a vision system. The cell would be designed to be able to machine a family of parts (this was discussed earlier in sections 14.3(b) and 14.3(c)).

21.4   Other CIM elements

As well as CAD and CAM there must obviously be other aspects of the manufacturing system that need to be automated if full CIM is to exist. Some of these have already been mentioned in previous chapters, e.g. material requirements planning and manufacturing resource planning, the construction of a common database including the bills of material for all products, and the overall management information system with labour performance reporting, costing, and quality statistics, etc. One aspect not yet mentioned is the link between CAD and CAM necessary for complex products; this is computer aided process planning or CAPP. This requires selection of machines and processes, determination of methods to be used, selection of tooling and fixtures, specification of speeds and feeds for machining, estimation of times and costs, and the use of this information as input for capacity planning and scheduling systems. This is a complex

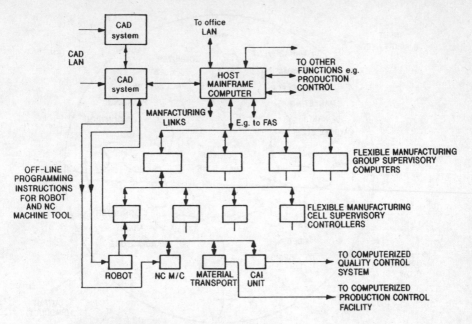

Source: Prentice-Hall

Figure 21.12   Information flow in a large FMS

procedure when done manually; it therefore follows that it is very difficult to use computerised methods to create sensible process plans automatically. A considerable amount of skill and experience has to be transferred to the software, thus necessitating the use of expert systems; in fact, there is usually at least some degree of manual input even in the most automated systems.

The CIM concept is shown in Figure 21.13. This shows how all of the previously mentioned elements integrate with each other and how the common database is central to the concept. Figure 21.13 implies that a number of computers will require to be linked to each other. This linking is carried out within the factory by using a 'local area network' (LAN) which uses coaxial or fibre optic cables to communicate data. One of the main problems with interconnecting computers and other machines is the **compatibility** of equipment and communications protocols used; industry standards are emerging which will ameliorate this problem. When computerised communication links are expanded to link other factories, customers, and suppliers on a nationwide basis these are termed 'wide area networks' (WANs), but these are as yet only partially implemented in manufacturing industry.

In conclusion, therefore, it can be seen that it is theoretically possible to automate all aspects of manufacture from product design through to final assembly and despatch, customer orders can be automatically received and

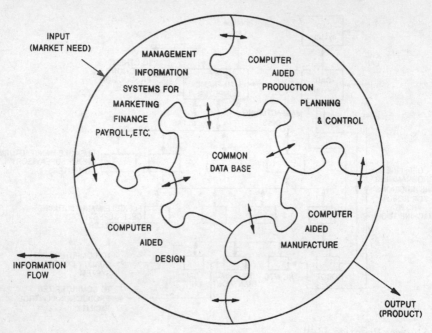

Figure 21.13   The CIM concept represented as a 'jigsaw'

processed, orders to suppliers can be automaticaly generated for raw materials and parts, and work can be scheduled and monitored as it passes through the plant. The two greatest factors preventing achievement of total CIM and its benefits are the enormous cost, and the fact that humans still have many advantages over machines – including computers. It is for these reasons that only those aspects producing the largest returns on investment will be automated.

21.5   The future

What of the future of manufacturing? Chapter 2 on manufacturing history took us to the close of the 20th century. Consider manufacturing technology, its management, and the social environment within which it operated at the beginning of the century, and compare this with the situation now: the changes that have occurred would have been almost impossible to predict. These were exaggerated by accelerated development of technology due to war, and by unique leaps in technology such as the development of solid state electronics. If we assume that this pattern is repeated in the 21st century, then we can see how difficult it is to predict even ten years ahead.

Looking to the near future, the development of enhanced, composite, and entirely new materials will produce new possibilities for products, and hence new challenges for manufacturing technology. Progress in computing technology will continue to have significant consequences. For example, 'virtual reality' has already been used to assist design engineers. It will be possible for the designer to walk around and into his or her design, make changes, and observe the results in the simulated world. Low volume production of components of varying complexity can now be made directly from CAD data without machining by using photopolymerisation and metal spraying processes. Developments in this field may allow products to be faxed around the world, assuming that the receiver has an appropriate machine and material, in just the same way as written messages or video pictures are sent today. In the social context, increases in the developed nations' productivity and the growing use of automation will continue to reduce the percentage of the population employed in manufacturing. However, no matter how many people actually work in manufacturing it will continue to exist as an essential creator of wealth and prosperity!

Review Questions

1 What is meant by the term 'Computer Integrated Manufacturing' (CIM)?
2 What is the most important part of CIM – computerisation or integration? Give reasons for your answer.
3 CAD is one major element of CIM; describe another **three**.
4 List **six** advantages that CAD offers over manual design and drawing techniques.
5 What are the basic hardware components of a CAD system?
6 Discuss fully the basic software elements of a CAD system.
7 Describe the **three** most common methods of representing an object in a CAD system.
8 Discuss the advantages of CAM over manual methods, and the use of special purpose machines.
9 What is the significance of the number of axes of an NC machine tool or an industrial robot?
10 Describe the construction of the control system for one axis of an NC machine tool.
11 Discuss the types of motion control available for NC machines and industrial robots.
12 What do you understand by the terms NC, CNC, and DNC, with regard to machine tools?
13 Define the elements that comprise an industrial robot.
14 Describe the major functions of an industrial robot.
15 State **three** types of robot configuration, and the type of work to which each is suited.
16 Describe **two** methods of 'on line' programming of robots.
17 Discuss the advantages of 'off line' programming of robots.
18 List **three** guidance methods for AGVs.
19 Describe **three** areas of application of industrial vision systems.
20 Describe the elements, and the operation, of a vision system.

21 Describe **three** types of Auto ID systems.
22 What is the function of a PLC within a CAM system?
23 What is the purpose of an FMS?
24 What is the purpose of CAPP systems, and why are they difficult to create?
25 Do you think that 'total' CIM is possible, or desirable? Give reasons for your answer.

___ Further Reading ___

1 'Computer Integrated Design and Manufacturing', by D.D. Bedworth, M.R. Henderson, and P.N. Wolfe. Published by McGraw Hill, 1991.
2 'Implementing Flexible Manufacturing Systems', by N.R. Greenwood. Published by Macmillan, 1988.
3 'Flexible Manufacturing Cells and Systems', by W.W. Luggen. Published by Prentice-Hall International, 1991.
4 'Computer Numerical Control', by Hans Kief and Fred Waters. Published by McGraw Hill, 1992.
5 'Computer Numerical Control of Machine Tools', by G.E. Thyer. Published by Butterworth Heinemann Ltd, 1991.
6 'Industrial Robotics', by Gordon M. Mair. Published by Prentice-Hall International, 1988.
7 'Introduction to Robotics', by Philip J. McKerrow. Published by Addison-Wesley, 1991.
8 'Programmable Controllers', by I.G. Warnock. Published by Prentice-Hall International, 1988.
9 'Computer Integrated Manufacturing – The Social Dimension', by Karl H. Ebel. Published by the International Labour Office, Geneva, 1990.
10 'Manufacturing Intelligence', by P.K. Wright and D.A. Bourne. Published by Addison-Wesley, 1988.

Index

Note: for topics with more than one reference any pages of greater significance are highlighted in bold.